JUPITER'S TRAVELS

Revised American Edition published in November 1996 by

Jupitalia Productions
25750 East Lane
Covelo, Ca 95428
e-mail tsimon@mcn.org

First published by Hamish Hamilton, London, in 1979
British paperback edition, by Penguin, in 1980
First American edition, by Doubleday, New York, in 1980
First French edition, by Albin Michel, Paris, in 1980
U.S. paperback edition, by Penguin, in 1981
First Italian edition, by Longanesi, Milan, in 1981
First Spanish edition, by Grijalbo, Barcelona, in 1982
First German edition by Rohwolt, Hamburg, in 1983
Second German edition, by Rohwolt, Hamburg, in 1993
Second British paperback edition, by Penguin, in 1995
First Dutch edition, by Arena, Amsterdam, in 1996
Third British paperback edition, by Penguin, in 2007

ISBN: 0-9654785-2-1
ISBN: 978-0-9654785-2-6

Printed in the United States of America by
Sheridan Books, Michigan

Also by Ted Simon

GRAND PRIX YEAR

RIDING HIGH

THE RIVER STOPS HERE

THE GYPSY IN ME

DREAMING OF JUPITER

Jupiter's Travels

by

Ted Simon

Jupitalia

**Covelo
California**

The Journey

A CALENDAR

1973
ENGLAND • FRANCE
ITALY • SICILY
TUNISIA • LIBYA
EGYPT • SUDAN
ETHIOPIA

1974
KENYA • TANZANIA
ZAMBIA • BOTSWANA
RHODESIA • SOUTH
AFRICA • SWAZILAND
MOZAMBIQUE
BRAZIL • ARGENTINA
CHILE

1975
BOLIVIA • PERU
ECUADOR •
COLOMBIA • PANAMA
NICARAGUA
COSTA RICA
HONDURAS
GUATEMALA
MEXICO • USA • FIJI
NEW ZEALAND
AUSTRALIA

1976
SINGAPORE
MALAYSIA
THAILAND • INDIA
SRI LANKA • NEPAL

1977
PAKISTAN
AFGHANISTAN • IRAN
TURKEY • GREECE
YUGOSLAVIA
AUSTRIA • GERMANY
SWITZERLAND
FRANCE • ENGLAND

How do you prepare for the unknown? I wanted to be as self-suffi-
cient as possible, but had little idea what I would confront. For months
I tantalized myself by trying to imagine what my needs might be in a
jungle, or a desert, or on a mountain top, and painstakingly I collected a myriad tiny items – from storm matches to snake-bite kits. Many
of them turned out to be quite handy. Some were simply absurd. But
gradually this mass of equipment settled down into working order.
Everything in this picture I took with me, except the tires. They were
sent on. And the umbrella? That was the photographer's, but eventually I <u>did</u> get one of my own, and it was remarkably useful. I strapped
it alongside, under the saddle and over a box on my right. On the left
side I carried a sword, but that's another story ...

The star of the show – my Triumph Tiger 100, fully loaded in southern Chile, after my first crossing of the Andes. The bike was capable of carrying much more than its own 390 pounds and still handling beautifully. The big leather tank bags – my pride and joy – held tools and spare parts, counterbalancing a lot of the extra weight at the back. It was in Argentina that I first felt confident enough to map out on one of my boxes the route I intended to take.I managed to follow it pretty closely, but Japan, and Indonesia got away. It would all look different today. But better? I doubt it.

Introduction to the new edition

Plus ça change...! The more things change, the more they stay the same. Since I ended my journey, almost twenty years ago, the world appears to have changed out of all recognition. Yet, as I read through these 450 pages again, I see that if I were to make the same journey today, everything that happened to me then could just as well happen now

Maybe they wouldn't imprison me in Brazil this time, but in Iran they might. Maybe they've stopped shooting people in the streets of Chile, but I hear there's no shortage of freelance gunmen in Afghanistan. Perhaps I would not find myself riding through revolutions in Mozambique and Peru, but there are plenty of other volatile areas on the map. Maybe they've paved the road over the Nullarbor, but I bet the tracks across Sudan are worse than ever. And in 1973 the principal problems confronting the world were ... poverty, terrorism, and environmental pollution.

As for the personal triumphs and disasters, the wonder and the ecstasy, the times of fear and despair, they are the stuff of human life and never change, but remain as new, bright and thrilling as the present moment itself.

Perhaps that's why this book has survived the fickle fashions of publishing. Most people I hear from say it reads as though it were written yesterday. Faithful readers (and I salute you all) who bought and read *Jupiter's Travels* fifteen years ago, when it first appeared in America, have remembered it and kept it alive, even though booksellers crowded it off the shelves. They talked about it, recommended it, sought it out in used book stores, had it brought over from Britain and Canada – where it has been selling briskly since 1980 – and elevated it to a cult. Finally they found a distributor on the East coast willing to import it and make it available. When my friends at Whitehorse Press put it in their catalog, they knew they were fulfilling a demand, but they were pleasantly shocked by the rate at which copies streamed out of their warehouse.

Whitehorse caters to a particular audience with a special interest in motorcycles, but this book is not just a "biker's tale" any more than I was a biker myself when I set off. It is a story of travel and adventure in many dimensions, and has been appreciated by thousands who never dreamed of twisting a throttle until they read it.

The mail I have received comes from people of all kinds and conditions, young and old, men and women, rich and poor, sedentary and mobile. Many have chosen to take to the road themselves, and to follow the same route. Occasionally they come to my door on their way around with reports on the state of Africa and Latin America. Some – quite a few – have told me that the book really changed their lives. So, as much out of respect for all these varied responses as out of my own natural affection for the book, I am producing this new edition of Jupiter's Travels, and will do all I can to bring it to a wider audience in this adopted country of mine.

Regardless of the wonders of technology and communication, our world is the same size as it ever was, and somewhere on its surface colorful, fascinating and unpredictable things are happening, just as they always have. The internet – and I'm on it, too – is a wonderful way for some of us to communicate certain kinds of information, but even at best it can never substitute for physical interaction, and at worst it is an escape from reality that can come perilously close to paranoia. Modern technology is a culture that cuts us off from the bigger world surrounding it. As human animals, we need to get out into that world, to feel it, smell it, think like it, to learn how good it is, and to feel free.

The book has been a great source of joy to me. Even now I recall with clarity my feeling, at the end of the journey, that it was the culmination of my life. All that followed could have been anti-climax, but the success of the book and its ability to inspire others has made the rest of my life part of the same journey.

One book could never cover more than a fraction of the experiences of four years, Large sections of the journey were unaccounted for. Swaziland, Argentina, Chile, Thailand, Assam, Nepal ... all were rich in memorable characters and events. Soon I expect to bring out another book, *Riding High,* a revised version of *Riding Home,* which tells some of those stories but was never published in the USA.

Ted Simon
Covelo, 1996

Jupiter

India would be unthinkable without its trees. The Neem, the peep-ul, the tamarind, countless others, stand at stately intervals along the roads and fields as giant witnesses from another age. By their presence they transform everything, framing the landscape, giv-ing it depth, variety, freshness, making green-glowing caverns under the sun and casting pools of dappled shade where people and animals can feel at peace.

When the fuel reserve ran dry too, and the engine choked and died, I guessed I was ten or fifteen miles from Gaya. The thought was disagreeable. It might mean spending the night there, and somewhere I had read that Gaya was the dirtiest town in India.

I let the bike roll off the asphalt onto the grass under a shade tree. The trunk of the tree was stout and twisted with prominent roots and a gray scaly bark. Drooping clusters of small dry leaves gave a medium shade. It was a common tree in India although I still could not remember its name.

I tucked my gloves into my helmet and stood by the bike looking up and down the country road and across the field of green wheat wondering who was going to help me this time, and what it would lead to. I did not doubt that help would come, and with it most probably some unexpected twist in my fortunes. It had taken years to achieve that measure of confidence and calm, and as I waited I allowed myself some pleasure in knowing it.

My thoughts brushed over the years and miles of the journey, tracing the fear as it had waxed and waned along the way, trying to hold it all together and reassure myself that there really had been a beginning. Without a beginning how could there be an end? At times, and more frequently now, I could feel the tiredness invading my bones, bleaching my retina and raising a mist on the horizon of my mind. Soon it would have to end.

There were many men walking along the road. Most of them wore loose cotton clothing, once white but stained right through by the reddish brown soil of Bihar. It caught the sun softly, and the people passed by under the trees like pale shadows taking up no space.

Few motor vehicles were on the road. Some men were riding bicycles, and a few drove ox carts or rode in pony cabs. There were some buzzing auto-rickshaws too, which are three-wheeled scooters with cabs for passengers. They were unlikely to have spare gas. In the state of Bihar you could get three or four meals for the price of a liter of gas.

A taxi came towards me full of people pressing forward. The driver was bent over the wheel with his dark face thrust against the windshield and all the expression squeezed out of him. The wheels flew up and down on the bumps, and the taxi slithered and juddered across the waves of tar as though trying to escape, drawn to its destination only by the concerted prayers of the people inside it.

By this time several men had stopped to observe me and then reluctantly walked on, but now one came who spoke a little English. His color and features indicated that he was a Brahmin, although his knotted cord, if he had one, was covered by his shawl and shirt. He told me straight away that he was very poor. I replied by telling him that I had no petrol.

"Village is there," he said. "Not far."

He stopped another man coming along slowly on a bicycle with a shopping bag slung from the handlebars, and spoke to him in Hindi.

"He says they will be having petrol. It is two miles. Not far."

I thanked him and waited. I felt sure there would be no gas at the next village but could not say so. There were more words spoken in Hindi.

"This man will go on his bicycle. How much petrol you are wishing?"

It did not seem to me that the man had volunteered but he appeared to accept the Brahmin's authority without question.

"That's wonderful," I said. "I will need a liter," and started to fish in my pockets.

"No, no, good sir. Afterwards you can pay. Now he will go."

The Brahmin's prophecy was instantly fulfilled. The man turned his bicycle and went. The Brahmin then mentioned again, as a matter of purely academic interest, that he was poor, this time adding that I was rich. I felt that he was striving towards some kind of dialogue which would result, without his even having to wish it, in my turning my fortune over to him and continuing on foot. This might well have happened in ancient Indian legend, but I was not the warrior he took me for, and he was not sage enough for me, although he had a sly air about him.

So I withdrew politely from the conversation and sat at the foot of the tree to write and take pleasure in the afternoon. It was February. The light was still cool and golden, and there was peace here too, a kind of detachment that I found only rarely in public places in India. It seemed a perfect time to put down on paper what had been accumulating in my mind since the day, four days back, when I made my great mistake.

In the three years of my journey I had never made an error like it.

I had planned to ride to Calcutta from Darjeeling, a long ride for one day on Indian roads, but the highway is better than most. It parallels the border of Bangladesh and, for part of the way, runs in company with the Ganges. What I had actually done on meeting the Ganges had been to take the highway that runs upstream to Patna and Benares. But had I done it? There was no recollection of choice. I had followed the holy river, secure in the knowledge that it was flowing on my right-hand side, unaware that I had crossed it in a confusion of streams and bridges and was on the west side and not the east. When I had noticed my mistake I had already traveled 150 miles in the opposite direction to Calcutta, a sufficient distance to change my life.

Why hadn't I noticed where the sun lay? Or which way the river was flowing? Or that I had crossed into Bihar from West Bengal? I prided myself that these observations had become second nature to me. Why had they failed me there?

This enormous deflection in my path had led me straight towards the heart and soul of India, to the birthplace of Buddhism and the most sacred Hindu places. On examination my reasons for rushing to Calcutta had seemed trivial, banal, although still, in my tired and confused state, desirable. Then, sadly at first, I had abandoned them and embraced instead this strange quirk in my destiny. It had led to remarkable experiences, the last of which had found me in a glider, high above Patna, whirling in a thermal current alongside a flock of big brown ferocious birds of prey.

All this took a while to record, and I still kept the pleasant sense of having been nudged towards some fateful event. My Brahmin had drifted away, tired of explaining me to every passer-by. His emissary to the village had not returned. I stood up and, as something to do, beckoned at an approaching car. It was a polished limousine driven by a chauffeur. Two fat women, lolling in the back, observed me with amusement, while the chauffeur intensified his glare at the road ahead and accelerated past me. At the same time a truck was coming towards them from Gaya. The truck moved farther out into the road, and the car was driven, screeching horribly, into a shallow ditch. The truck driver smiled at me and held up his thumb, and I grinned my appreciation.

A few minutes later two men on an Enfield motorcycle stopped just beyond me and walked back. The driver would have gone on, but the pillion rider insisted on stopping and, as it turned out, he was the owner of the machine. He was a young man, stubbily built and very short even in his stylish high-heeled shoes. He wore tightly fitting flared trousers, an embroidered yellow waistcoat and a magenta turban of the kind used by members of the Rajput or Kshatrya caste. His bearded face carried an expression of almost unbearable solemnity, like a boy trying to show respect at a funeral. At first I thought he was in the grip of extreme sadness, but the expression never varied, and in fact he was on the way to his brother's marriage ceremony and an occasion of great joy.

Eventually, between us, we solved my problem. It involved many people, including a retired vice-chancellor of Magadh University from whose carburetor we pumped the necessary liter, and it was very satisfying to all concerned. The shy cyclist also returned from the village, without gas, and smiled most happily to see us all at work. He would accept nothing but a warm handshake for his trouble. The vice-chancellor left for Gaya, having invited me to drop round for tea. Then I also rode off, with escort, on my way to a Rajput wedding.

And they brought on the dancing girls.

There were two girls, but only one of them danced at any one time, while the other sat between the *tabla* player and the violinist.

We were several hundred men sitting on sheets of thick white cotton spread over an area of twenty feet by forty feet or so. The day had gone, and the sky was replaced by a great multicolored awning lit with fluorescent tubes. Most of the men were in suits, though only the oldest wore their jackets. Naturally we all had our shoes off, and they were ranged around the edge of the tent. My friend, whose name was Raj, warned me mournfully to watch out for my things. Already, he said, four pairs of shoes and two suitcases had disappeared.

The air was at that perfect temperature in which the skin luxuriates, and scented by the incense sticks smoldering in front of the bridegroom. The groom lay back on a throne of bolsters and quilts, with his paternal grandfather on one side and the pundit on the other, both alert and upright and with bright yellow turbans on their heads. The groom seemed quite detached, his eyes only barely open.

"He has been fasting for two days," murmured Raj. "He will not eat until tomorrow after the wedding."

Two rifles lay on cushions in front of the groom, their barrels pointing over our heads. At significant moments they would be fired to frighten off hostile tribes, for the Rajput are a warrior caste.

The principal dancing girl held the floor most of the time. She was my favorite too, although her shape was far from my ideal. Her arms and shoulders were impeccable and moved with sinuous grace, and her face was full and pretty. The rest of her was wrapped tight in bodice and sari, but she proudly maintained an enormous and agile paunch, which seemed somehow to be much older than she was. I found myself watching it a great deal, amazed at the liberties it took, but distracted as I was by her belly I could not ignore her face. With true artistry she had created an expression of such supreme contempt for men that if I had been alone in a room with her I would undoubtedly have withered beneath her scorn. And just as surely, if it had softened towards me at all, I would have fallen into a state of deepest bliss. It must have been founded in bitter personal experience.

"They are prostitutes, you know," Raj whispered, in a voice charged with darkest meaning, and I saw that for him this had to be the most important thing about her.

The dance itself was a strange and fragmentary thing, and at first I thought it quite ineffectual and hardly worth the ten-rupee notes that she peeled off her audience and passed to the *tabla* player. She would stand, tapping one hennaed foot, shaking the ankle bells, swaying to the beat, and arrange her body into one of several positions, perhaps a hip and shoulder pushing forward, legs slightly bent, head tilted to one side. Then, catching a particular phrase from the musicians, she would shuffle forward across the cloth, moving whatever there was to be moved (the belly moving itself in perfect harmony) for just six steps, before straightening up, letting her arms fall to her sides and sweeping us with a stupendous pout that said quite plainly "There, you bastards."

In those six steps she said everything there was to say about men and women. Most of the time she merely swayed and sang, gesturing mechanically with her smooth, lovely arms, making not the least effort to put meaning or feeling into the song. Men shouted insults at her, elders castigated her for being too greedy or ordered her to moderate her behavior. She always did as she was told, but always her scorn triumphed. And I found myself longing to see, just one more time, those six derisive steps.

When she stopped to rest and her relief came on, and when I was not being cross-examined by other guests about every most intimate detail of my life, my eyes would seek out the father of the bridegroom. He also wore the brilliant yellow turban, but sat among the crowd. Clean-shaven and less solemn than Raj, he nevertheless had a tough and imperturbable manner and his smile was controlled and distant. I watched him because I had begun to wonder whether he was the reason I had found myself following such unexpected paths during the previous days. One of the first things Raj had told me about his family, when we stopped for beer on our way to the wedding, was that his father had great powers. He was a clairvoyant, a seer, he could read a man's soul and destiny.

"He will take your hand and tell you things about yourself. He has done this for many people. It is too important. He will do it for you." Raj was becoming morosely excited by the idea.

"Palmistry," I said.

"No. No. Not palmistry. You will see."

And several times after he had introduced me to his father he asked me:

"Has my father told you yet?"

But no, he had wanted to wait, for the right time, for a quiet moment, and since in their eyes I had become an important guest, having been gifted to them, as it were, by fate, and he had a reputation to sustain, I fancied that he was probably looking at me too from time to time when I wasn't looking at him.

Long after midnight, when the flow of ten-rupee notes had ceased and the dancing girls had wilted away, we all stretched out on the floor and went to sleep, with our wallets tucked under our heads. At the bride's house, a farm building about three hundred yards away where other festivities were being held, the loudspeakers were switched off and the last Hindi pop song went rolling away under the moon across the great luminous plains of northern India. The lights in the tent went out, but the curtain of colored lights that covered one whole side of the bride's house from roof to ground went on glowing, at least until I went to sleep.

The following morning, after we had all wandered off into the appropriate field, and washed at the pump, and breakfasted, the bride and groom came together at last. They were led into a small, cloistered courtyard which formed the heart of the bride's family house. There they sat on cushions with the bride's pundit between them and the groom's pundit on her other side, and as many of us as could manage crammed into the remaining space. To my amazement, and enlightenment, the chief dancing girl was also there with her musicians. The bride was obscured by veils, flowers and a brilliant wedding sari. The groom wore a paper hat from which sprouted and hung an extraordinary array of tinselly objects. To my Western eye he looked like something between a Christmas tree and an old-fashioned Martian, and his face also was invisible behind the things dangling from his hat.

The bride's pundit had some sheets of paper torn from an exercise book and covered with sacred texts which he read in a harsh jabber, stopping frequently to decipher an illegible word, or to seek counsel from the other pundit. Meanwhile the dancing girl and the musicians sang and played the same sexy songs as the night before, and people chatted loudly to each other, trying to make themselves heard. The groom also had to perform various ritual movements at certain points in the ceremony, like spooning milk with a folded leaf from a crock onto a pat of smoldering cow dung. At one time he had to do this with a cloth held in front of his face, though it is unlikely that he could see much anyway. I thought his ordeal was quite awful. Half starved, half blinded, stifled by far too much clothing, enveloped by the most shattering din and propelled through these complicated symbolic acts, I wondered whether any part of him remained quiet enough to know the meaning of it all. It looked to me like a ceremony devised by women in revenge for all the overbearing authority and pomposity that an Indian husband is capable of.

After half an hour no end seemed in sight and I left to walk outside for a while. Everything and everybody was at peace. I noticed clearly how all the man-made structures, the mud-walled houses and cow sheds, grain stores, tanks, irrigation channels and hay ricks were at one with the earth and the trees. A poor and backward harmony, some would say, best appreciated from a distance. But surely, I said to myself, there must be some middle way....

My appointment with destiny was approaching. Raj's father was getting ready to leave for his office in Patna.

"Come," he said. "We'll sit in the car."

We sat turned towards each other, and he said:

"Give me your hand."

I held it out, and he grasped it as in a handshake, but held it in his grip for several moments. Then, releasing it, he gave my thumb a quick backward flip, and murmured:

"Achcha!

"You have a very determined soul. This also is reflected in your mind.

"You are Jupiter...."

Why not? I thought. I like the sound of that.

Trouble with Mars

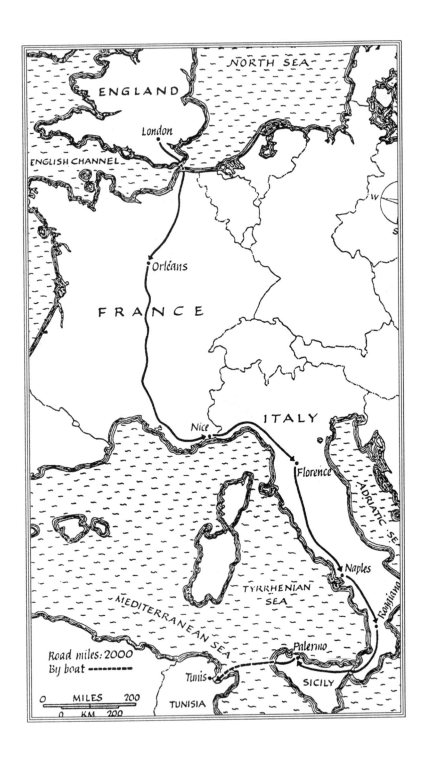

Officially the journey began at 6 P.M. on Saturday the sixth of October 1973. The announcement was to appear the following morning in the Sunday Times. I had just stepped out of the newspaper office with a last armful of film and other oddments, and I had seen the story in proof.

MARATHON RIDER OFF

Ted Simon left England yesterday on the
first leg of his 50,000-mile motorcycle journey round the world....

I really had to go.

It was not an auspicious day, far from it. Unknown to me it was the Jewish holiday Yom Kippur. More important, it was the day chosen by the Egyptian High Command to begin a devastating assault on Israel. Soon after mid-day the radio began to report massive attacks on Israeli positions in the Sinai. By the end of the afternoon the Middle East was at war again. The "Yom Kippur" War.

The war lay right across the route I had been planning and preparing for six months. I thought they had done it on purpose. Maybe you know how it is when you have decided to do something really enormous with your life, something that stretches your resources to the limit. You can get the feeling that you are engaged in a trial of strength with the universe. Dock strikes, assassinations, revolutions, droughts, the collapse of the Western world, all those things you usually say "ho-hum" to in the papers begin to look as though they were designed as part of your personal fate. I mean, I had trouble enough with the Ethiopians over their Muslim guerrillas, with the Triumph factory going on strike, with the Libyans running a holy crusade in their visa department. But a full-scale tank war, I thought, was going a bit too far.

The route of my first seven thousand miles to Nairobi had become so familiar to me that it lit up in my head at the touch of a button like those maps in the Paris Metro with their strings of little colored bulbs. I knew I was utterly committed to that route, by a thousand considerations, climatic, financial, geographic and emotional. War or no war, I would have to go through, but it filled me with trepidation. The only consolation I could find was that fate had obviously marked

Trouble with Mars ——————➤ 13

me out for something special. If the omens were dark, they were at least vigorous. It seemed uncanny. I felt blessed and cursed at the same time. Star-crossed.

I stood alone in the gutter with my laden Triumph in the black and rainy night, fumbling with my parcels and wondering where to pack them. I was wearing a lot of clothing I still had not found room for on the bike, in particular an old RAF flying jacket and, over that, a waterproof anorak. The anorak was too tight. To get it on at all I had first to stuff the jacket inside it and then struggle to pull this whole rigid assembly down over my head. It usually took several minutes and made an amusing spectacle at the roadside, but I was sentimentally attached to the jacket and did not want to spend money on another waterproof. The effect, once inside, was excellent for sitting still in cold driving rain, but movement was awkward and robot like, and produced a lot of heat.

Drops of sweat rolled into my eyes as I struggled and juggled with the packages, unable to put them down, because every surface was streaming with water, unable to find space anywhere, for every last crevice seemed to be packed with something.

A Good Luck postcard from a friend, which had touched me deeply, fell to the pavement and I watched helplessly as the writing dissolved in the rain and the inky water washed around my boots. This, I thought, was not the heroic departure I had envisaged.

I looked at the absurdly overloaded Triumph standing next to me in the gutter and had my first cruel glimpse of the reality of what I was embarking on. My vision had been dazzled by the purple drama of warfare and banditry. Now I saw, with awful clarity, that a large part of my life henceforth would be devoted to the daily grind of packing and unpacking this poor, dumb beast.

"It's impossible," I whispered.

For weeks it had been an enthralling game, a meditation, and at times an obsession, wondering what to pack and where to pack it. The major departments were Food, Clothing, Bed, Tools, First Aid, Documents, Cameras and Fuel. The Kitchen was pretty much established in one of the side boxes. I had a neat Optimus petrol stove in its own aluminum saucepan; a non stick frying pan with a folding handle; a pair of nesting stainless-steel mugs; some ill-assorted containers for salt, pepper, sugar, tea, coffee and so on; cutlery, a tin opener with a corkscrew, matches and a water bottle.

The problems were the same here as in the other departments. One had to fill the space completely and stop things from rattling, breaking, unscrewing themselves, leaking and rubbing against each other. The temptation was to stuff the spaces between the hard objects with odd items like bandages, spare gloves, toilet paper and socks. The results were impressive in terms of insulation, but as the software spread everywhere amongst the hardware it became impossible to remember where anything was, or to get at it, or to notice when it was missing.

The subtleties of packing a house and garage into the equivalent of four suitcases can be learned only with experience. At that time I was still at the loaded-wheelbarrow stage, and the bike looked and felt like it.

The Wardrobe was in the Bedroom, and that was in a red nylon rucksack which lay across the bike behind my saddle. The theory was that if ever I broke down in a jungle I would have a rucksack to walk off with. It contained a sweater, spare jeans, long woolen underpants, a number of shirts, socks and shorts, and an impeccable white linen jacket reserved for garden parties on the lawns of tropical embassies. The Bedroom consisted of a light one-man tent, a mosquito net the same shape that could be supported on the same poles, a down sleeping bag with a cotton liner and a small inflatable air bed.

Strapped down beneath the rucksack were two sealed gallon cans of oil intended ultimately to be used as spare fuel containers. The rucksack was high enough to act as a back rest, and was held by a long elastic cord.

Behind the rucksack was a fiberglass box. This was Casualty and Photographic. I was blessed with a medical arsenal of great power and flexibility, assembled by some very conscientious friends. As well as various antibiotics and other drugs and salves, I had bandages of every description, dressings suitable for amputations and third-degree burns, tweezers for extracting bullets and disposable scalpels for performing my own appendectomies. In screw-top bottles I was given some horrendous white stuff for body lice, and a strange mixture of cod-liver oil and glucose, which, they said, was an old naval remedy for tropical sores. Packed in with all this were two Pentax camera bodies, three lenses and three-dozen aluminum canisters of film, and under it all, to deaden the sound, lay a pair of carefully ironed and folded white trousers in a plastic bag to accompany the linen jacket at consular cocktails.

The Workshop was slung on either side of the petrol tank in two canvas bags, and the Office sat on top of the tank in a zip-up bag with a map holder. Annexed to the Office was the Bathroom, consisting of a rather luxurious sponge bag and a roll of paper.

The remaining side box had to cope with the biggest department of all, Miscellaneous. Here were two inner tubes, a piston, shoes, waterproof gloves, a torch, a visor and a hundred things I had collected that had no other home to go to.

I knew I had too much stuff, but there was no logical way to reduce it. Some of the problem was, of course, pure sentiment. How could I junk anything as unique and exotic as a mixture of cod-liver oil and glucose? It was worth carrying round the world, worth even cultivating a sore, to see whether it worked. But generally I was on the horns of the fork and spoon dilemma: if you take a fork, why not a spoon, if salt then surely pepper; if you are going to ride fifty thousand miles on a motorcycle then at least you want to lie comfortably at night. There was nothing I had not chosen carefully, and it always seemed that the least important things were also the smallest and lightest and least worth discarding.

How can one anticipate the unknown? Preparing for the journey was like living a paradox, like eating the cake before I'd had it. More than once I realized the absurdity of what I was doing. The whole point and beauty of the journey was not knowing what would happen next, but I could not help myself striving to work it all out in advance. My mind became a kaleidoscope of scenarios that I had conjured up out of my imaginary future, showing Me Crossing the Andes; Me in a Jungle; Me in a Monsoon; Me Fording a Torrent; Me Crossing a Desert.

The mystery deepened the more I tried to penetrate it. I bought and packed bits of this and that for emergencies which, when looked at in a different light, seemed like the purest of fantasies. A snakebite kit like a rubber thimble, a field compass, storm matches, a space blanket to stave off death on an ice field, all beckoned to me from the shelves of the big camping shops, and when they were small enough I took them. But it was beyond me to imagine myself steering a compass course across a wilderness, being marooned on a glacier or wanting to boil water in a cyclone.

And who can walk along the pavements of the city of London and seriously contemplate the prospect of being struck by a cobra?

I suspended my judgment and went on adding to my pocket universe like an agnostic crossing himself before battle.

In a linen belt next to my skin I carried £500 in traveler's checks. In a black wallet locked into one of the boxes were small amounts of cash in currencies ranging from cruzeiros to kwachas. In the bank, or promised, I had over £2,000. I considered that with all this I had enough money to go round the world, buy what I needed and take two years doing it.

Fuel costs I estimated at £300, shipping costs at £500. It was 1973. Gas in Europe cost around a dollar a gallon, and there were $2.40 to the pound. The war, which came to be called the Oil War, had just begun. Inflation was considered bad at 5 per cent. I could allow myself £2 a day, on average, for food and occasional accommodation, and considered that to be generous. Seven hundred and thirty days at £2 comes to, say, £1.500. Grand total: £2,300, leaving £200 for troubles and treats. Crazy arithmetic, but the best I could do. How was I to know the world was about to change, not having been there yet?

The idea of traveling round the world had come to me one day in March that year, out of the blue. It came not as a vague thought or wish but as a fully formed conviction. The moment it struck me I knew it would be done and how I would do it. Why I thought immediately of a motorcycle I cannot say. I did not have a motorcycle, nor even a license to ride one, yet it was obvious from the start that that was the way to go, and that I could solve the problems involved.

The worst problems were the silly ones, like finding a bike to take the driving test on. I resorted to shameless begging and deceit to borrow the small bike I needed. There was a particularly thrilling occasion when I turned up at the Yamaha factory on the outskirts of London to take a small 125-CC trail bike out "on test." I had my L plates hidden in my pocket, but first I had to get out of the factory gates looking as though I knew how the gears worked. Those were the first, and some of the hardest yards, I ever rode; now it can be told.

I failed my first driving test and I thought I might just as easily fail the second. Since that would not do at all, I obtained a fraudulent license and was quite prepared to go off with that, but fortunately it turned out to be unnecessary, and my life of crime ended there.

I was lucky to get the support of the Sunday Times, and in particular its editor, Harold Evans, and it was partly to acknowledge my good fortune that I chose to ride the Triumph rather than the BMW. The British motorcycle industry had crashed to its lowest point ever and I felt that a journey started in England and sponsored by a great British newspaper ought to be done on a British bike. The decision gave me some heartaches later on, but no real regrets. It always felt like the right thing to have done, which was all-important.

The bike was essentially the same Triumph that had been on the roads for decades: a simple, solid piece of engineering, difficult to break and easy to repair. It was a vertical twin, with pistons that moved up and down in unison and had a reputation for drilling the marrow out of the rider's bones, but I had low-compression pistons that allowed me to run on low-grade fuel and also flattened out the vibration. In fact it was a comfortable bike to ride. It was the 500-cc Tiger Hundred that had been used by the police. Its single carburetor was easier to tune and more economical than the twin carburetors of the Daytona. Good gas gave me fifty-five miles to a gallon, so that even the standard tank offered a range of nearly two hundred miles. It had high, wide handlebars so that I could sit up and take notice as I went, and good ground clearance to take me over rough going. And it was light as well as sturdy. Of all the bigger machines it was the lightest by thirty pounds or more, the equivalent of about three gallons of petrol.

We had planned all sorts of interesting modifications at the factory, a list as long as a sheet of foolscap, but when the time came to fetch it, I was lucky to get a machine at all. The workers had just decided to lock the management out, it was the end of the road for the old-style Triumph company and I think my bike was the last one to leave the factory for a very long time. It was totally unmodified, and so hastily prepared that a pint of oil fell out of the chain case on my way down the Motorway from Coventry.

I know Triumphs are supposed to leak oil, but this is ridiculous.

But it was nothing, a paper seal slipped in assembly, easily put right. You could stop the oil if you took the trouble. That was what British bikes liked, a bit of trouble. They thrived on attention, like certain people, and repaid you for it. Not a bad relationship to have.

We got on well together from the start. I thought of us as constituting a sort of space capsule that could travel at will, at least in two dimensions, unconstrained by the need for hotels, shops, restaurants, good roads, bottled water and sliced bread. I was aiming at self-sufficiency because I wanted to travel the way Livingstone did, or Columbus; as though anything could happen and all of it was unknown. It was going to be the journey of a lifetime, a journey that millions dream of and never make, and I wanted to do justice to all those dreams.

In spite of wars and tourism and pictures by satellite, the world is just the same size it ever was. It is awesome to think how much of it I will never see. It is no trick to go round the world these days; you can pay a lot of money and fly round it nonstop in less than forty eight hours, but to know it, to smell it and feel it between your toes you have to crawl. There is no other way. Not flying, not floating. You have to stay on the ground and swallow the bugs as you go. Then the world is immense. The best you can do is trace your long, infinitesimally thin line through the dust and extrapolate. I drew the longest line I possibly could, that could still be seen as following a course.

Generally the great overland journeys follow the Asian land mass east until the traveler is at last forced to take to the water at Singapore. I chose a different way because I was powerfully attracted by the challenge of Africa, and in great awe of it too. If I could conquer Africa, I thought, I would be able to face the rest of the world with confidence. So I chose Africa, and logic prescribed the rest. Cape Town led naturally to Rio de Janeiro. A cruise ship sailed that route three times a year at very reasonable rates, and as an act of faith I booked my passage for February 24, 1974. From Rio a long loop of fifteen thousand miles around South America would bring me up the Pacific coast to California. Across the Pacific the picture was more confused. China was interested in receiving only coach parties, and Southeast Asia was seething with the war in Vietnam, but there was Japan, Australia, Indonesia, Malaysia and Thailand. Coming home through India seemed absolutely right. That was a challenge I would be better prepared to meet after being loose in the world for a while.

Dutifully I collected information about Pacific fares and sailings, about road conditions in the Andes, ferry services in Indonesia, the weather in northern Australia, but it was all foolishness and at heart

I think I knew it. When I spread the Michelin maps of Africa on the living-room floor (and they must be the most beautiful road maps ever made), when I gazed down at the vastness of that continent, the physical variety and political complexity of it, and when I considered my complete ignorance of it, Cape Town seemed as distant as the moon.

What point, then, in worrying about the stars. It was enough to know they were there and that I was heading for them. I thought myself to be the most fortunate man alive to have the whole world almost literally within my grasp. There was no one on earth I would have changed places with.

Or so I thought – until that black night on the pavement of Grays Inn Road, when I stood dripping rain water, sweat and despair, crushed by the unwieldiness of the monster I had created, and the enormity of the prospect I had invented for myself.

Only three yards away, behind the thick glass doors of the Sunday Times lobby, was the bright and comfortable world that suited most people well enough. I could see the commissionaire, smoothly uniformed behind his desk, looking forward to a pint of beer and an evening with the telly. People in sensible light-weight suits, with interesting jobs and homes to go to, flaunted their security at me and I felt my gut scream at me to strip off this ridiculous outfit and rush back into that light and the familiar interdependence. It struck me very forcefully that if I went on with this folly I would forever after be the man outside in the gutter looking in. For a moment I was lost beyond hope, utterly defeated.

Then I turned away from all that, somehow fumbled my packages away, got on the bike and set off in the general direction of the English Channel. Within minutes the great void inside me was filled by a rush of exaltation, and in my solitary madness I started to sing.

All the way I was saying good-bye. Good-bye to parents and friends, good-bye to London. Good-bye to Snodland on the Canterbury road, always good for a laugh. Good-bye to the lambs and oasthouses and orchards of Kent. Good bye to Friday night piss-ups and Saturday football and Sunday roasts.

In Dover I bought a big blue and white golfing umbrella for £4. How can I explain such craziness? It fitted neatly alongside the bike.

Good-bye to the White Cliffs, to Boulogne and the sugar beet of Picardy, to Grandvilliers ("*Son Parking, Sa Zone Industrielle*") to the *saucisson* of Beauvais and the Paris *Périphérique*, all intimately known to me for a decade or more.

In Orleans I slept in a hotel and basked in the admiration of a garage proprietor. "I owned many English motorcycles, AJS, Norton, Matchless, Sunbeam. I wanted to make a journey like yours, but ..." He shrugged. "All this Japanese rubbish they make nowadays." Not true, but I appreciate the sentiment, so good-bye to him too, and to the fog over the tree-lined avenues and the high passes and the fairy citadel of St. Flour, all so familiar but all seen with fresh wonder because of where I am going, because of knowing that maybe, possibly, I might not quite make it back here again.

And the swoop down into Millau, where I just, and only just, miss being killed. With my lungs full of adrenaline I shout "Madman! Assassin!" at the blind commuter who overtook me in his liver-colored Simca and pushed me off the road toward a stone wall. I squeezed past on the dirt, very shaken. How can I possibly anticipate such insanity? Yet I must, somehow, to survive. I will survive.

Remember, then, that outside cities, in the evening, when the light is failing, people are driving home in a hurry, tired and bored by their work. And you will be going the other way, also tired. So at the end of the day, when you're anxious to go quick, SLOW DOWN.

Lodève. A Last Night in my house. How can I bear to leave something so beautiful? The contradiction is too painful, and the pain makes me anxious to be gone. There are other good-byes too delicate and too fraught with emotion to be written about in passing. On my way down through Europe I learn the value of the love I am abandoning. At times I experience a degree of misery and lovelessness I have not known since adolescence. I wonder whether I will have the capacity ever to bear such pain again. It occurs to me that that may be the condition for perpetual youth.

Good-bye to my unfinished dream, to the toasted vineyards of the Hérault, to Montpellier, Nimes and Aix-en-Provence. In Nice I have a friend who manages a "Grand Hotel" on the Boulevard des Anglais called the Westminster, slightly faded since its Edwardian heyday

Great expeditions, I thought, deserve grandiose departures. I tried to stage one outside this grand old hotel on the Riviera, with the entire staff lined up to wave goodbye, but the union would not allow it. All I got was my friend, the manager, and two waiters. Ah well, *sic transit gloria*. At least I was able to show off my luxurious leather chaps, before I lost them the very next day.

when expeditions like mine were undertaken by gentlemen. It strikes me as a suitable place from which to say a last Good-bye, and the "departing explorer" poses for a picture by the potted palm outside the revolving door. We had hoped to line the hotel staff up outside, but the union wouldn't allow it. So off to Monaco and the Italian frontier, good-bye to France, and . . . Shit! I've left my passport at the hotel. The departing explorer returns red-faced to depart once more. Dramatic farewells, it seems, are not for me.

Enough of this messing about, I tell myself. *It's time to take the journey seriously. For one thing, no more hotels. Tonight you sleep out and save money.*

Monaco, Genoa, La Spezia and, as night falls, Florence. I pick up a "Camping" sign and follow it to Fiesole, where I am ambushed by an English couple in a small restaurant who tell me to look up their relatives in Sierra Leone. If only I were going there.

It is late. The "Camping" sign leads up a very narrow steep hill, with a gate at the top. The gate is locked; the campsite deserted. The slope is too steep and the bike is too heavy. I can't turn it around. It falls over and I am too weak to move it. Disgusted with myself, I unpack it, pick it up, turn it around, repack it. Rain begins to fall. I will not go to a hotel. At the bottom of the hill is a small parking place. I put the bike up on the center stand, put up my umbrella and go to sleep in the saddle, lying forward on the tank bag. I am amazed how easy it is, how little I care what others may think, how little sleep I need. I am riding high on energy, like a surfer on a big wave.

To Rome on the autostrada, but the tolls are too high, and I get off it to go south through Latina and Terracina. Just before Naples, in the dark, I find a campsite that's open. During the last hours on the bike, my mood had plunged to despair, but the work of unpacking and cooking keeps misery at bay, and a bottle of wine washes it away.

To Naples and Salerno, and now the autostrada is free. It rides the bumps down the spine of Italy, a wonder of engineering, always either tunneling or soaring across great airy chasms. The weather is wonderful too, hot sun, crisp clean air. On the empty highway I begin to feel the rhythm of a long, uninterrupted ride. In most of Europe this is impossible, life is so dense, intricate, a million parishes joined up higgledy-piggledy and every patch intimately known to somebody for hundreds, sometimes thousands of years. I feel I am already leaving Europe, I can feel Africa there, so vast I am already within its aura.

The movement has a complex rhythm with many pulses beating simultaneously. Underlying it is the engine with its subtle blend of sounds, eighty explosions a second, cams on push rods, push rods on tappets, rockers on valve stems, valves on seats, ball bearings revolving and racing, cogs meshing and thrashing in oil, oil pumps throbbing, gases hissing, chains whipping over sprockets, all this frenzy of metal in motion, amazing that it can last for even a minute, yet it will have to function for thousands of hours to take me round and home again. Through all these pulses blending and blurring I seem to hear a slow and steady beat, moving up and down, up and down, three semi-tones apart, a second up, a second down; as I listen it grows clearer, unmistakable. Is it there or am I inventing it? Is it the pulse of my own body intercepting the sound, modifying it with my bloodstream? Try as I will I can hear no other pulse, no other pitch. There are other instruments in the orchestra, however. The lapel of the flying jacket flicks against my shoulder like a kettle drum, my overlong chin strap beats a more complicated tattoo on the helmet and undeniably there is vibration too, a faint tingle spreading from foot rests, grips and saddle, comfortable at fifty, distinctly unpleasant at sixty-five and then flattening out again at seventy. With 1,500 miles on the clock I consider the bike run in, and I'm riding at seventy and over. On the autostrada the load has no apparent effect, until I go up over eighty on a curve and feel the beginnings of a nasty wobble. I settle back to seventy and lean forward to hit less air. A full tank takes me almost three hours without a stop, three hours of contemplation and speculation, contemplation of past mistakes, speculation on future dangers. Why does my mind dwell so much on the down side of life, when the present is so exhilarating and satisfying? I find myself anticipating ghastly accidents, desperate situations, macabre and quite unreal challenges, like riding the bike over a rope bridge swinging across a Peruvian canyon, as the vines slowly untwist and snap, a strand at a time . . . shades of *San Luis Rey*. My heart is actually beating faster when I catch on to what's happening. It's the "B" movie syndrome. In my childhood they always used to show two movies, "A" and "B," though often they were both "B." In "B" movies everything spelled disaster. Windscreen wipers at night meant a horrific crash. A creaking door, a footstep, an oversweet smile, a "nice" stranger boded pure evil. Anything whatever to do with airplanes or of course rope bridges, and you were clinging to your seat (or girl friend) waiting for the spine-chilling consequences. Was that how I was conditioned to expect the worst? Or were the pulp movie-makers simply cashing in on an archetypal human instinct?

Is it possible, I asked myself indignantly, *that all these years you've been palpitating because of some cheap Hollywood con trick...?*

Something touches my foot, and I look down to see objects streaming onto the road surface. One of the canvas tank bags, loaded with tools, has sagged onto the right-hand exhaust pipe and caught fire. Half my tools and spare parts are spread across the autostrada. They are undamaged, the bag is easily tied up with string and I go on.

There you are, you see. If you had imagined this happening, you would have had the screwdriver through your foot....

At four o'clock, with an hour of daylight left, I turn off the autostrada to find a place to camp. The small road leads me through a hot and dusty land, horse-and-cart country still, Calabria on the instep of Italy, where the favorite color for clothes is still black. Rising toward the mountains, I come to Roggiano, a small town baked into the hillside, encrusted with age, inward-looking and shy of visitors. In the town square I halt, uncertain what to do but unconcerned. I have seen nowhere yet to put a tent, but my night under the umbrella has given me a strange confidence. I no longer care what happens to me. I stop the engine, pull off my helmet and, still sitting astride the bike, light up a cigarette and let peace settle about me. On the further pavement is assembled a small group of men wearing carefully pressed suits. Some children spot me and rush up shouting. Eventually I walk over to the men, who are dignified but curious, and at a slow and easy pace we exchange pleasantries until, at last, one of them suggests that if I go up the hill I will find an "international center." They will give me a bed. A swarm of small boys bears me and the bike like a carnival float up the hill.

The "center" is an assortment of low buildings set among trees and flowering bushes. In part it is devoted to the national campaign for literacy, but there is more to it. A handsomely bearded young man welcomes me without hesitation, as though such arrivals were commonplace. In a matter of moments I am standing in a communal hall drinking black coffee, served by a young woman in black, who stands by us gravely as we drink. A minute ago I saw her, with a vast bundle of laundry at least as tall as herself balanced on her head. She passed easily through a doorway with not an inch to spare anywhere. Such impressive poise. It should be an Olympic event.

The young man explains that the buildings were erected by people from all the fourteen villages of the Esore Valley in their spare time. There are bedrooms for those who come from a long way off. It has a full-time staff of four; his father and himself, another teacher and a secretary.

The father and founder, Guiseppe Zanfini, receives me in his study. He beams at me with such concentrated benevolence that I want immediately to vote him into office, any office. Then, without preamble, he launches directly and astonishingly into his story:

"When I was eighteen I was a Fascist from my eyes to my boots." His hands outline the ample portions of himself which that includes.

"I volunteered for the army to go to war. I was in an officer school, then in Sicily, and four years after came my first real battle. I heard the toot-toot on the bugle" – he goes "toot toot" into his fist – "that meant 'Prepare arms.' I was in the tent to pick up my gun and clean it, and I thought: 'This time it is not for paper cut-out figures. This time you will have to kill real men,' and I knew then I couldn't. Not to kill men with mothers like mine, with children – men who have come from homes like mine which will be in misery."

In a measured hush he speaks of love and brotherhood, his face flitting between solemnity and ecstasy. As the battle progresses he shows graphically how others lost a hand, an eye or a leg, and wipes imaginary blood – other men's blood – from his face. Tears tremble under his lashes as he relives his moment of conversion in front of me, at his office desk.

"Afterwards the colonel wanted to give me a decoration for staying on my feet through the battle. I refused. I told him I could never bring myself to kill another man. He said he understood and asked me only to keep my sentiments to myself. Three months later was armistice and I was able to go to university. In the new democratic Italy I studied to be a teacher and I came home to Roggiano to teach others that we must have peace not war.

"Then I saw that our men were returning from the prison camps to their firesides and talking about war. And soon the children in the square were rushing about going 'Bang, bang' and 'Boom, boom.' I saw that although we had already lost one war, we were in danger of losing an even bigger one around the hearth."

Zanfini is about to see his last and most extensive project realized. After seven years of bargaining and persuasion he has brought the mayors of the fourteen communes of Esore – seven Christian

Democrats, four Communists, three Socialists – together to agree on one school for the whole region. A school for children and adults too.

Zanfini rises like Caesar and unfurls his blueprint, which is magically to hand. "All this" he says, and there is a lot of it, some thirty or more buildings, sports stadium pavilion, theater and so on, "all this will cost only an eighth of what must be spent if each commune were to build its own necessary school.

"Calabria has agreed. Now we wait only for Rome and the Law."

He sinks majestically to his seat.

"Another march on Rome," I suggest jokingly.

"Never," he says. "There must never be another march anywhere." And that same ineffable sweetness floods over his face. "Peace and Love. Love and Peace."

I am absolutely convinced of his sincerity. His operatics only enhance the impression. If you really believe in something, why not give it all you've got. I am sizzling with excitement at having stumbled on something so rare and passionate. I know that somehow the manner of my arrival enabled me to draw much more out of this man and the situation. I feel alive to every nuance, every color, aroma and texture, even the soup stain on Zanfini's jacket.

I really did not expect the journey to start so soon.

In the morning I spend an hour repacking the bike. Every morning it's the same, but the improvement is always noticeable. I'm getting the weight where I want it, the bike feels better and there's more room as things settle into place. Today I want to get to Palermo. I know it is about 150 miles to Reggio, where the ferry crosses to Sicily, but after that I have no idea. It did not occur to me to bring a map of Italy, so little did Europe figure among my preoccupations .

The ride to Reggio is glorious, with glimpses of the Mediterranean, as from a small aircraft, and then the drop down to the sea. The ferry chugs across to Messina and a promising new autostrada points to Palermo. Then abruptly, after ten kilometers, the road becomes narrow, twisting, replete with roadworks and jammed with impassable trucks throwing undigested diesel in my face. It is 150 more miles to Palermo, much farther than I thought possible. Most of the way I crawl along in the dark. I arrive in Palermo at eight, very weary, and lose myself in a maze of impoverished streets.

I stop – I have to stop somewhere – in the Via Torremuzzo, and try to collect my wits. After a really long hard ride I feel my blood fizzing in my veins as though suddenly decompressed. I sit on the bike, for I dare not leave it, surrounded by a press of urchins, outside a noisy bar. In this strange period when movement has stopped but the noise and vibration are still ringing through my body I seem to have stumbled into an enchanted canyon populated by circus freaks and the odder characters of fiction from Rabelais to Damon Runyon. Dwarfs, giants, fat men, rubber men, sweeps, touts, pimps, slobs, whores and bearded ladies, throng in the spotlights and cavernous shadows, lurk behind bead curtains and make theatrical appearances on impossible balconies among outrageous articles of underwear. After a few moments my vision sobers down. Much of the effect is due to almost mediaeval street lighting, and a warmth in the night air that allows people to display a lot of skin, but even so Torremuzzo is a very flamboyant street.

I am beat. Too tired to think in English, let alone Italian. Where am I? No idea. Where should I go? No notion. The street life surges around me. I feel a hundred sharp and hungry eyes fastened on my bike as on a Christmas tree hung with gifts ripe for the plucking. Ashamed of my weakness, I can think only of the telephone number I was given of friends of friends. The Fat Man, playing cards on the pavement, says, Yes, there is a telephone in the bar. I carry the looser items of luggage in with me. The friends of friends are at home. They will come in a car and fetch me. I sit where I can watch the bike, and wait. What will I do when there are no friends of friends? I resolve to deal with this question later.

An Israeli approaches me. Yes, an Israeli, selling himself hard. Do I think, he asks, that if he goes back to Israel now they will put him in jail for desertion?

What would you do, I ask, if you arrived in a strange, exotic city at night and had no friends to turn to?

He goes away, disappointed. It's as I always thought. There are two kinds of people in this world: those who ask questions and those who answer them.

The street market in Palermo, Sicily, captivated me, and I took dozens of pictures of exotic displays of the most improbable foods, but it was the people who got me. They all seemed so bright and lively, especially this little boy, whose electric smile, I hope, makes up for the fuzziness of the picture

Africa

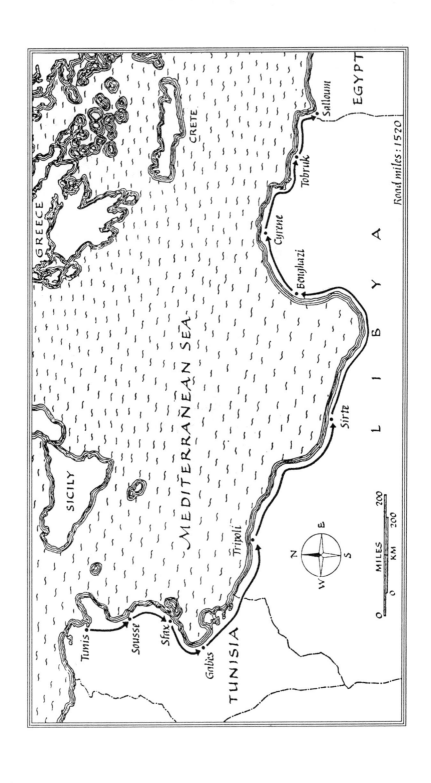

GREECE

CRETE

EGYPT

Salloum

Tobruk

Cyrene

Benghazi

L I B Y A

Road miles: 1520

Sirte

MEDITERRANEAN SEA

SICILY

Tripoli

N
W E
S

MILES
0   200
KM
0   200

Tunis

Sousse

Sfax

Gabès

TUNISIA

At first I thought he was a noisy, obnoxious fool. He was sitting on one of the green, slatted benches on the deck of the Tunis ferry, humming an Arab tune to himself and tracing the course of the melody through the air with fat and grimy thumb and forefinger joined at the tips like Siamese carrots. His face, all pits and wrinkles, wore the determined bliss of someone trying hard to get high. His head was the shape of a coconut and he saw me coming with eyes like black olives buried in old gray cheese. He wore a padded green combat jacket zipped up to the neck, patched gray trousers and old fashioned pointed shoes. His body seemed to be coconut-shaped as well.

"Ah, you, *vous, was machen. Sprechen Deutsch. Ich auch. Scheisse.*" Then a burst of Arabic, and "*Ich bin* Hamburg, Dusseldorf, Amsterdam. *Viel fraulein. Jolies filles. Einz. Zwei. Ja. Scheisse.*"

The wave of gibberish hit me as I walked towards him, and I thought it was some kind of invitation to talk, but he broke off again and went back to his trance-like singing. There were other Tunisians around, all grinning madly, and I felt embarrassed and annoyed. For me this ferry crossing to Africa represented a decisive leap into the unknown, a voyage of no return. Although the fighting between Egypt and Israel had by now stopped, I thought it might break out again at any moment. I was full of stern forebodings and in no mood for mockery, and I shied off to the far rail to talk to two effete Englishmen from Tangier who offered me the proper degree of respect. As far as I could see, we were the only European passengers. The crew members were Italian and wore fancy blue sashes around their middles, which I thought less than manly. The other travelers were evidently Tunisians going home from the great casual labor exchanges of the north, dressed by the flea markets of Europe and carrying their belongings in big cardboard boxes or papier-mache suitcases tied with string. As my friends gossiped about the goings-on at the court of the King of Morocco, I watched the thin, hardy men with their enormous bundles of stuff fighting their way along the gangways and through the hatches, the scapegoats of Europe, wearing our castoff clothing, hustled and slandered from border to border, available to do any job too dirty for a white man. No wonder they looked ugly and morose, except when grinning. No wonder I thought they had been mocking me.

Africa ⎯⎯⎯⎯⎯⎯➤ 33

After a while my smart friends decided to take to their first-class cabin for a snooze, and I went into the main saloon to see how I would pass the rest of the ten-hour crossing. The saloon was nearly full of Arabs, stretched out in the upholstered chairs and sofas trying to sleep. I started talking in French to my neighbor, a gentle Tunisian engine driver called Hassen, but it was only a few moments before I began to be aware of the barman. He was twiddling the knobs of the television set. He was angry. The thick white flesh of his face was set in an expression of stubborn conceit. He was literally pigheaded. The set had been tuned to a program of Arab music, but the channel he wanted was showing an Italian football match. The picture was indiscernible through the interference patterns and the sound was merely a crashing roar of static but it seemed to satisfy him. It was plain that he was not going to have any bloody wog music in his saloon. He was a short, fat man and his pregnant belly slung over the silly blue sash made him look unbearably pompous. As he steered his bumptious body back to the bar, he kicked aside the outstretched feet of sleeping Tunisians rather than walk around them. On his way he picked up empty soda bottles and flung them skillfully halfway across the lounge into a large cardboard box where they fell with a regular, shattering din. From then on I was unable to take my eyes off him. It was truly breathtaking to see one man seize upon an environment, which belonged, theoretically, to his forty or so customers, and use it for the complete expression of his own selfish and domineering nature. Behind the bar, his seat of power, he granted or withheld his favors as capriciously as any despot. Europeans he served with a ghastly conspiratorial grin. Others he refused altogether, loudly, rudely, with vulgar gestures. When some newcomer dared to tamper with the TV he flew into terrible tantrums.

His strutting and posturing were unforgettable. He treated the lounge and its occupants as his private colony and, with great energy, found a thousand ways of showing his contempt (mildly reflected in other members of the crew) while the rest of us submitted in our various ways, resigned, resentful or merely numbed. He represented in my eyes all that is brutal, greedy and corrupt in human behavior, and he was a powerful influence in stimulating my sympathy for the Arabs. Short of violence it was obvious that the man could not be stopped.

The singer came in a little later, when it started to rain outside. He sat at the far end of the lounge still chanting and smiling as though at some Sufi vision. In the confined space the songs were much clearer. Hassen said they were nonsense about girls and love, and he was apparently making them up as he went, but at least he offered an alternative kind of vitality to the terrible malignant power of the barman.

The Arabs nearest him began tapping and clapping along, and others drifted closer, but he continued for a while as though he were unaware of any of us, playing the fool for another audience that only he could see. The barman was noticeably annoyed and the tempo of his outrages increased, but although he still commanded two thirds of the saloon he did not meddle with the singer, whose territory was growing. I sat for a while on the border line of their two spheres of influence, and it was like looking out on two different worlds. To my left, shouting, hostility, the smashing of bottles and, from the TV, the gibbering howl of the ether. To my right, singing, laughter and a beat that was beginning to reach into me. Hassen and I moved across to the right.

The singer judged this the moment to come out of his private retreat, and began to respond to his followers. I could not imagine how I had ever thought him distasteful. At worst he was a simple clown, but his power now seemed to grow as the barman's dwindled. He interrupted his buffoonery with poetry, and Hassen told me it was original and good. The same thumb and forefinger placed the words in the air with a precision and meaning that I felt I could understand, though I spoke no Arabic. The songs also became longer, more lyrical. Slowly, over a period of several hours, the pitch of his performance built up. The barman by now was utterly effaced, the TV could no longer be heard. Everyone in the saloon was with the singer, his to a man, and yet he still seemed strangely detached from us, not feeding at all on our adulation in the manner of a Western "star." Nor was there ever an attempt by anyone to compete with him. He remained the focus of energy for the rest of the crossing.

Towards the end he moved from songs and poetry to oratory. It was a long speech, and if the rhythms were anything to go by, it was in the Arab equivalent of blank verse. His voice now was very muscular and gritty. The harsh, hard-nosed syllables flew out in formation and beat on my ear. His audience replied with moans and cries of agreement. I imagined the voice amplified a thousand times, a hundred thousand times, from loudspeakers on all the minarets of Islam.

The sounds conjured up an atmosphere of great ferocity, yet the sense of the speech, it turned out, was moderate. It had to do with peace and war in the Middle East. It praised the moderate statesmanship of Bourguiba, and poured scorn on the troublemakers who would fight, like Qaddafi of Libya, to the last Egyptian. Hassen said it was good sense, realistic and very poetic.

"I too thought at first he was just a fool, but now what he says is very impressive."

It was well after dark when the ship arrived in Tunis. By then I had made another friend, Mohamad, a young Tunisian who was one of the singer's most enthusiastic accompanists. He was more stylishly dressed than most, with a jazzy peaked cap on, which he never removed. His nickname, loosely translated from Arabic, meant "The Swell." He asked me where I was going to stay in Tunis, and I said I had no idea.

"Then you will stay with me. My family will be very honored. You will have everything we can offer. We will be extremely proud to have such a famous man in our house and our friendship will last forever. I have a dark skin but my soul is white as a lily. You will be safe and well in my house."

Before leaving the ship I happened to notice the barman. He seemed a rather insignificant person, cleaning up after us, hardly worth bothering with.

Arriving in Africa was, after all, pretty much like arriving anywhere. You used your imagination to make it different. There was a harbor, a passenger terminal, offices and officials, the usual formalities and indignities. Everyone spoke heavily pointed French against a background of murmuring Arabic. The ferry was a drive-on, drive-off ship and there was no delay in unloading. I took the bike outside the dock gates and waited for Mohamad. I had explained that there was no room for him on the bike and he had swallowed his disappointment and said he would find a taxi. I wondered whether he had invited me so that he could get a lift home on the bike. It seemed important to expose all these ignoble possibilities, to get a true mea-

The ferry from Palermo to Tunis carried many migrant laborers back to their families. Mohamad invited me to his crowded home in a makeshift suburb, and insisted that I sleep in his bed while he lay on the floor - my first taste of incomparable Arab hospitality.

sure of his hospitality. After all, I was going to write about it. I wouldn't want to say that a pure flame of generosity burned in his noble breast if all along he asked me home only for the ride.

I mean, let's get it right, shall we?

However, Mohamad and the taxi duly appeared and we wound round the streets of Tunis and out into the dark countryside for a bit, to arrive at the Cité Nouvelle de Kabaria. It was difficult to grasp it at night. Most of it was in shadow, but it appeared to have been recently built beside a major highway. I saw a maze of ten-foot walls, plastered white. No visible windows or roofs. Not like houses at all. Eerie. We plunged down a dirt alley and stopped by a door. The door opened not, as I expected, into the house but into a small cemented yard. Mohamad went first and then asked me to bring the bike inside. It barely squeezed through. The father was standing there in a fez, loose shirt, trousers and sandals. He greeted me very formally and politely, with few French words. The yard was maybe ten feet square, and the rooms opened off it on three sides, so the whole house was, in effect, a tiny walled fortress, with one door leading out. I could see already that the rooms were very small. I was ushered into a room opposite the street door, which was like a little cave. It was about seven feet wide, and half of it was filled with a brass bed, covered sumptuously by a shiny cotton pile rug. There was a bit of floor space and a chest cluttered with ornaments, like a shrine, with an oil lamp burning.

I was left to sit there for a while as whispered conferences took place outside, and I began to feel nervous about what was going on, so I went out to look. Mohamad's mother and two small children were there with him, moving about in deep shadow. The five of us and the motorcycle filled the yard.

Some hint of suspicion must have shown in my movement or expression.

"If you wish to watch over your motorcycle, please do, but I assure you it is safe," said Mohamad. He spoke gently and quietly, not at all the brash boy on the ship. I felt ashamed and went back to the room (just three steps away – everything was so close) to find that a supper had been laid out on the chest: Two small lamb chops in heavily spiced hot sauce with peas and pimentos, and some bread: No cutlery.

I ate the bread with the chops, and then made a mess having to scoop up the peas and sauce with my fingers. The sauce burned my mouth terribly and I could not finish it, and that made me feel bad too. I turned to the door and asked for water. The mother came in with a jug and a metal cup and I saw her face in the light, small and worn, but very calm and tender. This is definitely not a "B" movie, I told myself, and from then on felt absolutely secure.

The bed was Mohamad's but I was to sleep on it. I protested, but in vain.

"Whether you sleep on it or I, it's the same thing. If you sleep in it, it is as if I were sleeping in it," he said, offering it as a pleasure rather than a sacrifice, and although it was a traditional formula of hospitality, maybe, it came alive on his lips.

I lay down on it like a visiting emperor, with a small boy, Mohamad's brother, lying on the floor by my bedside, and I prepared to fall immediately into a deep sleep, but sleep would not come for a long time, and my skin, which had been itching nervously for some weeks, tingled even more than usual. Sometime in the night I came half out of sleep again to hear muffled drumbeats and what seemed in my dreamy state to be a procession of phantoms moving through the darkness.

I awoke with numb lumps all over my wrists and neck, and half my face. *Bugs,* I told myself. *Not nervousness, not heat rash. Bed bugs.* But I refused to believe it. That beautiful bed, infested? Never.

I slept on the bed three nights. The second night was just as bad. The third night I got out my nylon tent and wrapped it around me and that was better. The pleasure was Mohamad's, the sacrifice was mine.

So on that first morning I squinted through my swellings at an African day. Everybody was up and about early. They had nibbled at something before dawn because it was the time of Ramadan, and for that month no Muslim may eat while the sun is in the sky. The drums were to tell people it was breakfast time, but as a nominal Christian I was exempt and had a peppery fried egg.

In daylight the place seemed even smaller. There were two other rooms the size of mine. The rest of the family – mother, father, Mohamad and little daughter – slept in one of the other rooms, which was also a tobacco shop. The father had been a prison warder, and as a retired civil servant he qualified for a license to sell tobacco. It was not a roaring trade. How they all fitted together in that tiny space, why they weren't constantly colliding in the doorways was a matter for wonder. There was never a harsh word, no hint of impatience or frustration, the children kept to their own little world, seemingly content, looking up from a modest mud pie with big eyes full of liquid love.

They designed their lives around each other with the intricate harmony of an oriental carpet design. Obviously it required much submission, mostly on the part of the women. Was it submission or repression? Or a different view of space? I could not tell.

Just how uncrowded they felt became clear when I asked about their third room. They said that since their eldest children had moved out, they had so much space that they had offered their spare room to a couple of elderly poor relations who were still sleeping. So now we were eight.

There was one other door through which I passed after breakfast. Behind it was a square yard of cement with a hole in the middle, and a jug with a slender spout. I went to get some paper, and then returned and squatted down, rather puzzled, because it was obvious that nobody else used paper. I had been told many times, of course, that you should never greet an Arab with your left hand. It was a serious insult, because that was the hand they used to wipe their behinds, and I had grinned and said, Yes, I know, and somehow I had never really thought what it meant because everyone has paper. Don't they? No, they don't. They have a jug of water and a left hand, and the thought of having to touch my shit with my own hand disgusted me. God, it was bad enough having to stick your fingers in your food. So I turned my thoughts away from the whole problem, and choked up their toilet with paper, which was no easy thing to do.

There was no running water in the house and no electricity. The houses were as small as they could be, and built of the cheapest materials. The roads between them were dirt. Kabaria was a slum. A new, still uncompleted slum, or it would have been but for the people who lived in it, for a slum, I discovered later, is the people and not the place.

Just how mean a place it was became obvious when Mohamad's brother-in-law took me to visit his father in the country. We rode off down the highway and up into some low hills, lovely nourishing curves like the breasts of mother earth, planted with big shade trees and olive groves. I saw a brown cow suckling its calf, and a compound of thorn and cactus, and we turned in there to a couple of huts set at right angles. They were made of mud plastered over wattle and you could see where the hands had shaped them at the corners. The door frames revealed how thick and satisfying they were, like gingerbread maybe, topped with thatch, and at their base were two color-matched orange marmalade cats.

Inside, the spaces were about the same size as the rooms at Kabaria, but this was real space, under the rafters, with room for the imagination to grow. The old man sat down opposite me across a rough coffee table while his old lady busied herself behind me with a charcoal stove, always behind me so that I never really saw her. Behind her and filling the width of the hut was a wicker-work bed stretched on a wooden frame – less shelter for bedbugs.

The old man talked crazy nonsense to me about the world beyond his cactus fence, and he had a perfect right because it was a crazy world. I ate his bread and honey – his own wheat, his own hives – and heard about the Jews.

"These Jews," he said. "They have a strong smell. I can smell one a mile away." We were face to face, and half of me is Jewish. Maybe it's the rear half.

"I have heard of a Jewish tribe," he went on "which was conquered, and the invaders slew all the men, but the women allowed themselves to have children by their conquerors. '*Beshwaya, beshwaya,*' they murmured. 'In time. In time.' Secretly they taught the children to hate their fathers, and when they grew up they murdered them.

"As long as there is one left alive they will never give up."

He was a fine old man and his nonsense did not disturb me. Any Jew could come into his house and be as safe there as in his own home, as long as he came as a person and not a label. I watched him, listened to his voice rather than his words and drank in the scene. Everything fitted, everything was right; shape, size, color, texture, all the parts had grown together, into something that would shape the instincts of the people who made it and lived in it. What ever messages of hate he picked up and repeated, his personal dealings guided by those instincts would surely be all right. But what was there in Kabaria to provide the same inspiration, living in those shabby, cramped boxes, fighting for work on the edge of an overcrowded city? Perhaps the old man led a tougher life, perhaps at times he ate less or felt the cold. If so it had only done him good. But the kids couldn't see it. How could they? They had to get into that mess on the edge of the city so that one day some of them might appreciate what they had left behind. Did they choose or were they driven? Either way, I thought, they were the stuff that wars are made of.

In Tunis I worked the embassies. The Libyans gave me my visa, and took out one heavy anxiety, which the Egyptians replaced with another. There would be no possibility, they said, of crossing the border from Libya into Egypt.

I stared at the map. There was THE road, no other. North of the road was the sea. South of the road, the desert. Here and there tracks trailed into the desert...and disappeared, punctuated full stop by an oasis, or dwindling into nothing. There was no other way. A fourteen-hundred-mile cul-de-sac to Salloum on the Egyptian border, and I had to go down it, just in case...

On the third morning I was ready. The bike was packed. Mohamad had his gang around him, and they were going to escort me to the highway, and take ritual pictures on my cameras. Each time the bike had gone out into the street more people had seen it. By the third day every kid in town knew about it. As I rolled it along in first gear, overheated and dressed up to kill, the parade swelled to fantastic proportions. The Pied Piper or the Wizard of Oz could not have had a greater success, but I had nowhere to take this crusade and I began to get nervous wondering where it would take me. It was immodest, out of all proportion; I couldn't stop it, but I knew it had to go wrong.

As my army turned the last corner, in sight of the main road, the police came in and wound it up. They grabbed Mohamad, who was carrying my cameras, and told me to follow. The rest they sent scattering. There were only a couple of them, in dark and dingy suits, but they looked awkward and angry. When I got into their office on the highway one of them had already managed to find the release to open the camera, but didn't know what to do then, so I grabbed it, and closed it and rolled the film back into its cassette and then opened it for him.

Mohamad was looking very put down, and they were shouting at him. Then one of them turned on me, and accused me of being a sensation-mongering journalist trying to get pictures of Arabs stabbing each other in drunken brawls, exploiting their poverty and ignorance to sell my dirty rag. It was a good story. Maybe it fitted somebody else. Then they turned to accusing Mohamad of being out to rob me, and said I had been taking my life in my hands, and I said all the best things I could as convincingly as possible and tried to get the temperature down. So then they took us out in the street and told Mohamad to go home and told me to piss off.

I tried to make it all right with Mohamad before I went, but he was very chastened and didn't want to talk. I didn't like to go but I was a provocation just being there and so I said a sad good-bye and rode off into my cul-de-sac.

Tunisia rolls by. The first marvel comes in right after Kabaria, a huge Roman aqueduct swings alongside me for a few miles, crumbling but unconquered, like a monster from the depths of time. The rains are early and I see the water hanging in the sky ready to fall on me. The land needs it but I don't, and I hurry past wheat fields and over hills to beat it. Halfway to Sousse I know it's going to get me (it's a personal thing between the rain and me) and I stop to pull on the waterproofs. The land is very quiet, just a bunch of horses about a mile away. I wish I shared that calm.

As I ride along I'm thinking about Kabaria. Why did it end like that? It would have been prudent to leave the day before.

Yes, well it would have been prudent to stay at home. You have to let things go their own way, or why be here at all.

Still, I am uneasy. I have to find a way to be with people in a less spectacular fashion. I didn't see how Mohamad thirsted for prestige. He got drunk on it, and how can I blame him? It's all very well for me to go around feeling humble, but I must also be aware of the effect I am having on others. It could be potent.

Sousse is a big town of eighty-four thousand people. Hassen the engine driver lives here, but his directions are hopelessly inadequate. Maybe he never meant me to find him. Anyway, I have spent too long now looking for him, and it's too late to ride on. I come across a beautiful old part of town, and a hotel of mosaic tiles, frothy arches and cool interiors. A room for a dinar. Behind the hotel is a tiny lean-to shelter crammed with rags and boxes where I can put the bike. A man in a torn and dirty caftan watches me struggle to manoeuvre the bike in through a narrow gate, ten minutes of hard work, and then says: "One dinar."

I am furious at him. "You should have told me before," I yelp.

That's right, you tell him. Let's have some English justice and fair play around here.

I argue the price down to something reasonable. In the morning, where I thought there was room only for the bike, I see there are people sleeping too. The information hits me like a custard pie in the face. *God, Simon, you are a prick.*

There's a lot of water everywhere. The roads near the sea front are under two feet of it. Do they mention this in the brochures? I see a package of Nordic tourists washed up in a hotel lobby. The hotel looks as though it has absorbed its own weight of water.

Crossing overland to Sfax I see another antediluvian wonder rear up ahead of me. A vast wall shot through with rows of ragged windows bars my way like a small mountain range. At the last minute it veers off sharply to the right and becomes the remains of a coliseum.

El Djem is flooded. Sfax also. The watery grayness keeps me going. Along the coast now, more life, more traffic, mud-brick houses, market gardens, date palms, donkeys, camels, all the things you read about, see in pictures. When you get there you know none of it was right.

Riding cautiously in the wet, I have gone only 165 miles by mid-afternoon. I decide to stop at Gabes, very aware of the Libyan frontier coming close. I want to prepare for it somehow. Tunisia is not part of the war. It is a Western-oriented, tourist-conscious, bilingual country. Libya is belligerent, fanatical, oil-rich and runs according to the laws of the Prophet Mohammed, or so I am told. I decide to post all my exposed film off now, and at the last minute remember a document I'm carrying that has an Israeli stamp on it and send that away as well. Images of search and interrogation flash across my mind. They make me both shiver and laugh at myself. Extreme situations always seem absurd until they happen.

When does the "B" movie become a documentary? Back at the factory in Meriden we laughed about my untried, unprepared motorcycle. "Chances are," said one mechanic, "if you don't worry about it, it'll go all the way with no bother." I chose to worry. I took all the tools and spare parts I could carry, and half an hour later the oil fell out. Because I was prepared?

Does it rain because you carry your umbrella, or because you don't? It's a personal matter depending on how you remember it. The way I write my own history it's low on winning streaks. I never could gamble. I like to work things out in advance, but it bothers me to think of what I might have been missing. I've done too much hacking away against the grain of life. Without all that solemn effort, maybe, I could have gone further, faster, easier.

Remember what my headmaster said thirty years ago, that tar-stained old walrus: "Simon, you think too much."

Thinking's like a black tunnel. Once you're in it you have to think your way through to the other end. At least I think so.

The Libyan immigration man, if that's who he is, has a limp shotgun folded over his arm and hunting boots laced up around his trouser cuffs. He appears happy. He has several duplicated forms in Arabic, and points to where I should sign. I am being processed into Libya like a monkey, by sign language. I put my name to everything without question. He takes my passport.

"Helt," he says.

Helt? Oh, health. His first and only English word. I produce my vaccination certificates, grinning (like a monkey) and pass on. There's a lot of hanging about. Nobody will speak to me in a language I understand. The customs chief is in a shiny silver Italian suit, with a carton of Marlboros under his arm. He touches a few of my dusty things fastidiously.

"Visky?" he says. And that's *his* English word for the day. The Infidel monkey shakes his head and enters Libya. It is not that they cannot speak anything but Arabic. They will not. It is part of the Libyan crusade for Islam. We are not always kind to our foreigners and it is a sobering experience to have the tables turned. In the good old days, I suppose, one would have spoken English at the top of one's voice until the natives just naturally understood, but then we had Queen Victoria to fall back on.

On my left, a few miles of sand dunes and then the sea, blue fading to gray. On my right, desert, and nothing but desert. The map says there are 1,500 miles of it to Nigeria as the crow flies, if a crow could. Above, the sky is clear in all directions. Ahead the road is an impeccable two-lane tarmac. A mild wind raises a curtain of dust over the desert, nothing awkward, just enough to blur the outlines of a few camels. There is no trace of a human presence anywhere.

I stop to taste the emptiness, listen to the silence, like the hiss of a blank tape playing. It's a bit awesome. Although I could easily do the hundred miles to Tripoli before nightfall, I know that I must sleep out in a real desert tonight.

The city-bred boy in me is frightened, and all the usual alarm signals go off in my head. Can I ride on this stuff? What will happen if I sink into it? Is it safe? Who might come by in the night? A tingling mixture of fear and anticipation, waiting to combine into something like joy. Once the decision is made it's easy. I choose a spot among some dunes on the seaward side and prop up the bike, thanks to a metal disc welded onto the end of the swing stand, one good idea that did get carried out. Then the tent. Where? Which way? How anchored? Every action is part of a routine to be studied and perfected. How many times will I be doing this? Hundreds? It is worth getting it right. I use the bike to anchor one side of the tent, and find a boulder for the other side. What about the fly sheet? Will it rain? It seems impossible. The sky is clear from horizon to horizon, but still, just in case... Then in goes the bedding. The flying jacket folded inside out makes a great pillow. So it goes on. As I move around the bike I try to notice everything about it, chain tension, tire tread, anything coming loose, falling off, trying to build up a picture of it as it should be so that any change rings a warning bell . . . and sure enough there's a rocker box cap loose. I can see the thread.

Those bloody things. What a fucking awful design. Fifteen seconds of profanity to make their ears burn in Meriden. *Must remember to tighten it, with jointing compound. No! Do it now. You'll forget. And while you're about it, check the battery level.*

There's the Optimus stove to fill from the tank, a messy business because I can't see the level in the stove, and it's hard to control the flow of fuel anyway. Must find a better way. There are stuffed peppers canned in Hungary to eat with rice. The whole performance, unpacking, checking, cooking and clearing up keeps me moving and thinking for nearly two hours. I have almost forgotten where I am. With coffee and a cigarette I settle back into the astounding hush of the desert and remember, and then a really fierce flood of joy comes rushing over me.

Just look at me. Look where I am. Isn't this too bloody fantastic for words? It's me here, not Lawrence of Arabia, or Rudolf Valentino, or Rommel and the Afrika Korps. Me, and this little machine, we made it here.

The sun has run off into the sand somewhere in Tunisia. The stars are making unbelievably big holes in the moonless night. I am in a stupor of delight. If the journey ends tomorrow it will have been worth it, but a premonition sweeps away all doubt and for once I allow myself to know that the journey will not end tomorrow and that there will be many times when I will feel this same overwhelming joy. Tonight we are showing the "A" film.

Life never leaves well alone. I feel the wind change, see the lightning at sea, hear the thunder. In early morning the storm moves inland. It rains very heavily and I'm afraid the water may undermine the bike and drop it on the tent and me, but I did choose slightly higher ground and it should be all right. I decide to wait it out. At last a break in the rain. I pack hastily, the tent full of water and sand, and get back on the road to Tripoli.

All I know of Libya is The Road, a thousand miles of road, good fast highway, stretched along the African coast like a clothes line. Libya hangs from the line like a giant's bed sheet, pegged on by Tripoli and Benghazi, blistering in the sun. They say there are some lovely damp spots down below among the folds at Kufra and Sebha, but what I see from the road is outrageous.

Out in the desert I see a tent, the old kind made of hides strung on poles in graceful peaks and troughs where the Sheik of Arabee obliged our forebears to swallow sheep's eyes and murmur "delicious." Out of the top grows a television aerial. Alongside the tent are two gas bottles, and beside them is parked a new Mercedes limousine. The owner strides out in billowing white cotton, leaps in kicking off his sandals and presses a leathery foot down hard on the accelerator.

A little way along the road on the other side, are two camels tethered next to an airplane.

Every man in Libya, employed or not, single or married, gets a weekly oil dividend from the state. In the towns people are doing up their places. Every other shop sells paint. And every other shop sells audio/video gear from Japan. The Koran is proclaimed throughout the land on triumphal arches set across the roads. Alcohol, and women out of wedlock, are forbidden. Whisky is twenty-five dollars a bottle, if you're caught drinking it, and forty-eight hours in jail for a first offense. Women wrap themselves in a checkered shroud, cowling their heads and holding one edge of it between their teeth, so that sometimes only an eye and a tooth are visible. You must not look at the eye. (Who would want to? The one I saw glittered like glass.)

Tripoli looks as though it were recently bombed. It still has an Italian air about it, from the colonial days I think. Now the Italians are back with contracts. In my hotel red-necked Italian pipe layers lounge in the breakfast room reading comics. The hotel is very expensive and I have to go to the bank. There are three cashiers, but the man ahead of me in the line reaches into his plastic shoulder bag and brings out a pile of notes a foot high, mostly in tens and twenties. The libyan pound is worth one and a half of ours, and all three cashiers are counting his money. Halfway through a stack someone shouts a greeting, a cashier replies, has a little chat, loses count and starts again. It takes twenty minutes before they manage to get through it all without interruption. I draw one five-pound note and wonder why they don't just give me a handful.

From Tripoli to Sirte is three hundred miles, and next day I'm really flying with the engine singing for me and everything rapping along nicely. There's a lot of rain, but I'm less nervous of the wet now, on tar at least. The land and sea lie flat out forever, and I can see the weather coming maybe fifty miles ahead. I have never seen so much weather. I can see where it begins and where it ends; I can see the blue sky above, and the approaching storms and then the good times beyond. Remarkable. Like having an overview of past and future. I am a world spinning through visible time, and the weather is an evocation of history. Great forces meeting, interacting, discharging their energies. Over there the blackest of clouds is shedding doom on the land below. What does that poisonous-looking deluge represent? Plague? Famine? Civil war? Those who are under its terrible judgment can certainly not see beyond it. To them it must seem as if the universe is engulfed. While I can see that it is a momentary thing.

All morning I'm flying along under the weather, with my head down at seventy, left arm resting along the handlebar, listening to the rroomm-rroomm of the engine, the zappity-zappity of the anorak rippling in the airstream, the crackling of the visor on the open-face helmet. This part of the coast is more fertile: olive groves, thousands of date palms, settlements with paddy cultivation, many wells with curious stepped walls on either side of them. There are many big, white Peugeot taxis on the road. Outwardly they are the familiar blank modules of industrial civilization; inside, turbans, fezzes and veils huddled over bundles of rich fabrics. The effect is like a Frigidaire packed with shrunken heads, or a digital display that tells fortunes. Thousands of these taxis run immense distances between Tripoli and Cairo. Sometimes I see one leave the road without warning and plunge into the open desert. Only with shaded eyes can I see the dark speck of a tent on some distant rising ground.

Now it's getting noticeably drier and wilder. Soon there's only desert on both sides, and the wind is whistling clouds of it across the road. Sand flickers on the tarmac like flames and, in places, dunes are building up on the surface. Many camels graze at the roadside where, for some reason, there seems to be more shrubbery, lanky young animals starting away in fright at the unfamiliar sound of the bike. I see a sandbar across the road and relax on the throttle to slow down. No change. The engine races on and suddenly it's urgent. Brakes on, clutch out, and I lean forward to switch off the ignition, since there is no kill button.

The carburetor slide is stuck. I have to ride on like that for twenty miles, an interesting problem, until I get to Ben-Gren where there's shelter, gas, and a cafe.

My first roadside repair is easy enough once I get out of the flying sand. The garage owner is so intrigued that he gives me a free spaghetti lunch with meat sauce and grated cheese. There are very few strangers in Libya, and I am able to see how the absence of tourism allows people to take a natural and generous interest in travelers. I am highly privileged. It's dark long before I get to Sirte, and a road barrier looms up with a diversion arrow pointing off into the open desert on my left. My lights can pick up no track there, but the tarmac ahead looks fine, so I go cautiously ahead. The tarmac widens abruptly, and I begin to grasp that I am on an airstrip. After a while a jeep rushes up behind me and stops. It is full of army. A lieutenant in British style uniform takes my passport and searches through it with a torch. Their faces are most impassive, and I am expecting trouble. Instead they all take turns to shake my hand warmly and wave me on. A nice moment.

I have just decided to sleep out when I get to the police check point at Sirte. The guard insists that I go straight to a hotel. I ride up the muddy hill to spend the evening among men lounging in pajamas, curly slippers and tasseled fezzes, playing trictrac and smoking elaborate pipes. The clerk pretends to speak English and I ask him to explain the stepped walls alongside the wells.

"It is like this," he says. "From here is to Benghazi three hundred and fifty miles, and ..."

Ah. Yes. I see.

Three hundred and sixty-five miles – to be exact – is quite a long way on a motorcycle. I'm up early and flying again. After a few minutes of sun, the rain breaks over me. For three hours I ride through it, constantly grateful that the electrics hold up. There are two shaky moments on ridges of dried mud made soapy by fresh rain. Other than that I am only wet. The rain has worked its way through the seams of the rubberized waterproofs, and my boots are squelching.

When I come out from under the roof of rain cloud the desert around me looks like primeval swamp and the camels make suitable-looking monsters. Rivers of floodwater rush along the side of the road. Then, within hours, everything, myself included, is dry as a bone again.

Benghazi's tallest buildings are already in sight when I run out of gas. Evidently the gas is poor since it is not delivering the expected mileage, but I feel stupid and annoyed with myself for being caught like this.

I stand by the roadside to wave at the traffic and the first car stops for me. It is a little Fiat saloon with two young men in the front and a large bundle of laundry on the back seat which turns out to be not laundry at all but an elderly female relative.

The men are clean-shaven, tidily groomed in Western dress and energetically helpful. They shower services upon me. We siphon some gas from their tank. They escort me into town and help to find me a hotel. On the way, at a gas station, they fill my tank and absolutely refuse money. And finally they lend me a pound because the banks are closed.

The Oilfield Hotel is my home for a week. It costs one pound to occupy one of the three cast-iron infirmary beds in a room, but most nights the other beds are empty. Only once do I have a roommate, a coal-black Nubian cook on his way to work in an oil rigger's camp near Tripoli. His friendly chuckles when awake are offset by the loudest snore I have ever heard. In the night I throw everything at him, but the express trains continue to roar in and out of his nostrils. If he stayed one more night I would have to move out.

The Egyptian Consul confirms that it is entirely out of the question for me to cross into Egypt by road.

"I suppose I can always try," I say.

His smile is the one reserved for troublesome idiots.

"Yes. You may try."

I research all the other ways into Egypt. By ship? At best, time-wasting and uncertain, but now captains are refusing to take their vessels into Alexandria. By air? Terribly expensive for the bike and also, at present, uncertain. I could fly myself and road freight the bike, but I am warned that I might never see the bike again.

The Sunday Times has offered to send credentials to help me across the border. It seems worth waiting a bit. Benghazi is, at first, an enjoyable city. It has lovely squares with palms, pools and fountains, and a big bazaar, a gold market, cloistered shops full of desirable objects like ivory back scratchers and musical instruments.

In the same street as the hotel is a motorcycle repair shop. Kerim el Fighi, the owner, cannot do enough for me. I have the run of the place, and decide to paint the boxes green. The gleaming white fiberglass offends me now. I want a bike that loses itself in the landscape, rather than standing out. I even wind green tape over the bright chrome of the head lamp and handlebars.

It is easy to make friends here. There are so many young men around with nothing to do. They are courteous, inquisitive and good company, but very cut off from the world and from knowledge in general. They seem hungry for involvement, and prowl the streets like wolves, but there is nothing to occupy their minds except the latest film, which they are likely to see several times. The new money has liberated them, but for what? They seem very bewildered by the changes, and the obvious conflict between the religious values preached by Qaddafi and the Koran, and the New Age of technology. In any case it is all speculation, over endless rounds of fizzy drinks. In Benghazi, at least the women are freer of purdah, and many walk around in Western dress, but they are still quite unapproachable.

After a week of waiting there is still no mail from London. I can't bear the inaction any longer. Tomorrow I'll go to the border, right or wrong. An English technician tells me the border is a military one.

"They have very itchy trigger fingers. Shoot first and ask afterwards. Pouf! One more *Sunday Times* man gone."

I feel as though I'm going to the front, rather than crossing a frontier. Kerim tells me that there are some interesting ruins on the way to Tobruk.

"Roman," he says. " Very good."

Cyrenaica is where the coast comes closest to Greece and Crete, where the ancient Greeks and Romans gained their first foothold in Africa, but I knew little and cared less about antiquity at the time. I was quite convinced that in a few days I would be back in Benghazi, so I decided to take the shortest route to the border and do my tourism on the way back.

The road followed the coast awhile and then rose gently into the hills. The air was fresher and the land more fertile. There were farms all around and many small peasant huts. A man walked out of a hut and, three steps from his threshold, swept his robe up over his hips and squatted in a single, surprisingly graceful movement. Only afterwards did I realize what he had been doing.

"Good God," I said aloud. "So close to his own doorstep?"

The way wound among outcroppings of crusty white rock, enfolding pine woods, areas of scrub and gorse, patches of soft springy grass and streams with reedy banks. The landscape felt familiar and drew me irresistibly. I found a particularly luxuriant-seeming patch of grass shielded from the road by a row of low thorns and set up the tent there. No question, that land felt like mine, and I was entirely at home in it.

The moon was full and I realized for the first time that I had started my journey under a full moon exactly a month before. That night the moon seemed more brilliant than I had ever known it, and night was simply a reflection of day in a silver mirror. I ate and drank and smoked and wrote, doing all those things with great pleasure, and then lay down in the tent convinced that the day was over. As I lay, drowsily waiting for sleep, a male voice drifted across, seeming to come from the road. I heard a dog bark. The voice replied. They were moving along, but instead of fading, they grew stronger.

By now I was fully awake, trying to locate the position of the intruder and track his movements. Not for the first time I thought how hopelessly vulnerable I was, practically naked and inside this small nylon envelope. For a while there was silence, but I was increasingly nervous for I had heard nothing to suggest that he had moved away. Suddenly the voice broke out again, but very close this time and loud, singing a lusty song. This was too much for me. I scrambled into my clothes and prepared to struggle out of the tent, but as soon as I put my head out, my fears dissolved in astonishment.

I was surrounded by sheep. I looked out on a sea of silver fleece, a hundred animals or more. Not one sound had I heard to mark their approach. Well beyond them, farther away than I had thought and perhaps even unaware of my presence, stood two figures.

If everything in that light seemed to be painted in silver, their robes appeared to have been woven of the metal. Their faces were in shadow, but they carried their silver raiment with the majesty of kings. A window flew open on the past, on half-baked impressions left by Bible tales and Christmas carols which I had discounted then as silly fables and superstitions. Such things had no place in the crowded streets and classrooms of my childhood. They were only possible here, under this sky, in this light and on this land. This was Bible country, and on a night like this one could believe.

I walked over to the shepherds and exchanged the Arab greetings I had learned. We could do no more. We smoked a cigarette together peacefully and after ten minutes I returned to the tent and slept.

During the hours before dawn the temperature fell below freezing and I woke to find the frost glistening on the ground. The shepherds were still there, and now they were as remarkable for their poverty as they had been for their grandeur. Their faces were ugly and dulled by ignorance. Their robes were transformed from silver cloth to sacking. They were huddled on the ground, miserably cold, two ill-favored and pathetic peasants gazing in awe at the paraphernalia I was struggling to pack with frozen fingers. I would have made coffee for them, but there was no water left. The contrast between day and night inspired no lofty sentiments in me at the time. It was too cold for that.

I shared my last cigarettes with them and left. At the next town I realized that I was not on the road I had meant to take, but was headed willy-nilly for the antiquities. An hour later I was at Cyrene.

I meant to pay only a token visit. Roman ruins, I felt, were a bit too close to home, and my mind always seemed to be traveling several thousand miles ahead of my body. The entrance to the site was a wonderful gateway of honey-colored sandstone soaring above me. I entered and found myself in a vast forum, rows of columns reaching out beyond anything I could have imagined possible, and between the columns tantalizing glimpses of more marvels in every direction. I was alone in a great Roman city, certainly the only sightseer there. At one time I saw some robed women in an amphitheater, but they fled at my approach. I spent the day wandering, entranced, among pools and patios, gymnasia, temples, and in and out of the homes of ordinary Roman citizens. In one part an Italian archeologist was involved in restoration with some workmen, but they seemed to belong more to the city's past history than the present. Later in the afternoon the bubble burst for ten minutes when a party of very superior air force commanders swept round the ruins at the speed of flight, with their uniformed publicity photographer bursting blood vessels to break the record for exposures per minute. He was using flash in that blinding sun, which meant that he was interested only in their faces, and I thought that summed up their trip very well. Just faces.

I finished the day on the lower level of the city, with the Mediterranean spread out below me. As the sun itself faded, the light seemed to spring out of the stone, and the city glowed before falling back into the night. I knew that these experiences, the shepherds and Cyrene, were striking deep into me, that each day's events seemed to intensify the following day, and yet I had barely grazed the edge of my first continent. At the hotel I ate a meal with two French salesmen taking time off for a side trip. They were pleasant to talk to, informative about Arab deficiencies, but they seemed to me to have left their imaginations at home in Paris. Did I seem as ordinary, as uninspired to them? They were used to Africa, of course. To them, this was like visiting the Tower of London. It struck me that everywhere in the world I would meet people to whom being there would be an ordinary, everyday event. Was my journey really nothing more than a state of mind?

I slept out again that night, on the coast just beyond Marsa Susa, and I knew next morning that I would have to reach the border that day. By lunch time I was already in Tobruk, a dry bone of a city, splintering and powdering in the sun. I met an Irishman in the street. He worked for the "Aisle" Institute (the what? Oh, OIL) where he taught English (or Irish) to Libyan oil men. He was earning £500 a month, a fortune in those days, and with his savings he was buying an apartment in Rome, another one in Ancona and a farmhouse

Although I only came across them by accident, I was overwhelmed by the fabulous ruins of Cyrene. Libya is hardly a popular tourist destination, and during the Arab-Israeli war even less so. I had the privilege of wandering around this great Roman city entirely alone, immersed in a world that vanished almost two thousand years ago.

in Ireland. He asked me in for lunch with his Italian wife and small children. She hated the Arabs, and said her children couldn't play with their children for fear of catching skin diseases.

"I can't say I care for them myself," said the Irishman. "They seem to regard all Westerners as exploiters. But it wouldn't be so bad if they didn't treat us like Martians in the streets." They invited me to sleep there on my way back. I didn't know if I would. I felt rather sorry for them. These were nice people who seemed to have missed the point somewhere, but then I didn't have to live their lives.

I set off with the maximum of nonchalance, to do the last seventy-five miles, knowing I couldn't get through, but unable to forget what a fantastic triumph it would be if I did.

The first checkpoint appeared across the road about an hour before sunset, time for me to get back to Tobruk before dark. There was a barrier and a small, portable cabin. The guard looked at my passport, and the sheaf of Arabic documents, extracted the currency control form and handed the rest back to me with a grin. He slid the barrier back and said "Bye-bye." Obviously he was having his little joke. I laughed too, and went on to the real frontier. A small queue of taxis was lined up ahead of me a few miles farther on. I joined the queue, but a soldier spotted me and waved me to the front. He took my passport into the office with him and brought it back with the visa canceled. I began to get very excited and a little alarmed at what might happen when the Egyptians sent me back. Because surely they would send me back. I looked at the visas again, idly, and the ground suddenly seemed to slide away from under me. The Egyptian visa had an extra bit tacked alongside it, reading the wrong way on the page. In all the times I had looked at the passport I had somehow failed to notice it. The message was direct and shattering. It read: "Access to the U.A.R. via the coast of N. Africa & Salloum is not permitted." Part of it was almost obscured by the thick border of the principal visa stamp, but even so, if you were looking for it you could not miss it.

Well, either the Libyans had missed it, or they were playing me a sinister trick. There was only one thing for me to do, and that was to go on as though I hadn't seen it either. The gate swung open, and I went through, swallowing hard.

A hundred yards or so farther on was something that looked like a railway station, with three platforms, and two tracks for incoming and outgoing traffic, but first came another barrier. Always I was waiting for the hand that would rise before me and bar my way, Again I was waved on.

"You can go through."

'What? All the way?'

"Yes, you can go."

The station was in a ferment of activity. The platforms were piled high with mounds of carpets and cushions in plastic bags, being guarded or argued over by men dressed in every kind of robe and headgear and an army of officials in crumpled khakis. I rode straight through it all and out the other side. The guard at the gate there was about to let me through when a voice shouted "No Stop. Come back please." The guard pointed back and mumbled something. I turned to see a small roly-poly man with a shiny unshaven face, smiling at me through his whiskers.

"Come please," he said. "We cannot ignore the formalities. Can I see your passport please? You are going to Cairo? Welcome to Egypt. Now we must see the captain."

I brought out my newspaper cutting, almost a full page of the *Sunday Times* with a photograph of me, the bike and all my gear spread out around it. I talked about my journey as though the future of Egypt depended on it, and did everything to distract attention from the visa. Even so, I was surprised by the enjoyment it seemed to give them.

"I will do everything to help you," said Roly-Poly. "Would you like some tea?" With a glass of clear tea, sweet and delicious, in my hand, feeling like Alice in Wonderland, I confronted the first of the Eight Mandatory Obstacles between me and Egypt. The first man read my visa several times, paying particular attention to the "No Entry" qualification. He seemed to see nothing there of interest. Number two was the police. They read the visa again, but upside down, and then filled out a small form torn raggedly off a sheet of duplicating paper, having great difficulty writing in the XRW 964M. Numbers three and four had to do with the papers I had brought from Libya. There were flurried exchanges, and already I had difficulty finding a way to hold on to them all. At one point I lost sight of the first paper from the police.

"Is it important?" asked Roly-Poly.

"Well, I don't know."

"It is not," he said firmly. "Never mind." And he swept me on to change my money at number five, to pay for licensing the bike at number six. Then back to number three for an argument about the customs carnet, and on to number seven, where the Libyans discharged it. Finally, in an office well away from the crowd, a police officer sat behind the most venerable set of ledgers I had ever seen. They had been thumbed so often that their corners had been rounded off, and the paper was the color of the pyramids. They lay right along the length of his table like blocks of eroded sandstone, and I had no doubt that it was on these that the future of Egypt really depended.

He filled out my carnet and handed me two heavy metal number plates.

"Finished," he said. "Finished?" asked Roly-Poly. "Have you thanked the captain?"

"I always thank everybody," I replied, naively.

He burst into laughter. "Now," he said with special emphasis, "can I help in any other way?" I fumbled towards my pocket and then decided against it. Why should I assume he wanted a "gratuity"? I thanked him sincerely and turned away. His contented expression did not falter.

I went to the bike. I simply could not believe it. My heart had been in my mouth and was still there, pumping hard. I folded all the pieces of paper I had been given into my passport. Because the jacket had no pockets, I laid the passport on top of my wallet and some waterproof gloves in one of the side boxes. I locked the box. I found some wire and tied both plates on tight at the back of the bike. All the while I was expecting to hear someone shout "Hey. You. Just a minute."

I got on the bike, very deliberately, tickled the carburetor and kicked it over. Then I rode slowly through the gate into the town called Salloum. I delayed the moment of triumph as long as possible. Salloum was small but treacherous in the night. The road was narrow and bad, and there were cows roaming about loose. Ticking like a time bomb, I rode downhill through the winding street, and then, abruptly, I was out in the open spaces again and I could hold my ecstasy back no longer.

I roared and sang and jiggled with delight. I was in Egypt, and everything was different. The moon, the stars, the temperature, the smell of the air, all seemed to be subtly Egyptian. It was a wonder I stayed on the bike, I was so pleased with myself, as though it were some remarkable quality in me that had achieved the single-handed conquest of Egypt.

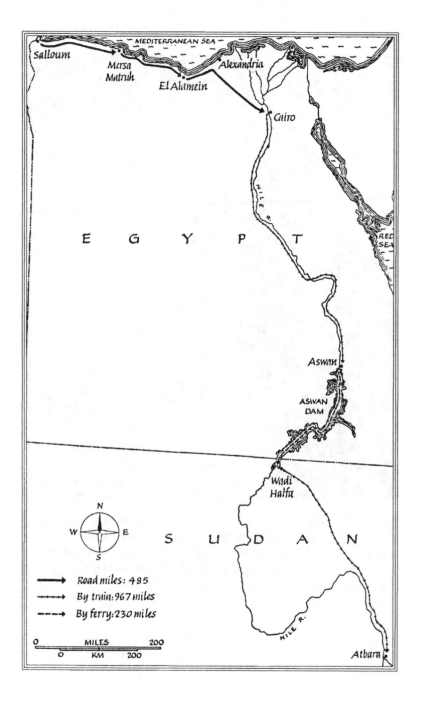

In Cairo, too, the war drove out the tourists, so I was able to spend half a day with this camel-driver and know him as a friend rather than as a "mark". In exchange for only a pair of socks he let me ride his camel around the pyramids for an hour, and I almost got the hang of it.Then we had tea together in his tent.

So sure had I been that I would not get through that I had not once considered where I would head for if I did. I had not even thought about gas. Holding my map under the headlight I saw that there was a pump at Sidi Barani, fifty miles along. I seemed to arrive there in no time at all. There was fuel, but nowhere to stay. The town, if there was one, had melted into darkness.

Eighty-five miles to Mersa Matruh. Nothing. I felt like riding all night, to Cairo if necessary.

Ten miles short of Matruh I saw some painted oil barrels across the road, with a hurricane lamp burning on one of them. Light shone from the doorway of a little hut. I slowed down and a soldier approached me. He laid his left arm across his right wrist and opened his right hand, palm upwards, in the sign that meant "Papers!"

I stopped, unlocked the box and brought out the passport. An older man in pajamas and fez came out of the hut.

"Please wait," he said. "It will be ten minutes only."

I heard a manual telephone cranking and lit a cigarette. After a while a third man came out and got into a black car parked beyond the barrier. As he started the engine and drove off the man in pajamas hurried over to me.

"Follow that car, please," he said urgently. "They will clear you in Matruh if you hurry, but they are just going to close down."

I was infected by the slight sense of panic and rushed off. The car was doing over seventy miles an hour and I had some difficulty catching it. Then, for the second time that day, the bowels of the earth slid open beneath me. I reached back with my right hand. The lid of the box had been blown off. Expecting to put the passport back, I had not locked it again. I stopped immediately. The wallet had gone. I looked at the mileage indicator. It could have happened anywhere in the last six miles.

The wallet contained driving licenses, vaccination certificates, credit cards, photographs, currency and an address book. Losing it seemed like an overwhelming disaster. Two cholera shots, a yellow fever shot and a smallpox vaccination would have to be done again. There were addresses I might never recover. The cash, the credit cards were extra layers of defense stripped away. But how far could I get without a driving license? Slowly I drove back, on the wrong side of the road, searching but numbed by this sudden reverse in my fortunes. I had ridden nearly four hundred miles that day, and the weariness hit me then. I tried to think clearly. The gloves should have been the last objects to fall, and as they were quite bulky I hoped to see them where a black wallet might not show.

For a mile I saw nothing. Then I saw light ahead, and the murmur of engines running. I came across two taxis, one coming, one going, stopped alongside each other with their interior lights on. One driver was in the middle of the road, a tall bearded man in white robe and turban. He stood in the space carved out of the darkness by the car lights, and seemed very much in command of that space. I wanted to stop and ask whether he had seen anything, but he waved me on peremptorily. His hand was raised in a threatening way and he stared at me fiercely. I felt too weak to resist, and rode on.

I went on searching vainly until I got back to the police post. A truck was coming through, and the police commandeered it to help me search in the much brighter illumination of its headlights. After a while I found the lid of the box. Then the truck driver spotted the first glove, and soon after I saw the second one. The wallet should have been between the lid and the gloves. I went up and down several times but found nothing.

I was in a state of despair out of all proportion to the disaster. Weariness, the end of a long day, me alone with the bike at midnight in a strange country at war; that was part of it. From Mark Antony to Charlie Brown in one thoughtless moment. I snatched at the lesson. As always I felt I could endure my tribulations if there was something to be learned from them. *Euphoria leads to thoughtlessness.* That's how fortunes are told. So O.K. No more mindless chasing after cars. *Is that all?*

No, that was not all. I went over the incident again in my mind, saw the Arab standing in that pool of light in the darkness, with his arm raised. Yes, but I had seen something else, before I had even known what I was looking at. I had seen him straightening up, that was it, straightening his legs. He had been rising from the road surface and I had seen him do it but I had not wanted to know because I was too tired. No! Not too tired, *too frightened.* I was too frightened of that imperious wave of the hand, of that fierce glance, to face up to the fact that he had just found my wallet on the road.

The discovery was devastating. I had thought I was a man. I had taken risks and come through them in the way a man was supposed

to, and yet here I was after all just a boy quailing before the first figure of authority that came my way. It went very deep in me, this fear
of authority, and it sickened me to find myself as vulnerable as ever.
I knew the robed figure would haunt me for a long time. It was the
beginning of a long struggle. Hard as it was to bear this moment of
self-realization, I found some kind of strength in it. I piled up some
stones to mark the place where I had been searching and rode on to
the checkpoint at Matruh where I was given back my passport. I
explained what I was doing, and went back to go on with the search,
but with no more success than before.

Then I started thinking. If the Arab had taken the wallet, he would
probably not keep it. He would take what was valuable and throw
away the rest. Where? Before the checkpoint. I rode up to the first
checkpoint again, and worked back. The driver of a car going to
Libya would throw something from his window across the road to the
other side. But no. In Libya traffic drives on the right, in Egypt on
the left. So it would be a left-hand-drive car, driving on the left of the
road. I followed the right-hand verge going towards Matruh. Fifty
yards along I saw a small bundle of paper against the root of a bush.
The wallet had been broken in half. No money. No address section.
No photographs. No credit cards. But the vaccination certificates
were there, and one international driving license. I could find nothing more in the area. Partly relieved, and a little better pleased with
myself, I returned to Matruh.

It was two in the morning. The police corporal received me with
genuine pleasure. He was short and unprepossessing, his uniform
crumpled and short in the leg, with some kind of blue and white band
around one arm. He was in charge of a small platoon of even more
ragged soldiers, but they were all obviously excited by the arrival of
a man on a motorcycle, and determined to look after me. They produced tea. Then a handful of dates much bigger than any I had seen,
and some corned beef and flat bread. The corporal's face was a landscape devastated by pockmarks. He spoke a little English and was
fiercely patriotic. He wanted me to know about the crushing defeat
Egypt had inflicted on Israel. As I munched my dates, sitting on a
rough bench near a charcoal fire, he stood over me repeating, fanatically, the same words.

"Nekesta week, brekfast in Tel Aviv. Nekesta week, brekfast in Tel
Aviv. Israel finish. Is good?" And all of them stared at me looking for

the truth in my eyes, but I wasn't going to let myself slip twice in a night, and I said there should be no war and that nobody wanted to fight on either side. By a charcoal fire in the Egyptian night the most banal remark can have the force of prophesy, and my words were received with wonder and agreement.

They built me a bedroom. Literally. While the corporal taught me Arabic, they made a soft-board roof over some heaps of brick and a platform to lie on. At four o'clock I was allowed to sleep.

In the morning I went back for the third time to the police post on the Salloum road, and found pages of addresses and photographs spread over the desert. They were all there. Only cash and credit cards were still gone. Most of my money was safe in my money belt. I thought I had been very lucky after all.

The road to Alexandria had military on it all the way. Immediately outside Matruh a very pukka officer with a dapper moustache sat behind a desk in an open tent. He asked for my permit to travel to "Alex". I brought out all my papers. The one he wanted was not among them, he said. I began to suspect that I might still not be in Egypt after all. Then, purely by chance, I found the scrap of paper that had been filled in by the semi-illiterate police clerk, that my roly-poly guide had dismissed as unimportant. It was, in fact, the only piece of paper I really needed.

On the road, the new war and the old one blended together. English, German, Italian – "Manqua fortuna, non valore." War cemeteries, thirty-year-old tanks, routing instructions for Monty's armies still scrawled on semi-ruined walls, and El Alamein, where I had a good lunch and a pint of beer for a dollar.

Matruh to Alex, one hundred eighty-one miles, the hottest miles so far. An older, narrower, bumpier road than the Libyan highway. The coast was absurdly picturesque. Turquoise sea, radiant sand. On a postcard one would have said the printing was far too garish. Small homesteads by the roadside, donkeys and camels plowing, turning over the top three inches of sandy soil with wooden blades. Graceful women in brilliantly coloured dress carrying water on their heads. Then, more and more houses, gardens, and just before the plunge into the city an extraordinary area of stone, whipped and carved and flung into waves and troughs like a high sea suddenly turned to salt.

Then Alexandria, and in the twilight an endless scramble through miles of cobbled dockside streets, tramlines, mad traffic and people in ever-greater compression, nowhere to go, nothing to aim for, except the center. The fate I escaped in Palermo caught up with me in Alexandria. I broke through the commercial areas at last and found a square on the sea front, and parked opposite an expensive hotel called The Cecil. As I nudged the front wheel against the kerb and looked behind me I saw black smoke around the exhaust pipes. I knew I was in trouble, but refused to think about it. A thin man in a blue jellaba and headcloth appeared at my side.

"You want hottle," he said. I agreed, and followed him around behind The Cecil and into a high old Parisian-style building. He asked me for a coin and fed it into a slot in the lift. The lift digested it slowly and began to rumble upwards. The landings were open and Alexandrian life seemed to reveal itself by layers. On the top floor was the Pension Normandie. I could not have asked for a better place.

It was cheap, clean, authentic, owned by a cuddly French widow and run on her behalf with doting indulgence by an elderly employee called Georges. I noticed only two other guests and both were French. One was a bluff middle-aged man with a handsome, ruddy face and fair hair turning to white. He adored competitive conversation, in which the object is either to sap or cap the last speaker's story, a sort of verbal bridge. His anecdotes were planned and delivered more with the intention of frustrating the opposition and keeping the play than simply to amuse, but it amounted to much the same thing, for he was a skilful player and his stories about the resistance were new to me. He taught French at a university in Cairo. The other guest, another French widow, had been married to a very wealthy Egyptian in King Farouk's time and was now retired on a small income. She also told languid tales of life in the days of sashes and cummerbunds and ten-foot wedding cakes, all very reminiscent of St. Petersburg under the czars, and could herself have been a Russian duchess, angular, erect, always carefully groomed and lightly varnished all over.

Mme. Mellasse, the owner, would kick off her slippers and fold her plump stockinged legs on the sofa; the widow sat under a lamp stand examining her carmine nail varnish and uttering brittle remarks; the professor, in good voice, dominated the proceedings, and I, I suppose, brought news from the front rather like a young cavalry officer on leave. We made a quaintly period quartet.

I carried out my first-ever major motorcycle overhaul in Alexandria. I found a cavernous garage near Ramilies Station, haggled bitterly over five piastres for the right to work there, and then received many times that amount back in tea, cigarettes, snacks and true friendship from the poor men who struggled to earn a livelihood in that place.

I took two days to do a job that might be done in two or three hours, but every move was fraught with danger. I dared not make a mistake. Already I knew that there would be no chance at all of getting spare parts in Egypt. Both pistons, I found, were deformed by heat, and I had only one spare piston with me (a piece of nonsense which inspired more waves of telepathic profanity to burn the ears of Meriden). The pistons had seized their rings, and I put back the less distorted one after sculpting the slots with a razor blade. It seemed the only thing to do. I prayed that I was right. I had no real idea about what had caused the overheating after only four thousand miles, and felt rather gloomy about it.

There were many British motorcycles pumping round the streets and some shops still had stocks of parts for them, but they were single-cylinder BSA's, Enfields, and AJS's of ancient vintage. It was warming to see all these old British bikes plodding on after twenty years or more, and obviously held in high esteem, but it was rather pathetic also. I knew that it was only economic policy that prevented them importing new machines, and that small Japanese bikes would be much better suited to them. If the Japanese ever got a foothold, British bikes would quickly become only a nostalgic memory. There was so much goodwill towards us that it seemed criminal to fritter it away, yet we had nothing to offer now in competition.

When the Triumph was all buttoned up again I tested it rather nervously. The first clouds of smoke frightened the life out of me but when the excess oil was burned away, it ran clean and sounded fine. Only then did I allow myself the luxury of looking at the city. It took me an hour to clear the grease out of my fingernails in the Normandie's bathroom. I admired the tiles, the old-fashioned fittings and, as I stood by the sink next to the lavatory, a bowl of Western design, I noticed for the first time a brass valve wheel sticking out of the wall. Its function was obscure so I gave it a turn to see what would happen, and a jet of water hit me in the chest. Shocked, I turned it off and looked for the source of the mischief, feeling like the victim of a practical joke. It took me some while to notice the slender copper pipe pointing straight at me out of the bowl of the lavatory. Once I had seen it I couldn't quite believe it, and had to play with it awhile, watching it, but even this latest sophistication in oriental toiletry did not convert me, and I went on leaving my paper trail across the face of Africa.

The obvious place to walk to from the Normandie was the sea front, only a hundred yards away. In my linen jacket and white trousers I strolled along the promenade, cameras slung ostentatiously round my neck, and raised the telephoto lens experimentally to look at the lighthouse. One moment I had been looking for someone to photograph, next moment I was surrounded. A hand seized my shoulder, a voice shouted hysterically close to my ear. People came rushing towards me. It seemed to me that they appeared from nowhere, out of the cracks in the pavement. The man who had me in his grip was much smaller than I. He wore a dirty brown fez and a jumper over a tee-shirt, something I have always considered a sure sign of bad taste. His face was distorted by hate, his veins and tendons stood out throbbing. "From where you come?" he screamed, again and again, and when I said England he went on screaming. "No. No. From where you come?"

The truth is I had completely forgotten about the war.

Fortunately there was a naval barracks just along the road, and some naval police arrived before the mob grew big enough to lynch me. They were all for treating me in a civilized way, but my captor insisted that they pin my arms behind my back and frog-march me off. He would have liked to see me blindfolded and led before a firing squad there and then.

As soon as we got into the navy yard, they let go of me and apologized profusely. The apologies were taken up more elaborately by captains, majors and finally a colonel who asked me to please not let this unfortunate incident color my good opinion of Egypt. Eventually a blue jeep was arranged to take me to the general in command of the defense of Alexandria.

The general, like all the other officers, had a bed made up in his office. His desk was burdened with a great quantity of patent medicines and tonics as well as paper work, and he looked dyspeptic, myopic and tired, but he received me with much grace, devoted ten minutes to discussing my journey, the merits of Pentax cameras and the publicity that Triumph would undoubtedly get. By now I had learned always to produce the *Sunday Times* cutting with my picture. It opened more doors than my passport did.

The general took the film from the camera, a new roll with nothing on it, wished me luck and returned reluctantly to his war. A brigadier next door gave me tea and talked fondly of the years he had spent living in London next to Harrods. I was returned to the promenade and let loose.

I went back to the Normandie, dumped the cameras, changed my swank jacket for a disreputable sweater and went out again determined to see something of Alexandria. Not far away, I found the sort of area I had been looking for, a poor working neighborhood crammed with tiny lockup shops; people caning chairs, plucking chickens, bundling firewood, counting empty bottles, scooping grain out of sacks into small cones of thick grey paper, beating donkeys, dragging trolleys, recuperating scraps of everything under the sun. A small boy in rags – no, in one rag, had his capital spread on the kerbstone in aluminum coins and was counting it solemnly as though about to make an important investment. A number of delicate gilt chairs stood tiptoe on the pavement, like refugees from a revolution, having their seats stuffed.

I was standing, fascinated, in front of a display of dried beans swarming with weevil when a hand fell on my shoulder. I turned to face a man in a grubby blue suit with a mourning band on his arm. He made the sign for "Papers" and I had to swallow my irritation, because I had left my papers in my jacket. He handed me to another man, similarly dressed but less shaven and more villainous. They had the same hard edge to their expressions that I had seen on the police in Tunis. They sat me on a chair outside a cafe. A crowd of people began to gather, murmuring "Yehudi." The proprietor came out with a bucket of water and threw it over them. They scattered and reformed, pressing closer. The "chief" decided to take me to his headquarters, a hutch buried under the staircase of a building across the road, eight foot square, windowless and lined with "wanted" pictures. It was the sort of place where "B" movie heroes are usually beaten up, and for the first time I began to squirm a little. During both arrests, I had surprised myself by remaining very cool and detached, and I was interested to see how disarming my behavior had been in the face of possible violence. Now, as I sat against a wall, facing the door, where privileged onlookers were allowed to peer in at a genuine Israeli spy, I felt less sure of my tactics. I watched a fire hose being dragged along the corridor to the street, where the crowd had evidently become a mob, and thought how helpless I was and how much I preferred being with the navy. Then the chief brought a cup of coffee, and the time for a beating had evidently passed.

The episode dragged on, however, for the rest of the afternoon. I was driven to police headquarters, then to the Normandie for my papers, then back to the police and at last let go. There was a lot of waiting, but no attempt at ugliness. I got to know a number of police and their relations, but to be arrested twice in one hour was enough to convince me that my third attempt might be unlucky. I got my bike out and rode to King Farouk's old summer palace, the Montasah, to sneer at the vulgarity of it, to admire the cool light inside and to be won over, finally, by the bathroom showers that operated somewhat like a modern dishwashing machine, and were no doubt supplied by Harrods.

The war news was not good. Tension was rising at Kilometer 101, where the opposing sides were discussing an armistice. I decided to hurry on to Cairo and Sudan. Already I guessed that I would be refused permission to ride the road to Aswan. Big troop concentrations, radar installations and airfields were said to lie along the road. If the train was my only way south, then the sooner I got on it the better.

I had my last lunch at the Normandie, washed up on the shores of time with my three exiles from better days. Speaking French, which was the hotel language, the professor entertained the ladies with an account of my escapades.

"It would be apparent to a babe-in-arms that our friend set out yesterday morning determined to provoke an incident. When his cameras and his obviously sinister wardrobe failed to do the trick, he climbed on a pedestal and pointed his telephoto lens at a Russian submarine in the harbor. However, his 'arrest' by the navy was disappointingly civilized and apologetic. He therefore exchanged his jacket for an Israeli sweater, deliberately abandoned his papers and sauntered off to the roughest neighborhood available to behave as much like a spy as possible. And in case that was insufficient, he made sure of popular hostility by drawing attention to a merchant's infested beans, saying 'In Tel Aviv, we have laws against this kind of thing.'"

There was much laughter, and perhaps a grain of truth.

At the end of the lunch, just as I was about to leave, a telegram arrived for the Frenchman. He opened it, drew a sharp breath and stared at it.

"My son is dead," he said. "I knew it."

He was petrified by grief. He was inconsolable, and immovable. None of us could find anything to say. I murmured good-bye, and left. On my way to Cairo I reflected, uneasily, that a lot of things were happening to me and around me. Every day it seemed added its quota of significant encounters, events and revelations. Were they already there, waiting to happen, or did I bring them with me? Could turbulence and change be "carried" and transmitted like a disease? I knew I had brought excitement into those three lives, but the news from the front was not always good. I wondered, unhappily, whether I was destined to leave a trail of grief and misery behind me too. "What colossal arrogance," I thought, but could not quite brush the idea aside.

From Cairo to Aswan the train ran for a night and a day. I boarded at the blacked-out station in a tumultuous rush of bodies to share a two-berth sleeper with a fat middle-class Egyptian in robes and turban. I also shared the sumptuous chicken feast he had brought bundled in a large white napkin, and he politely accepted a bit of my fruit. We munched together contentedly until it was time to sleep, undistracted by the efforts of conversation because he spoke only Arabic.

Most of the following day I watched Egypt and the Nile pass by from the dining-car window. I saw no missile pads or airfields, although a company of newly drafted soldiers came on board for a short distance. There was a bruised astonishment in their eyes that brought back sharp memories of my first weeks as a conscript.

I enjoyed the train, but resented the onward rush of it that rationed me to such fleeting glimpses of life outside. It was a quite different world, I realized, viewed through this thick screen of plate glass.

At one of the inexplicable stops trains make between stations I found myself looking down directly on a rice field beside the track where a grizzled old man and a boy were turning the soil with hoes. The man wore only a tattered galabia. As he leaned forward to chop at the mud it revealed the whole of his stringy body tightening with effort and his genitals swinging back and forth. Beside him stood a woman in a black robe and shawl, also old but slim and perfectly erect. In contrast to the old man's coarse, dull face, her features were exquisitely drawn. Her eyebrows, nostrils and mouth were arched like spring steel under tension, expressing complete authority and contempt for her circumstances. She held a long and slender cane, like a wizard's wand, and supervised the work with smoldering eyes.

Pharaoh's daughter could not have looked more handsome or commanding than this woman standing barefooted in a rice paddy. The group was quite oblivious of the train or of my stares. I saw that there was nothing they wore or used that they might not have had thousands of years ago. If I could discover, I thought, the secret of this woman's presence and the old man's submission I might have the story of Egypt, but before I could melt the glass with my eyes the train took me away.

The ferry is tied up at a wooden wharf above the Aswan Dam. It is not one boat but two; two small paddle steamers lashed together and run on a single paddle. The nearest one is first-class. I and the bike have to cross to the second-class boat. While this is no problem for me, I can see immediately that it will be impossible to manhandle the bike there. I can see that, but the porters can see only a glorious opportunity to earn a fortune in baksheesh by achieving the impossible.

"Yes, yes, yes," they scream and, in a flurry of brown limbs, they fight with the Triumph up a gangplank, over a rail into a narrow gangway, through hatches, over sills and bollards, four hundred pounds of metal dragging, sliding, flying and dropping among roars and curses and pleas for divine aid, while I follow, helpless and resigned. Finally the bike is poised over the water between the two boats. The outstretched arms can only hold it, but they cannot move it, and it is supported, incredibly, by the foot brake pedal, which is caught on the ship's rail. Muscles are weakening. The pedal is bending and will soon slip, and my journey will end in the fathomless silt of Mother Nile. At this last moment, a rope descends miraculously from the sky dangling a hook, and the day is saved.

For three days and two nights I drift up the Nile along Lake Nasser. The sunrises and sunsets are so extraordinarily beautiful that my body turns inside out and empties my heart into the sky. The stars are close enough to grasp. Lying on the roof of the ferry at night, I begin at last to know the constellations, and start a personal relationship with that particular little cluster of jewels called the Pleiades, which nestles in the sky not far from Orion's belt and sword. Really, those stars, when they come that close, you have to take them seriously.

I sleep illegally on the roof of the first-class boat, because the second-class deck is indescribable. I would rather swim than sleep there. Hundreds of Nubian camel drivers are returning to the Sudan, with their huge hide bags and whips, to pick up another consignment of camels and drive them remorselessly up into Egypt. They are all dressed in grubby white, and lie side by side among their bundles across the deck. The crevices between them are caulked with a mixture of orange peel, cigarette ends, and spit. The hawking and spitting, which is a constant background murmur to Arab life, here rises to become the dominant sound, louder than speech, louder than the ferry's engine, drowned out only, and rarely, by the ship's hooter. Lungs rasp and rip, you can hear the tissues tear into shreds, and the glutinous product flies in all directions. I am not ready for that yet.

During the first night we cross the Tropic of Cancer. During the second day a Turkish passenger goes mad. He has been looking more pale and drawn by the hour. Now, with his black eyes buttoned to the back of his brain, he begins to twirl in the saloon, stopping suddenly to point his finger and cast some fatal spell. He collapses, then rises to twirl again. His eyes have seen something too terrible to be borne.

The ferry ties up in the night somewhere south of Abu Simbel, and the Turk is taken ashore, but after much discussion he is brought aboard again and we continue. When we land at Wadi Halfa at midday he is quiet.

I meant to ride from Wadi Halfa, but the police say I must take the train at least as far as Abu Hamad, and I cannot get gas without the help of the police. I have made friends with a Dutch couple, and once on the train I might as well go with them as far as Atbara. What's a few more miles in the whole of Africa?

The train rattles on through beer, supper, songs, sleep, tea and English breakfast. In the oval engraved mirror of a colonial dining car I actually take notice of my face for the first time in a long while. Action has freed me from self-consciousness, and I am becoming a stranger to my own appearance. It is a very satisfying feeling. I no longer think of people seeing me as I see myself in a mirror. Instead I imagine that people can see directly into my soul. It is as though a screen between me and the world has dropped away.

Through the carriage window, the desert has been sweeping past, almost unbroken, for hours. I stare at it mesmerized, trying to imagine myself riding over it. Now there are signs of life. Some animals, more thorn trees, tents and huts. The train slows. Atbara Station. The corridor is jammed with people and bundles. My mind is in gear again. To meet trouble halfway, what disasters shall I anticipate now? Perhaps the bike has vanished off the train somewhere en route? Maybe half of it will be missing? Or I will be asked to bribe someone to unload it?

The wheels screech on the rails. The crowd tumbles off. The bike is still there. Nothing is missing. There are no problems. To me this is a sort of miracle. I wheel it to where my bags are heaped on the platform and pack them on as children peer into the speedometer where they believe the soul of the machine to reside. I flood the carburettor. *For God's sake start!*, I mutter. *Don't give me any trouble. It's too hot to wrestle with you now.*

One kick and she starts. *You lovely machine.*

First to the police, to be registered as an alien. The locomotive is hissing and panting in the station. I can hear it across the road. It howls and clanks into action. Plunk, plunk, plunk-plunk-plunk plunk as the train's vertebrae stretch. It rolls away to Khartoum, but now there is more noise, and agitation continues with a taxi for my friends, and the bike following, to find a hotel. The hotel.

Atbara is a frontier town; mud houses, wooden facades and the dirt road flowing around them and between them like a brown flood ready to reclaim it all. Here's a more imposing street with houses of red brick and cement. Is this the hotel? We stop. The taxi leaves, but the traveling noise goes on in my head. We're not there yet. The buildings look abandoned.

"Hotel?"

An old man sweeping leaves shakes his head angrily, and points down the street.

Alongside the next building is an alley. It debouches into a garden with tables and chairs rooted here and there among the weeds. A cemented verandah at the back of the building gives access to a series of closed green doors. Hotel! At a round iron table sit five men.

"Hotel?"

"Hotel, yes. Come and sit."

One last effort, to fetch the bike into the garden, park it against the verandah, close the gas tap, walk to the table . . . and sit.

The noise stops.

The sun is getting low now, the light is yellow and grainy. The five men are gathered like a conspiracy of pantomime pirates. One has a black eye patch, another a vivid scar. The one next to me, an Arab in galabia and turban, has a squint and a thin-lipped smile of artless evil. Every child in the audience knows he has a dagger under his robe. The table is laden with date-sherry bottles, all empty but one. With exaggerated hospitality the Arab sweeps up the sleeves of his galabia and pours out glasses for the Dutch couple and myself. Yo Ho-Ho and a bottle of date sherry.

The pirates are passing a joint around. The Arab waves it in the air and murmurs sibilant nonsense as though in a haze of mellow stupefaction, but his eye is much too bright. The scent of the smoke is delicious, the silence around us is like a cool bath. Is anything more relaxing than the hospitality of harmless villains? How do I know they're harmless? I don't, yet I do.

The Arab invests in another bottle of sherry and we sit for an hour as the sun goes down, lost in lazy contentment. During that hour I feel I have arrived in Sudan.

A muscular black man comes towards us, urgently, asks us to come to the hotel. The bar is open now, and a naked bulb is shining down on ugly plastic surfaces. I am very reluctant to leave the garden. The man insists. He has a tigerish body, too constrained in his neat shirt and trousers.

"I am coming to see ip you are all right, and I pind you sitting with a bad man. I am Pabiano," he said. "My name is Munduk, my brother is in the folice. That man is not good. He is a teep. He is only fretending drunk so that others will become drunk. Then he steal prom your focket. He has been in frison."

I look back to the table. In the last faint light the Arab has twisted in his chair to look at us, one arm outstretched towards us, the long cotton sleeve trailing, imploring us to return. I feel a sad affection for him. There was a kind of understanding.

Three nights in Atbara. From the ceiling of my room hangs an enormous propeller, slowly kneading the thick night air. During the days I prepare for the desert. There is an obstinate electrical fault in the bike. I take the lens off the headlamp, and it drops its wiring over the verandah, pitifully, as though spilling its entrails. I work on it, as martial music drifts across the wall from a school sports day. By evening the bike is repaired, the hernia sewn up.

I have been considering how to carry water. I have brought a collapsible plastic container, and can carry a gallon on the back of the bike, but I am not quite convinced it will work and I want a reserve. If I fill the aluminum bottle with distilled water, then I can use that for the batteries also. A garage fills the bottle for me. I have to cross 250 miles of desert to Kassala and the next gas pump. With three gallons in the tank, and the five-gallon jerry half full I should have enough. Tomorrow I will buy more, just in case. Today I can't because I haven't enough Sudanese money. It's Sunday, and the banks are closed.

I have asked everyone about the way to Kassala. They all say it is "*queiss*" – which means good. Thomas Taban Duku, the registrar of aliens, said so. It was more usual for people to go to Khartoum, but many buses go to Kassala, at least one each day. He could not remember anyone coming by motorcycle before, but then, he said, a motorcycle can go anywhere.

"If a bus can go, then so can a motorcycle, isn't it? And faster even? The road is *queiss*." He was quietly confident.

So is the man at the hotel. He says it's a good road, now the rains have gone. And the Michelin map calls it a marked and recognized track. Munduk also says it will be easy. He comes to the hotel, and

MILES

0 100

0 100
KM

N
W E
S

Atbara

ATBARA R.

NILE R.

Kinedra

Goz Regeb

SUDAN

Kassala

Khashm el Girba

Gedaref

Asmara

Doka

Metema

ETHIOPIA

Gondar

LAKE TANA

BLUE NILE

Road miles: 620

that evening, under a waxing moon, we visit his house to see how to make date sherry at home, and then to look at the Nile.

"Here is the Blue Nile," he says. "The White Nile is one day walking from here."

He is wrong. The Blue Nile joins the White Nile at Khartoum, two hundred miles upstream. How can he be so wrong about something like that? Who knows? Away from Western cities you get used to it. If you want to know something, you ask again and again. When many opinions run together they thicken to form a fact. Isn't that the essence of modern theoretical physics? So often it seems that every scientific principle has its counterpart in social behavior. Simon's Hypothesis?! Waves & Particles. Critical Mass. Fission, fusion, all of thermodynamics with Maxwell's Demon as the exception that proves the rule.... My head is flying and my feet slip into the marsh. Eye Pierce Heaven, Foot Stick in Mud. As I stumble out I see Munduk prowling round some bushes, more like a tiger than ever, sniffing the air, cocking his ear. He reminds me of Castaneda's Don Genaro looking for a car under a stone.

"Serpent," he says. "Or some animal maybe. I show you how we hunt in the bus'."

He and his six brothers, he says, fled to Uganda when the Muslims killed his parents in the war. They lived by hunting in the bush. Now all his brothers are famous. So he says. Why not believe him, until it becomes important?

Atbara is among the hottest places in the world. In summer it goes to 110 in the shade. In winter it simmers at a few degrees below ninety. Shops do their business early and late in the day. Banks, I thought, would do likewise. But no. In Atbara, as everywhere else in the world, bankers followed their own inscrutable whims. Opening time was nine-thirty.

It was already half-past seven. I was packed, paid up, booked out and ready to go. By ten the last cool hours of the morning would have evaporated. I thought I had enough gas. What need could I have for money in the desert? The time was ripe to begin my great adventure, to catch the tide.

I rode out of Atbara directed by dry, black fingers.

"*Queiss, queiss,*" said the owners of the fingers. "Road good. This way."

Atbara's only stretch of tarmac gave way to mud. I went past the Ethiopian prostitutes, alongside a last row of mud houses and came to a piece of stony ground surrounded by thorn trees. Spread out before me was a vast heap of stinking rubbish. No road. Not a sign of a road. I was not looking for tar or paving or even made-up dirt, but there was not so much as a track.

The difference between men and gods is farce.

During all the months of preparation, the girding of loins and steeling of resolve, the one feat which I thought would set me apart from mortal men was my single-handed crossing of the Atbara Desert.

And now I could not find it.

I rode back into town to ask again. Once more I followed the fingers, other fingers, along the same route. I could find no other way.

Twice I inspected Atbara's garbage, and twice I returned. I was in a fever of impatience and I felt completely ridiculous. If Neil Armstrong had lost his way to the launching pad he could not have been more frustrated.

There was a police station along the way which I had carefully avoided, but now I could think of nowhere else to go for an explanation. I was always afraid of involving myself unnecessarily with officials. Generally when a man in uniform has something unusual brought to his attention, his instinct is to stop it. Uniform is as uniform does. There are honorable+ exceptions however. The Atbara police delayed me, but they did not stop me, and they explained that

My first desert, south of Atbara, in Sudan. I was so impressed by the desolate scene that I did not notice – until I saw this picture three years later – that there were people sitting in the shade of the umbrella tree.

the road to Kassala did, indeed, go past the rubbish tip. And I began to understand, with some embarrassment, that in Sudanese English the word "road" has no mineral connections, it simply means "the way." I had fallen into the simplest linguistic trap, imagining that the road had a physical reality. There was no road; only an imaginary line across the desert.

By now it was nearly nine o'clock. I should have swallowed my pride, gone to the bank, cooled off and left the following day, but I was rolling under the momentum of my own folly, and I knew I could not stop or something might break. A dream for instance. This time I rode around the rubbish tip. Beyond it was a gap in the trees. Through it I saw the open desert. To the right of the gap was another heap of fresh garbage, and as I rode past it a big red eye met mine.

The eye was level with my own. It was inflamed, and encrusted with dirt. The dirt was sticking to the few vagrant hairs that remained on a bald and dreadful head. I was deeply shocked by it, and rode on before I had collected my wits and assembled the images. Then I saw that it was a monstrous bird, of human proportions, with a great pendulous beak and long and filthy white neck. I wanted to turn back, but I was carried on relentlessly by some inner current, and the bird became for a while a mythical beast and guardian of the desert.

I rode into the desert. It looked flat, but of course it was not. Nor was it sandy, but made of a rather greyish, fairly compact stuff half way between sand and soil, littered with small shards of stone. I found I could ride across it quite easily, and the faster I went, the smoother the ride, although stopping might be a problem.

The question was, which way to go? Ahead and to the left, the desert stretched to infinity, interrupted only by the well-defined profile of an occasional umbrella tree. To the right, however, perhaps a mile away, was a line of trees that I took first to be the edge of a forest. Then I realized that they were palm trees, and that they must define the bed of the Atbara River, which ran from Atbara to Kassala. My first great fear was dispelled. Obviously I could never be lost in the desert as long as I kept the river bed in view.

Also there were tire tracks, quite deep ones, made when the ground was softer at the end of the rains, but their direction was puzzling. Some headed towards the river, others made for the heart of the desert, none followed the route I thought I should take. I tried to move closer to the river, but the ground became softer and occasionally even drifted into dunes which would certainly swallow my wheels. I wondered whether the desert-bound tracks might be aiming for a better and firmer route away from the river, and I followed one for a way, but it showed no sign of bearing right, and as the river line was almost lost to sight, I thought better of it and headed back.

So I steered a middle course and, gaining confidence, increased speed until I was doing nearly forty miles an hour in third gear. Then, quite unexpectedly, two sets of wheel tracks converged and intersected in front of me. I could not avoid them, nor could I stop. I bounced through the first track but nose-dived on the second. I saw it coming, and was interested to notice that I did not say, "Christ", or "Fucking hell", or "Here we go, my darling", or even "*Sic transit gloria.*" I said, "Oops!"

Anything could have happened. I had never fallen with a full load at any speed, and I was prepared for a major disaster. The result was immensely encouraging. The bike slid along on its side. The Craven pannier, packed solid, took the weight with a few scratches, and I fell easily and without harm.

I was shaking with excitement and relief, but had to get the bike upright quickly before I lost too much gas, and for once I was able to twist it up from the handlebars without unpacking it.

Then I found out how hot I was. The effort, and the unused adrenaline, had me sweating from every pore. I was drenched. I looked at the odometer. I had come approximately nine miles from Atbara in just over an hour.

I continued more cautiously, rarely exceeding twenty miles an hour. Twice more I fell, but easily, coming almost to a standstill before toppling over. After a while I found a tire track that seemed to be following firm ground in the right direction. Occasionally it moved in towards the river, and once I thought I saw a hut among the palms, but immediately before the trees the ground was very soft, and dunes were reaching out into the desert. I stayed away from the river, and picked my track up as it came out again farther on.

Just as I was beginning to feel that I had found the winning system, it led me into a trap. A ridge of high ground formed on my left. The track veered right. Then suddenly a fence appeared. A fence in the desert! The track followed the edge of the fence, and the ground became softer and softer. I was forced to go faster to stay on top, and then it was too late and I was buried up to the axle in fine ash-coloured sand. Fifty miles in three hours. Another two hundred miles to go.

It was plainly impossible to move the bike, so I began to unload it. I noticed immediately that my water bag was empty, the plastic perforated, the contents drained away. Well, at least I had a liter of distilled water. With all the luggage off I glanced in the gas tank. Had it been possible at this stage to shock me, I would have been shocked. There was only a puddle of gasoline left, hardly a gallon. My fuel consumption was twice what it should have been, and when I thought about it, that was perfectly natural. Grinding along in second gear over a loose surface in such heat, it is what you would expect. Only I, of course, had not expected it.

By now I was assimilating information like a robot. Buried in loose sand, with scarcely enough gas to get halfway, one liter of distilled water, and no money. It was very plain that I was going to need help, the sort of help that was hard to come by in the best of circumstances. Where do you look for help in a desert?

There was no point in getting upset. All the riding and falling had emptied me of surplus emotion. I felt fit, and strong enough to survive a long time. If the worst came to the worst, the river was not too far away. There might even be water in it. I set about digging myself out.

Scooping the sand out by hand took half an hour, but I managed to make a lane back to the firmer ground. There was a bit of brush growing on the dunes, and I paved my lane with twigs. Then, inch by inch, I was able to haul the bike back to where I wanted it. Again I had lost a lot of sweat, and I got the water bottle out. It was warm to the touch. I put it to my lips, and then spat vigorously on the ground, mustering as much of my own good saliva as I could. The bottle contained acid. Battery acid.

It occurred to me that I might easily have taken a swig, instead of a sip. I knew many who would have done. At least I had that reserve of caution. In a silly, minor way I was encouraged, as though it entitled me to survive.

I started looking for a better way forward, and found one. With the bike repacked I went slowly along, hoping the fence might have something to do with people. After a mile the going got easier again. The ground flattened, hardened and opened out. I moved towards the river. There were buildings, a figure on a donkey, and murmuring voices.

The biggest buildings were two storeys high and stood inside a compound. The voices came from there, and I rode up to the compound gate, dismounted and walked inside. A young man in a blue shirt and khaki trousers received me gravely as though I had been expected, and we exchanged greetings – "*Salaam, salaam, salaamat, salaamat*," and so on for the proper amount of time, shaking hands the while. Then he fetched me a bottle of fizzy orange – and introduced me to the headmaster of Kinedra Secondary School for Boys.

When I had explained my circumstances, struggling between honesty and embarrassment, I was complimented richly on my courage, wisdom, initiative and good fortune, and the school was placed at my disposal. There were hundreds of boys and a staff of six young men, all anxious to devote themselves henceforth to my bidding. As far as possible I allowed them to continue with their normal routine, but it was clear that for the duration of my stay the functioning of the school became of lesser importance. Only one thing was demanded of me. I must stay. There could be no question of my going on.

Fortunately this coincided very well with my own ideas.

I was taken to the dormitory shared by the teachers, and a special meal was prepared and brought to me by the headmaster, with dishes of different meats and vegetables, in delicious peppery sauces. I did not disgrace myself. My fingers were nimble and my palate was thoroughly attuned. I ate with relish as the teachers sat around, admiring and plying me with questions. At other mealtimes they all ate from a common bowl of mutton, vegetable and rice, scooping up the food with pieces of an unleavened bread baked from millet and called kissera, but I was always brought specially prepared dishes. They were cooked by the headmaster's wife, but I never saw her.

We discussed the matter of gas, or benzene as they called it. Perhaps the district officer at Sidon might have some. He had a car.

Sidon? That was the town, three miles away. My concept of the desert was undergoing some changes. In fifty miles I had not seen a living soul, only the illusion of movement on the horizon where the heat haze bent the light and made it sway. That was the desert as I had imagined it since childhood, as I had wanted it to be, a place of awe-inspiring emptiness where only bleached bones could be at rest. Obviously it was that, but it was also a home for thousands of people who lived around it and crossed it frequently as a matter of course. Had I been extraordinarily lucky to stumble upon Kinedra, or was the world a more hospitable place than I had ever realized? My memory flashed back to the beastly bird guarding the desert. Suppose I had been stranded out there, on that baking ground, thinking about my bones bleaching in the sun, what a bird of ill omen that would have been. Instead I was being attended to like a lord. With little effort I could imagine the headmaster as a sheik, the boys as slaves, the walls as hides, the school as a great Bedouin encampment, and I was the honored envoy of a distant monarch. Such excellent fortune. Shouldn't I thank that red-eyed monster, and treasure its memory, for teaching me to drop my superficial judgements and let the world be what it was?

I tried to describe the bird to my friends, and at last they recognized it as something they called a "bous," and screwed up their faces in revulsion. I later learned to call it a Marabou, a stork turned scavenger, which appears with minor variations across Africa and Asia. I always thought of it with pleasure, and recognized it as a friend, although it was everywhere regarded with loathing. It joined the Pleiades as an ally on my journey. There were other creatures with which I had a special affinity. I was a great admirer of goats, donkeys and camels for their leathery determination to endure, and was always glad when they were around, but they had no magic power over my destiny, I felt. Just friends.

To show my gratitude I asked whether the boys might enjoy hearing me tell them about my journey. The teachers said they would arrange something that evening, but first they took me on a guided tour to see how their vegetables were grown and irrigated. An ancient Perkins diesel engine pumped water from the Atbara River in the winter, and so precious was the water that the owner of the pump got half the crop in payment. Even more wonderful though was the now disused wooden construction with interlocking vertical and horizontal gears, driven by an ox on a circular walkway. It hauled up water in buckets on an endless chain dipping into a deep slot in the riverbank.

They described how the houses were built up from slabs of wet mud, one row a day left to bake in the sun, tapering slightly to the roof, which was made of split palm and thatch and again covered with mud. The word "mud" in no way does justice to these houses. With their rich yellow colour, and the impression of enormous mass exaggerated by the inclined walls and absence of windows, they looked more like great ingots of gold. The space inside, dark, cool and mysterious, had more in common with the interior of a cave than a house. In fact, passing through the door of such a house from the desert at mid-day waslike dropping magically into some other dimension of space and time.

In the evening the teachers took off their Western clothing and put on galabias. The boys wore nothing else. In its simplest everyday form the galabia is no more than a cotton shift with floppy sleeves, and I also was given one to wear and to sleep in. That evening, however, the senior master wore a more voluminous and elaborate robe, crisply laundered, and a turban. He said the boys had been assembled to hear from me, and I changed back into my traveling clothes to give them a better idea of it.

I had given no thought to how it would be done, and I was rather taken aback. A rostrum had been set up outside on the open ground, with a lamp. The boys, all in white, sat on the ground in a huge circle, and beyond them was only the great velvet night.

The master translated my simple account into Arabic. The boys listened, and laughed at the right places. Then they asked questions.

"How often do you write to your mother?"

"Do you always wear those boots?"

"How do you get the money?"

And other sensible things like that.

The setting was dramatically beautiful, the whole thing had the air of a great theatrical event, and I was rather carried away by it, but the kids brought me down to earth again. Thank heavens for little boys.

Next day I took my five-gallon jerry and walked the three miles to Sidon, across paddies and through scraggly trees. The district commissioner received me with interest and changed a traveler's check for me, but he had only enough gas, he said, to get his own Land-Rover to Kassala. He thought I would be lucky to find any, because most of the traffic that came through was diesel.

I began to face the unpalatable truth: I would have to go back to Atbara for gas. Apparently a bus was due to come through from Kassala that evening. It would stop in the square.

The teacher accompanying me took me to the elementary school in Sidon, and left me in the care of a fiery headmaster called Mustafa, who tried hard to convert me to the Muslim faith, and kept me entertained through the afternoon. In the early evening he introduced me to another man who was also on his way to Atbara. We drank tea together, and then Mustafa left, saying:

"He is a rich merchant. He will take care of you."

I looked at the merchant with interest, but my curiosity was unrewarded. His face was smooth and unmarked, if a shade plump. He could have been any age from twenty-five to forty-five, although his status indicated age. His smile revealed two rows of excellent white teeth and nothing more. His body, probably well fed, was hidden by the folds of an expensive white robe and he wore a voluminous turban. He spoke no English and his expression was as controlled as it was courteous.

The square of Sidon is simply a piece of desert, as big and stark as a parade ground. Along one side is a line of low mud buildings with thickly encrusted roofs sloping into the square and leaning on pillars to make a sheltered walkway. The roofs, walls, and pillars flow together and the entire row looks as though it were made from one piece of clay by a giant hand.

At one end of the row was a tea shop, and we waited there as the sky dimmed and the heat subsided. Life in the square died down until there was only the proprietor of the tea shop and one other man. An oil lamp was lit in the shop, and by the thick yellow flame and the red glow of the charcoal burner I watched them. They spoke between long pauses. Occasionally one would roll up the phlegm in his throat and discharge it, staccato, to the floor.

The buildings across the square dissolved in the darkness and were forgotten. The night swallowed all except the little oasis of life by the tea shop. Soon even the shop closed. The merchant and I lay on the soft, dry sand, the only two mortals left in the universe, waiting.

We tried from time to time to speak to each other. I had a small vocabulary of Arabic, enough to suggest roughly the subject I wanted to discuss, but no more. He had a very few words of Italian. For the most part we lay in silence and I occupied myself with thoughts and cigarettes. I had almost decided to sleep and was lying on my back gazing at the stars, when the soft, careful voice asked:

"*Sudan signora queiss?*"

I was still wondering about the question, when I felt a finger tap my thigh, and the voice repeated, with slight urgency:

"*You Sudan Signora?*"

I could not think how to tell him that I had never seen a Sudanese signora.

"*Si,*" I said. "Yes," trying to sound offhand and academic, wondering what was going on and looking up towards the voice. A moon was just rising. The merchant's robes gleamed, the turban had been released to fall as a shawl around the shoulders. The face was quite invisible, only the even teeth shone white, as the disembodied voice spoke. What was the voice going to suggest next? A little shudder of excitement ran through my body, because I knew, at that moment, that I could not be sure of my responses. The strange, emptying effect of the desert seemed to have drained away all my conditioning. I did not know whether I was young or old, wise or foolish, strong or weak, and perhaps I did not even know whether I was male or female. But I did know that the tap on the thigh had released a current of sexual energy, and this invisible figure close to me had become mysteriously potent.

"*Sudan signor queiss?*" Ah, there it was. The voice went on softly, but with a sharp edge of interrogation.

"*You Sudan signor?*"

This time the finger tapped, very precisely, on my cock, which was already straining slightly against the denim.

Ted Simon was shocked. He wanted to do something to demonstrate. Nothing like that had happened to him in his conscious life. But I was already somewhat removed from him.

Don't be such a prig, I told him. *How often have you wondered, secretly, whether you were caught up somewhere deep inside by other cravings, by repressed desires and weaknesses. What about that other Arab on the highway? What about your problems with male authority? This is a moment when you have absolute freedom of choice. Morality has blown away into the desert, you are not accountable to anyone. This is a privilege you have never allowed yourself before. So, do you want a sexual adventure with this man?*

"*Sudan signor, queiss?*" repeated the voice, and the finger tapped again.

"*Si*", I said, but only to avoid offense, and I put myself out of range of the questing finger. "This way is no good for me," I said in English, relying on my tone to tell him.

It seemed to me that I really did not want it. That one important question had been finally answered.

There was no awkwardness, no break even in the mood. The episode seemed quite natural. It went one way, could as easily have gone another. I sat up with my back against a pillar and smoked another cigarette, lost in the mystery of it.

The bus came at midnight. Its light and sound preceded it far across the desert and it grew in noise and brilliance, approaching as I imagined the end of the world would come, or a landing from Mars. For all the long warning, its arrival in the square was very sudden. It stopped by us, and from its bright interior a horde of people jumped out. They seemed to be all men, and each one had a sword slung across his back. They wore sleeveless jackets over shirts over robes, and without further ado, they fell to the ground all about the bus and went to sleep, their swords hugged to their bodies. When I saw that the driver was among them, I did likewise.

At four in the morning we were all wakened. It was still dark, and now it was also chilly. I had not anticipated a night in the desert. My thin shirt left me very cold. The merchant and I sat side by side, the physical contact feeling rather odd to me now. Uneasily I began to ponder again on the meaning of our encounter for me. He must have felt me shivering slightly with cold, because he opened his shawl and laid it around my shoulders as well as his own. This paternal gesture seemed to offer some clue to what I was looking for. I was still uneasy. It was only long afterwards that the dark and inscrutable face of my own unknown father joined the mosaic of images that whirled around that incident, because I had forgotten that he, too, might have been taken for an Arab.

The bus juddered along into the dawn. I dozed and woke and dozed again. The two men in the seat in front of mine sat very upright, with their swords, in their strange, paddle-shaped scabbards, sticking up beside them. Their hair hung in greased ringlets over the collars of their dung-coloured shirts, and I smelled a particular, musty but not unpleasant odor, which might have been animal fat.

A little way outside Atbara, the bus made a stop, and all the passengers got out to stretch their legs and relieve themselves. The members of one family were getting off for good. They had small bundles of pots and pans, and took some poles wrapped in cloth off the roof of the bus. As they set their belongings down in the desert, I noticed that there were, after all, some women among them, carefully veiled from view. They all looked miserable and sick, coughing and shivering in very thin clothing, and their small boy, I realized, was the one that had been coughing throughout the journey. I was quite absorbed by their plight when the bus's horn called us aboard again. Only then did I realize that the merchant had disappeared. I could not understand it. There seemed to have been nowhere for him to go out there. I looked in all directions, but he had left my life as discreetly as he entered it.

By eleven I had my five gallons of gas and had found a truck going to Kinedra. By mid-afternoon I was back there. The truck set me down about a kilometer away, and a small boy on a donkey carried the gas as I walked alongside.

The warmth and generosity of the schoolmasters rose to a crescendo on my last night. In the morning they gave me a gift of money which they had collected among themselves to help me on my way. I knew that for them it represented a sizeable sacrifice and it was difficult to take it, but I felt that such gifts could not, and should not, be refused.

I had become close to them and it was a wrench to leave. They were very solemn in their farewells, giving the parting its full value as they did with everything and not shirking the emotion. A great crowd of boys had gathered to wave me good-bye. I would have been embarrassed if I had not known the feeling was genuine.

My feeling for the Sudanese was one of total admiration. Never had I met such unmotivated generosity, such a capacity for imbuing the simplest life with a touch of splendor. I had felt it straight away in Atbara. In the teahouses there it had been rare for me to pay, although I had tried. When it was time to settle I would find that someone had paid my bill and left before me. Only afterwards would I remember the quiet greeting from a stranger on his way out. Or the proprietor would refuse my *piastre*. They were small amounts, but they added great value to the tea and made it rich.

The desert contradicted my expectations in many ways. Fifty miles across a barren waste, where I had thought to find nobody, I stumbled upon a secondary school for boys. They were as enchanted by me as I was surprised by them.

The previous day I had been told that a district forest officer was taking his Land-Rover to Kassala for brake fluid, and had agreed to lead me on to the best route. When we met I asked him, naturally enough, where his forest was. He told me that this desert I was traveling through, which I had thought of as being as old as the stars above it, had become a desert only in the previous thirty years. Before that there had been grasses and trees, but the traveling herds of cattle had increased and stripped away all the natural vegetation, and men had cut down the trees. Now dunes were beginning to form, and soon it would be like the Sahara. The fence I had encountered the other day was to protect new plantations of grasses and trees to stabilize the soil once more. He was not cheerful about the prospect. "We are too few," he said, "and they are too many. The dunes will spread. We are like Canute against the waves."

At mid-morning he was ready, and we set off. From the start it was touch and go. His driver, over-impressed by the size of the Triumph, set a pace that was altogether too dashing. I managed to keep him in sight for several miles, but dropped far behind, unable to fly across the dips and soft bits as he could. It was while trying to catch him again, on a fairly easy stretch, that I ran into the same trap of intersecting ruts that had caught me on the first day. This time my "Oops" was a good deal louder. The bike came crashing down again, but much harder, ripping one of the boxes off its mountings and smashing the headlamp. My shoulder also took a fair blow.

Even so, all the important things were all right. The jerry was intact, the bike was functioning. My shoulder would manage. I found some wire and tied the box back on where the screws had torn through the fibreglass, taking my time, determined that I would get through somehow, and resolving that I would never again ride at anybody else's pace. Two such disasters, I thought, must teach me the lesson.

I was almost ready to go again when the Land-Rover returned. They had missed me, eventually. I explained that it was far better for me to ride alone, if they would just describe the route as best they could. They wanted to try to load the bike on the car, but I refused, and at last they did their best to draw me a diagram of what to look for, and left wishing me luck.

That was the beginning of the hardest and most rewarding physical experience of my entire journey.

If falling were a competitive sporting event, I would be a champi-
on. Sometimes, on deeply rutted tracks like this one between
Gedaref and Metema, it was impossible to avoid a fall. The damage looks worse than it was, but it was an exhausting exercise
because I could not lift the bike without unpacking everything first.

Falling
& Rising

The desert was full of spectacular sights, and none more splendid than these proud Sudanese tribesmen who posed for me at the Crocodile's Mouth. The man on the left is wearing his sword.

I am trying to keep track of the number of times I have fallen. Yesterday, three times. Today, twice, the hard fall that wrenched my left arm, and one soft tumble since. The arm is all right, but weakened.

My greatest problem is keeping up concentration. I have to watch the surface all the time, with only occasional glimpses at the longer views around me. The light is intense, but luckily I was given some Polaroid ski goggles in London, and they are excellent for the desert. When wearing them I sometimes have the feeling that I am traveling under water. They give everything that cool clarity you get in a rock pool.

Heat does not worry me, even in the jacket and the sheepskin lined boots. It seems crazy, but I don't feel it. It is not hot by Sudanese standards of course, but it must be nearly ninety in the shade. And I am not in the shade. It is very dry heat, easier to support. Does the clothing help to conserve sweat?

Goz Regeb, said Mochi, is the place to spend the night. It is still a hundred miles away, five hours at this present rate. I will not make it today.

Something is moving on the horizon, something live. I stop. Far away I see cattle crossing the desert, but they seem to be swimming through a silver lake. A mirage. A fantastic sight.

It is Thursday, the thirteenth of November. I have been traveling five weeks. How many days of actual riding? I count twenty-one. How far have I ridden? The clock shows 5,137 miles. Minus 867 when I started, leaves 4,170 miles on the journey. Average, two hundred miles a day. Not bad. Well, the average will start dropping now.

After three more hours I have come another fifty miles. In an hour or two it will be dark, but there should be a tea hut soon. I think it is called Khor el Fil, which is supposed to mean the Crocodile's Mouth. Spelling is very optional and distances are vague.

I have had one more soft fall, but each jerk on the wheel pulls the muscle in my left shoulder and prevents it from healing. I feel no hunger, no thirst. I am absolutely wrapped up in this extraordinary experience, in the unremitting effort, in the marvellous fact that I am succeeding, that it is at all possible, that my worst fears are not just unrealized but contradicted. The bike, for all its load, is manageable. I seem to have, after all, the strength and stamina to get by, and my reserves seem to grow the more I draw upon them. The natives, armed with swords and fierce pride, show me only the greatest respect.

Sometimes I wonder why the wilder parts of the world have always seemed so frightening, why the word "primitive" has always meant "danger." If it weren't so, would I be falling over tourists out for a day in the desert? Would I meet Len and Nell from Cranfield Park Road sitting under a tree at Khor el Fil, mopping their brows and writing picture postcards?

No, I must not forget why I am able to function here. These five weeks have changed me already. My stomach has shrunk drastically, my blood has changed, my sweat glands are adapted to a different regime, my palate has altered and my muscles have certainly hardened, to speak only of physical changes.

I have also had time to learn a confidence I never knew before, and surely my own confidence in the face of strangers must, in turn, increase their confidence in me. Then there is also the fact that I am proud of what I am doing. There is no denying it. I try to be modest, to say anyone could do it. But they don't, and I feel I have managed to pull off something special. It helps me to know that, as though I were plugged into a kind of power I did not know I had.

Why doesn't everybody do it? I don't think it's only timidity. I was as afraid as anyone would be. They have careers, of course, and mortgages. They say they would do it "if it weren't for the kids." I used to laugh at that, but why should I? It's perfectly legitimate. Much as they envy me, they are simply too absorbed in their lives to want to leave them behind. They are fascinated, as I pass by, to hear about my plans and my stories, but in the end they are happy enough to let me do it for them. Len and Nell can mop their brows under the pyramids for a week and leave the stomach shrinking to me.

Why you? Why were you chosen to ride through the desert while other men are going home from the office?

Chosen? I thought I chose myself. Were Odysseus and Jason, Columbus and Magellan chosen?

That is a very exalted company you have summoned up there. What have you got in common with Odysseus, for God's sake?

Well, we're all just acting out other people's fantasies, aren't we? Maybe we're not much good for anything else.

Looking back on what has already happened I can see that it would have the makings of a legend. Every encounter seems so significant, each one testing me and preparing me for the next. Zanfini; the Via Torremuzzo; the *S.S.Pascoli*; Kabaria; Sousse; Cyrenaica; Salloum; Mersa Matruh; Alexandria; the Great Bird of Atbara; and Sidon. And why did the Twirling Turk on the ferry point his finger at *me*?

In my childhood I was devoted to stories of men who overcame terrible obstacles to win the hand of the princess; dogs with eyes like saucers, dogs with eyes the size of dinner plates, dogs with eyes as big as cartwheels. They always came in threes. I did not know then that they were tidied-up versions of ancient mythology. In my childhood, nobody talked about myths and legends. They were just stories. The job of explaining life was left to science, but science eventually failed the test. So did politics, of course. And love. And property. And journalism just went on begging the question.

So here I am, still looking for an explanation, acting out those childhood stories which, perhaps, were always the most satisfying after all; making myself the hero of my own myth?

These are not so much sequential thoughts as feelings interspersed with memories, dancing in my brain as the bike rolls comfortably over an easier stretch. The symbols group themselves in my mind. The Yom Kippur War, the Turk and the Bird loom large as omens. What do they portend?

My thoughts are interrupted by the sight of a truck ahead of me. It is stationary. There are people grouped around it. Tracks start to sweep in across my path from the open desert, and following them around I see they converge near the river, by a group of trees and a hut. Khor el Fil, the halfway mark.

Nothing ever tasted more delicious than the tea I hold in my hand.

"Take the truck," they are saying. "You cannot go through. There are big dunes. Take the truck to Goz Regeb. It is not far."

I resist, but their concern for me is so genuine that I feel excused by it. Fifty miles in the truck, that's not too much.

There are four Bescharyin here at the teahouse with me, exotic figures, splendidly robed and armed, their hair teased out and glued into strands. I realize with a start that these must be the "Fuzzie-wuzzies" who fought so fanatically against Gordon at Khartoum The contact between us is instantaneous and overwhelming. There is a spirit in this tea, a magic solvent to wash away our differences. This is another reason why I am here: to experience (nothing less) the brotherhood of man. Imagine meeting these men in a London pub or an American diner. Impossible. They could never be there what they are here. They would be made small by the complexities, the paraphernalia that we have added to our lives, just as we are, although we have learned to pretend otherwise. I had to come here to realize the full stature of man; here outside a grass hut, on a rough wooden bench, with no noise, no crowds, no appointments, no axe to grind, no secret to conceal, all the space and time in the world, and my heart as translucent as the glass of tea in my hand. The sense of affinity with these men is so strong that I would tear down every building in the West if I thought it would bring us together like this. I understand why the Arab idea seems so perverse, so fanatical, so untrustworthy and self-destructive to the Western mind. It must be because the Arab puts an ultimate value on something we no longer even know exists. Integrity, in its real sense of being at one with oneself and one's God, whoever and wherever that God may be. Without it he feels crippled.

We Europeans sold our integrity for progress many years ago, and we have debased the word to mean merely someone who obeys the rules. A chasm of misunderstanding yawns between us. At this moment I know which side I want to stand.

The truck is being loaded by members of another tribe, the Raschaid. I gather they originate in Iraq, are known as nomadic camel herders and are supposed to be rich. This is a large family moving house by truck rather than camel. They have their tent wrapped up, great bundles of hide with the poles tied together; enormous heavy glass bottles slung in rope nets; the rest wrapped in carpets. Their women are with them, the first women I have been close to since Egypt. They wear finely woven silver veils over their faces, just below eye level. For them it is the mouth which must not, in any circumstances, be seen by a strange man. Their robes hang loose, their breasts are visible from time to time, it does not bother them. It does bother me, however, and I have to guard my expression carefully. I am helped in this by the playful way in which the head of the family toys with his rifle, as he sits on top of the truck and supervises the loading.

Four men load the bike without difficulty. I pay a small sum, and we're off. I sit jammed up against the members of the family, trying to ignore the sumptuous femininity jiggling so close to me.

There really are dunes. The truck has to put down metal tracks to cross them. I would not have had a chance here, but I might have made it through the trees.

All I can see of Goz Regeb, at night, is the big teahouse with many rooms. There is food too, meat and beans and kissera. There are wooden bedframes strung with jute to sleep on. All around me men fall to their knees in prayer, arms rising and falling, voices chanting:

"Allah Harkborough, Allah Harkborough" – at least that's what it sounds like. Then again the silence, the stars, and the early morning chill, but this time I am prepared.

Approaching Kassala at last, I can scarcely believe the skyline that rises before me. A range of high mountains with rounded tops like mounds of smoothly licked ice cream. I feel as though I am approaching an enchanted land, and more and more often I feel that I am acting out some fairy tale or legend. All I lack is a clear idea of my purpose.

In Kassala I seek out the forest officer, hoping to spend more time with him. The driver of the Land-Rover is the first to see me coming. His broad face radiates happiness at seeing me.

"You are a real man," he says.

I almost choke with the pleasure that gives me. It was worth it all just to hear that.

From Kassala there are two ways to go. The usual route, which I had expected to take, follows a big highway through Eritrea to Asmara. According to the Ethiopian Consul, the road is untroubled by rebels at present. I find the prospect rather tame. A real man has his responsibilities. I decide on another route, continuing south through Sudan for 240 miles and then crossing into Ethiopia at Metema.

On the map the road is graded one better than nothing as far as the border. After that it reverts to the same condition as the one I have just travelled, but I know now that this can only be the vaguest indication. All I am fairly sure of is that there is no more open desert.

The first stretch as far as Khashm el Girbar runs alongside the railway line. In fact it is part of the bed of the track, and made of dried mud, baked and cracked in the sun. At times it is raised above the surrounding brush, at others not, and it varies a great deal in width. There are some shallow ruts that reduce speed drastically, but worse still, most of the way is mildly corrugated.

The riding is not only as difficult as it was in the desert, it is also more uncomfortable and frustrating, as the bike rattles furiously over the bumps. The fifty-three miles take me three hours of hard work. There are teahouses on the way. I have made it a rule always to stop. At Khashm el Girbar I am rewarded by a teahouse with wonderful fresh fish from the reservoir there. Again the atmosphere is one of all-embracing intimacy. I have only to sit down in these places now to feel that I am among old friends.

The road to Gedaref?

"*Queiss*," they say. "Much better."

I reserve my judgement this time, but draw strength from their encouragement.

The road to Gedaref is worse. Much worse. Worse than anything I imagined. At times, in fact, I believe it is impossible, and consider giving up. The corrugations are monstrous. Six-inch ridges, two feet apart, all the way with monotonous, shattering regularity. Everything on the bike that can move does so. Every bone in every socket of my body rattles. Not even the most ingenious fairground proprietor could devise a more uncomfortable ride. I feel certain that it must break the bike. I try riding very slowly, and it is worse than ever. Only at fifty miles an hour does the bike begin to fly over the ridges, levelling out the vibration a little, but it is terribly risky. Between the ridges is much loose sand. Here and there are sudden hazards. The chances of falling are great, and I am afraid of serious damage to the bike. Yet I feel I must fly, because I don't think the machine will survive eighty miles of this otherwise. It is hair-raising, and then it becomes impossible again. The road swings to the west and the sun burns out my vision. I realize I must stop and make a camp, because I shall never arrive at Gedaref anyhow, today.

Between some bushes I set up the mosquito net, cook some rice and tea, smoke a cigarette, and sleep. I have been going from dawn to sunset, a full day of total endeavor, and I have come just under a hundred miles.

Something wakes me from my sleep. Huge shapes loom around the net in the darkness, threatening to squash me. I am petrified. A herd of camels is being driven through the night across my camp site. The camels obviously sense my presence though, because they avoid me daintily. After a minute I lose my fear and simply gaze up at them in wonder. They are really like ships in the night. Even so, I think I was lucky.

In the morning, refreshed, I lose patience with the corrugations and fly over them regardless. I find that I can control the bike better than I had thought. I still fear for the effect on the bike, but I am hopeful that after Gedaref things may improve. These corrugations are the result of heavy traffic, but beyond Gedaref, according to the map, the road is less important and may not be so deformed. I even hope, nostalgically, that it may be as pleasant as the desert track. At least, in the desert, I was able to think. Here every part of me is pinned to the road and survival.

I get to Gedaref in two heart-stopping hours, and find another place to eat fish, but this is a different kind of town from Atbara or Kassala, busier and more crowded, and the crowd is curious and pressing. They are all around me, peering at me, and I am glad to get away on the road to Doka. Until I see what the road is like. My alarm takes me to the verge of despair, and then turns to laughter. It is too ridiculous.

The washboard corrugations continue, as before, but not consistently. The ground here is obviously softer and heavy vehicles have been going through in the rain. The road is saucer-shaped, that is to say, it has a steep reverse camber. In the middle, at the bottom of the depression are deep slots, usually two side by side. They are only a couple of feet apart, and must have been made by trucks traveling with one wheel in the road and another on the bank. The space between the slots is not flat, but rises to a crown, and also narrows from time to time or disappears altogether as the two slots merge into one. It is not possible to ride between the slots without, soon, falling into one. The slots are fifteen inches deep and the same width. They might have been tailored to fit the bike. The pipes just fit inside them, the side panniers just clear the tops of them. I am forced to ride in the slots, but I see a great danger of breaking my legs against the side if the bike should lurch one way or another, and for much of the way I have to keep my legs raised in the air.

Where the slots are shallower or broader the ground is corrugated or covered with loose sand. For several hours I am unable to average more than ten miles an hour. My feelings have changed now, though. I see this as a part of what I must do, and I am resigned to the fact that each day the hazards will multiply until I meet the dog with eyes like cartwheels. My worries are now all for the motorcycle. With one suspect piston I am worried about overheating. Three times I fall; once when riding between the slots the bike falls into a groove and is almost upside down. Each time I stop and relax, and let the bike cool off. I'm trying not to let the riding overwhelm me so that I forget where I am and what I'm doing.

The soil here is pitch black, and flat, but far ahead I see it rising steadily towards the Ethiopian plateau. On either side of me are fields of cotton and millet, and the cotton is just bursting out of its pods in little puffs of white. Not a soul anywhere, not a vehicle or an animal or a person. What does it matter? I have water, rice, tea and sugar, and salt. I can take as long as I like, stop where and when I like.

So, plodding along, horseback fashion, I arrive in Doka just after four in the afternoon. The police offer me a large open space with a fence around it. I don't need their fence, but their hospitality is welcome and they share their food with me.

New day, new problems. The road is rising now, in short steep swoops. Where it rises the road is littered with big stones ripped out of the rock and flung loose. Something enormous has been traveling this road. Whatever it was has also ground the rock into a fine powder, a pink talc, like face powder, that reflects the sun and kills all contours. I cannot see the rocks before I hit them, and since climbing necessitates some speed and momentum, I find myself bouncing from one side of the track to the other, hoping to find a safe line through. Twice more I fall, spread-eagled across the track, and here it's worse because the rocks catch on the panniers, ripping them off, and denting the pipes. Once I am trapped with my foot under the rear wheel. The strap on the boot is caught on the axle, and at first I can't move. As I lie there, mustering strength, I remember the boy in the store selling me that boot. I asked him what the strap was for, and he replied, "for when you come off."

Why don't the tires tear to shreds under all this punishment? Why no punctures? I think a puncture might finish me, I'm so beat. Why doesn't the Triumph just die? Unlike me, it has no need to go on. It protests and chatters. On one steep climb it even fainted, but after a rest it went to work again. I hate to think what havoc is being wrought inside those cylinders. We have such a long way to go.

The morning passes in effort and short stops. The countryside is more pleasing as it rises among trees. The mountain kingdom of Ethiopia must be near now. The Sudanese side of the border is called Galabat. I see some men in uniform outside a building and ride up to them. They are soldiers and ask me to eat with them. We squat on the ground outside their garrison in front of a large bowl, scooping up the food with handfuls of kissera. All the usual politenesses and courtesies are offered, the symbols of mutual respect.

Soon I shall leave Arabia behind, and I suspect already how much I shall yearn for it, and Sudan in particular.

A deep dry gulch divides the two countries. The Sudanese customs official is correct and helpful, despite a lost document. His office is tidy and efficient, the compound neat and clean. He is shaven and wears a freshly laundered galabia. These are the things I remember as I ride down the gulch and up the other side into Metema.

The differences are shocking. Here in this crowded shanty town are slovenly unshaven soldiers, absentee officials, dirt, dilapidation and already a whiff of corruption. The army checks me out for explosives. It is three in the afternoon but customs, they say, won't be back until next morning. I ride up the road to find a hotel. Every hut is a hotel, or pretends to be with a painted sign in blue or magenta. "The Best Hotel in Town" is a square room under a tin roof, with rough daubed walls and an earth floor, a wooden bar, shelves of drink and, strange to see on an earth floor, some upholstered chairs and a sofa around a table. I had forgotten about upholstery. Then, the biggest shock of all. A woman, quite a pretty woman, in a plain cotton frock with an emancipated neckline and a hem just below the knees walks across to me, looking me in the eyes, and *shakes my hand*. It is as explosive as a kiss. I had forgotten about women too.

She gives me a small cubicle at the back. The culture change is too great for me to risk sleeping outside here. Metema has a true frontier town feel to it, and I smell lawlessness and a hint of violence.

I learned something about Ethiopia traveling through Sudan. The prostitutes in Atbara came from Asmara, and did a lucrative business. Occasionally the police rounded them up and shipped them over the border by truck, but the story went that the girls would bribe their way back and be in business again before the police even had time to get home.

Where the women of Islam are so concealed and repressed as to form virtually an underground society, the women of this most ancient Christian kingdom are shamelessly exposed, unprotected and exploited at the opposite extreme. Both the women in this hotel are prostitutes, and have several children. They keep their money in a big iron chest under one of the beds. Even the smallest sums are immediately put away there, and all their actions indicate that they must watch out for themselves constantly. They say they have saved to buy this place, that it must keep them in their older age. In the morning they make a poignant sight, nursing their illegitimate babies and their tightly rolled wads of Ethiopian dollars. I admire them and sympathize with them.

There is much more color here than in Sudan. Literally. A camel passes with two men sitting on it, back to back and laughing out loud. One is wearing a vivid carmine cloak. Another camel has birds sitting all over it, feeding off its coat. Even the birds have bright red bills.

At the border post they say, "No customs until the afternoon." Obviously it is not possible to believe them, nor am I going to make an offer, but I must have my customs carnet stamped. A policeman who seems to know what he is talking about tells me I can have it done in Gondar. I decide to chance it. The traveling is so hard that I must keep moving. I need the momentum to balance the hardship.

Gondar is the target, the point where I rejoin the main highway system. I cannot help thinking of it as Gondor, the gloomy mountain fortress toward which Tolkien's hero, Frodo, had to carry the Ring of Power. All my thoughts are still dominated by the physical battering that I and the machine are taking on this road. Before leaving today I have to clean up a terrible mess in one of the boxes. The vibration has loosened the lid of the cod-liver oil and glucose pot. It has also caused the aluminum film canisters to grind together and form a powder. Everything in the box is now smeared with a paste of cod-liver oil and aluminum, the most bizarre example yet of what vibration can do on a bike. Happily the cameras were no longer in there, and nothing is ruined.

The fourth day of the ride from Kassala begins. The road here is like a cart track on a mountainside, not bad on the level sections, but treacherous on the inclines with that same blinding dust obscuring loose rock. Gondar is almost five thousand feet up from here, but there is a series of lower ranges to cross, and the road is climbing or falling almost constantly. This much, however, I became accustomed to yesterday. What new monster must I wrestle with today? Here it comes. A river. I stop to look at it, and my heart sinks to my boots. How can I ever get across it? There is a ford about thirty feet wide. The water is not too deep, a foot or two at most, although fast-running, but the river bed looks impossible for two wheels. It is littered with black boulders the size of footballs. How can I possibly expect the bike to stay upright, even if the tires can grip the slippery-looking stone.

I am very frightened of what will happen, almost certain of disaster. Only the thought of those thousands of miles behind me forces me to confront the problem. I have never forded a river before. For five or ten minutes I walk up and down, looking for a better way, trying to stifle the panic in my breast and find some calm and resolution. It comes. The fear is somehow anesthetized. I know that if I am going to do it, it must be now.

"There is a first and last time for everything," I tell myself, and launch into it, trying to guess the right speed. There is nothing for me to do but hold on tight and pray. I'm going too fast to be able to change direction or choose a path. The bike leaps about like a mad thing. To my complete astonishment, I find myself riding up the other side. I stop, quivering with relief. All the strength has left me and my leg will hardly hold up the bike while I fiddle with the stand.

What a wonderful place this world is. It really does look as though I am meant to get through.

My boots are full of water, and I go back to the stream and wash my feet, wring out my socks, and take a drink. The ford looks more manageable now that I've crossed it, but there will be others. For sure.

There are four more that day, and the last one is the most monstrous of all. The bike stalls just before the other side, but I am able to keep it upright in the water. This ford is doubly unlike the others though, because here there are people. Some men come to help me drag the bike out of the river. They seem very friendly, and I discover they are building a bridge here and have a camp. They tell me to stay the night with them.

They are different from other men, these road builders. Some kind of *esprit de corps* animates them, as though the roads and bridges they make are only the physical symbols of a desire to help the world along. I have observed it many times before, in many countries.

That night I lie out under the stars again. The Pleiades are there winking at me. I am no longer on my way from one place to another, I have changed lives. My life now is as black and white as night and day; a life of fierce struggle under the sun, and peaceful reflection under the night sky. I feel as though I am floating on a raft, far, far away from any world I ever knew.

The men are gathered around a fire, talking. The language is Amharic, and quite impenetrable by me, but I can hear when they are just making conversation and when they are telling stories, because they have two voices. Comments are made in normal speech, but for stories they speak in a higher register, in a voice that trips and burbles along at a fast rate, full of mimicry and giggling laughter. I feel my raft floating right back to the beginning of time.

The fifth day out of Kassala, and the slopes are immediately steeper and longer. It is clear that the bike can barely cope with the combination of load, work and heat. The road is scarred and ripped to rubble. It's like following the track of some stumbling monster of destruction. Halfway up a particularly hard climb, I lose momentum and the bike simply dies on me. I don't know what's happened, what to do. I wait awhile and kick it over. It starts and revs up fine in neutral, but when I engage the clutch it dies on me again. I am quite near the top of the hill, and I unload the heaviest boxes and carry them up myself. Then I ride the bike up, and load again. The plugs and timing are O.K. What else can I do but cross my fingers, and try to keep up momentum.

Another long steep climb and I take it as fast as I can. When I get to the top, bouncing like a mad thing all the way, I find that I have lost one of my boxes at the bottom. It is way out of sight. As I walk down, I hear a big engine approaching. Farther down is the monster that makes this road what it is. A twenty-ton Fiat truck, with ten gears, is grinding uphill in first. It fills every inch of the track on its sixteen huge tires. The driver points to his left-hand side, then stops. He has the box with him, unopened, and I climb in beside him and ride back to the top, very grateful for his honesty.

It takes a while to fix the box, using largish pieces of flattened tin as an anchor where the fiberglass has been torn away. The road continues as before. I fall again, twice within a minute or two. The weak arm is wrenched again every time the stones snatch at the wheel and try to tear the handlebars from my grip. The climbing is intensely difficult. Up and down and farther up and down again and still farther up, always a new mountain ahead as the road rises through the eroded edges of a high and massive plateau. At one fall, some boys see me pick myself up from the dust, and they rush away, only to reappear with a kettle full of cold mountain water for me to drink. Another time, two boys in rags with gourds tied around their waists leave their cattle and come to watch. One carries a flute and hands it to me, but my brain is too addled by heat and effort to know what he wants. I hand it back and he plays the musical equivalent of a mountain torrent. His dexterity is astounding. He pours out notes with the speed and confidence of an absolute virtuoso, creating not a single stream of melody but a cascade of sound, which seems to be in several keys and registers simultaneously. He bathes me in his music and I know, as I listen, that I will never hear anything like this again. When he finishes I try to show my gratitude. We have not one word in common, and foolishly I feel it is impossible to repay such a gift with money. Afterwards I am ashamed to have made him the victim of my idealism. A dollar would have suited him better than my lofty sentiment, no doubt.

Still, his music is the sign that this ordeal is almost ended. A towering finger of rock appears, standing alone on the right of the road. Then I breast the final escarpment and run free on the plateau at last.

Chelga is the last village, about fifty miles from the highway, a mountain village, houses and people huddled more closely together, faces lined and angular, showing cunning and suspicion. There is a "hotel" that serves meals. The food is *injera* and *wat*, a variation on the Sudanese meal. *Injera*, the bread, is different. It comes like a pancake, or rather an enormous soft muffin, covering the whole of a circular tin tray. Under it is a small bowl of chopped mutton in spiced sauce.

Gathered around a table at the far end of the room is a group of men in Western business suits of solid dark worsted. Their skin is black, but their features are prominent and European. Several of them wear dark glasses. By their prosperity, by the way the hotel owner treats them, by their assumption of nonchalance and the careless glances they cast over me and others, I know they are some kind of power elite.

After a little while the hotel owner asks me for my passport. He

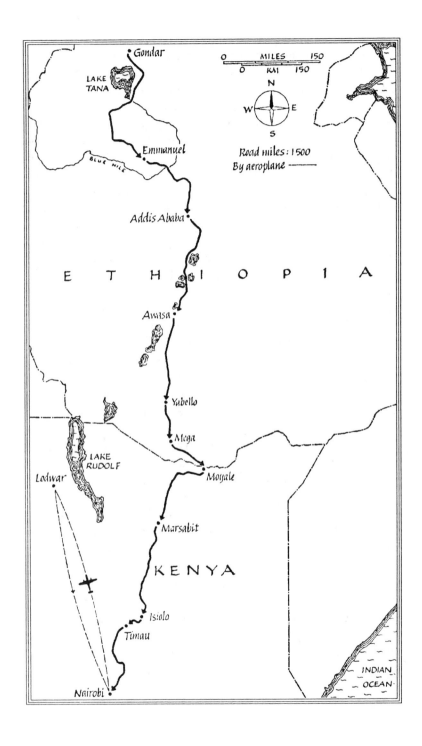

hands it obsequiously to one of the men, who studies it lightly, makes a laughing remark to the others and passes it back. The word that springs to mind is "mafia." When they have left, a bearded man to my right starts to speak.

"That man is a police general," he says, in good English. "I have to keep silence when they are near, but you will find that there are many like me who are ready to throw them out. Ethiopia is like France before the revolution." He is a teacher, and asks me to make contact with students in Addis if I want to find the truth.

"But look out for bad people on the road, who will try to stop you. If you joke with them they will steal from you. You must keep a good face. And it is not good to walk around Gondar alone.

"But after all your traveling you will have your own trick."

I am glad he says that. I know it is no good to go around expecting trouble. Better to hope that, in the last resort, you have found "your own trick."

The last fifty miles of road are shown on the map as "improved." The improvement consists of several inches of loose stone spread over the surface. I find it deadly, particularly on bends. There is one more ford, and one more fall. I feel by now that I have been treated to every variety of bad surface I could ever expect to meet. All that awaits me is to ride the same surfaces in the wet, but that privilege is deferred to another time and another continent.

At Azezo I ride out on to the highway and for the last eight miles I am on smooth tarmac. It is like a flying dream. I cannot feel my wheels touch the ground, and I enter Gondar floating through the air. I have ridden 450 miles from Atbara in seven unimaginable days, and in many different ways I feel I have arrived.

Ethiopia means trouble. Once on the highway to Addis Ababa, I sense it most of the time. Perhaps, unknowingly, I even symbolize it. The men I pass, stubborn-looking men with hard, impassive faces, sometimes raise their sticks as though torn between the impulses to salute and to lash out. Small boys, almost naked, crouch and raise their fists in defiance. Sometimes, under the condoning eyes of adults, they throw stones, and I feel sure they are acting out their parents' wishes.

It seems natural that something as rare and strange as a helmeted figure on a motorcycle approaching at speed should arouse whatever are the dominant emotions. Here I would have to say that the first emotions to spring to the surface are fear and resentment. In Wollo province, three hundred miles from my route, thousands are said to be starving to death, but I can see no sign of it. The live stock looks fat and grain grows everywhere, but the country is seething with rebellion and the Emperor's long, harsh and corrupt reign must be nearly at an end.

In a small village called Emmanuel, just north of the Blue Nile Gorge, after another difficult day riding through heaps of loose stones, I am forced to stop by failing light. Small boys gather like flies, as usual, and a bigger boy, who has learned some English, appoints himself my guide and protector. Their concerted efforts sweep me and the bike over the high threshold of a doorway in a wooden stockade. Within the stockade is a pinkly painted hut labeled "Hotel," and at last I am leaning back in a chair with my boots, grey from powdered granite, stretched out in front of me in a comic posture of relief.

At the bar on my right, on a high stool with her bare feet dangling, sits the proprietress in a pink dirndl dress and head scarf chopping up mutton in a dour mood. Opposite me, side by side in identical positions, sit four nearly identical men staring straight ahead, staves clasped with both hands and planted between their feet, elbows resting on knees, polished knees spread apart to touch the neighbours'. In their shiny black woodenness they might have been carved from a single huge ebony log.

I have not yet got the taste for home-brewed corn beer and am drinking a warm and expensive bottle of Italian beer, waiting for a meal, when the teachers come in from the street. There are three of them. The boys must have told them about me, because they come in noisy with good cheer and obviously determined to entertain me and have a good time. They are an oddly assorted trio. One is a tall handsome Arab. One is a short, black, wrinkled and canny mountain man. The third is true African, with a smooth oval head balanced on his neck at forty-five degrees. The African is in a beige gabardine suit and the others are in traditional Ethiopian dress with shawls edged by a coloured stripe.

The African is already drunk. He squeezes up beside me waving his arms around me and pushing his face close to mine. His eyelids are papery and taut and the same colour as his suit, his mouth splutters saliva and his breath is bad. It is hard to like him.

"What are your opinions about South Africa?" he shouts. "What can you tell me about this country? I am definitely short of opinions on this subject. What is your information?" and so on. He is so absorbed in his questioning and posturing that there is no need for me to reply – mercifully, since I have nothing to say.

The others are more restrained, and show willingness to be light-hearted and amusing, but in spite of themselves their questioning becomes hostile and suspicious and turns to interrogation, with demands for proofs and evidence.

"Where do you come from?"

"Where do you live?"

"But that is impossible. You are British. How can you live in France?"

"How old are you?"

"I cannot believe that. Show me your passport. I will not believe unless you show me in black and white."

"What is this? Born in Germany? How do you explain this?"

"What is in that wallet? Show me. I will not believe you are not keeping a gun in there. A notebook? What kind of notes? Let me see what you are writing down about us."

I refuse. Not because of what I have written, but because, by now, I am afraid of losing it under a flood of beer or vomit. The scene has a feverish significance that is heightened by the effort I have to make against my own weariness and to "keep a good face." The four peasants staring impassively, the sour woman ordering her skivvy about, and these three tipsy interrogators, their good intentions helpless against the tide of anger and frustration that wells up inside them, all that seems a quite excellent model of Ethiopia as I sense it from the road.

Food comes, and with it, I hope for some relief. I have to struggle to stop too much of the African's spit from falling on my plate, but most of it is dribbling over his food as he scoops up the mutton with fistfuls of injera and stuffs it into his mouth. Then I start back in horror as I see his dripping hand head straight for my own mouth. He tries desperately hard to reach me with it, but I am ducking and weaving like Muhammed Ali, and he has to give up.

The other two are severely amused.

"It is a custom of hospitality in our country that you may show your love by placing your food in the mouth of your guest."

That, I thought disgustedly, sums it up. Where else could a gesture of friendship become a repulsive act of aggression. In Ethiopia, for once, I allowed myself the luxury of a generalization. Two words described them all for me.

Fucked up!

In the south of Ethiopia, it's better. The roads are terrible again, but the people are softer and not so paranoid. Will it always be like that, better away from the highways?

The last stretch to the border of Kenya is partly a river bed, and I have seen some spectacular termite mounds, in red and white. The white ones, dotted all about the landscape, are like an outdoor exhibition of Henry Moore statues. Inevitably I think of Lot's wife and the pillars of salt.

The Ethiopian mood may be mean, but the high landscape has been magnificent. Now I am coming down again, into the African rift valley, and the desert provinces of Kenya and Somalia. Moyale is the border town. It's New Year's Day, and I am on the Ethiopian side, but a road engineer is in with the Kenya government brass and we get across for a celebration on the other side. Different world. An almost English pub, drinking Tusker ale and stout, struggling to catch the barman's eye while chatting with the district commissioner. The DC– as they call him – is a tall, stylish Kikuyu African called William. He tells me two things of great interest. One, that tourism is the only thing that will save African wildlife, since Africans themselves can see no advantage in keeping endangered species alive, unless it's to make money out of sentimental foreigners. Two, that Africans can't put up with "hippies." When an African sees five ragged Americans sharing the same bottle of Coke, he knows they all have millionaire fathers in Milwaukee, and he considers he is being conned.

Next day I cross the border officially. Two bus loads of Jehovah's

This sculptural form rising from chalky soil in southern Ethiopia was made by termites. There were many of them, in all manner of shapes, suggesting figures frozen in the landscape. Naturally, they took on the color of the soil - sometimes white, sometimes red. An engineer building the new road to Nairobi told me they were so strong that he had used them to winch trucks out of mud.

Witnesses are coming back to Addis Ababa from a congress in Nairobi. It surprises me to see how prosperous they look, but their circumstances are pathetic. All their belongings are strewn over the ground, and customs officials are going through everything mercilessly. Their literature is all being confiscated. Huge heaps of tracts, books, and "newsletters" are ready for burning.

From Moyale begins the last long run to Nairobi, three hundred miles of scorching semi-desert, and then the Equator. I'm very excited. There is a real road this time, part of a big new highway, but unsurfaced. It is heavily corrugated most of the way, but somehow that doesn't bother me so much anymore. Until, halfway along, the luggage rack on the back of the Triumph fractures, whipped to pieces by the vibration.

I'm standing there wondering how to get my stuff to the next stage to repair it when a Peace Corps man comes along in a pickup and carries my luggage on to Marsabit for me. There a gnarled Danish woodwork instructor with a workshop helps me to weld the rack together again. I begin to understand that in Africa, somehow or other, there is always a way.

This country is not properly desert, but savannah. There are bushes and low trees, and there is game. Already I have seen ostrich with glorious pink plumes, and then, just before Marsabit, I come across a herd of giraffe. When I stop, they observe me quizzically for a while over the tops of the trees, and then gallop away. I am absolutely spellbound. The only other kind of movement with which I can compare this incomparable sight is that moment when a big airliner, having just taken off, seems to hang over the end of the runway in complete defiance of nature. The giraffe glides through the air as though in free fall.

A hundred miles from the Equator, the ground begins to rise out of the desert. On January the fifth, and only thirty miles from the Equator, I find it hard to believe my eyes. I seem to be traveling through the south of England, Sussex maybe. The air is cool and fresh. There are flowers in the hedgerows. On either side, well-kept farms, with gates, cows on green pasture and country cottages with lawns, and on the gates, painted wooden signs announcing Smith, and Clark, and Thompson. At Thompson I cannot bear to go any farther and on impulse I turn into the driveway. It ends in front of a cottage built partly of stone, partly of wood. There is a dovecote on a post, a lawn with rose beds, a stream running past. Beyond the lawn, like a picture postcard in the sky, is Mount Kenya under snow. An African servant receives me. The master and mistress are not home yet. Please to wait, and have some tea. In a chintz armchair, among English country furniture, like a very self-conscious bull in a china shop, I wait and marvel.

Arthur Thompson and his wife, Ruth, seem not at all surprised to find me sitting there. They talk to me for a while, and invite me for the night. He was a soldier, from Northumberland, older, gray haired, with ulcers. There's a trace of a Geordie accent, mixed with colonial, and he puts much emphasis on the "classlessness" of the white community here. She is younger, plump, pretty, strong-natured. They grow maize, wheat, barley, pyrethrum, have eighty Jersey cows, a thousand or so sheep. All on three thousand acres.

"Had a good life for thirty years," he says, "but it's nearly over now. The Kenya Government is bound to buy us out soon. They're settling Africans out here now."

Where to go then?

"South Africa looks good. I can't see Europe letting that go. If they do there'll be no way round for shipping. Too important strategically. I think Rhodesia's bound to stay white for the same reason."

Wishful thinking, but it is January 1974. Even the Portuguese are still in Africa.

Thompson is direct, but not bitter. He does not strike me as a bigoted man. He feels for his land, like a good farmer.

"It's not suitable for settlement, for Kikuyu farming," he says. "There's not enough rain. The Kikuyu needs rain. His method is to exhaust a patch, then move on and let it go back to bush. He goes around in circles. He has a round hut. Then the woman grows yams around that. Outside, in a bigger circle, the man grows maize, and around that he hunts.

"But without irrigation he'll get nothing up here, and the land will be ruined."

True or false? I cannot possibly know, but I do feel his concern, and that, I know, is genuine. He is still reclaiming land washed out before he arrived, even though he is certain never to profit from it. I feel his identification with these acres, and wonder how he could ever tear himself away. All over Africa the white man is being pulled up by the roots. Weeded out. There will be much pain.

Falling and Rising ——————➤ *115*

Next day I'm in Nairobi. Halfway through Africa. Another magic milestone. Like all milestones, something to look forward to, something to look back on, but at the time, nothing more than a pretext for indulgence. Hotels, Restaurants, Drinks, Showers, Banks, Clubs, Publicity.

London to Nairobi. Seven thousand miles. Something to shout about. None of this means anything to me. Nothing of my journey means anything to anyone here. We are engaged in a conspiracy, pretending to understand each other. Isn't that what makes the world go round? I meet a man I once knew in London. He is pickled and preserved in the same urbanity, and rubbing his hands together over the same deals. Nairobi and London are joined by a silver tube that swoops through the pasteurized ether, and the same stuff pours out at each end.

I dress for the Muthaiga Country Club, a functioning relic from the days before the tables were turned. Anyone can join now, but in practice it's much the same blue-eyed crowd, still enjoying the privileges, without the power.

"Whatever they say, life's still pretty colonial here. The Africans pretend to object, but . . ." Dark polished wood, spacious rooms, parquet floors and pillars, and a wine cellar still intact.

Game fishermen, New Zealanders, talking about the marlin off Kilifi:

"Well, old chap, they say your boat's in absolute shite order..."

Smoked sailfish and lamb's kidneys *turbigo* for lunch, with a good claret.

At my hotel in the afternoon there are three people sitting near me, an African, an Indian in a turban and an Asian woman. I can't believe the conversation they're having, and scribble it down.

She: Look, you can see, one eye is higher than the other.
Indian: Well, your nose is crooked.
She: Yes I know, it was a bad accident I had. Very bad. Now
         I have the feeling when I look that one side is higher
         than the other.
African: You should take a hammer and straighten it.
She: You shouldn't think it's so funny.
African: It's better to see something than nothing. But if you lie
         on the ground I'll give it a good kick.

Later I'm on the terrace, at sundown. Two Africans in gray flannels and short-sleeved shirts have been sitting at the same small table since lunch time, with beer coming at the rate of three or four pints an hour. They are speaking Swahili larded with English phrases and words. "Anyway, let us compare this thing," or "We must analyze that thing." Rather the way we used to think it smart to use French.

"Is it better," one of them bursts out in English, "to make the wrong decision at the right time, or the right decision at the wrong time?"

I feel sympathy and kinship. I too am playing this white man's game, pretending it is important.

My host, Mike Pearson, the Lucas agent in Nairobi, rises above pretense. He is the real thing, a huge florid man with a big appetite who loves the life, the business, the whole ridiculous mixture.

"We've just bought a plane," he tells me. "Brand-new. Arrived yesterday. Thirty-four thousand pounds. Where do you want to go?"

"Well, there's this Irish doctor who invited me to Lodwar?"

"Fine. No problem. We'll take you there on Tuesday, fetch you back on Thursday. Suit you?"

Lodwar, in the northwest corner of Kenya, hundreds of miles from Nairobi, at the edge of nowhere. Desert to the north, desert to the west, desert to the south. To the east, Lake Rudolph, and beyond that, desert. The Turkana tribe lives here, alongside a river bed, now dry; long thin black bodies swaying indolently against a backdrop of hot sand and bleached grass. They have goats, grow some millet, live off the desert, help to make the desert. At night they dance, in a big circle, men and women, stamping feet, chanting a descending fifth – "Homm Hommmmm" The man in the middle jumps and sings – look I'm a giraffe, I'm a lion, I'm an antelope. And so he is, they all recognize him, see how he sets his shoulders, cocks his head. Higher and higher he jumps, our brother, our prey.

The Turkana were hunters, but hunting is illegal and there is almost nothing left to hunt. At night they dance, and wear ostrich feathers and ostrich eggshell ornaments, and ankle bells, and brightly colored tablecloths made in India, and the girls wear long goatskins painstakingly sewn all over with beads, and collars like bridles, and red mud in their hair. And sometimes, secretly, the men take their spears over the edge into nowhere, and raid somebody else's livestock.

During the day a blacksmith in a grass hut makes spears out of car springs for sale to tourists in Nairobi. I am the only white visitor here but I am made to feel like a tourist. The girls come, arms outstretched, begging and selling. For a few shillings I could strip any one of them bare of the little she wears.

Who are the Turkana?

"The Turkana are very treacherous . . . conceited and idle."

H. Johnston, 1902

"The Turkana is a careless and cruel herdsman and a most efficient liar."

E. D. Emley, 1927

"A feature of social life . . . is the continual begging . . . the only limits I am aware of are that a man may not beg another man's wife. Savage and wild as the country he lives in, so he will remain, in my opinion, to the end of time."

P. H. Gulliver, 1963

Time came to an end abruptly a few years after those last words were written, with the bad drought and cholera of the sixties. Until then the Turkana had been free of aid or interference. There had been no schools, no clinics, no administration. Only an occasional punitive expedition to control tribal warfare. But famine and disease persuaded the government to open up the Northern Frontier Province to the missionaries and aid societies.

Today there are flying doctors from Nairobi, mission clinics, schools. There are tin roofs, and souvenirs and the self-conscious assumption of haughty pride in front of the camera, followed by the outstretched hand for a posing fee. Life seems to go along much the same as before, the dancing and laughing and begging and lying, except that now there is more to beg for, you don't die so easily and there are white people fussing around in pants and dresses. Not like the old days under District Commissioner Whitehouse, who made native dress *de rigueur* for everyone, yes everyone.

And the Turkana still think nothing has changed. They actually believe they are the center of the universe. Listen to the old head man, the M'zee, talking:

"With one spear we can kill a lion or an elephant or a giraffe. Accurate at twenty feet. The Turkana will never change their customs. If any other tribe tries to overcome us we will beat them."

Savage and wild until the end of time? But the M'zee is wearing corduroy trousers, for heaven's sake, and a striped shirt. Old man, can't you see, you were bought and sold for a handful of white medicine and some ruled exercise paper. Your children will not kill a lion, not with twenty spears, not at twenty inches. Why did you want schools?

"So that children can get good jobs in the city and send money back to their parents. But they will never forget their tribe – only the bad ones."

Oh, there will be many bad ones in the shanties of Nairobi, where other tribes won the war long ago, and most of the good jobs.

In the District Hospital, Dr. Gerry Byrne from Dublin looks up from a patient's bedside and I diagnose astonishment all over his cherubic countenance. Six months earlier he had written to the *Sunday Times*: "Dear Mr. Simon, If on your journey round the world you happen to be passing near Lodwar . . ." but he never for a moment believed.

He is really chuffed, his big spectacles gleam with pleasure. Black bodies lie all about with modest green cotton wraps around their middles. It's the women's ward; wrinkled paps flapping, dust on the soles of their feet. There are lots of bright new bandages where they've been cut open, a batch of post-ops left to heal by the monthly flying doctors from Nairobi. Mostly they have had hydatid cysts removed, the local menace; they grow to enormous size, often in the liver or spleen, like clusters of grapes in syrup, and when they burst you die. It's thought the dogs carry it.

There's a pretty girl with spindly legs dying of a malignant tumor, but no one can be told, certainly not the family, because their rage, says Gerry, would be uncontrollable. Also, he says, when the grief is all burned out, there is nothing left. When Turkana parents know their child is dying, they leave it to starve. There never was too much food around. They don't bury the corpses. They put them out for the hyenas, to keep the meat in circulation, as it were.

It is hot in Lodwar, excessively hot. At times you can see the heat waving in the air.

Outside the hospital are many more patients lying on the ground with their families, not through shortage of beds so much as because they like it there and their families come and cook for them. Hygiene? So what? The rate of recovery is high. The pain threshold is high too.

"The men like having their feet cut off," says Gerry.

"What?" I almost shout.

"There's a thing they get that swells their feet up. We can stop it, but the foot stays big. But they prefer to have it cut off."

White Medicine Is Amazing, says Gerry, full of wonder and misgivings. It was never like this back in Dublin. Out here a miracle drug still does miracles. Penicillin is like it was in the days of Fleming: a shot cures just about anybody instantly, specially children. Trouble is, you ask yourself sometimes, what am I saving them for? Almost everybody in Kenya is under sixteen already. There's nothing for them to do, not much for them to eat, even in the prosperous parts of the country. To multiply the population out here, in the desert, seems crazy. Oh, my Hippocratic oath, says Dr. Gerry, I don't know. Why don't you ask the bishop?

The doctor's expenses and modest wage are paid for by the Medical Missionaries of St. Mary, and there really is a bishop in Lodwar, Bishop Mahon. Does he have the answers? Not on your life.

"I've given up thinking," he says. "I never did very much of it and now I don't bother at all. Just get on with it. Let the future take care of itself."

Spoken with humor, vigorous humility. He's got my number all right. If he did have the answers I wouldn't believe them.

He is quite ready to accept that he might be creating more problems than he solves.

"What can you do? You can't let people die. Can you?"

I'm not brave enough to say, Yes, it's being done all the time.

We are sitting in a house the bishop built. He knows exactly where to sit, with his back to an open-lattice cement wall that he designed himself from easily molded units. The breeze comes through to him, but fails to reach me, and I am abuzz with thirsty flies swarming fanatically into my lips and my eyes. I am uncomfortably aware that there are no flies on the bishop.

He's a strong, lean tough man with tobacco-colored teeth and straight silver hair, in shorts and a tea-stained shirt. Nine years in

Nigeria, six in Turkana and an occasional whirl around the States raising money. He has small hospitals in various outlying villages, staffed by Danish volunteers as well as his own home-grown Irish pastors and sisters.

He can't explain what motivates the Danes (it is certainly not religion) but says they are much better suited to the work, and less demanding than his own church folk. His nuns, he fears, are too often doctrinaire and officious, and their inflexibility makes it hard for them to withstand the pressures. All these naked breasts, for example – although they don't, anymore, go around persuading natives to cover up. The bishop smiles faintly at remembered scenes of outrage at the Norwegian-donated swimming pool where inflexible nuns in uptight swimsuits are exposed to the unself-conscious naturalism of supple Danes.

The bishop's "action man" stance has not blinded him to his responsibilities. Having wrought the miracles of modern medicine, he felt obliged to try for the fishes and the loaves as well. An FAO man reported that Lake Rudolph was capable of breeding and delivering between 50,000 and 150,000 tons of Nile perch a year, so the bishop got that one going. Ambitious Asian businessmen smashed an airplane and a truck bringing in the refrigeration. There was already an iron trawler in the lake, brought and assembled there by the British in more expansive times. They had good early catches, but then yields dropped and the scheme failed to fulfill itself. So he turned to loaves, with an irrigation scheme upriver.

"At next rains, in April, we should get about fifty acres under cultivation. We're aiming for several hundred, but it's hard going. They aren't all industrious.

"Without us there to direct them I don't think they could manage it on their own. I'm afraid the channels would soon choke up."

But that's worrying about the future, and we don't do that, do we.

Mahon relates the ups and downs of his missionary life in the way older men describe the hopes and disappointments of their sons, with a wistful fondness and faith in the essential goodness of the life and its intentions, whatever the outcome. He would not willingly return to Western life (nor would any of the volunteers – its selfish, indulgent nature is too blatant viewed from here) but he has few expectations. He is resigned to criticism of his "meddling" in nonmedical matters. One feels that the technocrats of Oxfam and the specialist relief agencies have often snubbed his people, and he feels they are all vulnerable.

"We project a terrible image on these people, going round in Land-Rovers, living in concrete buildings, but if we build in mud the termites work their way up the walls and eat the doorjambs and attack the roof. We've tried most things. There's a chap out there now living in a tent. He's happy enough, but I think he's doing harm because when he goes I can find nobody to replace him who would put up with those conditions."

He warns his people always about imposing their standards on the Turkana. "My only hope is that after a few years we can overcome the bad effects by showing them that we care as people."

Truly a pious hope.

My people are a treacherous, conceited, idle, careless, cruel, lying and begging people. Have you come to preserve us or to change us? Ha! My people are a tall, beautiful, vigorous, savage and wild people; our men can move like the lion, the antelope and the giraffe, and our women can move as your women have forgotten to move. Do you want us to care, as well?

Still, I like the bishop a lot, and I even prefer his nuns to the popeyed UN girls I saw Rovering around in Ethiopia in their solar topees and pretty safari suits.

And I really like the horrible Turkana. As well as all the other things they are, I find them very sexy. I should know, we danced together. Homm-Hommmmm I went, and stamped my feet.

They were determined to make a tourist out of me. All right, I said, I'll BE a damn tourist, and I bargained for everything in sight. At night I went to the stamping ground down beyond the grass huts, where the fire was lit, and watched them doing their magical leaping zoo numbers. Oh boy, I said. Pictures, I gotta have pictures.

The chief's son and heir-apparent and prospective Member of Parliament for Lodwar whispers gently to me through the hole they all have knocked in their front teeth in case of lockjaw.

"Two goats and some corn beer, and I think we could fix something," he says.

"O.K.," I say. "Get the goats."

Two sleek little black goats and enough corn for eight gallons of overnight beer cost ninety shillings, deductible on expenses. Emmanuel, the chief's son, is being nice to me. It's a knock-down price for a rave-up. His adjutant, the Minderbender of Lodwar, in khaki shorts and sandals, has a whole intrigue going already. Two goats, he says, will not feed a tribe, so we will choose only the best and bravest dancers, and the choicest and most nubile maidens, and we will make a secret rendezvous away over there.

Even I know there's not a chance of keeping it quiet. This fellow just loves to plot, and everybody's very happy to join in the mischief. Next afternoon the chosen few assemble. The men gather inside one of the compounds, where they pretend to be unobserved as they bring out their best warrior headgear and their finest table linen to wrap around their waists. The girls are already on their way, twittering excitedly like all girls everywhere going to a ball, the long goatskins, polished and weighted with red, white and blue beads, swinging dramatically from side to side, stretched and molded over each tourist-tantalizing buttock, so girlish and prominent that I can't help making the incongruous comparison with bustles in a Regency ballroom. As well as their finest beads, they are slung with necklaces and bracelets and ornamental aprons to indicate their wealth and marriageability, and they have fresh, glistening red mud on their partly shaven heads.

The newly fermented corn beer is in two square and shiny four-gallon cans called *debbies,* and two girls carry them on their heads with breathtaking ease and grace, making the cans dance with their bodies, investing those blunt tin cans with the elegance of the richest amphorae, leaving their arms free to trail enticingly through the air as they plunge forward, almost rushing, but beautifully controlled, to the dance. While the men stalk along, in a separate group, wearing their ostrich-feather crowns and brilliant cloaks like lords, and at this stage I don't care whether the tablecloths were made in Birmingham?

Of course the whole village knows there's something up. Little naked black spies have been buzzing around the compounds for hours. As we proceed across the dunes, a mob of the curious follow at a respectful distance. What puzzles them is the time of day. It's much too early for dancing, but I insisted on pictures by daylight. On the chosen site a big fire is started immediately, and the two innocent black beasts are ceremonially speared, gutted and tossed into the flames in one piece, hide and all.

The girls are rehearsing, hands linked in a line, singing a chant and making little runs across the sand. The men insist on posing for endless group shots, faces set in the sternest expressions, except for Minderbender, who fools about constantly in his khaki shorts, ruining the fake authenticity and making it real. Then they dance and I have to go leaping and squatting and rolling about on the ground with my 28-mm lens trying to remember how David Hemmings did it in *Blow Up*, until the light dies and it's time to carve the goats.

By now the camp followers have caught the scent of sizzling hide and are assembled on the rising ground watching enviously, and in their front rank are several ancient geezers with expectant expressions. The tribal butchers begin cutting the animals into lumps and laying them out on a table of branches and green leaves, but there's trouble in the air, and I hear voices raised among the warriors. Not too loud, as yet, because their mouths are full of meat and gristle, but as the meat dwindles away, the altercation becomes more heated and to my surprise half the first team gets up and stalks off, looking very fierce.

"Ah," says Emmanuel, "I am sorry but we must finish now."

There has been a schism in the tribe. A heresy has been exposed. According to tribal tradition, the goats should be sliced up in a certain way, and the choice cuts offered to the tribal elders first (who would undoubtedly accept). Fuck that, said Minderbender and his Revolutionary Council, why should the old geezers have the best bits. They weren't even invited. But some of his followers are not so staunchly progressive. Having licked their chops, they decide it's time to suck up to the elders, and they stage a Royalist Demo and Walkout. Under their tablecloths, it is whispered, they carry extra pieces of goat for later.

A good afternoon's work. I got my pictures; I have shown that the Turkana are indeed conceited, treacherous and all the rest. And I have demonstrated what one tourist and a couple of goats can do to rip apart the structure of a tribal society. Tomorrow the sightseers can come on their 747s from Frankfurt and Chicago and clean up the remains.

There is nothing left for me to do but to gather up my souvenirs and fly back to Nairobi. I wonder, would it have been like that if I had arrived on my motorcycle? No. I'm sure it wouldn't. Flying, I realize, can be very, very dangerous. I hear the purists mocking me. Motorcycles, they say, are just as alienating as aircraft, same technology sliced a different way. They don't understand. It's the effect

The Turkana bragged about their dancing. "All right," I said. "Show me". And for two goats and eight gallons of overnight beer, they did. The girls carried the beer cans on their heads – four gallons each – with such ease you might have thought the cans were empty.

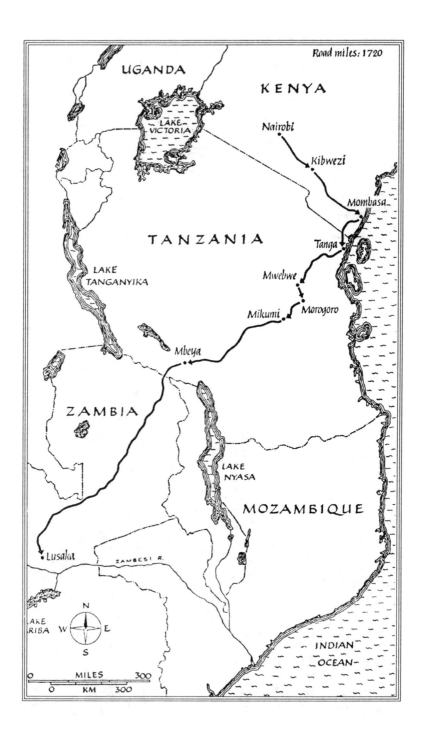

Road miles: 1720

on me I'm talking about. The long, hard solitary journey induces a different kind of respect. I mean to keep it that way from now on.

But then, I would never have got the pictures. Oh God, I don't know, and it's no use asking the bishop....

I wanted to get to Mombasa and drink a beer. I not only wanted it, I expected it. Life in Nairobi had softened me. Instead of a beer I had a flat tire.

"Bloody hell," I said bitterly. "Just the sort of thing you'd expect."

Petulant. Frustrated. I raised my voice. Why not? Empty highway. No one around.

"Isn't that just bloody perfect?" I shouted.

"Yes," said God, but I didn't hear him.

I swore at the top of my voice and the word lost itself in the tangle of weeds at the roadside. It became time to do something useful.

I was annoyed because I had just had two weeks in Nairobi to overhaul and repair the Triumph, to wash it and grease it and fit fine new leather bags on the tank, and new tires and tubes on the wheels, and here I was 150 miles down the road to Mombasa with a puncture, and a lot of dirty, uninteresting work in front of me. Furthermore it was mid-day and I was two degrees south of the equator and almost down to sea level at the hottest time of the year and wearing a flying jacket.

Hot as it was, I found the flying jacket comfortable to wear as long as the bike was moving. Its stiffness saved me from a lot of the fatigue that comes from being continually buffeted by the air, and I was spared the problem of finding somewhere to pack it. I knew it looked odd to be wearing sheepskin in the tropics and I enjoyed the effect, but when the airflow stopped, I had about thirty seconds before I reached boiling point, and my thirty seconds were up.

I trundled the bike carefully on the wheel rim off the edge of the road, kicked out the swing stand, dismounted and threw the jacket to the ground. Then the gloves. Then the helmet. Then I started on the baggage.

"Not even a mad dog would do this in the mid-day sun," I thought.

In Nairobi they had warned me. It's a good tar road to Mombasa, they said, four or five hours in a car, but the road surface gets so hot that it causes punctures. In Nairobi I had let someone else fit the new tubes and he had pinched the rear one with the tire levers, making so many holes that I put the older patched one back instead. Now the heat had melted off the patches. That is what I thought had happened, and it gave me a good chance to put the blame on someone else.

"Bloody fool," I said. But the bloody fool was me, for being too lazy to do it myself, and for not starting earlier in the morning when the road was cooler.

Normally a puncture was not a disaster. With practice and an hour's energetic work it would be done. First I had to take all the heavy stuff off the bike, because with the rear tire flat it was impossible for me to lift it on to the center stand. And on a soft surface I had to find something firm to lay under the center stand as well. I got out the tools, and soap and water and a cup and a rag. Then the right exhaust muffler had to be dropped, which meant unscrewing a couple of small nuts with their washers and laying them carefully on the outspread rag. With this done the spindle could be unscrewed and withdrawn from the axle, and the spacer and wheel adjuster with it, and all put on the rag away from grit and concealing clumps of grass. I tried to think like a manual.

Then I had a good trick I had discovered. With the swing stand out as well, the bike would lean over to the left at a crazy angle and there was room to take the wheel off the splines and slip it out from under the mudguard. Without this trick, or something similar, it was impossible for one man to remove the rear wheel. It was called a quickly detachable wheel and it was certainly easier than taking off the sprocket and chain also, but it had not, I thought, been brought to a pitch of great refinement.

With the wheel off, having remembered at the last minute to detach the speedometer cable, there were the security bolts to loosen. These were two bolts that clamped the tire to the rim and caused many spectators to wonder why I had three air valves on my wheel instead of the usual one. The nuts could be hard to undo because of the filth that gathered on them, but I had two pieces of plastic tube over the bolts packed with grease so that, once loosened, the nuts could be quickly spun off with the finger. That saved about ten minutes each way.

New tires were harder to get off, especially with the rather small levers I was obliged to carry, but the soapy water helped a lot. Unfortunately when I pulled out the tube, the rim belt came with it, snapped. The rim belt protects the tube from the inside of the rim where all the spokes come through, and it is obviously safer to have one. I had no spare, another reason for cursing.

There was nothing wrong with the old patches after all. There were two new punctures on the inside of the tube, tiny slits, and near them I noticed score lines and places where the rubber had blistered.

"Shit and damnation," I said, and, *"Merde puissance treize."* I swore a lot in those days, in a rather dull way but with feeling.

Clearly the old tube was no good anymore, and I would have to repair the punctured new one. It was difficult in that heat, with the flies refreshing themselves on my sweat, to be thorough, particularly with the clumsy patches I was carrying at the time.

The best trick in my repertoire was provided by a company called Schrader in Birmingham. They made a valve with a long tube which I could screw into the engine instead of a spark plug. As long as you had at least two cylinders, you could run the engine on one and the other piston would pump up your tire. So I was able to pump up the tube, and it seemed all right.

I put the puncture routine into reverse. The tire rims slid snugly into place on the soap, and the wheel pumped up hard. Twenty minutes later I had everything back on the bike and was washing my hands in the last of the soapy water when I saw the tire was half flat.

The life drained out of me then. I could not even find the energy to swear. I dropped down on the jacket and pulled out my cigarettes, and tried to think about other things. It was very pleasant here, I thought, if you had nothing to do. Hotter than Nairobi, certainly. But not too hot. Not at all. And pleasantly dry.

I looked at the vegetation alongside the road, trying to recognize it or fix it in my memory, but I could not make out anything characteristic enough to attract my attention. There were various wild flowers that looked to me like wild flowers everywhere, and low shrubs and bushes that looked the same as any others. I was annoyed by my inability to see plants clearly and remember them. It was a great drawback. Above all things, a traveler should have an eye for natural detail, I thought, since that is what he sees most of the time. There was some bamboo and I was glad to find at least one thing I recognized, not knowing that there were over two hundred different species.

Beyond the low vegetation, where the land had once been cleared for road-making, were trees, equally unknown to me, leafy and of medium height. I walked to the edge of the wood to relieve myself and wondered whether some enormous beast was at all likely to come crashing towards me through the undergrowth. Probably not, I thought, since I had seen small farms through the trees as I rode along. In fact, just a mile or so back I had passed a gas station at a crossroads, with a sign. What had it said? I looked at the map. This must be it. Kibwezi Junction.

I was wondering what to do next when I saw Pius coming towards me, although of course I did not yet know his name. He was a fat man in the best sense of the word, not gross or obese or flabby or bloated, but of a prime meaty plumpness to make a cannibal's mouth water. His black body was enticingly wrapped in a gaily flowered shirt, and he sat astride his little Yamaha motorcycle on jovial terms with the world and with a measured sense of his own importance in it. I waved to him and he stopped beside me.

"Can you help me, I wonder . . ." I said.

"Absolutely," he said. "Most definitely. I see you are having trouble, isn't it. A spot of bother."

"Well, my tire's flat . . ." and I went on to explain.

"I will introduce you to Mr. Paul Kiviu," he burst out enthusiastically. "Definitely he is the very man of the moment. He is manager BP station Kibwezi Junction and he is my friend."

Mercifully the road was level at that point. As I pushed the loaded bike along on its flat tire, Pius bobbed around me like a butterfly, calling encouragement, imploring me to believe that my troubles would soon be over. His good nature was irresistible and I began to believe him.

In any case I was happy that something was happening and I was in touch with people. At the time it seemed to me that what I wanted was to have my problem solved quickly and to get on my way. I had a boat to catch in Cape Town and the journey was still the main thing. What happened on the way, who I met, all that was incidental. I had not quite realized that the interruptions were the journey.

Paul Kiviu understood my problem. There was nothing he could do about it, but he understood it, and, as they say, a problem shared is a problem halved. Pius did not so much understand my problem as appreciate it. He reveled in it, celebrated it, but Paul understood it because he had problems of his own. He was accustomed to them, and he was the first African I had met who was marked by them. He was small, thin and intense, and showed signs of worrying.

His BP station had a servicing bay and pumps. The main building was a sheltered area with colored metal chairs and tables, served by a small lockup kitchen where a girl in a head scarf pushed sweets and drinks and snacks across the counter. It was clean and polished and quite the most modern thing for miles around. We had some fizzy drinks and potato chips and thought about what to do.

It was simple really. I needed a new tube and it would have to come from Nairobi. The punctured tube could be repaired, of course, but there was a very long way to go before I could expect to get a new tube. There would be nothing in Tanzania, I guessed, or Zambia, and in Rhodesia, with the economic blockade, it might be difficult. When I saw how the old tube had perished it made me unhappy to be without a new one as well as an acceptable spare. So I would call Mike Pearson in Nairobi, and ask him if he could get an inner tube to me somehow. And a rim belt too.

Meanwhile the bike could be safely locked up at the BP station, and I would wait in Kibwezi.

"Definitely. This is the solution," exclaimed Pius, and we had another fizzy drink and some cigarettes. A little later, when a person could see his own shadow again, I sat on the back of Pius' Yamaha and we went into town.

Kibwezi was a jumble of painted wood-frame buildings with tin roofs, mostly single-storey, on a crossroads of baked earth. It was well away from the Mombasa road and could not be seen from there, but buses came in and turned around, throwing up a fine dust. Kenya was very dry and crying for rain. Many animals in the reserves had already died of thirst.

Prominent on the corner was "The Curry Pot Hotel." On the other corner was the main store, run as usual by Asian traders. There were other small shops and bars, and in the road were fruit and vegetable stalls.

Jammed between the store and the next shop, in a space no bigger than a large changing cubicle, was Kibwezi Post Office. Much of the space was occupied by a fine old wooden switchboard, and in front of it, earphones clamped over his head, sat Kibwezi's determined postmaster. He was scolding one of his customers on the telephone. For years he had labored to drag the people of Kibwezi into the twentieth century. He had lectured and cajoled them on the proper way to address an envelope, on the disrespect implied by sticking first the Queen's head and then Kenyatta's head on up side down, on the need, when sending a telegram, to have some idea of where it was intended to go.

"Who is this Thomas N'Kumu? I have no knowledge of this man. He is not the Prime Minister, is it? Prior importance must go to his place of residence. First we must know where is this N'Kumu, and then we can look about messages."

His patience was exhausted.

"That is the correct method for dealing with this matter," he shouted scornfully into the little black tube, and with the wrath of a god at judgment day he pulled out the plug.

I faced the tyrant with my number, exchange and name of party in faultless order and he had no choice but to proceed. He manipulated the controls of the machine through which he ruled the world and, with surprising efficiency, I was connected to Nairobi and my business was concluded. They would do their best to find the tubes and deliver them. A telegram would be sent me the following day. I took up temporary residence at The Curry Pot Hotel.

Pius took me back to the BP station to fetch my red bag with my toilet and shaving kit and clean socks. Most people in Kibwezi walked barefoot or in sandals, but I had not got any sandals yet and had read somewhere about parasites that burrowed into your feet, so I wore shoes and socks. Sandals would have been kinder to my sweltering feet and to everyone else around, as well as saving socks, but they were too far down on my list. I had a long list of duties that I meant to perform when I had time. They included notes, letters and articles to write, jobs to do on the bike, and modifications of my various "systems," and they took priority over sandals. Once I had had a pair of sandals but could not wear them because they took the skin off my toes, so they went right down the list again. I allowed only a proportion of my time to things I did not feel like doing, since I found that the list of things I ought to do was endless and would otherwise take all the joy out of life. If at any time I really wanted to do anything on the list, of course I did it regardless of priority, but sandals never came into this category because of the painful recollection of skinned toes. That by and large was how I arranged my life. The list was not written down, but in my head, and it tailed off down my spinal column where it sometimes gave me a backache.

Paul had another friend visiting at the BP station, a big well muscled man with a placid face called Samson. He was a policeman but off duty, so we whiled away the time until Paul felt he had worried enough for the day, and we set off for town together.

We went to the bar that was a few doors down from the post office. It was after dark and the room was lit by softly hissing paraffin lamps. I liked this light very much, preferring it to light bulbs and the horrific fluorescent tubes which have probably been installed by now.

The room was square, with a counter down one side and half a dozen tables on a plain wooden floor. The doors and windows stayed open, as they did everywhere else. There were already several groups of men there, and we took an empty table and ordered. The beer was served by bar girls, and there were three of them, so they were not very busy. They liked being there because they could sometimes get off with a man they liked the look of and enjoy them selves, and if the man was feeling generous they could get some shillings as well.

I did not know about the bar girls when we sat down, but found out about it as the evening advanced. The conversation was very animated, full of fun and laughter as they answered my questions and I tried to answer theirs.

The girls all wore the same loose pink overalls, buttoned down the front, and head scarves. Under the overalls they wore only a nylon half-slip. Of course I was completely used to nakedness by then, not just in the European way of feeling free of embarrassment and not going goggle-eyed at the sight of a thigh, but in the African way of not even discriminating between different parts of the anatomy because when they are all on display together a finely arched back or a beautifully poised head can be just as exciting as a breast or a buttock. Only the sexual organs were kept hidden.

The pint bottles of Tusker kept coming from the ice chest, and Paul was getting anxious to fix me up with a bar girl. At first I was only amused by his efforts. It had been several months since I had been with a woman, but I did not consider that a long time and, in another way, I had got used to celibacy. The traveling was so intense, I was receiving so much stimulation, that it was completely satisfying in itself. Once out of Europe there was little artificial erotic stimulation, particularly not in the Muslim countries, and I had begun to think that we made too much of it in the West. In any case, prostitutes would have been my only recourse, and not feeling the need and considering the risk too great, I let the whores go by.

But I liked these bar girls. I liked the lazy way they swung their legs around, the loose-jointed walk. And it was clear that they were choosy. There was a freedom of expression and movement that liberated me too, and one of them in particular appealed to me, so I told Paul and he redoubled his efforts.

"The problem is this," said Paul – itching for a problem – "these girls have not slept with a M'zungo before. They are afraid. They are thinking that a M'zungo will be different. But I will persuade them."

We laughed loudly at such preposterous ignorance, and eventually one of the girls promised to Paul that she would come back later, but she did not and I was a little sad.

In the morning there was a telegram to say that the inner tube would be delivered during the day to the BP station, so I walked down to the junction and got to work again on the wheel. The day moved by slowly and I let it, working a bit, and talking and watching people come and go at the pump. A van arrived in the early afternoon, shiny and brisk from the city, with two tubes and two rim belts, and I viewed Nairobi through Kibwezi eyes as awesomely efficient and remote.

So the hot hours drifted by in work and idleness, until it was dark, and drinking time again. The Curry Pot Hotel had several features that distinguished it as one of Kibwezi's principal landmarks. The first was a most imposing wooden grill along the counter which faced the visitor as he entered. It was here that I was given my room at ten shillings a night, and a form on which I wrote 535439A 10 Sept. 73 10 Sept. 83 London Foreign Office British Hamburg Germany St. Privat France Builder Nairobi Mombasa 18 Jan. 74 Edward J Simon without even looking at my passport or lifting my ball pen from the paper.

From there one walked through an open door into the bar, and from the bar into an enclosed courtyard. The arrangements at the bar were rudimentary but satisfying. You could have beer or toddy.

I dare say there was whisky and gin for the better class of clientele, maybe much more.

At the far end of the courtyard was another feature that impressed me. It was the gents' piss house, under its own tin roof, a very neat affair of charcoal in a cement trough. The guests' rooms were ranged down the far side of the courtyard. They were a series of compartments made of corrugated iron nailed to a wooden frame with a hard earth floor. My room had a mat, a bed with a sheet, a mattress still in its protective plastic wrapping, a small table with a jug and basin, and I think there was even a mirror. It was entirely adequate and I considered it rather high-class. The metal walls were painted silver on the outside to adorn the courtyard and give pleasure to the drinkers.

The silver paint glimmered softly in the lamplight as we all gathered again on the second night, Paul and Pius and Samson and I. Paul was wearing a white shirt and a perky little felt hat with a curly brim. Samson was dressed in black trousers and a midnight blue shirt with cloth-covered buttons. He was the darkest of the three, and as the night deepened he dissolved, black on black, into the shadows. Pius was, as usual, garlanded in floral print, and his broad pumpkin face gleamed brightly.

Paul and Samson had both been on duty until sundown, and were oppressed by thoughts of human bondage.

"Employment is really a bother," said Samson. He rocked his chair and thrust his legs farther under the tin-topped table.

"Oh it is a bother indeed," said Paul. He nodded his jaunty hat, and turned to explain to me.

"You see, this fellow is not free. He is going round town even after his duties are finished and some person may come at any time saying his attendance is sorely needed in case of a sudden crime, or it may be a fatal accident and what and what."

Paul himself was expected to be at his post at Kibwezi Junction from seven in the morning until seven at night every day of the week including Sundays.

"You saw I had to leave this company for two hours yesterday evening. I was forced to go, isn't it. Some stores came for the canteen so I must go to search the stocks. This can happen at any time . . . and I do not know if I have a job tomorrow."

The voice was neither angry nor complaining. It described in sorrowful tones the loss of tranquillity. Responsibility and guilt were eating into their lives, and brought not security but increasing uncertainty.

Thirty miles up the road to Nairobi was Paul's shamba, a plot of land where his wife and children lived. Once a month, roughly, he managed to visit there.

"What is needed here," he went on, "is a thousand and five hundred shillings. Then I can build a tank for water on my farm and grow many things."

Two hundred dollars, I thought. I was carrying five times that amount on me at that moment. What difference would two hundred dollars make to my future? Tomorrow I might lose it all, and tonight it could transform a man's life. I felt the excitement grow in me, but could not bring it out. Then what will you do tomorrow, I asked myself, when you meet someone who needs it to save a life? Isn't that it? Either you keep it all or you give it all away. How can you hope to travel as a philanthropist? I decided to think about it more carefully, later. At the back of my mind was the doubt whether things were exactly as Paul said.

Pius was enlarging, meanwhile, on an insurance scheme that Paul could not afford. There was something both touching and symbolic I felt about this trio, the small African trying to turn an honest penny, with the muscular forces of law and order on one side, and the plump power of finance on the other. Who was Samson really protecting, and who was Pius trying to con?

"What is this insurance you are selling?" I asked Pius, lapsing involuntarily into the dialect.

"Persons are looking to me for protection of life and property," he replied proudly.

I wondered what kind of accident was most common.

"Snakebite is a common matter. My policies are not covering for snakebite," he added, as though this were a point in their favor.

I saw that Samson was moved by this information. He stirred and said in a surprised tone: "What is this? You are selling accident insurance and you are not covering for snakebite?"

I was astonished myself

"The snakebite is not an accident," said Pius. "How can you say it is? The snake is not biting by accident. It is wanting to bite," and to our gathering amazement he went on to state his triumphant conclusion.

"Where it is the agency of a living thing, this is not accident. That is the policy of my company."

We all thought this outrageous.

"What about the man who was killed by a pig falling?" I cried.

"The pig was kept on a balcony in Naples, and the balcony broke, and the pig fell on a pedestrian and killed him. That was an accident!"

"This was caused by persons putting pig on a balcony," he said smugly. "Definitely this was not an accidental happening. It is all the same whether it may be a pig or a lion or a snake or what and what."

"Well," said Paul, "when the pig was hitting the man it may be already dead from heart attack, isn't it. So to be killed by a dead pig is an accident."

"There will be an inquest on the pig also, and a certificate showing time of death," Samson contributed darkly from the shadow.

"I am not insuring for pig falls or snakebites in the Kibwezi region," Pius said wildly. "Definitely."

"I hope you explain all this to your clients," I said.

"Absolutely. They like it very much," he said.

The silliness stopped and we sank back into the peace of the Kenyan night. More Tuskers came. It seemed possible to drink any amount of beer without much effect. The table was almost invisible now under the empties, but I felt only a comfortable affection for the company and a frequent urge to visit the charcoal bed.

They were sad that I was leaving. We had come to like each other quickly because there was no obstacle to our friendship. All we wanted from each other was time and respect. Of course they were flattered by my attention, and it would bring out the best in them. I, who had come so far already on such an unimaginable journey, had stopped and given my undivided attention to three men whose entire lives were described within a one-hundred-mile radius of Kibwezi. This would be no time for mean or petty behavior.

The Spirit Incarnate of the Great World of Dreams meets with the Three Wise Men of Kibwezi, and for forty-eight hours all is light and truth. A man could live up to his ideals for that long. And they did have ideals, these three, so we were equals, and they showed me true courtesy and paid for their share of the beer. And they shed a tear for the moment when the great bird would fly on.

I was becoming a carrier of the dreams of men. I gathered them like pollen, fertilizing as I went. But I had not yet quite realized my power, nor its transforming effect on people, and I still thought they were as I saw them.

Paul had relapsed into mild mournfulness.

"Tomorrow you are leaving, isn't it," he said.

"Yes. I have to go on to Mombasa."

He came to a decision.

"Tonight you must have a girl," he said, and called to the nearest bar girl. He was talking rapidly in Swahili and she came towards us giggling a bit and protesting, but she took several good looks at my grinning face. There were further skirmishes over the next round of Tuskers, and then Paul said:

"The matter is settled. She will come."

It was too dark to see her face clearly. I saw only that she was small and seemed to be rather fat. I did not worry because I was sure that, like the night before, the fear of the dreaded M'zungo would frighten her away.

Soon after, there was no room left on the table for more bottles and it was time to stop. My friends wandered off and I went into my room and lit the hurricane lamp. It was very warm even at midnight and the air was still. Happily there seemed to be no mosquitoes. I took off all my clothes and lay down on the sheet, ready to sleep like that. I thought for a moment about the girl and, although I knew she would not come, the idea excited me. Then there was a tap on the door. Repeated. I stood up and looked for something to hide my erection. Then I thought "to hell with that" and walked over to the door as I was and opened it cautiously.

The girl stood there, and she came in and looked at me with an expression of slight wonder. Then she tapped my stiff prick approvingly a couple of times with the knuckle of her forefinger. It stood the test. I was utterly amazed at my own behavior, and enjoying it enormously.

She had a nice young face, although I could not tell how young. She put her finger to her lips, appearing to be listening for sounds outside.

"Mama," she whispered. "I am coming back soon" – and she disappeared into the night.

When she returned she walked straight into the room and took off her blue overall and sat on the edge of the bed looking a bit shy and uncertain. She was not at all fat. The arching of her back was so pronounced that her firm breasts thrust the big overall out in front, and her prominent behind pushed it out at the back and between the two it seemed to conceal a huge tummy. In fact her body was lithe and lovely. She still had the half-slip on, but soon that was off too and another bastion of racial prejudice collapsed, for we seemed to fit each other perfectly well and nothing I did seemed to surprise her terribly either.

My first concern was whether or not to kiss her, but she didn't seem to expect it, and I kissed her body instead because it felt like a nice thing to do.

The main obstacle was not between us but beneath us. The sheet slipped and slid on the plastic mattress cover, and we glided back and forth on the sheet in an ecstasy of unpredictable motion. Perhaps it was like making love on skis. One way or another it seemed that we were bound to wind up in a tangle of limbs on the ground. Several times I saved us from sailing over the edge to disaster, but the voyage was finally and successfully accomplished. After a while she got up, trailing her hand lightly on my face, and left the room without a sound.

I never saw her again. I meant to look for her next morning but I was in great confusion then and did not know what to do. I was very taken with her, but I knew I had to leave and it seemed foolishly sentimental to make a fuss. She had not asked me for anything, not even a hint of it. I wanted to give her something and had nothing to give but money. In the end I simply emptied my pockets and piled what was there on the table. It came to seven shillings and some pennies. I wanted the arbitrariness of it to seem less like a payment, but it never felt right, and I left the hotel unhappy with myself.

I felt a fool for being afraid to look like one, because I wanted to find her and hug her.

"How I do tie myself in knots," I reflected sadly.

Riding along on the road to Mombasa I came across my first wild elephants. There were ten of them, about three hundred yards away, gathered close together under a tree. They were quite still. The tree was a baobab, and its smooth fat trunk rose well above the animals before narrowing abruptly and sprouting a broad fan of branches. The baobab is also called the bottle tree; its young leaves are used for soup, and its fruit makes a drink.

I stopped the bike and watched the elephants in silence for a long time, my heart bursting with emotion, not quite knowing why I was so profoundly affected. Although they were some way off there was nothing to obstruct my view. The land was savannah, grassy and lightly wooded. The sight of those elephants touched me with a yearning that seemed to stretch back forever. I could even believe that I was seeing again something once observed through a remote ancestral eye.

The elephants were brown, and I did not question the color at the time. It seemed quite right, it matched my image perfectly, and only afterwards did I remember that elephants were gray. Evidently they had sprayed themselves with dust. They had nuzzled up to each other, wonderfully satisfying shapes, smooth and solid, superimposed in a cluster of curves; all the more alive for being so utterly still.

Elephants sheltering under a baobab tree, a familiar sight on this earth for thousands of years, and one I had waited all my life and traveled so far to see.

Africa.

The road was easy, with no traffic. I could watch the country as I went. I saw more giraffe. Then an abandoned gas station apparently inhabited by a tribe of baboons. I stopped again, to watch them; the mothers nursing their babies, the older children playing boisterously, the fathers preserving their dignity. They were oblivious to me, couldn't give a damn.

Aren't they supposed to be vicious? What would I do if they rushed me?

The road dropped to sea level. Clouds formed overhead, and I brought the first rain of the season to Mombasa, a few fat drops in the dust. I stopped in the middle of town and an open minicar with a tasseled canvas top drew up beside me. The driver was a Dane called Kaj, teaching at the polytechnic. We went to the Castle Hotel for lunch, a seven-course blowout for fourteen shillings with enough hors d'oeuvres to choose from to make the other six courses redundant. Afterwards I got a cheap room at Jimeey's. Everyone was saying how hot it was but I didn't feel it for the first two days. Then it got very sticky.

Kaj took me to the Sunshine Club on Kilindini Street. The moment I stepped inside my senses began to tingle, and I knew why I never went to night clubs. It had what clubs in London and New York can never have, however much they spend trying to simulate it, because it's illegal. The Sunshine had Life. Lusty, licentious, disgusting, decadent life. It was a big, untidy place full of people and happy noise. There was a bandstand and a band going full blast behind a soul singer. There was a floor and tables and a long polished bar, all under a high roof, and at the end of the room there was more stuff going on that you couldn't quite see. The place had depth and intrigue, and a hint of danger.

There were sailors and tourists and hustlers and bar girls. For all I knew there were arms dealers, ivory poachers, currency swindlers, slave traders, Cuban military advisers and agents of the IMF. There were even men who just came for a beer.

The bar girls did not even pretend to serve beer at the Sunshine, they had waiters to do that. The girls swanned about in outrageous wigs and long slit gowns of silver lamé, or fishnet tights, or whatever other glamorous junk came their way, drumming up interest and heating the atmosphere. Kaj knew most of them. He lived in the Sunshine Club the way Toulouse-Lautrec lived in the Moulin Rouge, and the comparison was not too far-fetched. When the girls had no pressing business, they would go back with him for pleasure. He said the girls had fun there. They came from Nairobi or somewhere around there, leaving their kids with the other wives, and spent a few months in Mombasa having a good time and making some money to send home. Nobody was interested in telling them it was wicked, and they did not look as though they thought it was either. They had their blood tests every week and got their green health cards stamped. As far as I could tell, they were free agents and nobody had

Falling and Rising ────────➤ 141

the bite into them, but I couldn't be sure, and anyway it was obviously going to change and get nastier.

A big German travel agency had already discovered "Sun and Sex" in Mombasa. With revolting teutonic logic it was running a package tour for "bachelors" with a hotel on the beach and a black girl thrown in. There was bigger money in it, and the girls went, but they hated it. They hated losing their freedom to those creepy bachelors.

"And if I give that man a dose, that's my pleasure and he just gettin' what he's payin' for, isn't it!"

Mombasa is a great trading port on a beautiful coast, and seemed the ideal of what a tropical city should be. Since ancient times Arab, Indian and African worlds had mixed here. The Portuguese called it Mombaça and planted a massive fort, and later the English provided order and a minimum of amenities.

It had a genuinely cosmopolitan life and you could find it in the faces, the food, the music, the buildings and the stores. It was far less infected than Nairobi by the trashy images of international business, credit-card culture, bankers' baloney, ersatz ethnic, Hilton hybrid, and the rest of the fungus that spreads from the airports to rot away the world's capital cities. The sea trade kept Mombasa alive.

Kaj drove me around the port one night, under the lights. A Kikuyu guard in a sentry box said: "You can pass." We drove for a mile among the sheds and sidings, weaving among piles of copper ingots from Zaire, drums of oil from Kuwait, sacks and crates and long lines of Yugoslav trucks and trailers. Brilliantly lit freighters bristled with derricks, unloading under floodlights. A locomotive with one vast Cyclopean eye pursued us for a while.

Later we went along the coast to Fort Jesus and walked around it in the moonlight. It loomed above us, too massive to comprehend, huge and black and cruel, staring out into the Indian Ocean, and four hundred years were wiped away without trace.

Going home that night, under the street lamps, an African boy with a bright, appealing face came up to me, dragging a twisted leg.

"I am not asking for help," he said. "I merely want to find a kind-hearted person to appreciate my problem. I have certificates in maths, geography, history, English, woodwork, and I have to look for help where I can. I believe God will look after me. You cannot understand now, but one day when you are in trouble you will see. Do not offer me a cigarette. How can I want a cigarette when I am starving?

Even though I have not a cent in my pocket I will not ask for money, only some food. But if I had my fare to go back to my shamba I would not be forced to look here for help. Four shillings and fifty is all I need."

I appreciated his talent more than his problem and gave him a shilling.

"Now give me a cigarette," he said.

I did, and he lit it, and limped away smoking. A few yards down the road his leg became miraculously untwisted, and he began to dance.

The coast of Kenya is irresistible. I rode up to Malindi, and hopped a small plane to Lamu. There I met the first motorbike traveler who had gone anything like the distance I meant to cover. Meeting him was intensely interesting to me. He was a young New Zealander from Hamilton called Ian Shaw. In four years he had moved through Southeast Asia, India and Africa, doing some sixty thousand miles.

He had had one bad accident. A high-speed wobble in Thailand had sent him rolling one hundred feet on a dirt road and skinned him "like a potato." A Thai hospital had stretched him out and poured salt over him, then washed him, put on Mercurochrome and sent him off. He rode as fast as he could for Malaysia, hoping to get to more tender care before he set rigid.

He showed no signs of any ordeals when I met him, nor of the sleeping sickness he had caught and almost died of in Botswana. The Tanzanian police had threatened to shoot him, a mob had chased him through the streets of Karachi, but he was alive and thriving, although he thought he might have picked up bilharzia.

Naturally I was wondering how my experience would compare with his. I always assumed that, sooner or later, something very painful was bound to happen to me. Perhaps my appetites would be less aggressive than his, though. And already I thought I recognized how many incidents, especially those involving "hostile natives," seemed to be brought on by the victim's behavior. His riding style was certainly more extrovert than mine.

In other respects we understood each other really well. I knew from his way of describing places, people and events that we had both learned and felt similar truths. We were both having a rather comfortable time there on the coast, and we met like soldiers on leave from the trenches. When we left to ride off again, but in opposite directions, he said with half a sigh: "Oh, well, back into it again."

I knew he meant time to sweat out the beer and replace it with water, to shrink his stomach back to a handful of millet and mutton sauce, to forget about washing for a while and get back to the bare essentials. How good that will feel, I thought, once the withdrawal symptoms have gone and I'm comfortable again with the least I need to survive.

I fixed on a Sunday morning to leave Mombasa, to pack my things and go. When that morning came I was reluctant. The weather coincided with my mood. It was gloomy and uncertain. Any excuse would have done to keep me there another day, but none appeared and I did not have the wit to invent one.

The bike also felt off balance, as usually happened when my mood was unstable. I got an impression of confusion, as though the power was not being transmitted cleanly, and my ear picked up noises and vibrations that fed my doubts. The responses were fractionally less positive, the gears less than crisp, the handling felt off, and the whole thing seemed to rumble along in a disconnected fashion, instead of being the tightly integrated machine I was used to.

I was unwilling to believe that all this proceeded from my own mind, and I tried to diagnose faults. I checked the timing, the plugs, looking for loss of power, speculating on whether a jet was clogged or whether the humidity was affecting the mixture. I looked at the wheel alignment and several times snatched a glance at my rear tire, convinced that it must be flat.

There was nothing wrong and none of my speculations made sense, but my anxiety only increased. The road was wet from a recent shower and I moved over it gingerly, expecting to slide at any moment. There is a ferry crossing south of Mombasa, and I approached the steeply sloping ramp of wet planks with such nervousness that it almost led to a fall.

The road south was a good one and gave me no reason for concern, but I watched it as though it were a venomous snake, and felt presentiments of disaster growing in me. The cloud thickened ahead. Within minutes it grew black as pitch, and thundered ominously, and I seemed to be heading for the heart of the storm. I felt imprisoned by the route, as though it were a one-way tunnel I was doomed to go down come what may.

Waves of fetid air swept across the road from the forest, which had been newly drenched. It was the first time I had smelled that characteristic warm odor of rotting vegetation which previously I had known only in the hothouses of botanical gardens. It roused me and reminded me of the wonder and excitement I used to feel as a boy among those strange lush plants from the tropics, and I realized with a shock that I was sinking so deep into my state of alarm that I was defeating the whole purpose of being there.

So, for a while, I rescued myself from my despondency. At that same moment the road veered abruptly off to the west and took me safely around the storm, and the bike seemed to run much better. I could hardly resist the odd feeling that I had been rewarded by some invisible trainer, nudging and cajoling me with lumps of sugar and a touch of the whip.

I set myself to look for the sources of my anxiety. What was I afraid of?

Was I afraid of having an accident? It felt like that. I felt as though I expected to fall off at any moment. But why? The road was good. There was no traffic. The bike was functioning perfectly well, for all my imaginings. Was it the wet surface? How could it be? My tires were brand-new, and gripping the road fine. In Libya I had ridden hundreds of miles through rainstorms at much greater speeds without a qualm. And I had never fallen off in the rain yet. What was it then? Come on, dig! Was it the stories that Ian Shaw had told me? Had they unnerved me in some way? Surely not. I had always imagined that accidents would happen. I had imagined far more gruesome accidents than any he had described. If anything, his example was reassuring. Well, what about his nasty moment with the Tanzanian police? The border was only a few miles away now. What about that?

For a moment that looked likely. I always approached borders with great caution. They were potentially dangerous. Too much power in a few hands. Too much greed. Too little control. I was always wary of uniforms. And yet, I had never let the prospect of a border frighten me before. I had crossed five borders already in Africa, twice in quite unpredictable circumstances, and each time I was pleasantly surprised. My system clearly worked. I arrived early, ready for anything and quite willing to spend the day there if necessary. I was always received with curiosity and good humor. Why should this border be any different? And even if it was . . . I shrugged. That was not what was bothering me. I felt sure of it.

Well then, what? I tried to pretend that it was nothing, just a passing fancy to be dismissed, but I knew that was untrue. And I wanted to find out. It began to seem passionately important to root this thing out. There was a nameless dread in me, and now was the time to put a name to it.

When had I last felt like this? To my surprise I realized that it had been quite recent, during the second week in Nairobi, only ten days before. What had *that* been about? I could think of nothing, except possibly the prospect of departure. But I had actually left Nairobi in excellent humor. There was nothing I could pin it down to.

When else had I felt like this?

Immediately my mind flew to the moment at Mersa Matruh when I had come across the taxi driver picking up my wallet; when I had unaccountably, and shamefully, obeyed his command and passed by, pretending I had seen nothing. The incident rankled deep in me. I squirmed as though touched by something foul. Then the border at Lunga Lunga came in sight, and for a while my speculations had to cease.

The crossing into Tanzania seemed a delicate matter in only one respect, and that concerned the hostility between the Black African states and White Rhodesia. Mozambique at that time was still Portuguese, and Botswana was observing a profitable neutrality, but Zambia was in total confrontation with Rhodesia, supported powerfully by Tanzania and Kenya. The border with Rhodesia was closed, and I would have to make a circuit via Botswana to get there and eventually to South Africa. It was not at all clear in those days what the Tanzanian and Kenyan attitudes were to traffic in and out of Rhodesia. Officially they would be bound to disapprove, particularly Tanzania, with its heavily Marxist-oriented ideology and rigid administration.

What made travel in Africa so remarkable was that one never knew, from one week to another or from one frontier to the next, what was going on. The only way to find out was to go and see. I knew that a trickle of people had passed on the same route going north, and I had heard a few stories about how easy or difficult it was, but all I could deduce was that it was worth trying.

The customs officer on the Kenya side raised my suspicions by questioning me in detail about my journey, my plans, my views on

Kenya and about the changes in Britain since she had lost her colonies. It was almost certainly just harmless curiosity, but it felt like a polite political screening. I did not have to lie, but I was fairly economical with the truth until he let me go.

On the other side I was received by a schoolmasterish fellow in a light worsted suit and spectacles. I was relieved to find that he was only interested in my money. He asked to see traveler's checks, which had to be recorded on a currency form. Then he suggested urgently that he himself could change the bits of Kenyan currency I had left.

"There will be no need to record it on the form," he said, "for doubtless you will be spending it immediately."

Obviously he was planning to change the money himself at the black market rate and since it did not amount to much I let him get away with it, keeping only a few coins. While we did our business it began to rain heavily. I stood under the eaves of the hut looking mournfully down the road, which had changed to dirt. The rain water lay on it in sheets. It looked slippery and difficult, like red mud. It struck me that I had crossed into the monsoons now and that for several thousand miles I might be riding on wet surfaces. I had no idea how much of that would be dirt, but I was troubled by the prospect. I had had virtually no experience of wet dirt and it was not a good day to learn.

Also I was out of gas. The pump marked on my map at Lunga Lunga had been closed. As I waited, wondering what to do, two tall and expensively dressed Africans on their way to Kenya stepped out of a Mercedes saloon, and I dickered with them for a liter or two of gas to get me to Tanga.

"You'd better wait and see if they let us through first," said one of them. "If not, you can take the whole damn car." But they negotiated their passage, and I got my liter, grudgingly spared at a high price.

The route swung back to the coast and ran through a light-red sandy soil, banked and ditched to channel the floodwater. For some way back from the road, the ground was denuded by goats grazing. Huts thatched with coconut stood among the trees and palms, but very few people were out. Those I saw looked dull and morose. Although I found the going better than I expected, the damp gray skies and the sullen people threw me back into my earlier heavy mood. I passed close to a man walking with a panga swinging from his hand. He looked miserable and hostile. The two-foot-long steel blade, razor-sharp all the way around, gave me a start. I imagined the damage one vicious swing with that weapon could do. It could take my foot off, I thought.

I saw myself struggling with field dressings, riding the bike with one foot. An image flashed before my mind of a white-faced motorcyclist riding up to a hospital, collapsing at the entrance. "We never knew how far he had come," says the surgeon. The nurse pulls off his boot to reveal only a raw stump. "He died without regaining consciousness."

That's ridiculous, I thought The panga would have taken the boot off too.

With a shock I realized what was going on in my head. It seemed incredible that I could be riding along a dirt road in Africa engrossed in these macabre fantasies. What on earth inspired me to invent them? Anticipating difficulties was one thing, but spinning horror stories to make my own flesh creep was terrible.

It did not occur to me to ask myself whether I was insane. I knew I was more or less as sane as most people, for I had decades of experience to support the view. I could get along in society, and make a living. What other definition of sanity could there be?

Obviously what was going on was part of the same story that had been unfolding before; the anxiety of a lifetime slowly revealing itself.

I began to see that all these particular fears, of falling, of meeting with violent behavior, of wildly improbable hazards, were only excuses for a fear I could not recognize. They were false messengers I decided, concealing anxieties of a quite different kind. These noxious vapors arising from some deep well of doubt and despair writhed and curled into whatever shape was convenient to haunt me at my feast. I was making it easier for them by offering them ready-made disguises.

I decided I would have no more of it. From then on let them do their worst unaided. I would no longer lend them the props of my imagination.

So my rational mind issued its tidy instructions and was completely overwhelmed by the consequences. Fear simply roared up and engulfed me in a waking nightmare, all pretense thrown aside, shrouding me in a clammy gray terror to which I could put no name or origin.

It subsided soon after, and left me in peace for the rest of the day, and I felt some satisfaction at having at least flushed the enemy out. I was very excited by all this mental turmoil. It seemed clear to me that my journey, the entire concept of it, was closely related to my struggles with fear.

I had launched myself on a journey to circle the globe, but I seemed to be on another journey as well, a great voyage of discovery into my own subconscious. And I trembled a little at the thought of what monsters I might encounter there.

The cloud lifted and dispersed, and the road came back to the sea at Tanga. The difference between the two regimes became immediately apparent. The town had been spaciously laid out in colonial days and was physically unchanged. There was none of the bustle and enterprise of Mombasa. Little advertising, little traffic, fewer shops, fewer goods, a quiet provincial backwater in dignified decline, at least to my casual eye.

I sat alone in a fine old cafe where nothing had happened for years. Beautifully made furniture in wonderful African hardwoods stood and seasoned while the proprietor grew older and more lethargic, presiding over an ever more limited range of food and drink. I ate some *sambusas*, deep-fried triangular pastry cases stuffed with spiced vegetable which are the Asian equivalent of a hamburger. After a cup of tea I moved on. It seemed a pity not to stay, but I had been still too long and needed to make some distance.

From Tanga the road was once again a good tar highway, and struck inland to meet the main highway between Nairobi and Dar Es Salaam. The land was richly green, with mountains rising to the right of me, and great sisal plantations all around.

Then I took the turning south towards Dar and Morogoro, and sped over the green hills and under the overcast sky as far as Mwebwe by the Wami River.

There were two strings of huts, one on each side of the road. I was attracted by one on my right painted in a jolly color and called a hotel. Some pleasant women sitting outside and sewing smiled as I passed so I stopped and asked how much a bed would cost. They sug-

Falling and Rising ————➤ 149

gested five shillings and showed me a reasonable portion of partitioned hut. I hung my mosquito net and walked up the road to where the truck drivers ate. The staple diet was posho, a mash of cooked corn, like the Italian polenta. With it came a bit of chopped mutton and peppery sauce. You could have a spoon if you wanted. There were *sambusas*, and some sticky sweet stuff, and tea.

After nightfall the low-powered lamps and wicks ushered in the familiar mysteries of the evening, casting shadows for the imagination to fill. I watched shiny brown fingers dipping into the posho and rising to sharply profiled African faces, listened to the fluid chatter of African voices breaking every now and again into some quaint English cliché, and mused over my morning's discoveries. I knew that I had never known a more intense period of mental events. There was something almost physical about it, like riding a tiger in the mind. I was sure it could only be the beginning.

That night my dreams were interrupted several times by a threatening presence. I would be engaged in quite innocuous or cheerful activities when this dominating figure would rise up to overwhelm me with fear and helplessness. I could not recognize it, but knew it was male. Dark hints echoed through the tunnel of years from a forgotten childhood.

The next day the sense of fear lingered only for a little while as I consciously tried to penetrate the identity of the attacker, but it was followed by a sense of unusual tranquillity. I felt, without quite knowing why, that I had made a significant advance. There had been no victory, the battle would be resumed another time, but I thought I had caught a glimpse of the enemy within and knew that it belonged not to the present or the future but to my own buried past. I had not overcome it, but in that one episode it had lost much of its power to overcome me.

Those who find romance in communications, who delight simply in the idea of spanning vast distances, must dream of the highway from Cairo to Cape Town. If and when it ever comes about, it will certainly be one of the world's great thoroughfares, to compare with the Pan-American Highway and the Bombay-Istanbul route. The plan has existed for some time. I rode on some of its sections; in southern Ethiopia I saw parts of it under construction by Israeli and Ethiopian teams; north of Nairobi the bed was laid and in use although untarred. In the south the road was much more advanced, but in both hemispheres it was hopelessly compromised by political upheavals.

For myself, the mere idea of a highway running the length of Africa soon became tedious and without intrinsic merit. A book that I had found by chance in Benghazi and carried with me through Africa had some relevant things to say, although it was written on a different continent, in an earlier century, by a man who made a virtue of staying in the same place. It was a collection of the works of Henry Thoreau, including the journal he kept when he lived by a pond called Walden.

He wrote: "We are in great haste to construct a magnetic telegraph from Maine to Texas; but Maine and Texas, it may be, have nothing important to communicate."

If Thoreau were alive today he would have full confirmation of his fears. Instant information is instantly obsolete. Only the most banal ideas can successfully cross great distances at the speed of light. And anything that travels very far very fast is scarcely worth transporting, especially the tourist.

The highway from Dar es Salaam to Livingstone is 1,500 miles long. It was notorious in 1973 as a "hell run," known as the TanZam Highway. When Rhodesia and Zambia closed their border, it was the only natural route from Zambia to the coast. Primarily Zambia had to export copper and import fuel, and the TanZam Highway was put to maximum use. Unfortunately it was not, at the outset, in very good condition, being only partially tarred. Gas tankers raced down the highway at suicidal speeds. Maximum turnover meant big money. Reckless, half-asleep, drunk or drugged drivers hurtled over the dirt and, often enough, hurtled off it into the rocks, trees, gullies and each other.

This was the reputation of the highway when I got onto it from Mwebwe. I had no difficulty imagining a dirt road in the monsoon churned up by drivers willing to risk anything for an extra load.

The road when I reached it was worse than bad, it was in the course of reconstruction as part of a Canadian aid project, and consisted of almost continuous diversions into the surrounding countryside. fortunately that slowed down the rest of the traffic as well, and I found it manageable. By the time I got to Morogoro I was quite at ease.

Outside the bank there, where I had changed money at a suffocatingly slow pace, a European came over to admire the motorcycle. I liked him immediately, as I liked most of the white men who had chosen to go on living in African countries after independence. His name was Creati. He was an Italian who had been taken prisoner during the war in the desert, shipped to a camp in East Africa and who had taken up the option of staying after the war. He was a motorcycle mechanic and had a workshop in Morogoro. More astonishing still, he had recently bought the entire stock of parts from the Triumph agent in Dar es Salaam, who had been forced out of business.

It was a providential meeting, because a minor accident had ruined my speedometer cable. Registering my speed was hardly important. Speed limits, if they existed, were purely nominal, and in any case I knew what speed I was running at just by the feel of the engine. But I found it disconcerting to have no record of distance. Gas stations were far apart, and the quality of the fuel was poor. The octane value, I was told, might be in the seventies or even less, and I needed badly to know what my consumption figure was to avoid running dry out in the bush. Creati had one cable.

"It will cost you forty-five shillings," he warned.

I agreed readily. It was cheap at the price. Anyway, in such circumstances one does not argue about shillings. We went back to his shop and I told him where I had come from, and where I was planning to go.

"How about forty shillings?" he said.

"O.K. Fine," I said.

"I'll tell you what," he said, handing it to me. "Give me thirty shillings." I did. He drove a shrewd bargain, that Creati.

After Morogoro I was prepared for the road to get worse and worse. Instead it improved rapidly and, as Creati had promised, it soon turned into a spanking-new tarred highway.

Above me the sky was in a constant turmoil of clouds forming, condensing, collapsing to the ground and reforming. When it was not raining it was generally overcast. The air was very warm and moist. All around stretched the lush green grasses and trees of Mikumi

National Park. I rode on awhile and came across an elephant. It stood facing me a little way back from the road, arrested in the act of chewing a trunkload of grass. The grass stuck out on either side of its mouth behind the trunk like a cat's whiskers, giving it a rather undignified and lugubrious look. We stared at each other for a while. Then I got the definite feeling that it was fed up with me and planning to do something about it. I kicked over the engine and rode on.

Farther along a small troop of zebras also stood grazing, and again I stopped. All stood still as statues, heads turned to face me from whatever position they had been in. Their small, round ears strained upwards and seemed to tremble with the effort to pick up any slightest signal. Their markings were immaculate, as if freshly painted on with immense care. All wild animals gave this impression of a sharpness and clarity that was new to me, and I began to remember zoo animals as having lost this edge and looking faded and grubby by comparison.

Nothing ever enchanted me so much as coming across wild animals. I thought often how human society had impoverished itself by driving this element out of its life. In Africa I began to see the human race, sometimes, as a cancerous growth so far out of equilibrium with its host, the earth, that it would inevitably bring about the destruction of both. Not an original thought, but it came to me repeatedly.

Viewed in passing, the undulating country attracted me strongly. So far, I reflected, I had not once camped out in the African bush, and I stopped the bike to consider how I would go about it. Immediately the countryside took on a quite different aspect. The grass, which had looked so enticing, now looked long and coarse and extremely wet. In fact it was as high off the ground as my tent. I did not like the idea of camping close to the roadside, but on the other hand I did not fancy maneuvering the bike any distance over soggy ground I could not even see. Whichever way I went about it, it seemed inevitable that everything would get extremely wet, and that thought discouraged me more than anything else.

The Mikumi Park Lodge, when it came in sight, looked like the ultimate in luxury after Mwebwe. I felt even less like roughing it in the long grass, and I succumbed easily, without protest.

The rainy season naturally kept sightseers away and there were few visitors: two Canadian engineers working on power transmission lines alongside the highway; two American embassy wives on their way back to Lusaka, and a young Indian traveling, as all Indians seem to do, "on business."

The landscape pushed out to far distant hills, and below the lodge was open pasture and a water hole where an elephant stood in contemplation. Much of the afternoon I spent on the terrace watching and photographing a party of my old friends, the Marabou storks, on a hillock close by. Presumably they were hoping for kitchen scraps. They seemed bored and grumpy, and creaked about aimlessly on arthritic-looking legs, occasionally ruffling their seedy feathers. I try not to be misled by fancied resemblances between animals and humans, but the Marabous defeated me. With their wings folded behind them like the tails of an ancient dinner dress, and their stooping rheumatic gait, I could not help imagining them as a group of elderly soup-stained waiters hoping for employment.

The engineers were informative about Tanzania. The country had eleven million people who lived on a very primitive diet, mostly maize, although they said there was no starvation. There was no known mineral wealth and Tanzania depended entirely on agriculture. The gross product per capita came to about $60, and some efforts were being made to introduce co-operative farming. President Nyerere they believed to be scrupulously honest, and though there was some tribalism in government it was nothing compared with Kenya.

The Indian came to sit with me later at the dinner table. He was a young, intense fellow with a shock of black hair. I listened to his story with fascination. He had left Zanzibar, he said, after the revolution, which had been very unfavorable to Asian families. His Zanzibar passport was canceled when he left, but he had a British passport also, and with some friends he hoped to get to England. They tried first to get up through Sudan from Kenya, but were stopped at Juba and sent back. Next they tried Uganda, but again were sent back to Kenya. He then went to the British High Commission in Kenya, presumably knowing that it was a desperate throw. They took the passport and, he says, told him, "You won't be seeing that again." He thought they had burned it.

That had been in 1963. His life's dream now, he told me, was to build a raft of mangrove wood twelve feet wide and forty-four feet long (he had the drawing) with which he said he would float on the currents from the Zanzibar coast to Australia.

The scavenging Marabou stork cropped up throughout my journey, first as the ghastly guardian of Atbara's dump, later in the paddy fields of Asia. In Tanzania they looked to me like a bunch of arthritic old waiters in seedy tailcoats, hoping for handouts.

I left the lodge next morning eager to know the country better. The first stretch of road was particularly beautiful. The road ran beside low mountains on the left, and then crossed them. For half an hour or so, the Great Ruaha River tumbled past me, swollen and red from the rains. Tribes of baboons appeared occasionally at the roadside or on the ascending rock faces, and the country itself seemed alive with its constant changes of perspective, the rise and fall of the mountains, and the gushing streams. I rode 150 miles without seeing a single person. Sometimes I glimpsed a hut among the trees. Once I stopped, thinking that somehow or other I ought to make some contact with people, but the general silence, the overcast sky and the wetness sapped at my resolution. I fidgeted uneasily at the roadside, feeling like an intruder, watching the small settlement for some sign of life, and when none appeared I climbed thankfully back on my machine and rode away.

The rain held off and there was even a burst of sunshine at midday when I reached Iringa. I climbed up to the town, a busy junction on the direct Nairobi to Lusaka road. With trucks and buses coming and going it seemed very lively, but on examination there was really very little there. A few shops with the barest provisions, no buildings I could see of any interest, nobody who seemed worth approaching. I ate the inevitable *sambusas* with a kebab and a cup of tea, and set off once more. Almost immediately came the first rain, and I packed myself into my rain gear, which restricted me and cut me off even more from the world around me.

The countryside became flat and unvarying. A few small groups of huts appeared at the roadside from time to time, each looking more sodden and dismal than the last. Now and again came a square-built shack aggressively labeled "Bottle Shop." Only once did I stop at one hoping to find some life, but there was none. A counter. Wan American fizz in bottles so often recycled that the glass was opaque. Some cigarettes. And a man whose face betrayed not a spark of life or interest.

I rode on. The rain fell harder and longer. The clouds came lower and blacker. It became ever more impossible to imagine making contact with anyone. Without the sun to ease my way and bring a smile to a stranger's face I felt utterly cut off from these dull and miserable-looking people.

My last hope was a place called Igawa. The map indicated some primitive accommodation but I could find nothing. I rode up and down the row of huts, and gave up. Well after nightfall I arrived in Mbeya at the border and went straight to the European Guest House. There were Finnish agronomists to provide me with more information about maize crops and co-operative schemes, and more Indians traveling "on business." I had ridden 365 miles from one oasis of luxury to another. The next morning I crossed into Zambia.

Tanzania became important to me afterwards as my first real failure. In three days and nights I had crossed an important country as big as Venezuela, or ten times the size of Indiana. I had learned less about it than I would have picked up from any half-decent newspaper article, and what I had learned had been by hearsay. When I finally left I was astonished to have to admit that I had not talked to a single African national there except to pay rent and buy gas.

In part I blamed the highway. It was too fast, too good and took me too far away from the slow-moving people. But mostly it was because I had let the rain enter my soul.

The first ten thousand miles of the journey are completed halfway down the road to Bulawayo from Victoria Falls. It's an event of sorts, and the least I can do is stop and contemplate them for as long as it takes to smoke a cigarette.

Yesterday I came into Rhodesia, and I feel out of place. There's something weird going on here and I'm trying to get it in focus. Coming through Kenya, Tanzania, Zambia, I met white men, farmers, business people, professionals, who have lived their lives in Africa. Most were content to accept the inevitable and go on working under African rule. It was obvious that Africa could not belong to them and never had.

On the other hand, since Kibwezi I have been unable to meet with Africans on level terms. Their economic and social conditions were too primitive and, as I said before, the rain got in the way. We are like different kinds of fish in the same bowl, passing each other, even bumping into each other, but unable to communicate. Of course, I can always find an "educated" African to talk to, but he does not tell me anything because to talk to me at all he has to pretend to be white. I don't even know how to begin to pretend to be black. That's how stupid I am.

In Zambia there was a third kind of fish swimming in the bowl. The Chinese. There are schools of them alongside the TanZam Highway, building a new railway line to the coast. They are entirely deliberate in their apartness. When I stopped to admire their work and goggle at them, I was waved on by the clenched fists of a man in blue overalls of a darker shade than anyone else's. Perhaps he was the "people's representative." I should love to have seen the blueprint of that railway. I am almost sure it was drawn on a scroll with brush and ink, and most delicately shaded. The proportions of the stone viaduct I saw them building had a lightness that suggested silk gowns and parasols, rather than heavy goods trains. The Chinese built their own towns, did much of their own laboring, brought in their own women. The Africans respected them, but felt no warmth towards them. Cold fish.

If Africa has never belonged to the White Man (and will certainly never belong to the Chinese) it is also obvious that it does not belong to the Black Man either. He belongs to it. Normally unreligious people who have been here awhile say that Africa belongs to God. They say that if you just stop and listen for a moment the truth appears directly. No doubt this is because people are not yet numerous enough to jam the airwaves. There is still room for other messages to come through.

Near Lusaka, two thousand miles on from Kibwezi, I rested for a few days with an English family on a small farm. They were people whose lives were consciously and completely devoted to the service of the Christian God, and in the ordinary way I would have found such company uncomfortable. In the event, it was not. God entered into their lives, and they spoke of "Him" often in my presence, but it was like hearing about another member of the family whom I had not met, and nobody was surprised or upset that I didn't know him.

Their ambition was to extend, as far as possible, their capacity to shelter people who needed or wanted to stay there a while. They were rebuilding a house that had burned down, and preparing a campsite across the river. The household, with all its children, was in a chronic state of disorder, but the grounds were well kept. They had a large and growing network of friends throughout the world, and it seemed to me that they were really intent on stimulating what was good rather than what was holy. At any rate I could see nothing but good coming from it.

They were frequently threatened by financial ruin, but "He" always came to the rescue. Black Rhodesian Freedom Fighters went on lethal rampages from their training camp down the road, and the farm was a refuge for frightened local Africans, but no harm came to them. The inefficiencies and shortages and contradictory policies of a newborn country made farming frustrating and scarcely profitable, but for them all that was part of "His" design and they took pleasure in it.

To live in black Africa at all (and Nairobi doesn't count) you must accept a very basic existence. Most of the commonplace luxuries and certainties of the West go overboard. If you can shed your more sophisticated habits, you are so handsomely rewarded by the natural pleasures of Africa (I heard this often) that it is easy to see the hand of God at work.

For some, Africa is proof positive of God's existence. Although my own God remains as elusive as ever, my experience supports the theory in a practical way. It is a mistake to worry here. Let Africa do the work, and a solution seems to follow automatically. A problem here is like that slippery Norfolk town of Diss; as you approach it Diss appears.

I used to worry about how I was going to get from Zambia into Rhodesia, since they were mortal enemies.* No need. What you do is, you go to Livingstone on the Zambezi and spend an enchanted day wandering around the Victoria Falls and the old locomotive graveyard, and then alongside the river, watching the hippopotamuses, listening to the liquid sounds of the bottle birds and "The Shadow of Your Smile" coming from the cassette player in a red Toyota pickup,

---

* At the time, in 1974, the white government of Southern Rhodesia was defying British efforts to grant independence to the African majority. As a result the country was under violent attack from black guerrilla forces based in neighbouring Zambia (formerly Northern Rhodesia) and Mozambique. Eventually, in 1980, white resistance was overcome, and the newly independent country was named Zimbabwe.

and talking to this fisherman who has caught several catfish and bream, and is just pulling something else out now.

"This fis' we call croaker," and to prove it, as he pulls it off the hook and snaps its spines, it croaks.

Next morning you ride up to the guard on the Livingstone Bridge just in case, by chance, he should feel like letting you across, but he turns you away gently with his rifle, so you ride up-river for fifty miles or so and take the ferry to Kazangula in Botswana. There they sell you a mandatory insurance policy to cover you against collisions on the six miles to the Rhodesian border. And there you go.

I sometimes think about those two guards staring at each other from opposite ends of the Livingstone Bridge, and wonder whether they know each other's Christian names. They are undoubtedly both Christians.

The weirdness begins right at the Rhodesian border. First there is this bright new galvanized wire fence, all properly erected and secured, with no bits hanging off or rusting away. Then, on the other side of the fence, you see that there are no weeds. No superfluous or inappropriate growths whatsoever. The cement is smooth, the gravel swept and free of grass and everything has clearly defined edges. Squared off, shipshape and in absolute shite order.

I gaze at this model of propriety, this example of "how it should be done," like some grubby kid on the street with his nose pressed to the squire's window. Maybe my first inkling of what it's like to be black.

"Pull yourself together, man," I say. "Where's your passport? Your *British* passport."

On the other side of the fence, having entered the squire's mansion, is this office, all spick and span, but what hits you smack in the retina, what makes you want to shield your eyes lest they melt in their sockets, are these two White Men. Man, are they White! They are dazzling, like angels or something. And they are White in White. They have little White socks, and elasticized White shorts, perfectly cut to those plump White thighs and tight White tunics. I swear, once I appreciate that they are real and alive, I don't see people. I see flesh, and I know it's White right through, like pork or chicken, done up in frilly White wrappings the way it comes ready cooked from the delicatessen.

Well, one of these amazing beings has got a gun that he is carrying against his chest, with the barrel pointing straight up past his nose. I don't know what he's got in this gun, but it could be full to the brim with instant atom-bomb powder or something, because he is clutching it with both hands and walking on eggs as though a variation of one degree from the vertical could blow us all to Zimbabwe.

He's got a prissy prep-school face that's saying, "Look at me, Daddy," and "God, don't let me mess my pants" simultaneously, and he proceeds, entranced, behind the counter and through a doorway like one of those toy figures on an old clock tower. Then the other being turns his po face to me and says, "Can I help you, sir" in a funny strained voice.

My eyes are growing accustomed to the glare, so I face up to him quite well.

"Do you have Rhodesian Third Party Insurance, Mr. Simon?" he asks, knowing bloody well I don't.

"No," I say. "Can I get it at Vic Falls?"

"Trouble is, the road from here to Vic Falls is bad. If you had an accident you might not have a leg to stand on."

There is no horse laugh after this uproarious remark. Perhaps the Rhodesian sense of humor is unconscious. Even while all this is going on, as I marvel at it, I am aware that but for the journey I have just made it would seem perfectly normal. This is how a white immigration office ought to be run, given a little extra spit and polish for the current emergency. Obviously I have been colored by Africa without realizing it, and I see that all those white people I have been meeting recently, while they are not really African, have lost the edge of their whiteness, and blend more or less into the racial spectrum.

Here I see what White really means. The experience continues into Victoria Falls. The butcher sells me a delicious fillet steak for a derisory price and says:

"Surely you must believe, as I do, that we are the victims of a world-wide Communist conspiracy."

What we have here, I see, is a White Tribe. What are their customs? Rigid adherence to the standards of Britain before the Fall. Efficiency, cleanliness, husbandry, *pro bono publico,* monogamy and cricket. Like the Turkana they believe that as long as they stick to their customs and rituals they must prevail. There is no alternative. I can easily imagine a black anthropologist visiting Rhodesia ten years ago and writing:

"Arrogant and superior as the country he comes from, so he will remain, in my opinion, to the end of time."

Time is running out everywhere, but it is not only pressure from outside that threatens this culture. A woman yesterday asked me, with a satisfied smirk on her pretty face, whether I knew that Rhodesia had the highest divorce rate in the world. Adultery, the Enemy Within.

As I finish my cigarette a figure is walking in my direction, on the other side of the road, an African wearing a cloth hat and a white coat like a tent buttoned at the neck. The country stretches forever all around, an open and empty plain, as it has through Tanzania and Zambia. Two thousand miles of empty land. I would not have believed there was so much space left in the world. The road is asphalt, and very hot. The African is barefoot.

"Where are you walking to?" I ask him.

"I am going to Bulawayo to look for work."

He asks me where I have come from, and says:

"Oh, my goodness! You are very clever, sir."

Bulawayo is a hundred miles away. When I think of walking barefoot to Bulawayo my own achievement seems less spectacular.

From Bulawayo to Salisbury the impression persists. The farms are beautifully managed. The cities run like clockwork. "We will not let go. African rule would be a disaster. They would massacre each other in no time. Everything would be in ruins. Anyway it's too late now. Who would buy our property? We will stick it out. We'll win through in the end. Someone will come to our aid. Britain. South Africa. Someone. They can't let us down."

From Umtali to Melsetter a road runs through the mountains along the Mozambique border, famous for its beauty. Halfway along is the Black Mountain Inn, known throughout southern Africa. It has recently changed hands. The new owner, Van den Bergh, is a Dutch man who worked in Indonesia and has retired from business.

He and his wife are taking a chance coming here, but they wanted a change of life.

"You'd never believe the bigotry round here. Not in the towns so much, but in the fringe rural districts and among the Afrikaners. There's a farmer they call 'Baas M'Sorry. He brings his labor in from Malawi under contract – a lot of them do. When his new batch

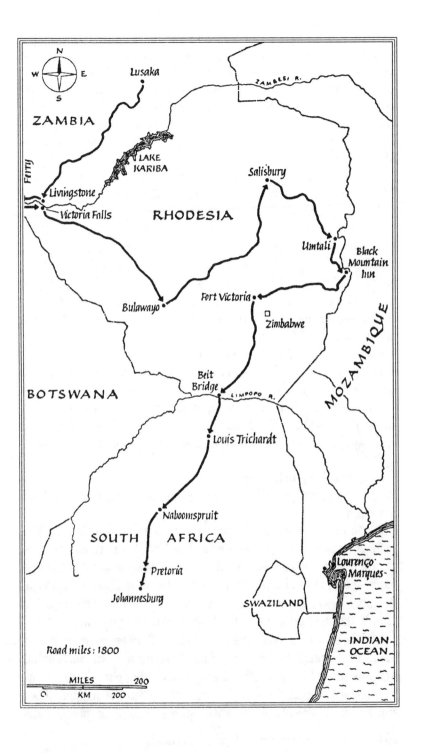

arrives, he puts each one in a jute sack and weighs him. Then he arranges the feed according to their weight. Like cattle.

"He wears those big snake boots, you know, knee-high leather boots, because there are snakes in the fields. If he comes across a cheeky Mundt – that's a Kafir who answers back – he steps on his foot and grinds with the heel of his boot until the fellow says 'Baas M'Sorry.'

"You know there's a law now that blacks are supposed to be called African Gentlemen and African Ladies. 'African Ladies?' says this feller. 'There's no such thing. Just Kafir bitches'."

Van den Bergh's stories come pouring out like a vaudeville routine. He hasn't met anyone for a while who would understand.

"When we first arrived we went to get meat for us and the servants. 'Oh,' they said, 'for them you want boy's meat,' and they produced this chopped-up bone and gristle and sinew. It was cheaper than meat for the dog. We thought, 'We can't give them that,' so we bought them steak. After a while there was a mutiny because we weren't giving them the proper meat."

Things are a bit risky around here, especially at night. There are raids across the border, both ways.

"The police are in here every night getting drunk. The army's the same. I'm afraid the Rhodesian whites are too flabby. If they ever came up against a really motivated black army, well they'd get rolled up."

So what's going to happen?

"The blacks will get independence eventually – but it'll take about ten years."

The inn is a lovely place, in far better taste than anything else I've seen, set among flowers and lawns. The Van den Berghs seem like the right sort of people to have there too. It's sad to think of the fate hanging over them. I think his forecast is too optimistic. In Chipinga, the next town, a businessman called Hutchinson, who says his grandfather was governor of the Cape Province, agrees with me.

"My date is 1980," he says. "There'll be African government by then." His arguments are convincing. He seems to be in touch. What Africans think I have no idea. I keep hoping that chance will throw me among them as it did in Kenya, but it does not happen. They appear before me only as servants, figures performing menial functions. All I hear is Yes Sir, No Sir, Three Bags Full, Sir. They inhabit some other world that I can't get in focus.

On my way back to Fort Victoria I stop at a black village on the Tribal Trust Territory. The site has some magic. There are huge, smooth rocks piled on each other, like symbols of power and protection, with sheltered patches of ground among them. I'm not very far from Zimbabwe itself, and there is a kind of sorcery in the land, but all I see are endlessly outstretched hands, begging. One dumpy lady runs frantically to fetch her big copper pot, and balances it on her head in the hope of getting a posing fee. Her haste is such that she gets it on wrong and has to stand with her head crooked to keep it up there. The anxiety on her face is comical and leaves a bad aftertaste. No, lady, that's not what I came for.

Fort Victoria is Rhodesia's tourist trap for visiting South Africans. It funnels them right into the curio shops.

"Get yourself something Unique, something Arty!" beckons one of them.

It's a long, dry ride south to the South African border. Above me I see a million storks make a swirling, towering column in the sky, marshaling themselves for the flight to Europe.

The South African Immigration and Customs authorities at Beit Bridge can afford to be a good deal fussier than the Rhodesians.

"Do you have your return ticket out of South Africa, Mr. Simon?" says the first official.

What *can* he be talking about?

"Well, hardly. I was booked on a ship to Rio, but the sailing was canceled."

"In that case I must tell you that you are classified as a *Prohibited Person.*"

He gives me a leaflet and a form, and I see that there is hope here even for prohibited persons. All I need do is make an interest-free loan to the South African Government of $600 for the duration of my stay. This money can be used to purchase a non redeemable ticket, or it will be refunded at the exit point. Ho-hum. I suppose they're good for the money, but I *know* there will be complications. Luckily I've got the $600.

Now for customs. I get this young fellow, full of bounce. He is even Whiter than White, but of course I am used to it now. He's got on the usual white gymnastics outfit, but unlike all the other officials who have some mark of rank on their epaulettes, he does not even have epaulettes. He is so junior he hardly even exists, and he's trying to make up for it.

First he packs me off across the road to get a road safety token, whatever that may be. On my way back I see them all gathered around the bike. I'm so accustomed to the sight that I imagine they are admiring it, as everybody else does.

Inside the office Billy the Kid fixes me with his dull blue eyes.

"Now, sir, have you got any meat, plants, firearms, drugs, books or magazines, cigarettes or tobacco?"

"Yes, I have a book on Christianity."

"*Christ-i-anity?*" He is incredulous.

I ask if he's heard of it, but he's too busy thinking about his next move.

"Have you anything else to declare?"

"No."

He has a thin voice that shoots into an upper register on certain words.

"Then *why*, sir," he pounces, heavily, "do you not declare *the sword?*"

The sword? Good God, yes, the sword. I forgot I had a sword. It's not my sword. I met a man in Cairo who wanted to emigrate to Brazil, but he was not allowed to, so he was trying to get his stuff out of the country first. He gave me $2,000 to send to his brother, and then asked if I could carry his father's ceremonial sword. I thought it was a genial idea, and I attached it on the opposite side to the umbrella. I never gave it a thought.

The Kid shows me his collection of confiscated arms. He is very proud of it, particularly a three-inch dagger he took only the other day. But a sword! That's a real prize.

"I shall have to take it away from you, sir. I'm very *sorry.*"

He sounds delighted.

"I'm afraid you can't," I say. "You see, it isn't mine. Anyway, it isn't actually a weapon. It is a family heirloom."

"I cannot let you take this sword, I am *sorry.*"

"Well, how will I get it back? Obviously I cannot just abandon it. It does not belong to me."

"We shall see if we can wrap it and send it *under seal* and at *your expense* to Brazil."

I can tell he's improvising now. The ground is slipping away under his feet.

"Why can't I collect it at customs in Cape Town?"

He is looking very confused. His neighbor at the next desk, who has a broad gold band on his shoulder and seems to be keeping an eye on him, leans over to him and says softly:

"Why don't you go and ask your father?"

Daddy, of course, is the boss. ("Ach, please, Daddy, let me go to customs, and confiscate my life away like you.")

A party collects in his office to inspect the weapon with enthusiasm. Daddy draws it from the scabbard and makes a few experimental strokes.

"How can we stop the natives having them if we let you in with this," says number two.

Does he imagine the "natives" engaging in knightly combat, cut, thrust, parry, according to the rules of chivalry? "Natives" don't need swords. They have pangas, which they use to cut cane, and grass, and if necessary, throats. I think these white knights are mad, but this is not the moment perhaps to say so.

Now Daddy has an idea. "Son, see if you can seal it into the scabbard, and then wrap it up well so no one can see what it is."

The Kid is happy. He's got his orders, which he can carry out to the letter, to the very serif.

"Come over here, sir, *please.* Now, sir, you see I am going to wire this hilt to the scabbard, and seal it. You see there is a number on this lead seal. If this seal is broken you go *straight to jail.*"

"What happens," I ask, "if someone should happen to steal it from me?"

"You go *straight to jail.* Same thing if you lose it or sell it. *Straight to jail.* Now, sir, I am going to wrap this sword up in brown paper which will carry the customs seal also, and I am bound to warn you that if it is tampered with in any way . . ."

"*Straight to jail,*" we cry in unison.

He manages quite well with the paper, but the sealing wax is too much. Little drops of it keep falling on his plump white thighs and he's dancing with pain and frustration. He is able at last to get some wax to stick to the paper, but it is obvious to me that the first rain storm will soak it to a mash.

"Usually," he says, primly, "we get the natives to do this sort of thing. Now I must ask you for a deposit so that we can be sure you will declare the sword in *Cape Town*."

But this is too much for me, and I am glad to see the older man shake his head, silently and repeatedly.

"All right," says the Kid, as if it were his idea. "You can go."

From Beit Bridge it is only 350 miles to Johannesburg. I imagine that I will arrive there tomorrow night, and set off to get as far as I can today. A considerable range of mountains, the Soutpansberg, bars the way, and the road climbs up into a cold cloud. There are tunnels to pass through, and on the other side, some rain. At a small town called Louis Trichardt I decide to stop and treat myself to a hotel, which proves to be memorable because of the dining room. This is a large square room, with a smaller room inside it, like nesting boxes. The smaller room has glass panes for walls and is the kitchen, and all the cooking can be watched from the dining room. In a London restaurant this could be an ingenious and even attractive idea, if rather courageous. Here in South Africa it has a gruesome feeling, because the kitchen staff, naturally, is black. We, the diners, are white. The owner patrols the dining room in a planter's safari outfit, and oversees both parts of his business simultaneously. I watch the "galley slaves" with a sick fascination. They do not talk to each other, or show the slightest expression of pleasure, fatigue, self-consciousness or, indeed, any emotion at all. The scene, to me, is so highly abnormal, and to everyone else it's so completely normal, that I feel I have wandered, by chance, into a land as strange as any Gulliver ever visited. I make a conscious effort to reserve my judgment. The logic of the arrangement is all too obvious.

I am now only 280 miles from Johannesburg, an easy day's ride. The significance of this day's journey is great. Since Cairo I have been riding with a damaged piston. It seems scarcely possible that the engine has been able to survive this far. Not only the distance, more than seven thousand miles, but the conditions of heat and effort, especially in the north, must have put the machine to a very severe test. Now, one day's ride from here are all the facilities I need to overhaul the cylinders, rebore, put in new pistons and do anything else. Up to now, at best it would have meant shipping parts from England with great delays and bureaucratic entanglements. Most of the way it would have been impossible.

My confidence in the Triumph has gone beyond surprise and gratitude. I now rely on it without question, and it seems past all coincidence that, on this last day, the unseen fate working itself out in the cylinder barrel should manifest itself. It is not I who am looking for significance in these events. The significance declares itself unaided.

Just beyond Trichardt, in the morning, the power suddenly falters and I hear, unmistakably, the sound of loose metal tinkling somewhere; but where? Although the power picks up again, I stop to look. The chain is very loose. Could it have been skipping the sprockets? I tighten the chain and drive on. Power fails rapidly and after about four miles the engine simply stops in first gear. There's a strong smell of burning. Is it the clutch? It seems to have seized, because even in neutral it won't move.

Two friendly Afrikaners in the postal service stop their car to supervise, and their presence irritates me and stops me thinking. I remove the chain case to look at the clutch, a good half hour's work. Nothing wrong, and then my folly hits me. I tightened the chain and forgot to adjust the brake. I've been riding with the rear brake on for four miles, and the shoes have seized on the drum. Apart from anything else, that is not the best way to treat a failing engine.

I put everything together again and set off, but the engine noise is now very unhealthy. A loud metallic hammering from the cylinder barrel. A push rod? A valve? I'm so near Jo'burg, the temptation to struggle on is great. At Pietersburg I stop at a garage. The engine oil has vanished.

"That's a bad noise there, hey!" says the white mechanic, and calls his foreman over.

"Sounds like piston slap. The piston's seized."

"Can I go on like that?"

"As long as it's not too far. You'll use a lot of oil."

From Pietersburg to Naboomspruit is thirty-four miles. I stop for more oil, but the bike won't even start again properly. I realize I must give up Jo'burg. It's 4 P.M. on Thursday, 21 February. I calculate that with the bike running well I could still have made that original sailing date in Cape Town. The thought gives some satisfaction.

I spend two days at Naboomspruit working on the engine. On the first day I take the barrel off. The old piston has shattered its skirt. The crankcase is full of broken metal. The con rod is scarred, the sump filter in pieces, the scavenge pipe knocked off center. The sleeve of the bad cylinder is corrugated. I have kept the old piston from Alexandria, and put it back thinking it might get me as far as Jo'burg. With everything washed out and reassembled, the engine runs, but no oil returns from the crankcase.

The second day I spend on the lubrication system, picking pieces out of the oil pump. On Sunday, in bright sunshine, I set off again, for twenty blissful miles before all hell breaks loose. The knocking and rattling is now really terrible. I decide that I must have another look, and by the roadside I take the barrel off again and do some more work on the piston and put it back again. By now I am really adept and it takes me four hours. There's a black fellow sitting there with me most of the time, just happy to be there and watch and have little things to do. He comes off a farm nearby, and I go there for water just as they're eating lunch. From the kitchen I can see into a small furnished room built separately from the house, where a young girl is eating alone. I catch sight of her only for a moment and see nothing describably wrong but it is obvious that she is mad. Intuition works so fast in some matters, why not in others?

My work has not improved things. The rumbling continues and the trouble is evidently in a bearing. I limp slowly to Nylstrom, and plan to take a train to Jo'burg, but Nick the Greek at the Park Cafe is very friendly and finds a fellow with a pickup willing to take me to Pretoria, using my gas.

This fellow is an Afrikaner butcher, but although he subscribes to apartheid, I find him unusually tolerant and good-tempered. It turns out that three years ago his wife, driving this same road in a van, was blown off by wind and crushed almost to death. She has now recovered all but the use of her left leg, which is still bound up. I met her too, a cheerful, handsome woman. His story of those three years, during which he also built his own house, is very touching. It occurs to me that these people would be good to have on one's side in adversity, and then to wonder whether they choose adversity for that very reason. Is that what is meant by the "lager mentality"? If so, there is less hope for South Africa than I thought.

He puts me down at Mader's Hotel because it has a large car park, suitable for unloading the bike. Mader's is a great cavernous place, like a railway station, and intensely gloomy. I'm ten minutes too late to eat. No dinner, no drinks after 8 P.M. I have to fetch fish and chips from a shop and bring them back. As I sit under the green light issuing from a morbid aquarium I see a couple sitting nearby. He is gray and shriveled, his face mud-colored by sun and alcohol, in a slovenly safari jacket. She is fortyish, with black-frame spectacles and biggish breasts packed into a sleeveless blouse. Then the man beckons me over.

"She likes you," he says without preamble, pointing at her. Then, after a pause: "You can sleep with this woman tonight."

I excuse myself, lamely, but he wanders off, apparently unconcerned.

"He makes my life a torment," she says. "He's my husband but he is still in love with his first wife."

The word "love" falls to the floor like a cigarette butt, waiting to be trodden on.

I was in Jo'burg for three weeks, and lived in style and comfort. I saw the sights, lived the life, visited the black township, and learned something of the good and bad side of South Africa. As in Nairobi, I found that the experience was in a different coin to the experiences on the road. In these big cities, where most people confront "real" life, struggling for money and security, I was not able to find much that was new or fundamentally interesting. I was happy enough to fall into the easy way of it, absorbing pleasures and information like a sponge and getting by on conventional truths. All forms of life are fascinating, but "The Journey" seemed to float in another dimension.

Joe's Motorcycles on Market Street, as agents for Meriden, took the engine to pieces again and sent me off with a rebored barrel, two new pistons, a new con rod, main bearings, valves, idler gear and other bits and pieces. The broken metal had penetrated everywhere and again I was struck by the force of the coincidence that all this havoc had been wrought virtually within sight of Johannesburg. I was very susceptible to "messages" and wondered whether someone was trying to tell me something, like, for example, "I'll get you there, but don't count on it."

A good deal of my time in Johannesburg was taken up in trying to find an alternative sea passage to Brazil. The Yom Kippur War still

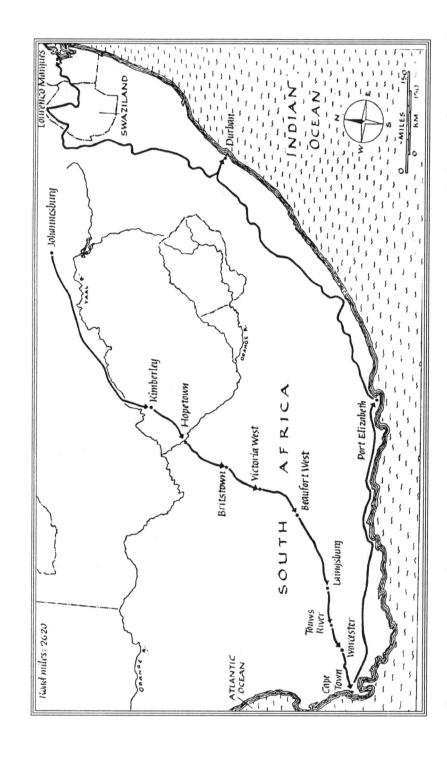

dogged my destiny. Since the war, Arabs having turned from open warfare to economic aggression, oil was twice the price, shipping was totally disoriented and passenger berths were suddenly unobtainable. At last, through a contact in a big trading concern, one ship came to light that could take me to Rio. The *Zoe G*, a small cargo vessel under Greek ownership, would be sailing out of Mozambique for Rio de Janeiro at the end of April. It would cost me the same as the air fare, but the bike would go free. I was delighted. It could not have suited my idea of transatlantic crossing better. I had time to travel to Cape Town, and then to ride around the south coast of Africa to Lourenço Marques, and a quite different aspect of Africa, a Portuguese colony. It is an ill war that blows no good. Loaded with addresses of friends of friends, I left on the last long leg to Cape Town and the Southern Ocean.

The weather played tag with me, and I was dodging between storms and rain clouds all the way from Johannesburg. On the second morning at Kimberley it looked wet from the moment the sun came up. The light was the color of reflections in floodwater, but the sky was a clear eggshell blue when I set off at eight. Although wisps of cloud began to marble it, I thought I would probably stay dry until noon.

These calculations were becoming second nature to me since entering the heavy rains south of Mombasa and my record of accuracy was improving steadily, to the point where they offered a sort of workmanlike structure to the day. I still needed this reassurance, although it made no practical difference to my behavior. I would ride on whether it rained or not, and only the most violent showers would stop me. It was not cold, the waterproofs worked well enough and the road was good level asphalt, but I had still not taught myself to enjoy the prospect of rain. Whenever it threatened to fall, a vague uneasiness would begin to squirm somewhere below my stomach. Nothing much, but enough to remind me that there was still plenty of anxiety waiting for a pretext to engulf me, and my encounters with the weather continue to be like reconstructions of a personal struggle on an epic scale.

On the broad landscape of Africa, under the bright tropical sun, a bank of cumulus cloud appears out of thin air and grows with stealthy speed into the solid likeness of doom itself. In an otherwise clear sky one of these monsters straddles the road ahead, growing at a mile a minute, like an airborne octopus of mythic proportions, its base filling with inky blackness, already feeling out the ground with stray tentacles. To leave the sunshine and ride underneath this devouring creature with its fetid breath and bulging carcass is like challenging the Dark Tower; as impudent and terrifying as that. To know with the intellect of what flimsy stuff this thing is really made does not disarm it when you have already fought to exhaustion with even flimsier devils of your own making.

Perhaps there are men raised in peace and lucidity, with no phantoms on their tails, who see nothing in a storm cloud but convection currents and water vapor. In any case I would not change places with one of them. What grandeur there is in my life blossoms out of my own mean beginnings. What times of peace I know are a thousand times more precious for being interludes. And there is much more. For example, the fascination with which I watch myself come closer and closer to merge with the world around me, dipping first a toe, then a foot, then a limb. Although I am made of the same stuff as the world, it used to seem that I might as well have been born on an asteroid, so awkward and unnatural was my place in the scheme of things. I remember my clumsy efforts to simulate "normality," to win acceptance by any false pretense, and my desperate betrayals of my own nature to avoid detection. Then the gradual discovery (born, I think, out of some irreducible core) that others were twisting and cracking under the same strains, and that behind the apparent conformity of daily life was a world of "all things counter, original, spare, strange."

Then began a long apprenticeship, to become something certain in my own right, from which to see and be seen. Beyond that came the search for connections, freely offered and accepted, to confirm that the world and I, after all, were made of each other.

There are in me the seeds from which, if necessary, the universe could be reconstructed. In me somewhere there is a matrix for mankind and a holograph for the whole world. Nothing is more important in my life than trying to discover these secrets.

Now, with the engine running beautifully, I ride along the edge of the Orange Free State towards the Orange River. My waterproofs are crammed away confidently in a pannier, and my flying jacket is beating off the cool wind. On either side, among clumps of marshy grass, water gleams pale after the rains of a few days ago, when parts of this road were eighteen inches deep under floods. This enormous plain I am crossing, which will eventually become the Great Karoo, is supposed to be dry as a bone, but the whole of the Southern Hemisphere is awash this year. Here and there are cattle settled among a surfeit of greenery. Around them and over them hop cattle egrets,Q the slim white birds which live with the cattle, like private nurses, gracefully relieving them of their ticks.

The sky is still only faintly streaked with clouds when I pass Modder River, but on the horizon to my right I see the beginnings of a sinister change. Hundreds of miles away across the moor land the sky is changing color from light blue to gun metal, as though a vessel of dark pigment has been pricked by the western point of the compass and is seeping out into the heavens. Surely it is not merely fanciful to read apocalyptic warnings into the sky like this. Out on the veldt, miles from even the nearest tree, there is no escape from the momentous events unfolding themselves above. Unknown to this human speck making his snail's track across the floor of a vast arena, another spectacular has been prepared. Pressures and temperatures have plummeted, winds veered and strengthened, and when the first stain darkens the western sky the thing is already all but accomplished.

The climax is so quick and subtle and on such a vast scale that my eye cannot follow it. The sky is light, then dark, then cloudy, then black. I am still hoping for another half hour's grace when the first drops fall splat on my goggles. Cursing, I pull up at the verge and begin the ludicrous business of putting on my waterproofs. Then I am in it.

The rain hardens to an obliterating downpour as I cross the Orange River, and I notice that the river reflects a baleful orange light from its charge of suspended red silt. Then into Hopetown, slowing down to look for shelter, cursing again as the goggles mist over without the fast air stream to clear them. Peering through the mist, I see two gas stations, one on each side of the road and, astonishingly, two rival sets of African attendants grinning madly and beckoning me with theatrical gestures to patronize their pumps.

Like the donkey that starved between two bales of hay, I get several times wetter before deciding to stick to the party on my own side of the road.

Calling at a gas station is an event, particularly on a motorcycle with a foreign number plate. In southern Africa everyone plays the number-plate game. You can tell instantly where each one comes from; C for Cape Province, J for Johannesburg, and so on. My plate begins with an X, a mystery all the deeper because some pump attendants belong to the Xhosa tribe.

Peeling off damp layers of nylon and leather, unstrapping the tank bag to get to the filler cap, fighting to get at the money under my waterproof trousers which are shaped like a clown's, chest high with elastic braces, I wait for the ritual conversation to begin.

"Where does this plate come from, baas?" asks the man.

"From England."

A sharp intake of breath, exhaled with a howl of ecstasy.

"From England? Is it? What a long one! The baas is coming on a boat?"

"No," I reply nonchalantly, knowing the lines by heart, relishing them rather. "On this. Overland."

Another gasp, followed by one or even two whoops of joy. The face is a perfect show of incredulity and admiration.

"On this one? No! Uh! I can't! You come on this one? Oh! It is too big."

The wonder of it produces a pleasing sense of intimacy but it is illusory. It leads nowhere. He is safe in his attitude of admiration while I consent to play my heroic role. It is not a role in which I feel comfortable. I am learning, as I make my way through my first continent, that it is remarkably easy to do things, and much more frightening to contemplate them. I am embarrassed by exaggerated respect.

This black fellow in his boiler suit props me up on my pedestal and feeds me on a White Man's diet of flattery and indulgence until I ooze benevolence like a green fly tended by ants. African wildlife is full of these symbiotic relationships, and that may be one reason why apartheid can be entertained at all in South Africa. As a practical system it has its advantages, and not just to one side, but the underlying suggestion that it makes a convenient arrangement for two different species to get along is such a travesty of the human ideal that

I wriggle with embarrassment at being placed in such a false position.

From the shelter of the gas station, looking along the sodden streets of Hopetown and into the swirling gray storm clouds above, there seems no hope of the rain stopping. In my mind's eye the blanket of wetness lies across the Karoo from end to end, and no effort of the imagination can raise so much as a corner of it. So out I go across the mud and puddles, resigned to the advance of moisture through the pinholes and seams of the waterproofs, past the leather and sheepskin and denim, through the worn soles of my boots, saturating trouser pockets and their forgotten contents, leaving a mash of match heads, a pulp of currency, turning hastily scribbled notes to an inky wash.

Yet only minutes from the town the gray brightens from lead to mercury and a last flash and flurry of droplets recedes into rainbow, leaving a tranquil blue vastness ahead. Once again the cosmic drama has been staged both to chide me and encourage me. The light and warmth were waiting. I had only to ride out faithfully to find it. Somewhere the same chorus is murmuring the same inexhaustible theme of light and dark, hope and despair and renewed hope, a world where everyone can be a hero, where there is an absolute guarantee of renewal which will be broken only once in a lifetime.

For me this is a landscape and a time to bank up courage in a craven heart, to carry a greater fund of joy into the next cloud of sorrow, to learn even to love the sorrow for the pleasure it divides, like the black notes of a keyboard, or hunger between meals. Perhaps even to discover that pain and pleasure, since they cannot exist without each other, are really the same thing.

I strip off my waterproofs and bundle them away, feeling a great, heart-pumping pleasure at being let loose on this shining land. The wind rushes through my clothes, whipping away the last shreds of mist and moisture, and I sing loudly about Shenandoah's Daughter and the Rio Grande.

Strange things peer at me across the corn and pasture, wind-driven pumps, tall silver objects on three legs with mooning, fan-shaped faces, straining for a puff of airto agitate their rusty bearings, to tug their long slender roots dangling into the ground and suck up moisture. Poor senseless creatures that can't comprehend the abundance, the superfluity of water that has descended all around them. They remind me of people I have known; of the old news vendor on my high street who died at his pitch leaving a fortune; of the big winners who'll be "clocking in at the works as usual on Monday."

Far away over softly undulating marshes a cathedral rears up to the sky in splendid isolation, blankly astonished by its limitless diocese. Where is the bishop? Who are the flock? It is an immense grain store, with a central tower and four silos flanking it on either side. What a harvest festival will be celebrated here from these streaming fields. South Africa anticipates the heaviest crops in memory as the result of these rains, and there is no end to the good fortune of the ruling Nationalist Party and its Afrikaner backbone.

Soon an election is to be fought – well, teased would be a better word. There is no contest. The price of gold has never been higher. Terrorists on the borders give patriotism just the necessary injection of the vital jingo serum. The election is a foregone conclusion. In Jo'burg dispirited Opposition supporters throw up their hands and say they are tired of fighting God. The grain cathedrals of the Karoo proclaim his presence. So do the astonishing yellow mine dumps rising above Johannesburg, monuments to gold the father, gold the son, and gold the holy ghost. All is ordained.

I am grateful for one of the White God's ordinances. He has kept most of the traffic off the road. The world oil crisis (more power to this god's elbow) has brought a nationwide speed limit of fifty miles an hour. It is enforced with dour efficiency. Khaki-clad policemen everywhere leap along the hedgerows and roadside ditches uncoiling wires for their speed traps. The fines for speeding are draconian, hundreds of pounds in some cases. At weekends all gas stations are closed, and woe betide him who is caught with more than two gallons in his trunk.

For me fifty miles an hour is a perfect speed, the golden mean between dawdling and drumming vibration. At this excellent rate I can spin and tumble along all day in comfort, and see where I'm going. There are now some five hundred miles between me and Cape Town. By nightfall I should be well within a day's ride. I fly past Strydenburg and Britstown feeling like Pegasus on wheels. In the early afternoon some clouds mount a few scattered fortresses in the sky but I am able to ride under them before they can release their leaden charges. Now the heat is building up and the road is steaming. The sun drilling through the haze begins to poach my eyes in a hard diffuse light, and I stop for a few minutes to lean forward on the handlebars and doze, cocooned in still, warm air and the song of the black, long-tailed Sacabula birds perched like crochets on the telegraph wires.

When I open my eyes I see that the day has turned to afternoon, the light has a golden touch to it and a big bank of cloud has stretched across my path reflecting glimmers of lilac and purple at its ragged, rolling fringes. The bar is rooted in the west among distant, shadowy hills in a black corm veined with lightning. I can see under it and beyond to the first peaks of the ranges that weave across the southern tip of Africa, with their strange Gothic names – Grootswartberge, Witteberge, Outeniekwaberge – and a hint of Frankensteinian menace.

Thinking I can easily ride under this cloud bar and out again before it breaks, I leave Victoria West behind and rush on. Then, just as I am about to congratulate myself on one more storm avoided, the road swings to the west and I find myself still under the cloud and headed to the very heart of it. Still gambling, I think maybe it will break and disperse before I get to it, and so I pass Beaufort West as well and keep going. Quite unexpectedly, in late afternoon, it breaks on top of me, a roaring mass of rain and wind laced with lightning.

I seem to be in the heart of the cumulus, and the forces are terrifying. Inches of water rise immediately on the road. I have to stop, and shelter under the umbrella. The wind snatches it from me, and I recover it with difficulty. Lightning is exploding everywhere, and I am seriously concerned about being hit. Rivers of brown water are already racing down either side of the road, and for half an hour I have to stand there and wait for the clouds to empty themselves. The rain lets up only as the last light fails, and I continue in the dark, damp and anxious to stop. The first town, Laingsburg, seems to lie downhill from the highway on a series of descending terraces. In the darkness, and still under the influence of the storm and the mountains, they remind me somehow of a Hieronymus Bosch painting. There is something bizarre going on down there. I arrive to find myself in a plague of locusts. The air is thick with them, crashing about in the fluorescent light, a wild, mad scene. They crunch disgustingly underfoot and one hits me in the eye, quite painfully, before I can get inside the hotel.

Kimberley to Laingsburg is 461 miles. That leaves me with only

170 miles to go to Cape Town. I like to arrive early in big cities, so that I can get a feel for them and relax a bit before it gets dark. Also I have people to find, friends of friends. I'm up and away just after dawn, planning to have breakfast at Touws River and fill up for the last lap. When I get there it hits me. I forgot it was Saturday. No gas. I last filled up fifty miles before Laingsburg. That leaves me just two liters short of what I need.

No one at Touws River can help – there is hardly anyone there, anyway. I ride to Worcester, another forty-five miles, through a lovely valley planted with vineyards. The last range of mountains is piling up ahead of me now. There's a tremendous crosswind blowing too, and I have to lean right into it as I go, but it's steady and no real problem. I can feel the approach of a milder climate, and an easier life. More houses, gardens, people.

Worcester has a very nice small hotel. Its name is the Arab word for hotel, but the owners don't know it and seem unsure whether to believe me. They are very helpful though and, at last, we find a legal way out of my fuel problem. The man next door lets me take two liters out of his lawn mower. Breakfast is a great pleasure, and everything is feeling very good. I am letting it creep into my conscious mind now that very soon I may actually come to the other end of Africa. It is not certain. I don't allow myself such expectations. Many things can happen in eighty miles, but it is a distinct probability.

I have a very confused impression of Cape Town. I imagine that I am now on Table Mountain, and that when I come to the edge I shall look down on the city, but the valley soon narrows and I come to a pass called Du Toit's Kloof. On the other side I look down from five thousand feet to land that looks fertile and busy with farms, vineyards, prosperous towns, with the ocean still hidden by the haze. I free wheel for miles and miles to save gas and feel my heart lightening all the way. Somehow I know I'm going to make it, and that Cape Town is going to be wonderful. It is a rare and beautiful feeling, that certainty that nothing can go wrong.

The great freeways sweep me on past Stellenbosch and Belleville towards the ocean, into the suburbs of Cape Town, winding me down effortlessly and without error as though on an automatic flight path to the heart of the old city and setting me down in the plaza beside the ocean. My joy is almost hysterical as I park the bike, walk slowly over the paving towards a cafe table and sit down. I have just ridden that motorcycle 12,245 miles from London, and absolutely nobody here, watching me, knows it. As I think about it I have a sudden and quite extraordinary flash, something I never had before and am never able to recapture again. I see the whole of Africa in one single vision, as though illuminated by lightning. And that's it. I've done it. I'm at peace.

Among bright flowers and flights of shimmering blue and green birds I came over the high mountains from Swaziland and down to Mozambique on April 28. The *Zoe G* was due to sail on May 3.

There was the friend of a friend in Lourenço Marques, but I arrived too late to find him. In the twilight I searched for the hotel that a casual acquaintance had suggested, enjoying my first experience of a Portuguese colonial city, and getting lost.

Four kids stood idly on the pavement outside a bar and I asked for the Carlton hotel. The one who answered me was the natural leader of the group, and about sixteen. He wore a very short, tight red sweater and flared trousers the color of strawberry ice cream running down the inside of a trash can.

"Hi man," he said, with an indefinable mixture of strange accents. "How ya doin'? I'm sure glad to meet you. Sure man. We're all friends here. We don't care about the color here. I'm just at school. Sure. But I'm in the bar here, fuckin' plenty of businesswomen. Plenty, sure. Businesswomen from Mozambique. Sure."

His face was smooth and brown under a woolly black fleece, and his breath smelled of whisky. He didn't stop talking. His three companions clung to him silently, hoping to learn the trick. One was a white Portuguese with a sensitive face, and the others were wispy in-between kids. I mentioned the name of the hotel again.

"Oh you want a room to sleep. Sure, I can show you. Great place. All South Africans go there. That one you talkin' about is shit, man. That all Portuguese shit, shouting and noise. I show you. I can take you all right. Maybe fifty 'scud, I don't know. It was, three months ago. We are smoking too, man, you know? Grass. Green grass. You know what I mean?"

We set off along the streets, dark and deserted. As we walked, one after another they opened their trousers and sprayed the pavements and the walls with wide arcs of silver piss.

Across the Republica and up two blocks we turned into a doorway and up a green and brown stairwell to the first floor. Two Africans sat in chairs facing the stairs, backs to the wall, with a table between them. The nearest one had large holes in his earlobes, but they were empty and he was dressed for business. His skin was hard and dry and close-pored like old walnut. He wouldn't speak English although he plainly understood it.

His price was 120 escudos for the night. For Portuguese it was only fifty, but for South Africans and lesser foreigners it was 120. That was a fixed price, he said, the same all over, and could not be altered in any circumstances. For this price I would get one of four army beds in a nine-foot-square cell. Each one was 120 'scud, which meant he was looking for £12 or $28 a night, plus a free meal for his insects. The effrontery of it had me laughing all the way down the stairs. My whisky-drinking, grass-smoking, businesswoman fucking schoolboy friend seemed rather crestfallen. But he put on a brave show. He maintained that all peoples should be treated alike, and that economic discrimination between races was a gross injustice. In consequence he said he was unable to persuade me to accept the price.

The Carlton, when I found it, was just what I wanted, a big old-fashioned hotel with a bustling restaurant in the Latin style downstairs. The handsome double room for ninety escudos seemed like a gift after the previous offer, but it was still a lot of money.

The following day I resumed the search for the friend of my friend, and found him in his shoe shop. He took me for lunch to the Clube de Pesca, and we sat at the bar playing dice while his fishing cronies told filthy jokes and stories about the war. Everyone was talking about the war. It was obviously coming to a crisis. When I was in Salisbury I had had a firsthand account, clearly authentic, of the true position of the Frelimo independence movement in Mozambique, and it was clear that the Frelimo were more advanced than anyone in white Africa believed. It would have to end soon, somehow.

The man next to me at the bar started telling me about it, swearing boastfully in Portuguese Afrikaans English, which is in itself ugly enough not to need emphasis.

"I was in it bladdy three and a half years. That's a bladdy long time. I tell you, we were losing men all the bladdy time, man. Maybe one man a day. Well, there's four bladdy lots like our fuckers, so that's four bladdy men a day, so in seven bladdy years, man, we lost a lot of bladdy men."

There were already rumors of crisis in Lisbon about the losses sustained by the Portuguese in Angola and Mozambique, and the white Portuguese colonists were not happy either. They were milked economically by Portugal and believed that, given their own independence, they could do a deal with Frelimo.

"The bladdy worst was, we couldn't bladdy fight the fuckers. They had bladdy grenades and Kalashnikovs and bazookas and bladdy mortars behind, and they would bladdy kill some of our fuckers and then bladdy run away.

"We were walking forty bladdy miles in a day looking for the fuckers, but when we find them we can't shoot them, we got to bladdy bring them in to question. That's no bladdy good!"

A satisfied grin crossed his face then, as he swallowed his drink.

"Not the navy men, though. They were bladdy good. They landed and bladdy shot everything. They didn't care if it was us or the bladdy enemy. They kill anybody, you just get out the bladdy way."

I could see his point. I thought that maybe, after three or four years of being shot at, I might want to kill everything in sight too.

Remarkably enough, the very next day the army in Portugal overthrew the old dictatorship, and Mozambique began its first revolution as though for my benefit. There were passionate meetings in streets, squares and cafes. Veins throbbed and fists clenched as orators screamed about independence, liberty, autonomy, equality and so on. It was noisy but peaceful, a largely white affair of leaflets and polemics, and the colony was given self-governing status, but the war with Frelimo continued.

My sailing date was postponed from day to day, as the *Zoe G* waited for a loading berth. I spent time with journalists who had flown in from London, but felt remarkably remote from them and, I know, looked like a freak to them. Other times I spent in Rajah's Snack Bar, a splendid Indian establishment where I was received almost as a son, played innumerable games of chess and consumed unnumbered *sambusas*, most of them free. Rajah himself felt none of the euphoria of the white population. He foresaw great trouble and could not quite decide whether or not to cut his losses and go. It was the

Indians in Mozambique, as elsewhere in Africa, who saw a political reality that few others recognized, but theirs was a sterile understanding, for they never joined in the process either way but stood on the sidelines, self-made outcasts, consoled by their profits.

Another Indian I got to know a little was the shipping clerk in charge of manifests at the agent's office. He took me to the *Zoe G* the day before she was due to sail. First we walked past the station, with its swollen Baroque cupola, blown up just beyond the limits of decency like an over-ripe fruit. The whole thing was a piece of pure Lisbon dropped from heaven on the shores of Africa. Facing it stood a heroic stone mother figure, bearing Portugal's burdens with a sorrowful expression. She might have been welcoming new comers. More likely, I thought, she was wishing she too could catch a train and get the hell out of there.

Beyond the station were the dock gates, and then the endless sheds, and rolling stock and heaps of everything under the sun, including rubbish and flies. The *Zoe G*, when I first saw her, dented my morale severely. Evidently she could float, because she was tied up at the quayside, and wobbled as they put a thousand tons of copper aboard her, but it seemed unlikely that she would float for long before the rust gave way somewhere to the sea. Not a clear painted surface or a gleam of brass could I discern anywhere.

Under the night-loading lights a great chasm gaped in her deck among the debris. In its depths, black stevedores in khaki shorts chanted and heaved among sleeper-sized bars of metal. There was some magic down there, but in the saloon were only sleazy seamen in attitudes of despair. I dumped my bags and fled.

Next day, Amade the clerk and I returned before dark, and things did not look quite so bad. I was shown a cabin, the "owner's cabin," which was far better than I expected, and had a small drawing room attached, and a proper bathroom, dilapidated but very acceptable. In its better days this ship, once Danish, would have been entirely suitable to Agatha Christie. It had had accommodation for twelve passengers and a miniature grand staircase sweeping down to a saloon with engraved glass swing doors. If it was now more appropriate to Graham Greene that was, in a sense, all to the good.

I sat later in the captain's office and talked to Amade as we waited. The captain, in cream shirt and gray flannels with a zip that wouldn't quite close, was tapping out letters on a prewar Standard

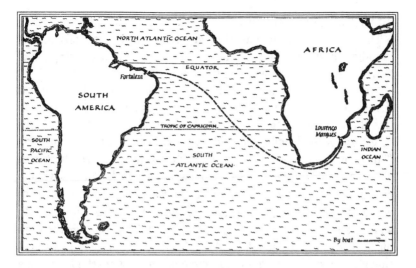

typewriter and filling in forms. Amade had noted the loading for fuel and water, the draught fore and aft, the anticipated mean draught at Fortaleza and the expected time of arrival.

"Where is Fortaleza?" I asked.

"In the north of Brazil," he said. "You will call there first."

It was the first I had heard of it, and an idea slowly formed that I might get off there instead.

We went on talking about the future for Mozambique.

"There will be trouble," said Amade. "You will see. You will hear about it. There will be no arrangement with Frelimo. There will be bloodshed."

He was a tall Portuguese Indian with a liquid charm and a wry smile suggesting always that behind the apparent reality lay an altogether different reality which promised little good. He listened politely to my counter-arguments, but they carried no weight and didn't convince me either. The poignancy was overwhelming.

"I was four years in the army fighting the war," he said. "I left university to go to the army. When I finished fighting I gave up study, there was no time anymore. It was necessary to put my feet on the ground. Now I am married. I have children. Am I going back to the army now? We can fight this war for four, eight, twelve, sixteen years, but we will have to give it away in the end."

The pilot appeared in the doorway, bearded in a heavy coat. He was shrouded in darkness and mystery, a portentous figure.

"Are you ready, Captain?"

The ship had been shivering gently for hours, a soft, almost inaudible rustle in the paneling, like the breath of a sleeping child, flowing and ebbing, flowing and ebbing.

Amade uncrossed his legs and smiled encouragingly at me as though it were I and not he who was facing the miserable uncertainties of Africa. We shook hands and he jumped ashore from the rail.

"Go up on the bridge," he said. "You will see it better from there.

"The pilot was on the bridge with the captain. Above them was another open deck where the funnel simmered. I heard the whistle and chatter of walkie-talkies and the stern swung clear of the bows of the next ship in line. Amade, on the quayside, gave a last wave and walked away across the sidings, away from the lights, over the coal-black dust, into the night shadow of the yard. I'm going to Rio, I thought. He's going nowhere. An immense sadness reached out to me and faded as he moved out of sight among the goods wagons.

Over the starboard side a long tugboat was hauling the stern into the harbor. My excitement surged up in a choking flood, as I saw the full line of vessels stretched out in both directions as far as my vision could stretch, all brilliant, glowing under a thousand lanterns, tantalizing, promising joy, like department stores at Christmas time, like a giant fairground. Nothing, I felt, gladdens the heart like lights shining in the darkness. I was so overjoyed that I leapt up and down and shouted, wondering what the captain below would make of my antics.

The tug let go of the stern and its bulbous, padded nose slid along the shore side of the ship and rammed into the bows, chugging furiously, swinging us around to point to sea. Behind me the funnel belched, and the ship's Burmeister engines took the strain. The tugboat streaked away to port, flaunting her power.

Ahead a trail of blue-flashing marker buoys perforated the black water leading out past other floating fairylands at anchor.

The prospect of Brazil, the pleasure of seeing massive objects in effortless motion, the lights which leave so much to the imagination, all this was a benign magic shaping the world for my special pleasure. My first great sea voyage had begun.

I woke feeling fine although the ship was already wallowing in a heavy swell, and sat down with confidence to a breakfast of eggs and bacon at seven. By ten a gale was blowing, the sea was much bigger and I was beginning to feel uneasy. The ship was seesawing and rolling heavily. With alarming speed I was launched into full scale seasickness, which I had never experienced before.

There was only one place where I could bear to stand, on the starboard gangway at the pivotal point of the pitch. There, at least, the possibilities for violent motion were reduced by one. Exhaustion eventually forced me to try lying down, but my stomach went into a floating wobble, something gripped my throat, my mouth flooded with saliva, like a beast of prey at full kill, and there was just time to get to the rail. The croaking, despairing noise that issued with my breakfast was the worst of it.

In the brief moment of peace that followed I took up my station on the gangway again watching the sea. It was in an unbelievable turmoil. Lumps of black water with white crests rushed about in aimless fury, colliding with each other. The wind whipped up spray, the clouds discharged rain, the two met and the sky and sea merged all around me in a swirling fusion of air and water.

It was impossible not to think of the sea as alive. There was a life force at work in it. The waves were mere cloaks for Neptune's raiders as they tore about below the surface, and the crests were a froth whipped up by their tridents. The *Zoe G* was some four hundred feet long and weighed about four thousand tons. She rode up on the swell and fell again through at least thirty degrees. When she came down to hammer the sea with her bows, the sea rushed off screaming vengeance and pain, showing vivid bruises of pale blue where the ship's hull had smashed air and water together so hard that they remained entangled in the wake as far as one could see.

Looking down into all this made me grasp the rail very tight. I knew nothing could survive in that cauldron, and I thought my ordeal would never end. It gave me only the slightest satisfaction to know that the ship's engineer was as sick as I was and, with a belly twice the size of mine, was presumably twice as uncomfortable.

The next day was clear and blue, the sea was calmer, but I was unable to eat anything until the evening. Most of all I was afraid of sitting down in the saloon, which was heavily permeated by the smell of diesel oil and cooking.

I picked nervously at a tomato salad. It went down with no trouble at all. Every mouthful made me stronger. There's roast lamb with garlic and greasy roast potatoes but nothing can stop me now. Beer as well. Delicious. Marvelous. It's over!

The great gale (and it was an unusually violent one, they told me) was like purgatory before paradise. The Southern Ocean was blue and mild, under scattered cloud, as we floated around the coast of South Africa. I was the only passenger and passed my days happily on deck teaching myself Spanish, watching the big sea birds that came to swoop around the ship and contemplating my journey and its meaning.

On the fourth day, Cape Town, veiled in gray mist, drifted past to starboard. I stared at it as though at a fairyland doomed to vanish under a spell, feeling the most painful regret. Then we floated free into the Atlantic and began the long sweep up to the equator.

Those days were among the most precious of the journey. To balance the discipline of learning a new language I was reading *Memories, Dreams and Reflections* by Jung, given to me by a friend in Cape Town whose perceptiveness I was now beginning to appreciate.

The book met my needs in the most extraordinary way, dealing so freely with thoughts and feelings outside the realms of logic and reason. All through Africa I had felt growing in me the belief that what was going on around me, the weather, the sudden appearances of animals and birds, the way I was received by people along the way, was somehow connected to my own inner life. Here was a man of great experience and erudition not only discussing the subject and describing similar experiences from his own life, but actually providing a word for it which he had himself coined: "synchronicity," meaning, for example, "when an inwardly perceived event is seen to have correspondence in external reality."

What, all my life, I would have called foolish superstition was being pressed gently home to me by my own experience and interpreted for me by Jung. The book goes much further, of course, into ideas of afterlife and a collective unconscious. All of them connected precisely with thoughts that had come spontaneously out of the journey. I was specially startled to read Jung's remarks about mythology and the need of the individual to have some story or myth by which he can explain those things which reason and logic cannot account for. It seemed to me then that I had been close to the truth in thinking of my role as a "myth-maker," and not just for myself perhaps.

The book encouraged me immensely, and I spent a large part of the ten-day Atlantic crossing re-examining my past life and writing furiously about my discoveries. At the same time I took ever greater delight in the creatures that appeared around the ship as it moved into warmer waters. A particular albatross that followed us seemed to have become quite familiar with me, and soared close by me again and again, showing me his broad white breast and the immense wings which he (or she) used so brilliantly. Flying fish sprang from the waves, like small bejeweled rockets, dashing over the water for seconds at a time, their wing-like fins whirring with an almost invisible swiftness.

At night the Pleiades appeared clear and bright to remind me of the magic of Sudan, and my dreams were rich with mysterious symbolism.

One event then crowned that whole series of discoveries and reflections. I had come to a point in my thoughts where one day, on the deck, it seemed to me that I had uncovered a fact about myself and the world, a way of looking at my relationship with others, that promised a great liberation.

"If I can just fix this thought," I told myself, "I shall find a wonderful new freedom for myself."

At that same instant, below me in the sea, a great shoal of flying fish burst out into the sunlight. It was an incredible display that described exactly how I was just then feeling. Up to then I had never seen more than one or two fish at a time, nor did I ever again. It was a dream come true.

Brazilian fishermen on their sailing raft photographed in the bay at Fortaleza as I arrived on the *Zoe G*. This craft must be the precursor of the wind-surfer. It is cheap to make and efficient, but highly dangerous in a storm. Even so, the impoverished *pescadores* often stay at sea overnight, unwilling to return without a catch.

America

Land was nearby and the world was closing in, muffling sounds and thoughts. Thick humid air pressed around the ship and bore it up between ocean and sky. Clouds of silver and lead boiled above, speared like marshmallows on the slanting rays of a mid-morning sun. A soupy green sea slurped softly below. I stood above the bridge waiting for South America to appear.

Perhaps I was expecting the whole continent to come over the skyline in a simultaneous rush of cathedrals, revolutions, llamas and carnivals. Instead I saw the horizon thicken into smudges of dark green and brown. We drifted in. The smudges stretched but remained low. A last flying fish swooped over the waves. I caught the movement from the corner of my eye and moved just in time to follow it at the end of its course. That streaking spray of light had become as charged with mystery and hope as a shooting star. I felt a great reluctance to leave the ship and wished I could go on dreaming of a landfall that never came.

A line of buildings appeared at the ocean's edge, and I made out two or three spires pricking the pale sky. I forgot about South America and began to think about Fortaleza, on the northeast coast of Brazil, four degrees south of the equator, and five hundred miles east of the Amazon. More than a million inhabitants, they had told me, and yet I had never heard of it. I felt that I had slipped off the edge of my customary world.

A red cutter came popping towards us and the *Zoe G* slowed to let the little boat nudge alongside. The harbor pilot came aboard. He was a disappointment too. He did not even look Latin. We swung to port and headed for another part of the coast where I could already see a grain silo and some cranes. The shoreline embraced us and I saw that we were in a broad bay. The only other craft in motion were narrow rafts, four logs lashed together with a rudder and sail. Most of them carried one or two men; small men, barefooted, in chain-store nylon shirts and trousers. The shirts were loose, open and torn. The trousers were baggy at the behind, narrow at the legs, short at the ankles, patched and split. They were fishermen, of course, *pescadores*. A raft came by no bigger than the others but crowded with people, shoulder to shoulder. Even as I watched I knew it was a physical impossibility that it should stay afloat, and realized that in this new world there were also new laws.

I should have been excited by the prospect of landing, but I found that I was nervous. Maybe I had a premonition, although it did not figure consciously as such. I simply balked at the complexity of the process that lay ahead of me, knowing that the motorcycle would create difficulties and involve me in long and painful exposure to bureaucracy. I had two prejudices about Brazil: that the bureaucracy was totally corrupt, and that the police were violent and suspicious, particularly where journalists were concerned. Although I was not traveling as a journalist, my connection with the *Sunday Times* would have to be declared since they were guaranteeing the bond on the motorcycle. I felt wrong-footed. Vividly in my mind were accounts of police brutality and torture that I had heard in London. Like all strong prejudices they not only prepared me for the worst. They paved the way.

Captain Fafoutis already had the crew at work opening the hatches. Winches whirred. Derricks clattered into position. Deck hands hammered and shouted. There were four massive tarpaulins to lift, wedges to knock out, planks to throw about, girders to hoist and lower and temporary hatch covers to position so that a sudden shower could not destroy the cargo in the holds. The ship rattled and banged from stem to stern.

At sea the *Zoe G* had begun to seem quite respectable, even passing fair, with her freshly painted green decks and white bulkheads, the rust and grime effaced and the filth of Lourenço Marques washed away by the Cape gales. Now her corsets were coming undone again. She opened her mouth and showed her blackened stumps, and the satisfied hum of her engine gave way to raucous dockside obscenities. At sea she was a lady, but in port she was a trollop.

Her holds were about to be raped of fifty thousand bags of cashew nuts, each bag weighing as much as an average man. It was supposed to be done in two days and the job meant hauling out the bags at the rate of eighteen a minute for forty-eight hours nonstop.

They had to be loaded onto trucks and carted off to a warehouse. Was anyone in Fortaleza capable of running such an operation? Captain Fafoutis shrugged. "If not," he said, "they will have to pay penalty."

The docks were more clearly in view: A row of big gray sheds, the silo, a cobbled quay, the rails running along it, the big traveling crane on its four stiff legs like a great creature frozen in prehistory.

One other ship, smaller and rustier than the *Zoe G*, lay there tied up and lifeless. The sky was uniformly gray now, and heavy. Soon it would rain.

The ship winched herself alongside, a rough gangplank went down and the port doctor came aboard, followed soon after by a stream of officials. I went back to my cabin to gather the last few things together, and felt a slight sense of panic at something being irrevocably over, felt the powerful attraction of this little floating universe of peeling veneer, frayed cloth, unvarying routine and familiar faces. I peered into the captain's cabin, next to my own. The atmosphere had become so dense with smoke and dealing that it oozed illegality like a prohibition honky-tonk. I wanted badly to be part of what was going on next door, to be one of the gang.

I went out to look down on the quay and saw a small wooden table move past below me. It was covered by a transparent plastic pyramid that shielded a display of colored souvenirs and shells. As it moved along, the sandals of the man beneath it became visible, and he parked it against a wall and fussed over it with a duster. Another man in torn cotton clothing arranged custard apples against the colossal steel base of the traveling crane. They resembled green hand grenades, and he handled them with appropriate delicacy.

Trucks were already arriving from the dock gates, and stevedores poured into the ship over the gangplank. Within minutes the derricks began rumbling and the first net full of bags swung up from number two hold, with numbers one and three soon discharging too. The bags came up a ton at a time, with three trucks loading together, and a fleet lined up and waiting. Somebody, I saw, was determined to beat the penalty.

Eventually a deck hand came to fetch me to be interviewed by the police. I followed him to the gangway outside the captain's cabin, where two men stood watching the unloading. They were ridiculously sinister, figures from a fantasy. They belonged to an age of crime which I thought had long since passed, and which to be truthful I thought had only been got up for films and television. The boss was a big ungainly man in a black leather jacket. He wore dark glasses with shiny metal rims, and his face was not only swarthy, pockmarked and scarred, but disfigured by lumps large enough to rival his natural features. He seemed to draw on two quite separate traditions of violence and could have been cast as a hit man for Himmler. His companion was stunted and weasel-faced, and could only be described as a sidekick.

However, they were quite civil, and asked me to fill in a form typed on a piece of rough paper. Among other things it had a space for my mother's Christian names. Then we went to my cabin to inspect my things. The big man was jovial enough but spoke no English, and the little man translated clumsily. They asked me several times about "scuba." They were determined that I had underwater diving equipment somewhere and my denials obviously surprised them. They seemed baffled and suspicious. After a little while they asked me to go ashore and have my passport stamped.

I walked along the quay, on firm ground again, absorbed in the strange illusion that the cobbles were sliding beneath my feet. Two more men in plain clothes received me in a wooden hut. Unlike the first pair they were not caricatures. The younger one introduced himself as Samuel and spoke school English, mostly in the present tense. He had a handwritten list of details he was supposed to get from me, and they included my mother's Christian names, which are a little unusual. I began to think of them assuming a life of their own and traveling forever in Brazilian official channels. My father's occupation was also demanded again, and I replied with overemphasis: "He is dead!" as though they had been caught walking on his grave. This, I found, gained a little extra respect, although in reality I had hardly known my father.

Samuel also asked about my diving equipment, but seemed content to hear that there was none. He then gave me the same form to complete as I had already filled in on the ship, and it included all the questions he had just asked me. I did it without comment. It seemed pointless to object to frontier officials wasting one's time, since they are perfectly placed to waste as much of it as they wish. One just tried to make sure that patience was not seen as servility, a fine distinction.

In all this life-consuming rigmarole of irrelevancies, common to all frontiers, one new fact stood out clearly: The idea of going round the world on a motorcycle meant nothing to these men. It was doubtful even whether they believed me, and their disbelief disturbed me more than it should have done. I expected people to look at me and know that I was genuine. Without this tribute I became cold and defensive. How else could I explain my presence, my strange clothing? Like a real cowboy stumbling accidentally into a fancy dress party, I wanted to shoot to prove my gun was loaded.

My passport kindled some interest. It had already been stamped through fourteen pages of visas in Africa, and the police lingered long over the Arabic and Amharic scripts. Finally, on page nineteen, I got my stamp: BRASIL ENTRADA 22.05.74 TURISTA, signed João Z de Oliveira Costa.

"Can I go now?" I asked.

"You are free to go anywhere," said Samuel. This proved quite soon to be a wild exaggeration.

My cabin was still locked as I had left it, but I saw immediately that someone had been searching my things. A tube of salt tablets was lying loose on the bed. Whoever had looked did not care whether I knew. Nothing appeared to be missing. Had they been looking for drugs? Or was it another attempt to discover my diving gear? I began, even then, to think I might be walking into a trap, but the idea seemed hysterical and I tried to dismiss it.

With Captain Fafoutis I shared a taxi into town, and we followed the shoreline around the bay. I had never been anywhere that looked so wet. It was not the quantity of water that impressed me, but rather the way it seemed to have permeated everything. It covered the road in lakes, partially concealing great subsidences. In other places sand bars lay across our path, swept down from the dunes on the left. The buildings alongside seemed sodden to the point of dissolution, their stone surfaces eroded and spongy, their plaster long since fallen away. We drove a long way, slithering and bouncing. The people on the sidewalks, moving along their own obstacle course, did nothing to lift my spirits. Their tobacco-colored skin was all that distinguished them to my jaundiced eye from the population of any industrial suburb, with their downcast faces and ill-fitting, mass-produced clothing.

The shipping agent's office was of the old-fashioned brown variety. With different furniture it could as well have been a bedroom or a salon. The agent, an elderly man, listened impassively as though I were a young nephew reciting my homework. My loose shirt and jeans, and the funny belt with the pouch on it, did not qualify me as a serious client.

"The customs need a bank guarantee against the importation of the motorcycle," I told him, "and this guarantee is being provided by the *Sunday Times* in London. You have heard of it, perhaps? The newspaper?"

His expression indicated a mounting distaste. I hurried on.

"The guarantee was lodged in Rio de Janeiro. Now I must tell them to have it transferred here to Fortaleza."

The agent began to turn away towards the door.

"So I would like, with your help, to send a telex message, unless" – I caught sight of a telephone – "unless perhaps I could telephone."

This last remark seemed to penetrate where nothing else had.

"Impossible," he said.

"I would reverse the charges, of course."

"It is impossible," he repeated with a voice like a rubber stamp.

The telephone was one of those ancient models with the mouthpiece on a stalk like a Bakelite rose. It did not seem adequate for reaching London, and I let the idea go.

"Well, when can I get a telex message off?" I asked.

"You will not get through," he said.

"Why not?" I asked.

"Impossible," he said. "You must use the telex."

"Yes," I said. "I would like to send a telex message. Do you have telex?"

"Of course," he said.

"When can I use it?"

"It is too late," he said. "Please wait." And he left the room.

I sat down in a brown chair and considered how much time I should donate to this useless exercise in order to make sure that the agent did not actually block my progress. I roughed out a short message to the *Sunday Times*, and allowed the agent to enter and leave the room once without demanding his attention. When he returned ten minutes later I felt I had shown enough humility and asked him where the telex machine was. He avoided the question and left the room again, but an elderly clerk was obliged to remain and I harassed him with questions about time differences and routing details until, in frustration at not being able to understand me or dispose of me, he took me downstairs to the street and into another office a few doors along. Within this office was yet another smaller office, and when the door was opened, icy air struck me, freezing my sweaty shirt to my skin.

Where before I had seen only brown wooden desks, I now saw green metal filing cabinets. A young man in a tight-fitting suit, and a shirt with shootable cuffs, was using a telephone of recent design. Through the hum I heard a pronounced "clack" that focused my eyes immediately on a bright new telex machine chattering its pre-taped message to its remote counterpart across the globe.

Walter Sá, the son of the owner, was a grave and fashionable young man who spoke good English and, apparently, also got things done, for he was the man in charge of beating the penalty at the *Zoe G.* He agreed immediately to send my message. He warned me that there might be no line open until later, and I should not expect a reply before the following day.

I should have thanked him cordially, relaxed and left his refrigerated office to go about my proper business, which was getting used to the climate, seeing something of the strange city and learning the language. I did not. What I had already seen of the town depressed me. The strange behavior of the police frightened me. I wanted to get away from both, but as long as the bike was locked up in the customs shed I could not move. I became obsessed by the need to speed up the process, and could think of nothing else. I sat for hours in the artificial atmosphere of Sá's office watching the clock, willing the channels to London to open, willing the message to arrive, willing the answer to return there and then. It was absurd. The message went out as expected at 4 P.M.; that was 7 P.M. in London, and too late for a reply to be possible until the next day.

My back was stiff with tension, and the chill air had done it no good. I took a token walk up the hill into town, but my heart was not in it. Torrents of rainwater were rushing down the street, making a muddy river over wildly uneven surfaces of flagstone, cobble, cement and earth. Halfway up the hill was a bridge being either restored or demolished, it was hard to know which. Above me loomed a gray granite wall retaining the embanked garden of a colonial fort, and on the wall stood a soldier, wearing a waterproof cape and carrying a rifle. As I passed he gave me a malevolent stare, locking on the wallet at my waist. So, I noticed, did others. I began to learn that in this part of America one thing you looked for on a stranger was a gun.

Then the clouds began to weep again, and I lost what heart I had and scuttled back to the ship in a taxi. The shower had stopped when I arrived. The storm covers were being removed from the hatches and the cashews were swinging out. The work continued under flood-lights through the night. My dreams were modified to include the rhythmic rumbling of the derricks, and the pace of it kept my own anxiety alive.

In the morning, over an oily egg fried in garlic, which I had come to appreciate, I learned that I would have to leave the ship that day. The *Zoe G* was expected to sail the following morning before dawn. I took a taxi back to the agent's office but there was no message, and I took another aimless walk into town. It was a shock to discover that the Spanish I had learned was no use at all. Even when I read out the Portuguese words from a menu at a fruit-juice counter I could not make myself understood, a blow to my self-esteem because I had always been good at picking up the "feel" of a language. In revenge I developed a senseless dislike of Portuguese and determined not to bother with it, telling myself that I would soon be in Spanish-speak-ing America and that to learn Portuguese was a waste of time.

As soon as I reasonably could, I returned to the shipping office and sat, frozen inwardly and out, waiting. They were patient and toler-ant. I was offered frequent little cups of sweet black coffee, *called-cafesinho,* and bottles of Fanta.

Shortly before mid-day the message came.

It was in three parts.

The bank guarantee had been arranged with the Banco do Brasil in Rio de Janeiro.

I was introduced to Father Walsh at the Acão Social of São Raimundo, with an address and a telephone number.

It was suggested that I go to a town called Iguatú, where there had been a serious flood disaster, and write about it.

I was delighted to have some information that might lead to the release of the motorcycle, for the bike was the key to my freedom. The introduction to the priest, who I gathered must be a Catholic missionary, promised at least a foothold on this slippery shore, and gave something more to look forward to than bureaucratic entangle-ments.

The reference to Iguatú scared me. I had no doubt that telex messages were monitored by the police. In due course they would read that the *Sunday Times* had asked me to report on a flood disaster in the state of Ceará. "This," they would say, "is an odd way for a tourist to be carrying on. Let's ask him again where he's hidden his snorkel. Or something."

Sá gave me the use of his phone, and I dialed the number in the telex. A woman's voice sang in my ear.

"*Quem esta falando?*"

The words meant nothing to me, and I asked for Padre Walsh. There were some scuffling sounds, and a man came to the telephone who by pure chance turned out to be Walsh. I explained how I had heard of him. In a brisk, young voice with a powerful Irish inflection he established quickly where I was and what I needed, and arranged to meet me with a car an hour later.

"If I'm not there on the dot, don't worry. I'll be stopped somewhere on the way with my head under the bonnet. We have the most egregious collection of cars you'll ever see. I'll bring the *jatāon–* that means jet liner – it's a flashy performer but it has black moods."

The *jatāo* was on schedule. Walsh leaned across the empty seat to shout my name through the window.

I liked the look of him immediately. He was a vigorous man of about thirty in a loose shirt and sandals with a friendly but shrewd face. I climbed into the green VW and he suggested lunch before I had even begun to wonder how to mention it. We went to a fish restaurant on the beach. The food was delicious, the beer was good and cold and Walsh was a grand talker. His speech came fast and furious and often his accent made it hard for me to catch, but by the end of lunch he had illuminated the political landscape of northern Brazil, the Church's history, the changes forced upon it and the present role, as he saw it, of a Catholic priest in Ceará. He was witty, comprehensive and wonderfully free of humbug or pious rectitude.

Perhaps the major surprise for a pagan like myself was that he concentrated so thoroughly on the pragmatic approach. As a reaction to the shameful history of the Church's indifference to its poor flock, it was refreshing. When Walsh spoke about the Church or his mission it was with the excitement of someone engrossed in a stupendous theatrical production, though whether as actor, director, stage manager or critic was unclear. Presumably the show was put on for the greater glory of God, but the presumption remained tacit. Walsh had one criterion for a smash hit, and that was, "Would it send the people away better off?"

He seemed (and I surely wronged him here) to care nothing for that part of his duties which required him to wear his cassock unless it made money.

"You should see our Wednesday novena," he said. "The Wednesday Show, continuous performances through the day, the most fashionable thing in town. All the cream of Fortaleza is there. The takin's are somethin' glorious."

The takings went to support social welfare schemes and were spent on things as prosaic as food, clothing, building materials and tools for self-help projects. I listened bemused and grateful for the torrent of information. If I spoke at all it was token stuff to show my appreciation and give the man a breather. I showed him my telex message, and mentioned my fears. To his credit he did not try to convince me that they were groundless, but simply suggested putting them away since there was nothing to do about them anyway. In his company that seemed a most natural and intelligent course to take.

He drove me to the docks and helped me to fetch my things. A measure of his influence was that the *Zoe G*, which that morning had felt like home, now looked the seedy old freighter she would always be when viewed from shore. I said some farewells to the crew, trying to breathe a little of the old camaraderie into them, but the replies were so offhand that I saw I had long ago been unloaded and forgotten in their minds, relegated to that other world which the *Zoe G* always sailed away from sooner or later.

Walsh and I rattled off to São Raimundo on an endless and tortuous route. At times we seemed to drive out into the country, only to plunge again into some waterlogged and sand-strewn suburb. The greater part of the city consisted of single-storeyed brick buildings undulating and crumbling on loose foundations. I felt the earth was determined to shake itself loose of an unwanted encumbrance.

Towards the end we ran along a major road whose surface had all but disappeared, with ditches running alongside and across it. There were cars and many taxis on the road, all looking as though they had been recovered from the wreckers yard. They flashed as the sun struck the multifaceted dents in their body work, and the doors jiggled visibly in their frames. They slalomed skillfully but recklessly, in a triumph of temperament over common sense, because vehicles in Brazil were supremely expensive.

We climbed a sandy embankment, crossed a railway line, stumbled over some more ditches and arrived at São Raimundo.

For the next few days I ate with the priests, and slept in a hammock down the road in the caretaker's home. Antonio Sá, the caretaker, was a tall, happy man, brown-skinned and handsome, who lived with his wife and children in a small brick house. They ate in one room and slept in another, so the third room was available for letting. I shared it with another Englishman, Ian Dall, who was visiting São Raimundo, and we paid Antonio a few cruzeiros to help him out while he studied to become an electrician. Ian showed me how to use the hammock. It was a revelation to find that by lying diagonally across it, one could stretch out straight and be comfortable rather than be folded up like a banana.

The next day I presented myself at the Banco do Brasil to see about the guarantee. The bank took me by surprise. I had expected the older style of shabby and discreet banking. Here was a large airy banking hall full of up-to-date office machinery and animated people, promising bustle and efficiency. I found my way to the right official and explained my problem with a translator and several eager minions standing by. The man had a keen, expressionless face of European paleness. He wore spectacles finely framed to foster the impression of a man whose mind ranged far beyond his immediate responsibilities. His suit was an immaculate lightweight gray, and his shoes gleamed on the comfortable carpeting beneath his table. Above all I was struck by his opulent linen. His shirt and handkerchief had that soft and spotless luxury which only dedicated servants can provide and which no amount of Western money and machinery can duplicate.

He listened carefully and his entourage gazed on respectfully. Then he spoke. The translator informed me that what I wanted could not, unfortunately, be done. The official addressed himself to his papers, and the group obviously expected me to vanish marvelously without another word. The rudeness of it astonished me. I demanded an explanation, and the official raised his head and looked at me as though I really had reappeared from thin air. He smiled at some private and infinitely subtle joke and even laughed, lightly and delicately. He repeated that it would be "quite impossible," meaning that only a half-wit could have imagined otherwise. I still refused to evaporate, and was shunted off to others, but nobody seemed capable of even hinting at an explanation.

When I was finally ejected onto the pavement, I realized that the *Sunday Times* would have to start the process again from London, and I sent off another telex and prepared myself to wait.

São Raimundo consisted of the church, a large college for boys and girls and the parish house where Walsh lived with three or four other priests. The priests were strongly built Irishmen, chosen in part for their fitness. They had adopted Portuguese names and were known to their parishioners as Padres Mario, Eduardo, Brandão, Marcello and so on. The slightest of them all, physically, was Marcello, a visitor from a country parish who had come to Fortaleza some time back to convalesce from a long illness. We were passing the plastic box of corn flakes around the table at my second breakfast when I heard that he was returning the following day, by bus, to his parish in the interior.

"Where is that?" I asked idly.

"Iguatú," he said.

But for that chance I don't suppose I would have gone to Iguatú. Having the name thrust before me again in such a pointed way made it difficult to refuse, although quite whom I was planning to oblige I didn't know. The notion of allowing a degree of randomness in my movements was already established. My arrival in Fortaleza was itself a fateful accident, and I was intrigued to see how one happening led to another in such a way that, somewhere along the thread of events, it seemed as though a pattern was being woven. I felt impelled to let the pattern emerge, however ominous it seemed.

"Why don't you come and have a look?" Marcello added, as I knew he would. "It'll only cost you the bus fare."

"All right," I said, and lightly for Walsh's benefit: "Might as well be hung for a sheep as a lamb."

Iguatú is 250 miles from Fortaleza on the Jaguaribe River, and the journey took most of the day. The countryside moved past like an endlessly revolving backdrop of the same oil palms and swamps and glistening red laterite soil. Signs of that year's massive rainfall were everywhere visible. The road, newly built, was already broken and potholed, and in places had been swept away altogether so that we were in any case forced to take a longer route than usual.

There was a stop for lunch in a barnlike restaurant serving the staple Brazilian meal of steak, rice and coarse, floury *manioca* fried with the meat. After another short stop in the afternoon the bus arrived in Iguatú, just before dark.

That evening I sat in Father Marcello's small house brushing aside mosquitoes while he tried to give me some idea of the life of the people in his area.

Most of them are among the thirty or so million peasants in the north of Brazil who are as close to destitution as any in the world. Since they do not own the land, their condition is virtually feudal, and the tiny resources they have are sufficient only to see them through from one day to the next. When the great natural disasters occur they must succumb, and disasters in the tropics are as regular as the seasons. Cyclone, flood or drought take their toll annually, and because of this inescapable punishment, the victims have been known for generations as the *flagelados*.

Their original language is Guaraní, an Indian language that was widely spoken in Brazil, Argentina, Paraguay and parts of other neighboring countries. They are of Indian descent mixed with Portuguese, and have well-defined cheekbones and broad faces. They are short in stature and have fine smooth skin like toffee, delicately engraved by age.

Iguatú is a Guaraní word meaning beautiful water. It was on Sunday, 24 March, that the beautiful water had suddenly risen and flooded across the banks of the Jaguaribe. The flood lasted for three days and swept many houses away. During the following weeks the victims salvaged what they could from their ruins and took shelter temporarily in the already crowded houses that had survived. So far it had been an ordinary disaster. Then, on the third Sunday, the water rose again but this time much higher and much faster.

As with the first flood, the water took three days to subside. It had risen forty feet, to touch the lower girders of the big iron railroad bridge. Some people in a barge had been torn from their moorings and trapped for a while under the bridge. It was said that they had lost a child. Miraculously that would have been the only known casualty. The second flood left four hundred houses either ruined or totally demolished. Hundreds now had no place at all to take shelter, but on the following Thursday, before any useful measures could be taken to help them, the river rose yet again to its previous highest level.

I arrived a month later, towards the end of May. In a normal year the rains would have been over, the sky long since cleared and the soil already scorched and dusty in the heat of the dry season. But 1974 was exceptional, as I had already seen in Africa, and the sky was as gray and soggy as wet flannel.

Iguatú is a sizable small town of several thousand inhabitants with a pleasant and prosperous center, running rapidly to seed at the edges. It is built on higher ground on the south side of the river and was largely untouched by the flooding, although the river did undercut the bank in places and brought down a few improvised dwellings. The major part of the damage was on the lower north bank, where poorer people had access to land.

In the morning Marcello and I walked across the bridge to have a look. On the other side we followed a path that curved away to the left and brought us back to the river and an open sandy expanse littered with debris. It was here that hundreds of homes had recently stood. Most of them had been small two-roomed constructions, some built of brick and others of wattle and daub. The later houses, ostensibly stronger and made of brick, had collapsed altogether and nothing remained to show where they had once stood. There was a moral here somewhere.

It was obvious that the houses on these shallow banks invited destruction by their very presence. The people cut down the trees for building and for burning. They kept animals, a goat, a donkey, perhaps a cow, which denuded the ground of grasses and shrubs. When the river rose the soil slipped away like sand with nothing to bind it. The process must have happened many times, eating farther and farther into the land. There was only a limited area available to these people. Beyond were more prosperous houses with walled and fenced gardens.

We stopped by two old people who were recovering the round clay tiles from their ruined home. The house was now a transparent structure of wooden uprights supporting the roof, and the river had laid three feet of sand over the original floor level, so that the old man, short as he was, stood with his grizzled white head through the rafters looking at us across his own roof.

His name was Manuel Subino dos Santos, and he was a fine, tough old man with a dried and salted look. He told us that he was about seventy years old, sixty-eight or seventy, he was not quite sure. He wore a loose and faded blue tee-shirt and shorts, with a string of brown beads around his neck and some kind of silver object hanging at his waist. He was handing the tiles one by one to his wife, Ignacio Zumira da Conceicão, who looked as old and wiry as her husband but said she was only fifty. She wore a printed cotton dress and white headband and she was stacking the tiles. They planned to rebuild their house elsewhere.

They looked quite indestructible, and seemed calm and at ease with the world.

"Some other land has been allocated to the homeless for building new houses," Marcello told me. "It is on higher ground beyond the town. A committee was formed to cope with the disaster. There's the Volkswagen agent, a businessman with some stores, a local farmer who has some political pull. Then there's the bishop and the parish priest who's another Irishman, and three county councilors and two doctors.

"There's a national organization too, called Ancar, which is responsible for rural development and they have three people on the committee. I must say they were really quite energetic, and the governor of the state has put a lot into it."

It was very pleasant now by the river, with the water running safely far below. On the opposite bank women were slamming their laundry on stones and spreading it to dry on the sand, making a big and colorful patchwork. Upstream a man was fishing. A good place to live, within reach of the water. One could put out a net and keep an eye on it. Handy for cooking, and washing. If only they could find a way to protect the grasses and shrubs, to keep the bank stabilized and resistant to flooding. Why not?

"Ignorance, perhaps, or apathy. In the past whenever they made an effort to make something better for themselves it was always taken away from them; if not by the elements, then by landowners, soldiers, the powers that be. Over the generations they are left with little desire for improvement. They are hardy and uncomplaining. They take what comes."

I took pictures of Dos Santos and his wife, and other less fortunate families whose houses had disappeared entirely. Then Father Marcello went off on his duties and I wandered along the river banks looking and photographing.

The self-help program for flood victims was centered around a concrete slaughterhouse, newly built and not yet functioning, on the other side of town. Some families were housed in the building. Others took shelter in hutches of black plastic sheeting draped over wooden scaffolding. The families, although large, occupied tiny areas of space and had only the most meager possessions. I should have examined them more carefully to see what had been rescued, what objects of veneration stood guard over the mat, the saucepan, the water pot, but I was too hot and too distracted by my own discomfort to make the effort.

This same heat, which I found stifling, was the saving of these people. In a temperate winter, given their circumstances, their scanty food and clothing, most of them would have died of exposure. In the tropics, with shelter from the rain, one can subsist a long time on remarkably little. What lacks most is hope and initiative, and this was being supplied, in practical form, by a machine for making cement cavity bricks. It had been designed by an Englishman working with the Oxfam charity, and it was set up in front of the slaughterhouse. Homeless men who were not working at the time were employed on it, and a great many bricks were already piled up and waiting to be used in the houses that they planned to build for themselves on the new land.

So they had been given some sort of a promise of a better tomorrow, but it was terribly fragile, just as it was painfully obvious that these people were really not needed. They were unskilled, uneducated and destitute. The big landowners would never want for manual labor; they had their pick from millions.

Some had been given low army tents to sleep in. Here was a woman with six children, cooking outside her tent. She had built a small but pleasing shelter from woven reeds and grasses to serve as a kitchen. In it her smallest child lay in a cardboard carton. Her husband was at work laboring for ten cruzeiros a day, which was just under a dollar fifty. She did not know for how many days he would be employed.

"Yes, sir, I would like to send my children to school, but how can I? They have no clothes."

I asked Father Marcello whether he believed her.

"Oh, I think so. Schooling is cheap enough, it only costs thirty cruzeiros a head and that includes a snack for lunch but she would have to find a hundred cruzeiros at least for clothing, and then more for paper and pencils."

"Ten cruzeiros a day doesn't sound like much," I said.

"No," he replied, looking almost apologetic, as though he were to blame. "It will buy three kilos of rice or beans. It's actually well below the legal minimum, but they are not in a position to complain."

Needless to say, the people in the north of Brazil were all thin.

The bus rattled me back to Fortaleza next day. Alone this time, and going over the same route, I dozed a good deal of the way, with the senseless music of a transistor radio mingling with the bus's roar and enveloping me in a tunnel of fantastic noise.

It was still only mid-afternoon when I got back to São Raimundo, and I was restless. It was my seventh day ashore and at last I was beginning to feel more comfortable with the climate. My curiosity had come to life again in Iguatú and I was no longer a traveler in limbo with one foot at sea and another on land.

Walter Sá had a telex message from London to say that the *Sunday Times* was making arrangements for a guarantee with the Bank of London in Fortaleza. Father Walsh said he knew the manager, a Scotsman named Alan Davidson. I called the bank and made an appointment to see Davidson. Meanwhile Samuel, the young policeman, had left a note at the house asking me to call at the Maritime Police with my documents. There were some details they had forgotten to fill in.

"My mother's Christian names again," I said wearily. "I suppose I'd better go."

"I suppose so," said Walsh.

"Well it can wait until tomorrow," I said, and set off for the older part of town.

I found remnants of the old fortifications, a small but pretty park with delicate fences and ornaments, old sidewalks still paved, surprisingly, with marble flagstones. Lights beckoned from a vaulted gateway set in the middle of a fine old stone building, and I followed faint sounds of music and conversation. The building had been the old prison and was now converted into a museum. Huge rooms with ancient and lustrous hardwood floors were turned over to examples of local art and custom. Behind the prison was a garden of small lawns and pools, with fountains playing and lights concealed in bushes and among palm fronds. Alongside ran an arcade of shops trading in leather work, woven goods and other handicrafts. At scattered chairs and tables young couples or groups entertained themselves with a seemingly endless repertoire of humorous anecdotes, the rattle of speech building up into spasmodic climaxes of laughter. The kids were all impeccably turned out in the pop fashions of the late sixties, miniskirts, brightly colored flared trousers, tailored shirts and blouses, three-inch platform soles. Physically they were no different from the peasants of Iguatú, but they were planets apart.

I sat for a while, but it was an atmosphere that emphasized my solitude. Without the language, and with no bike to establish my credentials, I felt too shy to make contact. I was about to leave when my attention was seized by two guitarists sitting side by side against the wall of the arcade. They had both begun to play, and one was singing. His voice sent shock waves through me. He took the syllables of the first line and hammered them out with distinct and equal emphasis, like blows on an anvil, before leading into the melody that completed the verse. Then his companion replied in the same manner. The effect was wonderfully potent. I felt the same astonishment that always overtakes me when with a few bold strokes something familiar is made strange and thrilling again.

For the first time since landing in Brazil I experienced something I could call beautiful, and it gave me a place at last in this strange new world and made me hungry again for life. I understood only afterwards the significance of that moment.

Suddenly immersed in the tropical poverty of Latin America, I was struggling not only with personal problems but with moral and ethical questions of great complexity. How poor is poverty? How rich is rich? Should priests tend bodies or souls? In whose interests were they acting? Would the Indians be better or worse off in a democracy? Can a democracy function with an illiterate population? What kind of aid helps, and what kind is useless, and what kind corrupts?

Yet underneath all this clinical questioning, what concerned me really was a much more direct and personal doubt. What I wanted to ask was, "How can I or anyone possibly live a good life amidst all this squalor and humidity and decay and indifference? Where is the point of it? What is there to lift up the heart and the spirit? What can an individual pit against the power of nature and the apathy of others? Where is the value that lasts?"

I badly needed some ground in which to root my feelings and the singers gave it to me.

I had heard Father Walsh say, with honesty and due consideration, that he could not rate beauty very high in his scheme of things, and I had reproached myself for letting it bother me. When there were people sick and starving and homeless, how could it matter whether they ate off china or plastic, whether their roof was tile or tin, whether the priests lived in a harmonious and pleasing home or a soulless echoing institution? Wasn't it enough that these men gave themselves utterly to the poor, and taught them how to grasp at just a few of the material benefits of the Machine Age, which had left them so far behind? Wasn't there enough beauty in the hearts and actions of these raw-boned foreigners to offset all the ugliness of their new pragmatism?

I saw peasants coming from hand-made houses to receive help from men who lived in squared-off boxes lined with inert substances and lit from corner to corner. Naturally they would fix on this bright new rectangular life as their ultimate ambition. While in my world millions of descendants of Europe's peasantry were longing to struggle out of those same sterile spaces and back to something resembling a life with natural things.

Was the whole "underdeveloped" world queuing up to be put through the sausage machine, to come out uniform and plump and covered in the same shiny plastic skin. It was not the first time I had seen the human condition in such mean and aimless terms. The same depressing vision had overwhelmed me in the slums of Tunis, the tin huts of Ethiopia, the shanties around Nairobi and the black township of Soweto. Try as I would to imagine a rosier future, I could see only ever-increasing numbers of people determined to seize on the resources of the earth and pervert them into greater and greater heaps of indestructible concrete and plastic ugliness, only to look and learn and retreat in penitent dismay before the next wave of "developing" citizens. And there seemed to be nothing that I or any individual could do that would make a jot of difference to the outcome. I met many who shared my pessimism, and some who felt personally insulted by it, but I never heard anyone propose a convincing alternative.

It was my weakness to become obsessed by these gloomy abstractions. I made it my duty to save the world, and each time I failed I felt as lifeless and meaningless as the gray army of unborn billions whose future I was trying to settle.

Again and again I had to be taught that one single life-giving act is worth more than a million speculations. Once, in Ethiopia, I was restored by nothing more than a smile. As I rode out of Gondar a woman walked towards me dressed in pink and carrying a parasol. When she saw me approaching (and I was an unusual, perhaps frightening sight there) her face was transformed by the most extraordinary smile I have ever seen. It shone, it beamed towards me with such life and depth that I was her son, her lover, her savior all in one. She bowed quickly but deeply several times as I passed, but maintaining that same radiating quality of happiness, so that I was raised to the Gods for a long, long time.

In Fortaleza it was those two men with their urgent, sad voices who reminded me what life was about and what made it worth living.

I met the manager of the Bank of London next morning. He was a fair-haired, youngish man who seemed to exude without effort all the qualities of superior competence that the man at the Banco do Brasil had tried so hard to project, but of course I was heavily biased. In his studiously furnished sanctum we drank sweet black coffee. He asked intelligent and flattering questions about my journey and described his life in Brazil. He enjoyed Fortaleza and was physically comfortable there, and being with him raised my morale another notch. I expected that we would meet again some evening and I looked forward to being drawn into the life of the city while I waited out the formalities. Meanwhile it was clear that the problem of the guarantee could be safely left with him.

To encourage my rising optimism I treated myself to the luxury of a restaurant with clean linen and flowers on the table. The weather conspired with me and waited until I had taken my seat before sending the mid-day rain smashing down on the flagstones outside. I reveled in the freshness of the prawns, and discovered stewed cashew fruit. The rain continued. I smoked several cigarettes and copied the menu on a paper napkin, determined now to begin learning the language. Still it rained, and eventually I could put the visit to the police off no longer. In a corner of my mind they continued to agitate and disturb my peace. I wanted to be shot of them.

By the time I had found a taxi my clothes were wet. I was still unsuitably and obtrusively dressed. My shirt sleeves were long, my jeans too hot and heavy. I still had no sandals, and my shoes and socks quickly became soaked in the streams of water gushing over the pavements and gutters, but I expected the afternoon sun to dry me out.

Samuel received me with profuse apologies, looking younger than ever.

"Now you come for Policia Federal. It is nothing. Some questions only. Nothing. I am so-o-rry. I will be your friend."

We sat side by side in the back of a shabby black police car and returned the way I had come, as Samuel continued to soothe me.

"Policia Federal is not very long away. I shall like to talk you more for my English."

I saw the cathedral pass by, and then the car stopped before a white villa set back from the road with a flower garden in front.

It was a large and irregular building distinguished from its neighbors by a web of aerials above the roof. We walked down a red tiled corridor to a small reception area at the back. I was surprised by the clean and prosperous look of it all, as though they were doing good business. We sat on modern black plastic cushions and gazed at wood-paneled walls, and waited.

We waited more than an hour. Finally a young woman came up to me. She was slim, pretty, hardly more than a girl really, and dressed for a holiday or a date with a boy friend. She seemed very composed, and smiled easily at me.

"I am Franziska," she said. "I will interpret for you. Please come."

This can't be so bad, I thought irrelevantly, as she led me into a very small office. It seemed to be full of men packed in cigarette smoke. I was seated at a desk facing a small, tough-looking fellow in shirt sleeves. Franziska sat on my right between two other men, her green miniskirt well above her shapely, coffee-colored knees. I smiled at her. She looked grave, but not too grave.

Then the man across the desk began shouting. He made me quite nervous. He sounded very belligerent indeed.

Franziska began to translate.

"He says: 'You have been to Iguatú. You have been taking pictures.

Who were you with? What pictures did you take? Who were you talking to?'"

Franziska's nicely modulated voice did nothing to dispel the brutal impact of the little man as he sat staring angrily at me, or the menace of the other two, who seemed to be counting my vertebrae. There was obviously no point in denying anything or refusing to answer. I admitted the charge, explained as graciously as I could and added with genuine innocence: "Why not?"

I got no answer. The man bellowed at me again.

"Are you a journalist?" said Franziska.

It is one thing to have this put as a polite question, and quite another to be accused of it as if it were a capital offense. I felt the first twinge of hopelessness and fear, because it was a question I was incapable of answering honestly and credibly. Yes, I had been, and maybe I would be again. But now, on this journey? No, I was not.

My older passport, which identified me as a journalist, was tucked into the linen money belt at São Raimundo, together with a correspondent's card that had been useful in Cairo. If I had had those with me I would never have dared to deny the profession. Was I or wasn't I a journalist? Was it better to tell the truth and risk being made to look a liar, or tell a lie and have it believed? I remembered vividly being told in London that foreign journalists were often given short and painful shrift by the Brazilian police. I decided to tell the truth.

"No," I said firmly, "I am not a journalist, but my journey is supported by the *Sunday Times* and I write articles about my personal experience."

Now came the problem of the telex. That bloody telex, I thought savagely, sending me off to Iguatú. Any minute now they'll produce a copy of it. And why, oh God, was I stupid enough to go? And I thought about being watched at Iguatú and wondered where else and for how long they had been watching me. So I decided to show them the telex straight away, like the frank and forthright fellow I was, hoping I could confuse them over the wording of it.

The telex was tucked inside my working passport. With it, unhappily, was a black and white snapshot taken by Father Marcello, showing the Jaguaribe River in full flood beneath the bridge. As I drew out the telex, the photograph fell on the desk.

If there is one thing dictatorships hate (and with reason) it is foreigners taking pictures of their bridges. The interrogator seized upon it. Pointless, again, to deny what it was, who it had come from. I began to feel terrible. How could an innocent snapshot begin to assume such sinister significance? Yet it undoubtedly did. And now the priests were tangled up in this too: Marcello in Iguatú; Walsh in Fortaleza because he was mentioned in the telex; even Oxfam was there as an incidental reference. I was astounded by the complexity of the situation, although the game had scarcely even begun. I realized later that even the most elaborate fictional spy plots would be childishly simple compared with the real thing.

Franziska struggled to translate the telex. I explained that what it *really* meant was that the *Sunday Times* already had a story about Iguatú. The message was for my information only, and I had gone there merely to satisfy my curiosity because the opportunity offered itself. It sounded too complicated to me. I did not think that they would believe a word of it.

The little fellow was getting more businesslike now, and not bothering to frighten me anymore. (I was frightened enough.)

"Where is the film and camera?"

"At São Raimundo."

He had Samuel in and told him to take me to the priest's house to get the camera and film, *todos as coisas* – "all the things" – and bring me back.

It was dark and wet, but not raining. As the car rattled across town Samuel talked a little, gentle as ever, protested that he knew I was innocent of all wrongdoing and let me think.

What did they mean by "all the things"? Was Samuel going to search my belongings? Somehow I had to get those other documents hidden, but how? When we arrived, fate seemed to be going my way at last. The house was empty and locked, but I knew where the key to the back door was kept. I muttered something and dashed around the side of the house while Samuel waited patiently for me to come through and open the front door for him. On my way I got the money belt from my room and, looking around wildly for a hiding place, slipped it under the refrigerator in the dining room. It never occurred to me that I might not be back that evening to recover it.

I let Samuel in and under his gaze I collected my cameras and six rolls of film that I had shot in Africa. He showed little interest in anything else, and I wished I had hidden the film as well. Before we left, Father Walsh returned and I told him what was happening. He showed only polite interest, and I could hardly blame him. I wanted him to stay detached, but his apparent indifference deepened my gloom, nonetheless.

At the villa I was taken to the head of the political department, notorious in Brazil by the acronym DOPS. An elegant man lounged back in a revolving chair and put his fingertips together. He had formed the unnecessary idea that my meeting with the priests had been somehow secretly prearranged. He asked me to explain the films. Five of them were Kodachrome, and could not be developed in Brazil. I told him where they had been taken. Then, to my astonishment, he asked me to write out my mother's Christian names. He dictated a series of messages to Brasilia and Interpol and, still through Franziska, said I would have to wait until he got replies to his inquiries.

"Maybe this evening," she said.

An orderly took me back to the entrance hall where an agent was always on duty, and then through some louvered doors into a large office. There were several desks and filing cabinets and an electric fan. Two other doorways, barred by locked wrought-iron gates, led to the street and to a back yard. The agent in the hall could communicate with the office through a shuttered hatch in the wall. The floor, I noticed, was tiled and sloped gently towards a drain in the middle. Looking up, I saw that the roof was really just a canopy raised three feet above the walls, and that the room must once have been an open patio.

The office was obviously in use, although its people had gone home, and I was alone. Somewhere nearby I could hear a telex machine, and a loudspeaker emitting messages in Portuguese or an occasional burst of Morse all interwoven with crackles and howls of static.

The orderly came back after half an hour with a small chipped enamel dish of rice and beans. There were some fragments of chicken and bone among the rice. Eventually the DOPS inspector came to confirm that I would be there for the night. He pointed to the corner where there were some collapsible beds with straw mattresses. He was polite but curt, and left quickly.

I could not decide whether my situation was mildly inconvenient or extremely serious. I tried hard to divine how it would seem to them. On the face of it, it was ridiculous to suppose that I would have ridden a motorcycle the length of Africa in order to engage in a spying mission in Brazil. But how would they confirm the truth? And for all I knew they might find the truth even more ridiculous. In my present position even I found the idea of traveling around the world on a motorcycle a shade absurd.

I was determined to remain optimistic. After all, I had been arrested before in similar circumstances, once in Tunis, twice in Alexandria, and each time I was turned loose again very soon. And, damn it, I was in an office wasn't I, and not moldering in a cell? Yet even during the short time that remained before I thought I could reasonably hope to sleep, I found myself being sucked into a vortex of speculation which seemed to drag me always down towards doubt and fear.

As the evening wore on there was another crashing downpour of rain. Some splashed in under the roof, some rose up through the drain and water rushed and gurgled all around the room and under the floor as though we were being swept to sea. I heard later that it was the heaviest fall of rain that Fortaleza had known in sixty years.

It was a surprisingly uncomfortable night. I had only the clothes I had arrived in. My jeans were still damp, my shoes and socks almost wet and my shirt sticky with the day's sweat. Two walls of the office were saturated with moisture by the deluge. The open doors and roof encouraged a night breeze which, normally, would be a blessing but was a curse for me. Although there was a mattress there was no sort of cover. The moving air was cold, and the exposed parts of my body were chilled even further by evaporation. I slept only for minutes at a time, with the noises from the radio room distorting my dreams into nightmare shapes. Eventually I put another mattress on top of my body. It helped a bit, stiff as it was, but covered me with a fine straw dust which stuck to my damp clothes and skin.

In the morning I felt gray and unappetizing. An orderly took me to a bathroom where there was a shower but no towel or soap. There were some scraps of lavatory paper to dry on, but they did not go far. It was useless to ask for anything, for it was all too easy for them to brush me off with a blank, uncomprehending stare. I did not feel strong enough to make a demonstration, thinking that quiet dignity might serve me better. I expected to be free again that day.

So, on an empty stomach, I watched the staff drift into the office.

The Policia Federal, it seemed to me, was like a Brazilian FBI staffed by *agentes* (agents), men and women in plain clothes with a reasonable education who drew good salaries and were encouraged to study for higher qualifications. I saw them more often with text books than with guns, but the gun was always tucked away somewhere in a waistband or a purse, and the textbooks usually dealt with subjects of a slightly Machiavellian nature like *Mass Communications in the Modern State.*

The uniformed police in Brazil, as in most Latin American countries, were at a much lower level, the departments staffed largely by semi-literate ruffians who busied themselves with petty crime, extortion and gratuitous violence. The *agentes* were above all that and had a more sophisticated function in controlling fraud, smuggling, drugs, vice, forgery and so on, but I was concerned more with its other job of enforcing the political repression of Brazil on behalf of the army.

Brazil was a dictatorship ruled by army generals. Their main priority after taking power in 1964 was to depoliticise the country, meaning to stop anyone engaging in, or talking about, or even thinking, politics. Football, yes; the Samba, si; Politics, ninety million times NO. Political opposition to the generals was punished by imprisonment, deportation, torture and death.

Naturally such a government would watch most carefully over an area like the state of Ceará, where so many had so little to lose and where there might be real potential for subversion and revolt. It was into this high-tension grid that I had stumbled off the *Zoe G* in my outlandish dress, with my strange vehicle, my cameras, my telex messages, my quixotic mission, my passport full of Arabic text conveying hints of terrorism and my much advertised promenade into the interior.

Facing the door, with my back to the wall, I watched the *agentes* assemble around me. There was a bitter humor in my predicament, and I made the most of it. Which of them, I wondered, would be the one to pull out my fingernails or attach electrodes to my genitals? What about that fresh-faced young fellow over there in the sky-blue pants and fawn shirt with the tidy auburn hair? I watched him set down a pile of books, draw a small automatic from under his shirt front and drop it in his drawer, perch one buttock on the edge of the desk and, rather stylishly, light a cigarette, swinging his well shod foot. Surely not!

Or this older man with the wavy gray hair, the comfortable paunch and the face of a family doctor who sat at the desk marked "TOXICOS"? Ridiculous! I became fascinated by this unusual view of humanity. Were any of them capable of real menace? It wouldn't be the girl across the room, typing. She was the complement to Franziska, shorter, fairer, plump and softly appealing.

Well, how about the fellow at the DOPS desk? Surely he would be my man. The Department of Political and Social Order, a bland title for the administration of terror and thumbscrews. He was another man of mainly European descent, probably German. I watched him talk and smile, watched his blue eyes and, to my disgust, I found I liked him.

I could keep the game up no longer. They all looked like reasonable people. More than that, there was something familiar about them, their restlessness, a touch of vanity, a subdued energy suggesting that they were just marking time, that their real business was elsewhere. The parallel came to me immediately. It was the office of a daily newspaper where I had once worked; a roomful of reporters fiddling reluctantly with their expense sheets, waiting to be sent on a job. The comparison was faultless and rather disturbing. Clearly there was little to fear from these people, they were the glamorous, acceptable and perhaps naive face of the machine. If I needed torturing there would be specialists to do the job, somewhere else. From the corridor I had already noticed steps and an open well leading to a gloomy basement area where I imagined the cells to be. Hurriedly I put them out of my mind.

The agents behaved as though I were invisible, and I guessed they were used to finding all sorts of riffraff lodged there for the night. I hated, hungry and filthy as I was, to be present among a group of well-dressed, freshly washed and breakfasted people gathering for their morning's work, to be totally ignored by them, to have to submit to the status of an "untouchable" and yet be obliged by fear to remain and endure it in silence. I learned a rare lesson in the nature of serfdom.

The chairs had all been seized and I was forced to stand. After two hours frustration made me reckless. A rough-featured sergeant figure had come in from time to time and finally I told him, as best I could, that I wanted to see the inspector. He dismissed me with the usual grunt and turned towards the door. Incensed, I followed him, insisting loudly. He turned again, his face working with rage, and shoved me back against the wall, roaring *"Fica!"* Then he performed a brilliant mime which demonstrated in a few seconds that I was a spy who took photographs and therefore beneath contempt.

Nobody in the room appeared to have noticed anything untoward. My hopes slipped even further.

Then there was a break. First, an orderly came in with a tray of coffee, and the agent nearest me offered me a cup. And then, suddenly, Ian Dall, the Englishman from Antonio Sá's house, came in with the DOPS inspector. He walked straight across to me and shook my hand.

"I've come to help with your statement," he said. "They thought it would be better – that it would be better if the fathers stayed away from it. They hope you understand. How are you? Are you all right?"

He seemed reluctant to say more. I tried to tell him how I was. It was impossible. Somehow it all translated into "not bad." Anyway, all the misery of the previous sixteen hours lifted at the pleasure of seeing him.

"Do you know what's going on?" I asked him. "Are they going to let me go? I can't make out what's happening. It's terrible not being able to talk to anyone. I can't even get breakfast . . ." I heard myself talking and it began to sound rather pathetic, so I stopped.

"I think it will be all right," he said. "They don't seem very concerned. I expect it will be over soon."

We walked, a civilized little group of three, to the inspector's office. We might just as well be walking out into the street, I thought, so why don't I? But I didn't. There was a lot of talking and repetition, and the inspector passed several sheets of longhand to a secretary and then took us to a bigger office where Superintendent Dottore Xavier lounged in a bigger revolving chair with armrests.

This man evidently spoke some English, and enjoyed practicing phrases, but for the most part Ian translated from the Portuguese. He made an eloquent statement about security and his role in protecting Brazil from the international conspiracy of the Communist press. I said the *Sunday Times* would hardly be considered part of a Communist conspiracy. He made some reference to *Le Monde*, which Ian found unnecessary to translate.

"Mr. Simon will have to stay until we have replies to our inquiries."

"Am I under arrest, or what?" I asked.

"You are only detained," he said. "You will have full privileges."

"What privileges? How about starting with breakfast?"

The good doctor appeared shocked that I had missed my breakfast. Why, he declared, I could be taken out to restaurants for meals if I wished. I had only to ask. And policemen would buy things for me, like cigarettes or sandwiches. I had only to give them the money. And yes, I could have clothes and washing articles brought from São Raimundo. And of course the British Consul would be told. Indeed this very friend, Senhor Dall, would no doubt perform that service straight away. One might have thought I had deliberately chosen to sulk in a corner instead of coming out to have fun with the rest of the boys.

"The trouble is," said Ian, "I have to go back to Maranhao. My bus leaves in three hours' time." My yo-yo heart flopped again. "But I will manage it somehow. There is a vice-consul here. He's a marine biologist called Matthews. I'll do my best. The police have already offered to drive me to the bus station to save time."

I could not help my spirits rising once more. They had fallen so low that they flew correspondingly high. Some notice seemed to have been taken of me at last. I was an individual again, with rights and an identity. We returned to the inspector's office where the typed statement was waiting for my signature. Ian translated it, and it seemed all right. Prominent in the first paragraph were my mother's Christian names, correctly spelled. There were three pages in triplicate, nine signatures in all. I took a pen to the first page and found, to my horror, that it went entirely out of my control and produced an unrecognizable scribble. I had to work very hard to get my signature back, and even then I thought it looked more like painstaking forgery. I was very aware that the inspector seemed to regard this as quite normal.

As Ian left he tried to encourage me again, but I felt his uncertainty. "I think it will soon be over," he repeated.

I was put back in the general office. It was lunch time. The staff began to drift away. I waited for someone to take me to lunch. The room emptied. An orderly came with a dish of rice and beans. This time there was no chicken.

"I want to go out," I said angrily. "Where's the superintendent?"

The orderly shrugged and left. My morale collapsed yet again. It was all lies, that stuff about privileges, meals, clothes, all talk to sweeten the Englishman. All fantasy just to get my statement and send Ian Dall on his way. Dall was my last chance of contact with the outside world, and he was taking a bus to a place hundreds of miles away on the Amazon. What could he say to the police if they took him to the bus and said: "Leave the consul to us." Nothing. And the priests? What could they do? Nothing.

The door had been left open and I saw the superintendent coming down the corridor. I shouted at him and he surprised me by coming in.

"Don't you like our home cooking?" he asked silkily. It was a rhetorical question. His smile was very close to a sneer, and he left quickly. I was speechless with black fury. The food was irrelevant. It struck me forcibly after he had gone that even if the prison served truffles and caviar I would prefer to be out for five minutes to buy my own rice and beans. There is no relish like freedom.

I was heavily inclined to expect the worst, and when a strange *agente* came for me in the afternoon and took me down those grim steps to the basement I really thought the worst was about to happen. But it was only to have photographs and fingerprints taken.

"Do you play the piano?" asked the *agente*, with a grin. Perhaps it was meant as a compliment, but I could hear it only as a threat conjuring up an image of broken fingers.

The agent who took my photograph told me happily that he had developed my pictures. "Very nice," he said, "good pictures " As we walked up the stairs another man stopped on his way down, and grinned. Everything was a joke to these fellows.

"You will be deported," he said. "I have seen your passport. Visa is canceled."

As the afternoon dragged on I tried to understand what was happening. My real problem was that I had no way of knowing what was likely, no experience of the country, no feel for the way things usually happened there. On the other hand I did know that anything was possible. They could free me or, if they wanted to, they could kill me. There was no point in denying it. The question therefore was: Why should they want to kill me? Not gratuitously. That would hardly be worth the trouble it might cause. If they wanted to get rid of me they would simply deport me, as that last agent had promised they would, but for some reason I was not ready to believe that, quite.

No, I had raised the specter of death and now I would have to deal with it. They would kill me either by mistake, or to cover up something else. They seemed to believe I was on some kind of revolutionary mission. They would look for evidence. They would find nothing conclusive, for there was none, but they would turn up the hidden passport and that would excite their suspicions even more. So they would come to me for evidence. I would have to deny it. I couldn't invent it if I tried. They would have to use torture. That too would be a miserable failure. And then? It might well be too embarrassing to let me go; easier by far to feign an accident, say I disappeared, rather than have me fly home to tell my story.

During the following twenty-four hours I could conceive of only two possibilities: I would be deported, or I would be tortured and killed. As time passed I became increasingly pessimistic. I could get nobody to talk to me or listen to the simplest request. The staff left for home. I got another bowl of rice and beans, and then . . . nothing. By the end of the evening I knew my attempt to reach the consul had failed, and the implications of that were overwhelming. It became impossible then to believe that the way they were treating me was merely through accidental neglect. It had to be deliberate. I could no longer accuse myself of paranoia.

The walls were still soaking. During the day it was not noticeable. After nightfall I began to freeze again. By morning I was shivering, slightly feverish and had a cold. It was Saturday, and as the minutes built up into hours I realized that the office would be empty for the weekend.

I searched for any means to relieve the monotony. I tried to recite poetry, and was appalled by how little I could remember. I counted the tiles on the walls and on the floor (including fractions). I tried to work out a feasible plan of escape. It occurred to me that this might be expected of me (from the top of a filing cabinet I might have clambered over the wall, but into what I had no idea). I began to look for secret surveillance, a closed-circuit TV lens, perhaps. All the time I was aware of my fears being almost entirely self-induced, and that in itself made things worse for I could not shake them off.

Real terror came over me in waves, about once an hour. I found I could not sustain it any more than I could sustain hope. My thoughts might be mercifully far away and then some trick of the mind would produce, say, a mental glimpse of the lumpy-faced policeman on his hands and knees at São Raimundo with his hands under the fridge; and suddenly sweat would pour off me as the thought carried me on to unmentionable consequences.

After several hours of this Franziska came into the office and said she wanted to practice her English. I could have exploded at the absurdity of it, but I was far too suspicious. Every question she asked seemed loaded. Although I was grateful for the distraction and wanted to believe in her goodwill, I dared not. She brought out a tube of vitamin C tablets and offered me some. I refused. God knows what might be in them, I thought. She promised to ask about being taken out to lunch and about the consul, but when she left the rice and beans came as usual, and silence.

The silence was broken in mid-afternoon by another strange event. The radio started a great noise of whoops and wails and crackling, as though someone had just turned up the volume. Then a voice spoke, loudly amplified, very slowly, repeating everything in phrases so that even I could understand most of it.

"We have the films of the coast," it said. (My black and white roll included pictures of the coast taken from the *Zoe G.*)

"Marcello . . . the Englishman . . . to Rio . . . *deportacão*."

Up to that moment I had kept alive a last flicker of hope that my danger was all imaginary. At this point it died. Not only had they apparently deported Father Marcello, but they had wanted me to know it.

From then on a dramatic change came over my hectic mental life. It feels immodest, even distasteful to say, after the event, when I am still so much alive, that I prepared myself for death, but that is undoubtedly what I did. There seemed no purpose in trying to guess anymore. I might as well make my mind up about it, be ready to handle it as well as possible.

Death itself, I soon realized, was not such a bad prospect. In a way I had invited it by embarking on this journey, and could hardly complain. My life, when I thought about it, had been full of interest. Not a very finished life, perhaps, but evolving nicely all the time, always changing and generally, I thought, for the better. It was not really death that bothered me then.

It was pain.

By chance, on the bookshelf at São Raimundo, I had found a copy of Graham Greene's *Travels with My Aunt* and read it. Greene's stuffy suburban hero finds himself seized inadvertently by the police in Paraguay. A policeman hits him, but he scarcely feels it. Then there follows a sentence which, in my hypersensitive state, I must have stored for emergencies:

"Physical violence, like the dentist's drill, is seldom as bad as one fears."

As a sentiment it might not seem very reliable, nor specially emphatic. The point was, though, it was a piece of objective, dispassionate advice. It was not a piece of my own fevered imagination, and I built on it as on a rock. I contemplated the possibility that the fear of torture might be worse than the torture itself, and it seemed possible. And given the laughable folly of doing the torturer's work for him I managed somehow just to let the fear go. Instead I composed a letter to someone I loved; not a very good letter, I realized afterwards, for it was surprisingly full of clichés and banalities, but it brought a delicious calm like the answer to a prayer. I owe Graham Greene a great deal for that afternoon.

My newly found composure continued. I seemed to have discovered a way to endure, and I watched myself carefully to avoid slipping back into the old spasms of hope and despair. A few hours later, well after dark, I was seated at a desk, studying scraps of Portuguese on the waste paper from the bins, when the hatch slid open and a face appeared. It was a squarish face with a gingery beard and hair, and a weather-beaten complexion.

"British?" it asked.

"Yes," I replied, surprised.

"Matthews," it said. "British Consul."

For an instant I believe I actually resented his interference. It was a stunning shock.

"How do you do," I said, and: "Won't you come in?" and: "I'm very glad to see you," and other foolish phrases. Then the relief and joy swept through me like tidal waves.

It was ridiculous. It made me long to laugh. This small, bristling, upright man had poked his head through a hatch, and I was delivered. Through him I was joined again to the world I knew, a world in which I had a certain value, where efforts would be made on my behalf. I could no longer vanish without trace. I had condemned myself to death on circumstantial evidence and the honorary vice consul had brought my reprieve. The very fact that the police had allowed Ian Dall to get his message to Matthews meant that all my fears might prove groundless. I was restored to life and it was a most bewildering experience. I stood blinking in the light like any newly hatched creature.

Henry Matthews was plainly not there to become enmeshed in an emotional drama. He was a busy, practical man who had just returned to Fortaleza after a long and tiring journey. He was deter mined to do his duty and then, as soon as possible, get back to supper and bed with his family.

We stood by one of the desks under a fluorescent tube, and as I looked around my "prison" it became again just a pleasant, clean, well-lit office in which I had spent hardly forty-eight hours.

For a while I could not think what to say. I wanted to describe the fear, the humiliation, the despair that I had suffered in there, and I knew it was impossible. I might as well have launched into an account of a bad dream. To Matthews it would surely be quite incredible and I was afraid of losing his sympathy. So I stuck, as best I could, to the facts, explaining who I was and where I had come from.

"I will see what I can find out," Matthews said, and left the office. I watched through the hatch as he telephoned the superintendent at home. He was polite but not obsequious, and I awarded him full marks. When he came back I noticed, for the first time, that his English was heavily accented.

"He says it is something very big. He will explain it to me on Monday."

My fears, it seemed, were not groundless after all. There was some consolation in that.

"He says you have full rights and privileges" – I could not restrain the cynical smile – "but unfortunately you must wait for the outcome.

"I will come back to visit you tomorrow, but is there anything you need now?"

It was kind of him. He would have liked dearly to put me off until the next day. There were many things I wanted badly; a clean shirt, a towel, a shave, a cover to sleep under, books to read, paper to write on, dry socks, but I could not concentrate my mind sufficiently to remember where they would be. I begged Matthews to go to São Raimundo to fetch my red bag, hoping that what I wanted would be inside it, because what I craved most of all was news from the priests' house, to know what had happened there and to Father Marcello.

Dutifully Matthews toiled out to São Raimundo and back. Of all the things I wanted, the bag contained only my razor. However, the news was as good as it was baffling. No police had been to the house, and Father Marcello had certainly not been deported. Matthews promised to return next day with books and a towel, and I lay down for the third night in the same shirt and trousers.

Next morning the hours passed as slowly as ever. The dampness was getting deeper into me now, and the fever and congestion were worse. Despite that, the consul's arrival had stimulated my imagination again, and once more I could find no escape from doom-laden speculations.

On reflection, the consul's arrival seemed less of a miracle. I tried to draw up a new balance sheet of my prospects. On the credit side, the police were not after all trying to keep my presence there a secret. But then, why should they? They were the law. If they needed a pretext for holding me, they would have no problem finding one. If they wanted to implicate me in some sort of conspiracy obviously they could do so. My trip to Iguatú gave them plenty of ammunition.

By now I was beginning to wonder whether there was more going on in Iguatú than the after effects of a flood. Perhaps there really were small centers of resistance to the regime, struggling to survive. And where better than in a disaster area?

And those radio messages? I had not imagined them, with their references to an *Inglês* and Marcello and deportation. They must mean something. Why the concern with "photographs of the coast"? Were they afraid of foreign intervention? From Cuba, perhaps.

I recalled the agent on the cellar steps and his offhand remark about having seen my visa canceled. It simply did not sound like a lie. Why on earth should he have invented a lie like that? Did that mean that the best I could hope for was deportation? Yet there had still been no attempt to question me further. And most mysterious of all, they had shown no interest whatever in my belongings. They had my passport, but my address books and papers, carried openly in the same wallet, they had ignored. Surely if they suspected me of conspiracy with *"subversivos"* they would at least go through the motions of examining my address books. None of it made sense.

Several times I had the strange impression of being two quite distinct people; one innocent and the other guilty. As though it were, in a sense, my own choice that would decide the matter. I tried to remember more clearly something I had read or heard about there being people who were "torturable" and others who were "untorturable." Was it Kafka? Or one of the Russians? No matter. I decided to devote myself to being innocent and untorturable. And immediately I stumbled over my own guilty secret, which was the passport under the fridge.

A thousand times I cursed the impulse to put it there. The prospect of the police coming upon it in a search was so disturbing that I even considered confessing its existence voluntarily.

What stopped me was an even more awful prospect. Suppose the maid in the meanwhile had swept the dining room and come across the belt. And handed it to Walsh. And what if he, then, had decided to hide it elsewhere on my behalf. What then would the police think if, after all, it was no longer there? Would not that indicate the very thing I was most afraid of, evidence of a conspiracy involving the priests? I absolutely dared not take the risk of implicating them. During all the time I was held by the police, the one thing which constantly undermined all my resolution was the image of that hidden package being discovered.

Matthews came at lunch time as he had promised, bringing books and a towel. I racked my brains to think of ways to profit by his presence, as the underprivileged do when given brief access to power. I dared not tell him about the second passport, so at last I recalled the superintendent's facile promise that I should go to dine in restaurants. It struck me then as a ludicrous idea, as futile to propose as a journey to the moon, and I expected him to laugh when I mentioned it, but he took it up immediately with the agent in the hall and again I watched their faces through the hatch.

The *agente*, who had never even glanced at me before, turned to me with a smile of electrifying sincerity and said: "Of course," and "Why didn't you mention it earlier?"

I was astonished. I walked out into the sunshine and experienced for the second time in twenty-four hours a shock of ecstasy. The sun reached directly into my bones. I felt the moisture boiling off my clothes and skin. The relief was overwhelming, and only then could I measure the effect of the dampness in the building.

To anyone coming and going my complaints might have seemed hysterical, although the cold and the fever were real enough. It came as a revelation to me that real physical and mental harm could be inflicted on a person, quite subtly, in the "nicest" circumstance, while civilized observers would see nothing particularly wrong. I was lucky to have had only a taste of it.

The *agente*, from being a faceless guard, turned into a genial family man recently transferred from Rio. He seemed genuinely anxious to please and asked me where I wanted to eat.

"Fish," I said, "somewhere on the beach."

In his car we drove to the coast south of the city, to a busy restaurant on a terrace. I was crazy with delight at the sound of voices around me, the traffic, the clean linen, the sea rolling in on the sand. The *agente* impressed me even more by paying for his own meal. The cold beer (Brahma Chopp *"estupidamente gelada"*) which we shared, I took on my bill with pleasure. In its way, that lunch of soup, grilled fish, fried potatoes, salad and coffee was the grandest treat I have ever had or hope to have in my life.

It also marked the beginning of a new phase in my prison life. Matthews' real value was that he had broken the ice; the *agentes* began to take an interest in me and, at the same time, I picked up a few words of Portuguese and learned to sing them so that I would be understood.

The books Matthews had brought me were by Agatha Christie, published in the twenties, and held together by transparent tape. I devoured them all in a nonstop orgy to give my restless mind a break, and fell back gorged onto the bed with the taste of Hercule Poirot's brilliantine still on my chops. On Monday, Matthews returned, and this time he brought clothes, a sheet and some more serious books from São Raimundo. I was able at last to change my shirt for a clean one after four days and nights, and to plunge into a history of the decline of the Spanish Empire.

Predictably, Xavier had nothing very remarkable to tell Matthews after all except that they were determined to hang on to me. I was still unable to get breakfast. At mid-day, I was brought a small dish of rice and bones, and again I protested loudly, but this time Franziska was there to help me. Finally one of the younger *agentes*, called Daniel, was persuaded to take me into town, and Franziska came along. From then on, for a while, I had no more difficulty going out. And it was about this time, too, that I knew Franziska was watching me with more than ordinary interest. It was the hardest thing to judge.

During the first days, when I imagined myself to be under sentence of death, or worse, I found her curiosity about me obscene. It offended me that a good-looking girl with a gun in her handbag and almost unlimited power over my fate (as I imagined) could expect me to swagger and crow over her favors. Now that my fears were receding and I felt the blood flowing a bit warmer through my veins I was intrigued but extremely cautious.

It was impossible to know whether she was acting on her own initiative or someone else's or both; and the confusion stifled the excitement I might have felt. As the days dragged on she would come in, often at odd hours when the office was almost empty, and question me about England or other places I had seen. I knew that my answers were not what interested her most, that her real interest was more personal, but the game seemed full of danger and I dared not even think about playing it.

Instead, as the novelty of my new privileges wore off and I became increasingly angry and frustrated at the waste of my days, it was she who bore the brunt of my bitterness. She seemed authentically surprised by my complaints.

"Why are you so angry?" she asked. "It is going well for you. You will be free soon, I think."

"When will I be free?" I asked harshly.

"I don't know. I am not involved in your case."

"Then how can you know I'll be free?" I said with fine contempt, refusing the offer like one who has been fooled too often.

"I don't know. We can tell. Daniel, the others, they all think so." Almost as though I were a medical case showing signs of remission.

She always looked me straight in the eye. She was never demure or evasive. At any other time I would have known she was telling the truth, but my instincts were warped and I saw her as Sarah Bernhardt playing Mata Hari.

I was sick and tired of coping with my fear and resentment. My twice-daily excursions into town no longer appeased me. I was in a rage of impatience.

"It's ridiculous," I said. "You know I'll be free. They know it. But how can I believe you? They must know who I am by now. It's disgusting to keep me locked up here, imprisoned, for no reason."

I had meant my outburst to be intimidating. I would have liked her to burst into tears. But she was simply amused.

"Nobody is free," she said. "Everyone has a prison. Wife, parents, children, they all make prisons."

I was astounded, insulted, to have my ordeal compared with petty domestic trammels, and I ranted on about the principles of justice and liberty, but my speeches had no visible effect. And I was feeling far too self-righteous to accept the simple, shocking truth that she presented to me.

Matthews came again on Tuesday, to be told once more that the police were waiting for a reply to one last cable. He told me he had to leave Fortaleza for four days. The superintendent had promised that my case would be resolved before his return.

That night a customs house clerk joined me in custody. He was twenty-eight years old, frail, timid and very unhappy. He told me he had flown in from a town somewhere up the Amazon and had been discovered without any identity papers. He said he had left them at home by accident, and was worried because his wife would be expecting him back next morning. It was remarkable how much we could tell each other with the little scraps of language we had in common, but after his arrival my grasp of Brazilian improved more rapidly. He was called Ignacio, and he called me Tedge. Like most Brazilians he was incapable of pronouncing the "d" in "Ted."

On Wednesday, Ignacio developed toothache and a big swelling, and I made a fuss about getting him treated, but with no effect other than to occupy my mind. While I was obviously now in favor, the clerk was despised as a petty criminal. Franziska knew nothing against him specifically, but just felt sure that he was up to no good.

At lunch time there was an unusually vigorous burst of activity in the office. Everybody, including the girls, went out on some operation, all with guns. The guns were neat brown things with tiny barrels. The men tucked them in their waistbands beneath their loose shirts. The girls put theirs in their shoulder bags and teetered off on high heels in the best traditions of television crime series. Franziska later told me it had to do with smuggling, and in the afternoon three flashily dressed men joined us in the office, followed soon afterwards by a black man with eerie pale eyes. They seemed very boisterous and confident. With six detainees in the office, plus a full staff, the game of musical chairs became hilarious. Even with two of us to a chair they were not sufficient. As the oldest inhabitant I felt entitled to a chair of my own, but in the end it was too much trouble to hang on to it, and by evening the intruders had swaggered off, leaving Ignacio and me to ourselves.

I made a chess set from scraps of paper and we played an elementary game. When Franziska saw us, she rushed off to fetch a set of dominoes from her office. She told us that there was going to be an eclipse of the moon that night just after dark. We saw it clearly through the gap between the roof and the walls, and Franziska and I stood and wondered at it. I could not remember whether I had ever seen one before, and it struck me as odd that I should see it in these circumstances. The rainstorm on my first night there had also seemed significant to me. The tendency, newly discovered on this journey, to connect unusual natural phenomena with my personal fate, continued, although I had no idea how or in which direction the influence might flow.

Then there was another flurry in the office, a big briefing session, and they were all off again into the night.

By Thursday morning things had progressed to the point where, when I wanted to go to the bathroom, I simply walked out of the office without a word or an escort and was unchallenged. In principle I could have let myself out of the back door of the kitchen and walked away, although it would have been supremely silly to do so. Then the barometer swung back suddenly from Fair to Horrible. It happened at 4:30 P.M. after exactly a week in captivity. The fair blue-eyed operations chief who usually sat at the DOPS desk had moved to a seat near the door. I was standing not far away, having again been tricked out of a chair. Then an *agente* came in who was only rarely seen in the office. He was one of the two agents I had noticed who looked really vicious, the other one being the lumpy-faced fellow who had met me on the ship and whom I had never seen since.

This man was an Arab whose face was ravaged by pockmarks, which did nothing to soften the meanness of his mouth or the shifty glitter in his eye. He and the *chefe* spoke in whispers, which caught my attention straight away, for it was quite unusual. Worse still, the blue eyes kept flicking towards me, and I was allowed distinctly to hear the word *"inglês"* several times. I had already begun to believe that I was watching some kind of charade, when to my amazement the other horror with the lumpy face walked in, complete with dark glasses and his weasel-faced assistant. They all made a great show of conniving together. Until that afternoon I did not know it was possible to be amused and terrified at the same time. The *chefe* said *"inglês"* and *"passaporte"* and "São Raimundo" and *"espião,"* which means "spy," and "Ask the woman" and "If it is there . . ." and then he made one of the most eloquent gestures in the human repertoire; he scooped up an imaginary fly and crushed it in his fist. I didn't know whether to laugh or cry, but a deep-down sense of the absurdity of it all saved me from doing either. It was a hilarious melodrama with a chillingly serious message. For whose passport could they possibly be after at São Raimundo if it was not mine, and who was the spy if not me?

The three villains slunk away on their theatrically appointed mission, and I watched myself carefully to see how I would take the new threat. After all, I told myself, this was where you came in. To my relief I found that I simply lacked the energy to be terrified again. It was too exhausting. "If it happens, let it happen," I thought, and went back to reading history. From then on, although I was expecting painful news from São Raimundo at any moment, I was able to push the thought from the forefront of my mind. It was encouraging to discover that in coping with terror, as with any other human skill, one improves with practice.

The *chefe* came back into the office later, like a hound on the scent, asking his staff whether anyone had heard of *"orshfam"*, which had to be Oxfam pronounced in Portuguese. Nobody had. I found the spectacle utterly comical and began to wonder whether they were all just incompetent, but that thought was too uncomfortable and I dropped it. Then the fuss was over for the day and they all went home.

There was a simple policeman with a merry disposition who sometimes took me out to eat when there were no *agentes* to spare. In the office he appeared to have adopted me as a pet, and whenever he saw me he shouted, "'ta boã?" at me several times in the exaggerated way that one calls "good boy" to a dog. I humored him, as he humored me, with a laugh or a smile, since I couldn't bark. It never occurred to him, I'm sure, that I might one day learn to speak to him and in consequence his company was quite undemanding and peaceful.

It was a glorious evening, dry and bright. As we walked towards the cathedral I smelled night-scented flowers on the breeze. The cathedral stood two blocks from the police station, a monstrous thing more like a fortress than a church, built long ago out of millions of dark waferlike bricks. It was far from beautiful, but its size and squatness gave it a power which impressed me more every time I passed. It overlooked a broad cobbled area where several roads met and many small bars and restaurants traded, and it was here also that prostitutes gathered towards evening.

My escort knew most of the women. He shouted *"ta boã?"* (which sounds like "ta bong" and means "How're ya doin'"?) at them and they exchanged familiar insults. Each time he would turn to shout *"ta boã?"* at me too, to distribute his good nature evenly. He led me first, on his invisible lead, to a small brightly lit shop where bets were taken for a national football pool called Loto, and he pondered heavily over his card, licking his faulty ball pen until he had finally decided between the rival merits of Santos and São Paulo. Then we went up some stairs to the back of a cheap eating house and he watched affably as I ate my favorite dish, a rich dark pork and bean stew called *feijoada*.

When we came down the moon was shining full onto the black facade of the cathedral. Beside me on the doorstep of a bar a man lay back with his legs apart and his eyes closed in blissful drunkenness. The gray material of his trousers was so threadbare that a fountain of crystal urine passed straight through it and rose up sparkling in the light of the street lamps. On the pavements the refugee peasants from the flooded interior were already stretched in sleep, as motionless as the stone beneath them. Some had pieces of cardboard to lie on, others not. Some lay in couples, back to back. Some had a few belongings, others none. All seemed utterly at peace, faces tranquil, bodies classically composed as though they had paid special attention to the placing of their shining brown limbs before letting the world fade from sight.

I looked out on this scene, and, for once, felt part of it, not just an idle spectator. As a prisoner of the Policia Federal I felt I had business there, although God alone knew what that business would be. At least I had come to terms with the uncertainty, and there was some satisfaction in that. My senses and my curiosity were both sharpened. Nobody was being sorry for me, and I was not obliged to feel sorry for anyone else. I felt I was within reach of experiencing a genuine emotion born, for once, out of the moment itself.

We walked across the cobblestones and the policeman drew me to the right so that we would have to walk behind the cathedral. After chatting with another group of women, he beckoned me towards some stone steps. There was a mass in progress in a chapel in the crypt of the cathedral. My first view inside was like a hallucination, as though the rough black masonry itself had split to reveal a glimpse of paradise. A roseate glow washed over the pure white walls and low vaulted roof, and bathed the priest and his small congregation. The chapel, in its gleaming simplicity, was the opposite of everything that Fortaleza had seemed to me to be: A cool, clean and infinitely desirable vision. Anyone who could enter there, I thought, would lead a charmed life.

Perhaps that was why we stayed outside. The policeman stopped at the threshold and knelt on the steps, laying his forehead on a low stone buttress. He was a young, strong man and I was moved by the way his body folded naturally into a sculptural form of complete humility.

I stood beside him, a cigarette still smoldering in my fingers, unable to take part but hoping vaguely that there might be a small surplus of grace to take care of me too and whatever might be waiting for me at the station.

Walking back the last hundred yards he told me that he was a married man with children and came from Bahia, and that this day was his thirtieth birthday. The station was quiet. The night passed peacefully. Occasionally I woke up to imagine an agent with a lumpy face and dark glasses furiously ransacking São Raimundo. Then I dismissed him and slept again.

The unnatural calm lasted until mid-day on Friday, and then it was broken by another triumph of melodrama and corny characterization. I was already on my way to lunch with another policeman, when a big, battered black car making terrible noises from its exhaust screeched to a halt beside us. The driver had obviously escaped from a gangster movie of the thirties. He was what they used to call a runt. He was weedy and wore an overpadded suit, and on his face were two huge pieces of sticking plaster, in a cross. Al Capone must have sent him personally, for he was full of urgency and self-importance. I was bundled into the back, and the wheels started spinning before the door was closed.

We shot off in the direction of São Raimundo, and my adrenaline made valiant attempts to rise to the occasion. Surely this must be IT, I thought, but then the car made a surprise left turn and in a moment we were back outside the police station. I was rushed inside and along the corridors into the superintendent's reception area, where Xavier himself was standing and talking on the telephone. Then Franziska came in and told me there was a call from the Foreign Ministry. They wanted to talk to me.

I could hear Xavier saying that I had been there four days and I became quite angry suddenly. I raised eight fingers, and said *"ocho"* loudly, but Xavier took no notice. After a while he passed the receiver to me with a smile.

"You can talk to Counselor Brandão in Brasilia," he said, and walked into his office.

Brandão spoke good English and sounded concerned.

"I telephoned the customs about your motorcycle – a technical problem of ownership – and they told me you are in custody. What is your position? What are you doing? Are you a journalist, or not? Why didn't you tell them?"

I tried to explain to Brandão who I thought I was, but with little success. It began to occur to me that the subtle distinctions I had thought so important might be invisible to the naked eye. If I was to be connected with the *Sunday Times* at all, I would be considered a journalist, and it would be useless to deny it. Normally there was no need to reveal the connection, but in Brazil, because of the guarantee on the motorcycle, it was inevitable.

"I don't understand," Brandão was saying. "You say you have been there for four days . . ."

"No, that was Xavier. I have been locked up here for eight days."

"Eight? I still don't understand. Haven't you got a document from the *Sunday Times?"*

I took a deep breath and said: "Yes." For better or worse I could stand the complications no longer, and with the Brazilian Foreign Office involved I felt safer. The conversation lingered on. With each passing moment I felt more certain that at last the knots would untie and I would be free. I put the phone down with Brandão's civilized assurance like music in my ears.

Xavier had returned and was sitting near me.

"I have a *Sunday Times* correspondent's card," I told him. "It is at São Raimundo, and I should explain it is with another passport . . ." but Xavier had already got to his feet.

"We will get the card in the afternoon," he said. He was in a remarkably jovial mood. We might have been making a date for tennis. He put his arm around my shoulder and swept me towards the door.

"Now it is time for our lunch," he said.

I tried one more time to talk about the passport but he would have none of it.

"See you later, I think you say." He grinned, and disappeared. I still did not like him very much, but I was glad to see him happy. Neither the card nor the passport were ever mentioned again.

In the afternoon my optimism appeared to be justified. Not only did Matthews arrive unexpectedly – "I was worried, so I came a day earlier" – but with him came Alan Davidson from the bank and Father Walsh from São Raimundo. It seemed impossible that I would not be walking out with them when they left.

Davidson had received the guarantee for the bike and had arranged for an agent to get the bike out of customs.

I told them about my talk with Brandão. Like me they seemed to think that must be the end of it, and Matthews went to see the DOPS inspector, who was technically in charge of my case, to ask for my release. Meanwhile I told Walsh about the strange scene of the day before and the references to São Raimundo. Once again he insisted that nobody had been there, with or without lumps, pock marks or plasters. What surprised me more was that he seemed to attach no significance to it, and I wondered fleetingly whether they all thought me a bit peculiar.

Matthews returned and said they refused to let me go until they had a reply from the Policia Maritimi. I was terribly shocked and I cursed loudly and angrily while they waited for my symptoms to subside. When I was rational again, Matthews lowered his voice and went on:

"They say they have grounds. They say they have been looking for an Englishman, a lawyer, with the same names as yours. He is called

John Simon Edwards and they say he has been involved in subversive activities."

At first it sounded like an outrageous fiction – another damnable pretext for hanging on to me. I was convinced that they hated to let people go. Just the fact that you were in there at all meant that there had to be something wrong with you. Eventually they would find some way to justify keeping you. Ignacio, the clerk, seemed to know it. He did not behave like a man who had been deprived of his liberty, more like a patient in an institution waiting to hear whether he was cured.

Yet the story was almost perfect in its way. It explained nearly everything, the messages, the snatches of conversation about "*Inglês*" and deportation. Even the odd feeling I had of being two people must have come from my frenzied effort to make sense of the mystery. The canceled visa must have been in his passport, but if they had his passport, where was he? Had they thought he was hiding at São Raimundo? Why hadn't they been there? But then São Raimundo was a district, not just a church. Was it only coincidence? Too much coincidence, I thought. And if the story was true, I could see how my arrival would have confused the police as much as it confused me. Was Mr. Edwards a keen underwater fisherman? I wondered. I should have liked to meet him.

"But now," I said, "now they *know* there are two of us, so why do they have to hang on to me? It's crazy . . ." and I went into another fit of fury as futile as the first.

My friends tried to comfort me, but there was little they could do. Apart from freedom I had everything I needed. I had clothes, books, the use of a shower, cigarettes, money, access to restaurants, a fairly comfortable bed and a companion to play chess with and talk to. Yet the time dragged by as heavily as ever, and now there was not even fear to spice the hours. Another full weekend at least, alone with Ignacio, with not even the antics of my captors to amuse me. It seemed intolerable.

However, entertainment was unexpectedly provided by the management, in the shape of a lawyer called Andrade. He made his first appearance briefly that evening when Xavier brought him to the office. I saw a tall man, thin and gray-haired, who looked as though he had just seen his life fall into ruins.

"You can stay here if you like, but you must not talk to these," said

Xavier, indicating us. Miserably, the man shook his head and mumbled something, and they left together. He was all the more pathetic because he was so well dressed and groomed, and obviously accustomed to comfort and respect.

Next day he was back, but in much better spirits. His coming was a revelation to me, an example to us all. He brought with him a leather bag and a small pigskin case, and his first move was to unpack a brightly coloured string hammock and hang it across a corner of the room. To my astonishment the hooks were already provided in the walls, and in my eight days there I had failed to take notice of them. There were silver-backed brushes, toilet water, an elegant robe and slippers and hints of other unidentified luxuries.

The silence lasted only half an hour, if that. Within the hour he had told the clerk his life story, but it had gone too fast for me to catch more than a tantalizing detail here and there. We played two games of chess, he won the second, and I persuaded him to tell his story again slowly. As best I could tell it went like this:

He was from São Paulo, Brazil's biggest, busiest, smoggiest city, where he had been employed as a lawyer in the state government. Then in 1964, after the military coup, the brother of the governor of São Paulo betrayed him or slandered him in some way and he went to the governor's palace to protest and demand satisfaction. He accused the brother to his face of his reptilian behavior, and the brother replied in terms which he, Andrade, could not tolerate. He therefore delivered to his persecutor a punch on the nose, at which the cowardly fellow drew a gun and sent Andrade sprawling on the marble floor with a bullet through his calf. However, as he lay on his back, propped up on his left elbow, he was able to draw his own gun, and he shot the governor's brother once through each shoulder and once through the leg.

Andrade's account of this event was marvelously vivid, as he moved and spun with the progress of the story, and he concluded by hoisting his right trouser leg to reveal a penny-sized scar on one side of his calf and another on the other side. The scars gave him great satisfaction.

As a result of this incident, he said, he was unable to earn a livelihood in São Paulo. He lost his job, all doors to private practice were closed and he was labeled politically undesirable. In 1970 he exiled himself from São Paulo and went to Ceará, a sufficient distance away to outrun the slanders. In Fortaleza he built up a new reputation and took part in the creation of several important enterprises, including a water-treatment plant and a cemetery. He associated himself with the Ceará branch of the company that sold Larousse encyclopedias in Brazil, and it became the most profitable branch in the country. His boss in Ceará became his closest friend.

Then in 1973, just before Christmas, he was suddenly dismissed. The principals in São Paulo refused to see him or communicate with him, but he decided to take no action. Then some months later his former boss in Ceará was also dismissed and accused of fraud. This man invited Andrade to help him prepare a case against Larousse but in the meanwhile Andrade had discovered that it was his supposed friend who had originally denounced him in Sáo Paulo as a swindler. Andrade therefore gave evidence against his former friend instead.

Now he himself had been arrested. He was told that criminal charges, brought against him years ago in São Paulo, had gone to trial. He had been convicted in his absence and sentenced to five years. He was now waiting to be sent to prison. He seemed to be quite without hope.

That evening he received a visit from his son, a young man in casual but most expensive clothes.

"Papa!" he cried, and they fell into an emotional embrace. They were given a private room somewhere to talk, and Andrade came back beaming. He carried a plate of roast chicken joints wrapped in a clean red and white napkin, and a bag of other assorted foods and fruits, which he shared with us.

His son and his friends, he said, had been researching in the records at São Paulo. The whole story of a prison sentence was a wicked lie disseminated by his enemies. There had never been a judgment against him he said. Soon the truth would emerge and he would be free again.

I found it as difficult to believe in the new rosy dawn as I had in the black picture of despair he had painted a few hours ago, but he was so exhilarated by his prospects that I pretended to share in the wonder of it all and congratulated him heartily on his imminent release.

"At least," I said, "you won't have to escape." He laughed. Earlier he had spent some time discussing ways of breaking out of the station. Compared with the prison at São Paulo, he said, it would be very easy. I did not ask him how he knew.

His euphoria carried him through until Monday morning. When I returned from the bathroom, I noticed Andrade and Ignacio both standing by the wall in a rather curious position, and could not at first make out what it was that was so odd. Then I saw that they were standing in such a way that the morning sun, passing between the wall and the roof, shone on their faces. They were both very serious about it, and it struck me as the sort of thing one might do if one had spent long periods in prison.

Shortly afterwards Andrade was taken away. He returned briefly later to collect his hammock and other things, and his face had fallen once more into the bitterest dejection. He said nothing and neither did I.

Monday was a poor day for me as well. There was no sign of my release. Ignacio was taken away too during the day, heaven knows where. At lunch time I was refused permission to go out, and put back on the prison diet of rice and beans. Franziska was nowhere to be seen, and nobody else would explain. In the evening there was a strange *agente* on duty and again I was not allowed out. Even worse, I was given nothing to eat either, and the effect was very depressing. In the mornings, I had established a routine whereby a policeman fetched me a sandwich, coffee and cigarettes, but on Tuesday morning even that system failed. I was dumbfounded. It was as though the whole bloody business was starting from the beginning again. All my carefully cultivated special relationships had withered. At lunch time all my usual companions vanished. Nor was anything brought to me. The anxiety I felt then was unusually corrupting, for it undermined all my expectations. I could not attribute this new regime to anything. I could not even be sure it was deliberate. It simply left me with a sense of total revulsion against every one of the bastards, from Xavier down to the cook; I no longer cared whether they were cunning, incompetent, corrupt or naive, it made no difference. The result was a rotten, soul-destroying mess and from that moment I buried the benefit of any doubt I might have had about any of them.

In the afternoon Matthews and Davidson came to tell me that I was free. I was to be delivered officially into the arms of the British Consul with Davidson as witness. It should have been a moment of joy and celebration, but by then I was so deep in resentment and misery that all I could think was, "About bloody time too."

In gratitude to the others I tried to look happy but it was hard going. I wanted only to get away, and the formalities dragged heavily. At the last moment, when Davidson had already left, Matthews and I were standing with Xavier by the entrance. Xavier looked at me with an indulgent smile and said:

"Now you can write the story."

"Ask him," I said to Matthews, "whether he is finally convinced that I am innocent."

Of course Xavier had to say yes, but I was watching his face and I shall be indebted to him always for a superlative specimen, in its finest flower, of the variety of human expression known as the Sickly Grin.

But it was I who was sick.

During those last days something inside me twisted and strangled the source of my vitality. Up to then I had imagined, without realizing it of course, that the entire Brazilian police apparatus was devoted to my case. My very existence depended on whether they found me "innocent" or "guilty." It must have been some time on Monday that they found that they had no further use for me. From that moment I was not even worth my rice and beans.

They ceased to recognize my presence. They lost interest to the extent that they did not even bother to feed me. Then I saw that without them I was nothing. Worse than nothing. A dog that cowers at the feet of a brutal master grateful for any acknowledgment, whether it comes as bones or blows. I became disgusted with myself and loathed them for showing me to myself in such a shameful light.

So they demonstrated their power to me in the end, in a careless, offhand way, without really trying. They were indifferent to the consul, to the *Sunday Times*, to their own government even. But they found me mildly irritating, and spat me out. Some other time their attention might be attracted and they would suck me in again. I felt a great and malignant shadow hovering over me and I wanted only to crawl under a stone and hide.

The consul's brother Charles drove me back to São Raimundo and the priests offered me a room in their own house. I felt it was wrong of me to stay there, but they were quite confident and it was so much what I wanted that I could not refuse. As soon as I was alone I went to the dining room and looked under the refrigerator. The belt was there, among ringlets of dust, as I had left it.

I could not shake off the sense of fear and revulsion. It was as though I had been squeezed too hard. Although the pressure was off, I had no resilience left to resume my former shape. Never before had I been unable to find the resources within myself to respond. I cowered inside my shell like a shriveled homunculus, and I was worried that it had affected me so deeply.

But nothing actually happened to you, I told myself angrily. *What is this nonsense? It was only twelve days. Now get on with life.*

But I couldn't. It was important to write an account of the experience quickly and send it off, but everything I wrote seemed false and trivial. I tried all the tricks I could muster to find a different perspective, to climb out of myself just for a moment. Physical exercise. Detective thrillers. Getting among crowds of people.

Progress was slow. I watched a lot of television on a big color set, in a recreation room upstairs. It was a World Cup year and Brazilians were in a frenzy about football. The Brazilian sugar monopoly was one of the main sponsors of football on TV, and its advertisement, a growing mountain of sugar, seemed to be on the screen constantly. It was one of the first things I laughed at, because the country had been struck by a sudden and severe sugar shortage, and Brazilians cannot drink coffee without it.

Or I sat in the cane rocking chair talking to Walsh, or stood in the dark of the balcony watching the huge fruit bats swoop around the jack fruit tree and scoop out the pulp. Sounds of music and laughter drifted in from the neighborhood, and oil palms in a back-yard plantation brushed the night sky with their feathering silhouettes.

During the day, with paper and the parish typewriter, I burrowed into every available corner of the house, hoping that a change of space would unblock my mind. I no longer thought much about the aesthetic merits of the building. It provided shelter and safety and that was all I cared for.

For a while I worked in an office just inside the front door, with a hatch opening on the hallway where I could watch the mothers come for a gossip and to help with the duties of the parish. They had little crushes on particular priests. Sometimes they telephoned and then they would do their utmost to get their favorites on the telephone, while the priests in turn defended each other fanatically. When I was alone in the house I sometimes answered the phone.

"São Raimundo," I announced in my best Portuguese.

"Quem esta falando?" sang the shrill, intriguing, matronly voices.

"Padre Eduardo," I replied gravely. That perplexed them for a while, but the flurry of sounds that followed would be too much for me usually, and I would wait for a pause to say *"Si, Si"* and put the receiver down.

On the third day I tried the game in reverse. The phone rang and I got the question in first. *"Quem esta falando?"*

A woman's voice answered: "Franziska. Can I speak to Ted, please."

I felt sick inside and would have told her to go to hell if I had dared.

"How are you?" she said, and: "Are you happy to be free?"

"Of course."

"I have been thinking about you. Have you thought about me?"

"I have been thinking of many things."

It was a noisy line. We both had to shout.

"I would like to see you. Will you come here?"

"Where?"

"At my home. When I finish working. When you will come?"

"I am very busy writing."

"Tomorrow I am free."

"All right."

What the hell do you think you're doing? I asked myself as I took the address. *You can't seriously expect to make love to a woman who carries a gun in her purse and works for the forces of evil.*

At the docks the customs put thirteen men on the job of discharging my motorcycle. They were keen to show me where the police had cut the saddle open to explore the foam rubber underneath. "Looking for bombs!" they said contemptuously, but I said no, they were after scuba equipment.

There was no love lost between the two services. As a victim of the Policia Federal I was an honored guest and treated to an elaborate coffee ceremony in the chief's office. They were all brown men in brown offices with brown ledgers. Theirs was the old, suffocating kind of bureaucracy that I detested, but they only imprisoned things, not people, and for once I appreciated their more human qualities.

Having the bike back was an important step towards freedom. I arrived at Franziska's house feeling stronger than I had the day before. Among her own family it was almost possible to forget what she was. She radiated innocence, and they all treated me with great affection. There was never a hint of how we had met, or that I might be in any way a dubious character, but while my insecurity was soothed a little, a new problem arose. I had no idea what the moral customs were here. A respectable Catholic family in a provincial city, I thought, would have rigid standards of behavior, and if I violated their sense of propriety . . . ?

Underneath it all the same question lay, sapping my puny confidence. How could I be sure that a woman scorned, or a woman outraged, would not think to avenge herself through her connections? Or perhaps the whole thing was set up, and not necessarily by her? Even while I was certain that these were fantasies, I had come so recently from a world of fantasy that they inhibited me terribly – and yet undeniably she was attractive, and far from silly, and her attitude towards me was directly inviting.

It was too ridiculous. I wanted to break through the web of suspicion, but I was scared. I touched her, familiarly but awkwardly because my heart was not strongly in it. There was a brief flash of fury.

"If my father sees you he will be very angry."

I felt like a puppy having its nose tapped. Embarrassed, I retreated into platitudes and neutrality. I could not figure it out. Undoubtedly it should have become a love affair, but it always faltered on the brink.

I took a week to finish my piece for the *Sunday Times*, and I had to relive all the agony to do it. I was greatly relieved when it was written, but by then I had developed an infection of the gut which slowed me down for several more days. It was the first illness of the entire journey. In Africa my health had been perfect although I had eaten and drunk everything that came my way. There is nothing worse for health than imprisonment and frustration.

Franziska and I met several times, but my fear continued to make me as shy as a fourteen-year-old. My last days in Fortaleza were the beginning of the festival of São João, a week of celebration throughout Brazil. We went to a dance on the beach where I felt sure I would be able to overcome my faintheartedness. A big crowd sang and danced and drank at wooden tables under a broad, tiled canopy. The moon was full, the air warm on the skin, the coconuts swayed on the shore. Everything was auspicious . . . until I saw her friends from the office, two policemen I had last seen when I was their prisoner. I even caught a glimpse of the guns in their waist bands, and my ardor froze to ice again.

We sat for a while, much later, side by side on the beach listening to the waves. I longed to touch her smooth long legs, to feel her skin against mine, but I was paralyzed, thinking:

"Once I start, where will it end?"

I knew it would be our last meeting. We found a taxi after walking a long way, and in the taxi I kissed her for the first time and knew it would have been all right. But by then it was too late.

The priests had all been summoned to a diocesan conference at Maranhao, a long way away. Father Walsh had told me they would all be leaving in three days' time. He did not say I would have to leave, but it was obviously time to go. I was hoping they had not had to invent the conference to get me out of the house.

I was packing the bike in the back yard on the morning they left for the bus station wonderful, kindly men whom I would be most unlikely to see again. An hour or two later I left myself. The thought of going made me nervous. I saw myself as a target for every idle policeman on the two thousand miles of road to Rio, and it was not unlike the very first departure in London. In some ways I felt even more vulnerable than I had then.

At the first police checkpoint on the highway leaving the city they checked me out but gave me no trouble. I had an impressive temporary driving license, with a picture of me looking utterly villainous, and they liked that. Still the cloud of anxiety traveled with me down the highway. Then gradually the familiar movement, the sound of the engine and the rush of air built up my confidence as nothing else could. I sat up and took notice of the bright green forested hills, and the streams and lakes that reminded me of Tanzania.

I began to remember who I was and what I had already done and the strength came pouring back into me. By the end of the day I had crossed from Ceará into the state of Pernambuco, and somewhere about there the cloud detached itself and floated back to Fortaleza. After a month of misery I felt free. At last.

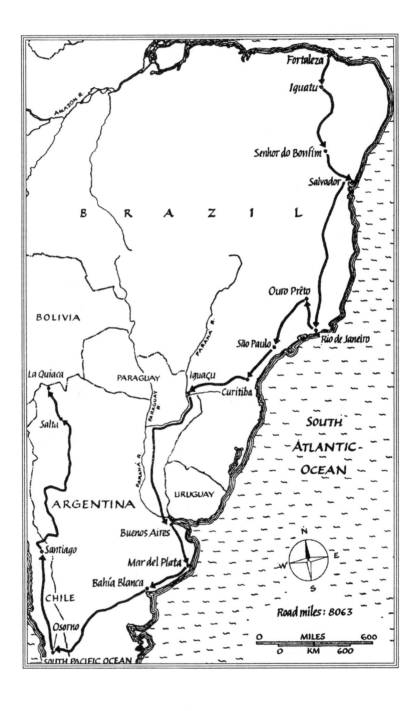

Fortaleza

Iguatu

Senhor do Bonfim

Salvador

B R A Z I L

Ouro Prêto

São Paulo

Rio de Janeiro

BOLIVIA

La Quiaca

PARAGUAY

Iguaçu

Curitiba

Salta

SOUTH
ATLANTIC
OCEAN

ARGENTINA

URUGUAY

Buenos Aires

N

Santiago

Mar del Plata

W   E

Bahía Blanca

S

CHILE

Road miles: 8063

Osorno

SOUTH PACIFIC OCEAN

0   MILES   600

0   KM   600

I was traveling south from the equator down the east coast of America on a parallel track to my journey down the east coast of Africa. It was a magnificent geography lesson. If Ceará resembled Tanzania, then inland Bahia was similar to Zambia, while Minas Gerais, the next great state on the southward trail, was startlingly like Rhodesia, with those same massive rectangular rock formations, old gold mines, gemstones, broad skies, dry air and peaceful lambent evenings. As an introduction to the size and diversity of Brazil it was breathtaking.

The life of Brazil though seems to have little in common with Africa, even with such a large proportion of Africans descended from former slaves. There had been Europeans here for hundreds of years, imposing themselves on the native Indian population, building churches, fighting over the spoils, interbreeding, creating complex hierarchies, becoming rich and destitute, leaving the traces, layer upon layer, of their passions and virtues.

When the first foundations were still being laid in Salisbury and Lusaka, the Portuguese palaces and cathedrals in Brazil were already ancient, and the coastal states were peppered with thriving communities.

The towns portray their history. In the middle they aspire to the church. Around the square where citizens met and festivals were celebrated and where, occasionally, armies were mustered, the tallest houses vie with each other for the most ornate facade. Great efforts were made and many lives expended to cut, haul and lay the stone that paves the roads and clothes these buildings. Radiating outwards the roads soon turn from cobble to dirt, and the houses shrink and decay until they meet the modern highway system where a newer kind of wealth makes a new stand in cement and girders and asphalt, garages, bus stations and newly dilapidated hotels.

The streets are muddy in the rain and smell of garbage and urine, laced with coffee and cigar smoke. Buses and trucks splash through on broken suspensions, spouting black exhaust, their wooden coach work gaudy with fairground colors and macho slogans like "A woman is like a truck. She goes faster when you put your foot down."

In the evening the streets swarm with people of every color but pure white (for the pure white keep apart). During the hot, dry and dusty afternoons, the streets sleep. It was a hot, dusty afternoon when I came to Senhor do Bonfim, a small inland town in Bahia, a day's ride from Salvador. I came early, wondering whether to stay, and walked through narrow streets looking in on barber shops, billiard saloons and people sipping coffee in *botiquinos*. The week of São João was just ending. Loudspeakers on street corners broadcast music, announcements and advertisements by the town tradespeople.

I liked it, found a room near the railroad, parked my bike in the street, dragged my luggage up to the first floor and flopped down on the bed to doze for a while. Birdsong and chatter invaded my half waking state, followed by other, stranger sounds. There was a noise like muffled tin cans falling in a heap coming repeatedly from the yard beneath the open window. Then I heard an even stranger wailing musical sound, winding up and down the scale, now loud, now faint, as though blown from a long way off by a fickle wind. I opened my eyes lazily and saw a blue figure of a man, legs and arms outstretched, float up to the sky to disappear above the upper edge of the window frame. Such benign mysteries, I thought, are what make traveling infinitely worthwhile. Everyone else in the hotel knows exactly what these sights and sounds are, but I am free to imagine anything I choose.

It was easy afterwards to spot the turkeys in the yard, and to guess that the balloon man was something to do with São João, but the skirling music remained a mystery. At dinner downstairs I heard it again. The hotel owner came towards me, agitated; something to do with the motorcycle. It was in danger, he said.

I went outside to look. The music was growing into a metallic howl, but I saw only the usual small boys gathered round the bike, prodding it and staring fixedly into the speedometer. The music had the eerie quality of an approaching storm. Then there came round the corner, at the bottom of the street, preceded by a pack of dancers in violent motion, a most spectacular thing. A thing emitting light and sound on a scale of intensity I had never known, so intense that it took a while to focus on its various parts and identify it.

There were two objects shaped like rockets floating ten feet in the air, and they were about thirty feet long. They were built entirely out of brilliant fluorescent light tubes. Beneath them, a myriad clusters of coloured bulbs flashed on and off, each cluster being set into a loudspeaker. Rising above the glare of the rockets were three men in bright clothing, bowing and grimacing like marionettes high above us all and plucking furiously at tiny electric guitars. On sumptuous galleries below the rockets, running all the way around this phantasmic object, were floodlit drummers dressed in satin, gesticulating, like an animated frieze, as they hammered away. All of it seemed to be borne along by a throng of hypnotized dancers jerking their elbows and twirling to the music, which poured out in solid waves, having no beginning or end.

The thing drifted past at walking pace, carving a great tunnel of light and fury out of the night, and like everyone else I was sucked into its wake. It came to rest beside a large ornamental park, with trees, pathways and a fountain. All around were huts lightly built of palm fronds on wooden frames selling refreshments. Middle-aged peasant ladies in heavy bodices squatted by charcoal braziers roasting skewered meat and corn cobs. A roguish old man in a velvet jacket and gaucho hat operated a crown and anchor game, with heaps of toothpaste tubes and soap as currency. A raised wooden stage had been built in the park and, facing it, a bank of seats for ticket holders and notables. The rest of us stood among the trees or wandered around the stalls.

On the stage some young people were performing comic dances, and a man in a striped shirt and bow tie stood in one corner with a microphone pretending to be an unusually crass American tourist and making absurd comments in pidgin English. Of real tourists there were none, but the people of the town and round about were there in their thousands, enjoying themselves enormously.

But obviously the best was yet to come. A shock wave travelled through the crowd, and the dancers hastily left the stage. Another man came to the microphone and said something urgent about the "*Fogo Symbolico de Republico.*"

"Fireworks," I thought. The police were making a lane through the crowd, pushing people back mercilessly to connect the stage with the outside world. There was a great air of expectancy. Whatever was coming would have to be sensational to justify it, after all I had seen already. The waiting dragged on. People came on to deliver speeches of thanks and tributes. We were all shuffling our feet impatiently. A group of youngsters in gym clothes ran rather self-consciously from the road, through the cleared lane and up the steps to the stage, having much difficulty trying to keep in formation. On the stage some of them stopped. Others ran on the spot. Those who stopped, started again with embarrassment, just as those who had continued thought they had better stop. Then I saw that the front runner had a torch in his hand with a small flame, and a voice boomed out again about the "*Fogo Symbolico.*"

The applause was the absolute minimum necessary to be audible; evidently everybody found it all much too symbolic, and I wondered how far down the road they had struck a match and lit the torch. São João went out with a whimper, and I thought I had never attended a greater anticlimax in my life. I went back to the hotel to kill mosquitoes and sleep, but there were not enough blankets and it became surprisingly cold. Between patches of sleep I tried to reconstruct that fantastic music, a continuous melody played at the speed of a banjo, with some of the feeling of an old barrel organ, thickened and amplified to a frenzy of excitement. For a while I thought I had it, but in the morning it was gone.

Only much later did I discover that I had met, in Senhor do Bonfim, one of Brazil's most celebrated institutions, the unique and illustrious Trio Electrico from Salvador, which was the glowing heart of the Bahia Carnival.

For six more days I moved south towards Rio. I began to study Portuguese seriously, reading menus and advertisements, and learning the road signs by heart. "*Não ultrapassar quando a ligna ezquierda for continua,*" I repeated again and again. The one I could not understand said: "*Conserva as placas.*" Often it was riddled with bullet holes. I learned later that it meant "Do not destroy the road signs." I recalled other odd signs from Africa: The one that greeted me as I was about to take a high viaduct over the Blue Nile Gorge, leaning out from the mountainside thousands of feet above nothing.

"Drive slowly and carefully," it said. "This viaduct has begun moving."

Or the one painted on the roads in South Africa, just before traffic lights in the right-hand lane.

"Slegs Only," it warned.

"What on earth are slegs?" I asked.

"It's Afrikaans for 'only'," they told me.

The last two days before Rio were glorious, riding through the state of Minas Gerais. That rolling ranch country drew me irresistibly. I walked in the evenings past the cattle pens, admiring the solidity and workmanship of the stout black fences with their white-capped posts. Mounted cowboys sauntered by with carefully laconic faces. The sun set in splendor leaving an air of great tranquillity over the land, and I swore that one day I would return there.

Then the emerald-clad mountains carried me high up to Teresopolis, and soon I was standing next to the Finger of God, and looking down over the bay of Rio de Janeiro, feeling exactly the same happy premonition that I had had coming through Du Toit's Kloof and looking down to Cape Town. I knew Rio was going to be wonderful, and Rio did not disappoint me.

The friends of friends lived in luxury in Ipanema. I was welcomed into their apartment, and stood in my black boots and clumsy gear on their white carpet among priceless paintings and fragile modern art constructions, feeling as though every move I made would cause irreparable damage. "Fantastic," they said. "Wonderful" – as though what they most longed to do was to buy a couple of bikes and come the rest of the way with me. I was used to some of the things that wealth could do to people, and I found their swashbuckling innocence a great relief. They were generous beyond measure, but in a way that made it seem natural, nothing to make a fuss about, something between friends. I found myself installed, for as long as I liked, in a small flat within a hundred yards of the beach, above a ballet school that they ran. Every day I was invited to lunch or dine or visit with someone. Almost everyone they knew seemed to have been the governor of one state or another, or related to some famous pioneer in Brazil's history. I was riding on Rio's inner circle, and the fact of what had happened to me in Fortaleza made it all seem not only unusually pleasurable, but entirely appropriate. I reveled in it.

So it was not long before I was a dinner guest of the best-known and most-liked politician Brazil had produced this century, President Juscelino Kubitchek. The dinner was attended by other powerful and more or less obnoxious people, all striving for mastery in strident Portuguese.

My lack of Portuguese forced me to sit on the sidelines and make do with whispered translations from my friends and Kubitchek's daughter, but I watched him, fascinated. A battle raged around him about the plight of the white Portuguese in Mozambique, which

Frelimo had by now taken over. I thought of my friends there, of Rajah and Amade, and "Vic," who had put me up. Given the monstrous nature of most successful politicians, I was surprised to find that Kubitchek was the only one there whose sympathies I thought could be trusted.

Later I talked to him alone, in French, and found him very pleasant and not at all overbearing. The army, of course, had rendered him powerless, but he maintained his dignity and showed no bitterness. This self-made, self-taught man with the pale, watchful face contradicted all my prejudices about South American presidents.

I was under the particular wing of a lovely dance teacher we called "Lulu," who was the most enthusiastic and intelligent companion any man could hope for. She had friends and relations in every direction, and we drove all over the mountains and beaches in her Volkswagen, Brazil's universal car, tasting every kind of fruit and sea food and exotic drink that Brazil could provide.

When she was teaching I wandered around on the bike and one day I found my way up a narrow road to a new vantage point called the Vista Chinesa. High above Rio, I looked down on the big lagoon and Copacabana. The mountains rise up tall and thin and rounded on top like the divisions of a papier-maché egg box, and the city is squeezed in among them. In the deep clefts the high-rise blocks rise higher and higher, adding always one more floor of priceless property on every lot, and the villas swarm up the mountainsides, clinging ever more precariously. The lagoon, as still as glass, mirrors it all. Rio should really be seen from the air.

Looking over the bushes in front of the mock pagoda, a stir and a whirr caught my attention, and a hummingbird appeared in front of me, the first I had ever seen. It flashed black and blue and green, the most marvellous thing. It was a pulsating masterpiece hanging on a blur of pure movement, its wings no more visible than a heat haze. It dipped its needlelike beak into a blossom. Then it vanished – I swear it almost did – and reappeared a foot away, motionless again except for the slight tremor in the enveloping air. My eyes would have swallowed it whole if they could. When it darted out of sight a little later I felt as though I had been rooted to the spot for an age. It was one of those few moments which I felt could justify one's entire life. I made a note that "magic was simply experiencing something for the first time." It occurred to me then that my purpose should be to increase the number of such moments until maybe, one day, everything could be magic.

It was spring in Brazil, and a perfect temperature for the beach. Lulu had a particularly well-placed relation with a house at Buzios, a most desirable beach because, by a freak twist of the coastline, it faced west instead of east, which gave it shelter and also a spectacular sunset. That weekend remained in my mind as probably the most idyllic of my life, and held the quintessence of what Brazil had to offer.

We wandered away from the main beach across to a smaller one, perfectly shaped, totally deserted. I swam awhile along the cliff face in the crystal-clear water, and then stretched out on a rock on the beach to read. She was standing on the shining wet sand, looking dubiously at her own footprints. Behind her the green mountains, patched with banana and cactus, rushed up into a blue sky.

"How is it when they do the triple jump?" she said.

She stood loosely, with the comical, awkward look dancers some times have when they are not telling their bodies what to do. She was frowning like a clown and running her index fingers around her thighs under her bikini bottom where it had ridden up. I noticed how, in the small of her back, the strong muscle held the edge of the bikini away from her spine.

"Oh tell me please, how does it go, the triple jump?" She pro nounced it tripee-el She had a way of pleading for things in her Brazilian English to make you understand that they were matters simultaneously of no consequence and of life and death. You could refuse, and nothing would be changed; or you could give, and earn undying gratitude. It was a great gift, which she had won by long effort and sorrow and laughter. It was the humorous residue of cravings which had once been corrosive enough to etch her face.

"Is that the hop, skip and jump?" I asked lazily from the rock where I was sitting and reading. I did not want to leave my rock. I had my left leg over the side with the foot in the sand. Every thirty seconds or so the movements of the water combined to send a wave swishing along the side of the rock, covering my leg up to the knee and cooling it. I felt the sun's heat flowing through me into the sea.

"I really don't know," I said. 'Why? What's fascinating you?" She had asked about the triple jump once before, I remembered, in Rio.

"I don't know," she said, each word long-drawn-out and husky. "I am going to try it anyway."

She pursed her mouth and did a coltish sprint along the sand finishing with both feet together. She stood for a while with the sun on her back, her face in shadow, looking again at the prints she had left.

I watched her still, exploring the shape of her body. I would have expected a dancer's body to be harder, to show more muscle. Her limbs were rounded and smooth, her thighs filled out and touched to make an airy triangle below the bikini, her belly curved down from a single crease at the navel. The smooth, firm, well-proportioned body of a twenty-year-old. Only, knowing she was thirty-six, I could appreciate what dancing had done for her. Funny though that her calves had none of that ribbed angularity. Funny too that I wasn't in love with her.

Fused with the wonderful, liquid warmth that flowed around me on the rock, so tangible that it felt like another element to complement the salty heaviness of the sea, was a warmth of feeling for this woman that was as close to love as the skin is to the flesh. Perhaps it would do as well, I thought. In some ways it might even be better. And she loved me. I knew that. Only . . .

I put *Islands in the Stream* face down on the rock at page 241. Strange to be reading Hemingway again, after so long, on this beach, on this coast. Just for a moment I could imagine his bleary heroes bitching at each other right here, game fishing for metaphors in these same blue crystalline waters, drowning in an eternal round of fancy alcohol, fucking up the place with their manly pursuits. The image was impossible to sustain. It must have died with him.

I walked over to where Lulu was standing, on the shining wet sand, with its faint brown wash of iron glittering with fool's gold.

"Look, I am going to jump again. Now, you watch me and see what I do."

She took a short run and jumped. I thought I saw the difference between a dancer and an athlete. The power was in a different place. I drew lines in the sand with my toe to mark off her jump. It was about six feet long. Then I ran and jumped too. My jump was scarcely better. A couple of inches, maybe. We laughed at each other.

"What do you expect from an old man?" I said.

"You are not an old man," she said, "and I am an old woman."

We ran and jumped some more, and I managed to put on another

Above, Tedjy, still smoking, and lovely, lissome, limber Lulu on the beach at Buzios. *Below,* In Iguatú the old church presided heavily over terrible poverty and disaster, while the new priests fought hard to make things better. The police did not appreciate my visit there.

two or three feet. Then I paced out the distance I associated vaguely with the Olympic record, and we looked at the faraway mark with awe.

She took my hand and said: "Oh, Tedjy." I smiled at her, but instead of pulling her down onto the sand I ran into the sea, playing for laughs with a silly, high-stepping trot, dragging her reluctantly behind me until we both fell into the water.

When we came out, she wanted to go back to the other beach. I would have liked to climb back on to my rock, to read some more about frozen daiquiris and "high bolitas," and impossible battles with legendary swordfish, but I didn't object, and we walked back, kicking the sugary sand, towards the other rocks where the little brown gully began that went up through the scrub and over the promontory back to Buzios.

There was a shelf of rock that sloped into the sea, where there were clusters of small mussels in the wash of sea water, their shells gaping like the beaks of fledgelings in a nest.

"We could cook some mussels," I said. "Have you got any matches?"

"Is it all right? We won't be killed?"

She was not really worried. She trusted me.

"Of course it's all right," I said, although I had never cooked mussels on a beach before. "You just have to make sure they're alive." What nonsense, I thought, looking down at them. You're not buying them off a barrow! How could they be anything but alive? Either alive or empty.

We found some bigger stones and built a fireplace against the wind. We pulled some dried sticks out of the scrub. They were as light as straws, and ants scurried out of them through little holes. She found a piece of round clay roof tile and I laid it so that when the mussels opened in the heat the juice would run off along the tile instead of putting out the fire. I became very excited by the idea of making a meal off this small area of rock, and as I worked I thought about living on a beach like this. The vegetation began immediately behind the sand, at the first rise of the ground. Bananas grew there in plenty. Other fruits would certainly grow there also. Vegetables too. The sea was rich with fish, prawns, lobsters. All along the coast were huts and shelters built of wood, split bamboo and banana-leaf thatch. My heart sang with joy just in the knowledge that such a life was possible. The world changed for me. From that moment on I would always know that there was a beach in Brazil, if not this beach then a beach, where I could go and become whole again. What a journey this has become, I thought.

The fire – it was really more like an oven, with a flat stone on top to reflect the heat down on to the mussels – worked very well. The first mussels were orange and meaty and she ate them readily, saying how good they were. Then there were some white ones and she did not like the look of them, so I ate the white ones, and later she did too. They were all very small. It would be hard work living off these, I thought.

"It's just about perfect here," I said.

"What a beautiful oven we have," she said. "It's so good, Tedjy. Let's have some more."

We got through about four dozen. Then she got some cigarettes out of the little pocket in her cap, which was made of scraps of old jeans and reminded me of the one Jeanne Moreau wore in *Jules et Jim*.

I watched a boat rush around the bay pulling a woman on skis. She didn't look very secure. Probably she should straighten her legs and lean back more, I decided. I had water-skied only once, just long enough to know I could do it. I had tried several new things in that way. I wasn't really interested in doing them, just knowing that I could. That wouldn't have been good enough for Hemingway, I thought. Well, Hemingway didn't ride a motorcycle 18,000 miles through Africa and Brazil. And I don't stop every hour for a frozen daiquiri either, I thought. Then I laughed at myself.

"What are you laughing, Tedjy?" I laughed again.

"Just happy," I said. I did feel very happy. I made a mental note that I wished I would give up smoking, but couldn't. Even that did not spoil my happiness.

I took a looping inland circuit from Rio to see the old gold-rush towns of Ouro Prêto and Tiradentes, and the lovely, ethereal church of Congonhas, before going south to São Paulo. There I delivered the sword to my Egyptian friend, who to my amazement had got there before me. I don't know which of us was more astonished. He told me that he had given sums of money to a dozen strangers like myself to post on for him, never less than $2,000, and every one had honored his promise.

The 250 miles from São Paulo to Curitiba were extremely uncomfortable, dirty and dangerous. The road was breaking up and ran along the crown of a range of hills often in cloud. Heavy diesel traffic charged the fog with oil droplets, and covered the visor with tar. Both the throttle and clutch cable seized and the ordeal lasted nonstop for eight hours. I arrived frozen, filthy and wet, but the natural balance of pain and pleasure was rapidly restored. A motor cycle enthusiast snatched me off the streets and gave me a warm shower, food, a bed and an introduction to the kind of civilization that southern Brazil can offer.

He was a fat, warm teddy bear of a man with a limp and a big bushy moustache, and his neat and pretty wife adored him. He and his friends, the "*motoqueros*," all owned expensive three-cylinder Suzukis, and kept every spoke polished. They gathered in a special place in the evenings, like a floating motorcycle showroom, and looked enviously at my scuffed and battered workhorse parked among them. I could not help being saddened that so much fine machinery was so completely underused. It felt almost sinful. If only machines could speak to each other, I thought, that would be a conversation I would like to overhear.

I noticed that my friend Marcio was not the only one with a paunch. Since Rio most of the men I met seemed well fed and fondled their stomachs often through their jersey knitwear. It struck me that I could scarcely remember a fat man north of Rio, but I did recall a conversation with a black shoeshine boy who had been amazed when I described how I travelled. He thought it would be impossible for me to get enough to eat.

"You have to eat so many more things than us," he said, patting his very hard flat stomach. I realized with a shock that he really believed I belonged to a different species and required a quite different diet. Now I had to admit that I did seem to be among a different species. and in a different country.

At Iguaçu, where Brazil, Argentina and Paraguay meet, I chose Argentina, and wandered down past the old Jesuit settlements of

After a long, wet, cold, filthy, and rather dangerous drive from São Paulo to Curitiba, I was glad to be spotted on the street by Marcio, a self-proclaimed *"motoquero"* He took me home, gave me a bed for the night, and introduced me to his friends. Alongside their shiny new Suzukis, which went nowhere, my Triumph looked like a war veteran. If bikes could talk to each other, I thought, that would be some conversation....

A wonderful book, *Don Segundo Sombra,* that I read many years ago first introduced me to the Gauchos, the cowboys of Argentina. When I met them I felt a strong kinship. It was in Argentina, I think, that I turned 'professional'. I was as comfortable in my saddle as they were in theirs. I knew what I had to do to survive, and felt a quiet confidence in my ability to take things, good and bad, as they came.

Missiones into the great beefy heartland of Argentina. The sad and violent history of Argentina was erupting all around me. There were daily shootings. Revolution and ever-greater repression were inevitable. Fine sentiments were like froth on the lips of a dying man. Every shout of "Liberty" drove another nail in the coffin, and "Democracy" came to sound to me like a dirty word.

Yet in this big open land all the vanity and venom of public life seemed like the squabbling of children in the wings of a vast and empty stage. Only the chocolate melancholy of the tango followed me across the Pampa.

I think it was in Argentina that I turned professional. I had been on the road for a year; I had been very high and very low, and everywhere in between. The world no longer threatened me as it had; I felt I had the measure of it.

It must have helped that I was in horse country. I felt very much that I shared something of the gaucho's view of the world, and my seat certainly fitted my saddle as closely as his. Riding the bike was as natural as sitting on a chair. It scarcely tired me at all. I could pack and unpack the bike with the automatic familiarity of shaving, and I did not allow the prospect of it to annoy me. The same was true for minor maintenance problems; a puncture, cleaning a chain, aligning the wheels, whatever it was. I did it without giving a thought to the inconvenience. These things were facts of life. I slept on the ground more often, and my bones began to arrange themselves accordingly. The air bed was punctured and I did not bother with it much. I had a hammock, a wonderful old hammock made for a married couple, and bequeathed to me by Lulu's grandmother. I treasured it and used it as often as possible, finding it very comfortable.

I felt very much tried and seasoned, and no longer expected to make silly mistakes or confront unexpected hazards. I had also developed a battery of useful instincts. I knew when there were thieves around, when the bike had to be protected and when it was safe. More often than not it was safe. I knew when to expect trouble from strangers, and how to defuse it. I knew what drivers of cars and trucks were going to do before they knew it themselves. At times I think I could even read the minds of stray dogs, although it was a rarity to see one on the highway that was not already a pulped carcass at the roadside.

In the natural paradise of the Southern Andes I crossed over to

In Villaguay I finally got the tank bags I needed. Here's Quiroz, the saddlemaker sewing them for me. While I was there, this normally sleepy town in Argentina's prime cattle country was rudely shaken by gunfire

Chile and the long-awaited Pacific Ocean. I continued my political education in Santiago, which was still in the grip of curfews and the throes of nightly shootings in the streets, torture in the prisons and starvation in the slums.

Then again I crossed the mountains, this time at ten thousand feet, to Mendoza. North of Mendoza the parched bones of the Andes sprawl in the waterless wastes of San Juan, Rioja and Catamarca. I rode from oasis to oasis, coming up at last to the fertile valleys of Tucuman and Salta, where I spent my second Christmas.

And in 1975 I began my journey along the roof of the Americas, in Bolivia at fourteen thousand feet.

and murder at the hotel, as the country's "dirty war" spread. *Below,* The deep soil grows wonderful grass, but is soapy slick in the rains. Ancient cars are prefered. Their big wheels, like cart wheels, do better in the mud..

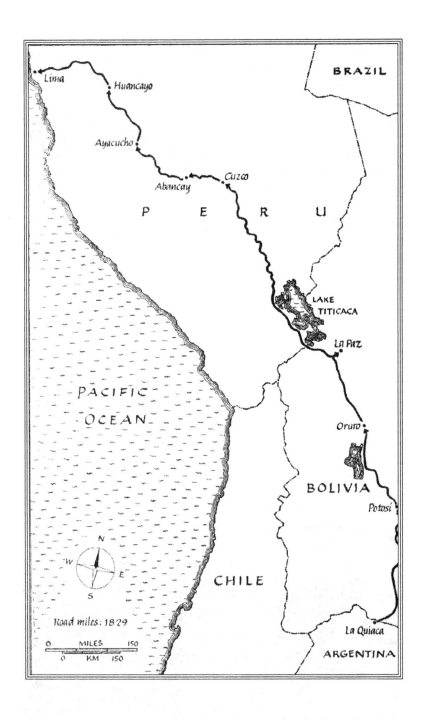

A ntoine usually did the shopping for the three of us. Bruno drove and nursed their battered Renault van. If I had a role on the motorcycle it was to explore the route ahead and find good places for us to eat and spend a night. And sometimes, coming into a small town, I felt like the advance man for a traveling circus.

It was mid-afternoon when we stopped in Abancay to buy food and, well, just to stop for a while. The streets were coming to life after the siesta. In those Peruvian valleys the sun rises at eight and sets at four, although light pours across the mountain tops for the normal number of hours. When the sun does become visible above the peaks the heat bounces down two miles of mountainside to collect at the bottom around the palms and cactus, to roast the big stones in the river bed, and to make the thought of movement disagreeable. The valley may be at six or seven thousand feet above sea level but at mid-day it is very hot. Dogs expose their bellies in the dust. Donkeys stand still as though stuffed, with their heads bathed in any scrap of shade they can find. In the silent mud-walled houses the shadow looks thick as molasses. But the valley is not a desert. Tumbling down the mountainside come streams of water. There are grains, fruit, vegetables and flowers in abundance, as there were in the time of the Incas.

We were parked along the kerb of the main street. Bruno was staring angrily at his engine.

"I've had it up to here with this heap of shit," he hissed in French.

Bruno treated the Renault the way he treated horses, with alternate admiration and contempt. I watched sympathetically, enjoying myself, sitting on the bike a few yards away and resting my forearms and knees. The long descents into the valleys over stony dirt roads were worse for me, a constant jarring from wrists to shoulders, with my knees driving into the leather bags slung across the tank.

I always liked watching Bruno. He did everything with an animal gravity which ended either in gleeful satisfaction or an explosion of rage. I was not far from thinking of him as my son. He had just lost his father and was perhaps still looking for him.

The men of this small town in Peru did not crowd around me as they would have in a city. The Indians, as always, appeared to be perfectly indifferent. Those with more Spanish blood showed their curiosity, at a distance. A large-bellied man in white shirt and trousers presented himself in a ceremonial fashion, as though his fat-ness entitled him to represent the other men, who were mostly thin.

"Where are you going on this *poderosa*," he said in Spanish, very condescending.

"I am going to Lima," I said, careful to maintain the same steady smile. Experience had taught me the delicate art of these exchanges. Eagerness could be an embarrassment. Better to keep a close mouth and savor the tension.

"*Y de donde viene?*"

"I come from England."

Once, in Bolivia, I had made the same reply, but the man I was talking to there had never heard of England. Now I watched to see what England might mean in Abancay. An Indian woman walked past with quick steps, dragging a small black and white pig on a string. Her gaze barely flickered.

"You have come on a long journey."

"Yes," I said. "It has been sixteen months."

"And when do you hope to regain your family?"

"In one year, or perhaps two."

"Good luck," he said. "You have much courage."

There was a flash of gold teeth, and he took off his hat. A crow dropped a small medallion of black and white shit on the crown of his head. He replaced his hat.

"Thank you," I said.

Antoine came back with his face smiling but inwardly composed. It was rarely any other way. His shirt was clean, his hair groomed and there was even a crease in his safari trousers. He was *soigné,* as though on active diplomatic duty. In fact they both had diplomatic passports, having been attached to the French legation in Paraguay. Bruno had bought the old van in Asuncion and wanted to drive it to Mexico. Antoine was sharing the journey as far as Lima. They both spoke Spanish with a fluent French accent. My accent was better, but my Spanish was horrible.

Antoine put back on the dashboard of the van the little Paraguayan bowl where we kept our mutual funds, and reported on his mission.

He had some tomatoes and eggplants and a strange giant bean. There was never much in the shops. We all shared the feeling that somewhere behind the somber shelves of soap and wire wool the good things were quickly hidden away when we came in view. There was

Bruno and his battered Renault van. We traveled the same route through much of the Andes, from Bolivia to Colombia. He is trying to treat a septic finger with boiling hot salt water - a painful remedy he learned from his grandmother. Hence the sour expression on his face.

Mourning becomes electrics. Among the dunes and bushes of a camp site at La Plata, south of Buenos Aires, I searched for an electrical fault. I never found it, but when I put everything together again, furious and frustrated, the fault disappeared. Not an uncommon experience.

no hope of finding meat at this time of day. There were no eggs. Bread was not a local food. We never saw any dairy products aside from tins of condensed milk, although there was a brand of indestructible thousand-year margarine.

"Perhaps further on we will find eggs and mangoes," said Antoine.

"There's a pump down the road, on the way out of town," I said.

Bruno slammed the lid on the engine. "The *salope* will never make it," he shouted.

"To the pump," I asked, or to Mexico?"

"In any case," he said, "we will never get up another mountain today."

I shrugged and put on my jacket and helmet and gloves.

"I'll go ahead and see if I can find somewhere for the night," I said.

From Abancay the road to the north rises steeply again, toiling over the ascending slopes for thirty or forty miles until it runs free at last with the llama and the eagles at twelve thousand feet. It would have been good to get about halfway up and spend the night among the greener trees, the sweeter springs and the fresher air. I wondered what was wrong with the van that it should lose so much power. We had tried many things, all the things that seemed most obvious. At times it went well, but usually it was sluggish and too hot.

I wondered whether to leave them and go on alone. It was always there as a possibility, quietly understood on both sides. I kept all my things on the bike, even though it would have been easier to off load some of them on to the van.

I remembered how we had met at La Quiaca, the Bolivian border town, drawn together by the frustrations of the customs house there. Afterwards we had eaten together in the big canteen over the bus station, soup and rice, and beans and sausage in a spicy red sauce. We were very happy to have finished with all the paper work and the payments of one dollar here, two dollars there for pieces of paper we did not want and would never need. Our hearts were light as mountain air, excited by the journeys we had already achieved, and by the ones that lay ahead.

It was natural for us to travel on together that day. We circled the rim of an immense bowl, thousands of feet deep. I had often anticipated in my imagination the vertiginous drops of the Andes, but had not expected so soon to find myself riding so close to the edge of nothing. I could see the van across this vast upside-down space, a whitish speck crawling along, and at times I imagined Bruno and Antoine inside, exchanging desultory comments. I knew it was dusty in there, and that their vision was limited, and I was glad to be outside and alone, free to escape from my own ordinariness and the train of other people's thoughts.

But at night it was fine to share a meal and talk, to hear about the things I had missed and the thoughts I had not had. So it went on, day by day, but always a thing of the moment. And when, in Potosí, Bruno wanted to go on to Sucre and I wanted to stay and write, it was the easiest thing to separate, perhaps forever, just as it was the easiest thing for us to find each other again, as if by chance, a week later in La Paz. We guarded each other's liberty as though it were our own.

Only sometimes it was not so easy, and you had to pay the price for company. On the third day after La Quiaca, just past noon and in bright sunshine, we came up the highest road I have ever traveled, perhaps the highest in the world, at sixteen thousand feet or more. Ahead of us a party of Indians were crossing the road in procession. Bolivian Indians are among the world's poorest and they lead a harsh life. Most of their clothing is homespun from hand dyed wool, yet no company could have looked more prosperous and content than these Indians as they appeared before us on the tenth of January 1975. We passed them by, and then stopped, entranced. The men were smiling enthusiastically and saluting as they came up to us. Most of them were carrying pottery vessels or cloth-wrapped bundles.

Bruno asked the leader where they were going.

"To Otaví," he replied, pointing over a long rise of stony ground, partly cultivated for maize, where houses were just visible.

"It is the Feast of the Kings. You are invited."

They seemed truly happy that we had arrived at this propitious moment, their happiness no less sincere for having been released by some of the corn beer they carried in the pots.

It was a wonderful chance. The Indians continued across the hill and we found our own roundabout way there.

Otaví is a small town of cobbled streets and adobe houses built on a steep hillside. We climbed the main street still buoyed up by the gaiety and splendor of the Indians we had met on the road. Then I began to realize that the village was in the grip of a quite different mood. There were many people on the sidewalks, standing, leaning, squatting. No one moved. No one spoke. I had the impression of walking through a museum of ethnic culture.

Of course there was sound and movement of a kind. People still breathed, and scratched themselves and raised coca leaves to their mouths. They followed us with their eyes, but a spell had been cast over them and it was like being watched by pebbles on a beach.

On our left was a house with a more imposing roof. A sign identified it as the *corregimiento*, or magistrate's office. The somnolent bystanders were thickest here. The doors were open to reveal people arguing and gesturing, in strange contrast to the entranced pavements outside.

We stood wondering what to do. Already I was absorbed in this world of stone, plaster, lime wash, natural wood and hide, sun bleached wool and bright vegetable dyes arranged in brilliant traditional patterns. Then another man looking as outlandish as we did, in a green corduroy jacket and a porkpie hat, came hurrying down the hill towards us like White Rabbit in Wonderland.

He spoke fluently and eloquently, which was unusual out there even in Spanish, and he was telling us about his fish. This was a fish he had brought from Argentina, but I was never able to grasp its significance because he was quite drunk.

Another man with a crazy black face came to join us then. He was too drunk to speak much, but he waved his arms in large meaningful swoops, and the two of them surrounded us and bore us away on a tour.

"Churchill, Franco, de Gaulle, Truman. I know them all," said White Rabbit. He spoke with abandon about economic imperialism, military juntas and exploitation, while Crazy Face conducted the flow of words with his arms. We strolled on past the rows of enchanted spectators, and it at last got through to me that everybody in town was simultaneously stoned and squiffy on cocaine and alcohol.

The *corregidor* had forbidden the annual procession and fiesta. Great negotiations were in progress while the would-be revelers could do nothing but drink their chichi, chew their leaf, and become silently blotto.

Two women walked past side by side, crooning and carrying white flags, followed by several children and an old man with a long curved bamboo woodwind, but this unofficial procession died before our eyes. The old man tried to play for us, producing three dismal honking notes and sprays of saliva as his drunken lips failed to hold on to the mouthpiece.

We inspected the chapel at the top of the hill. Most of the stucco had peeled off it, and old crones sat in the shade of the entrance leaning stupefied against the chapel walls.

Yet there were some energetic spirits and they were determined to create some sort of pageant around us, and they pressed us to stay and drink and wait for the fun to start. Inevitably we were nervous, wondering what would happen to us if this whole damned drunken town should spring to life in a full-blooded fiesta. We had to decide because we were a group, and if we wanted to get to Potosí that day we would have to leave soon. Somehow we let our fears speak for us in the name of wisdom and we left.

Alone, I would have stayed, and learned much more about those people. The chance did not come my way again.

There is a way to convert fear into positive energy. When I had discovered it for myself along the way, I used it quite deliberately to project confidence and sympathy. It had never failed me, and it gave me an unusual and exhilarating sense of power over circumstance. But it seemed to function only when I was alone.

So as I left Abancay and started climbing the dirt road I wondered whether it was time, again, to go on alone, not to go faster but because I thought I might lose my power in the group. Then I put the matter aside, satisfied with having brought it to my attention, thinking, "I'll know when the moment comes," and I set about looking for a place where we could cook and eat and sleep.

The least we needed was a level area to park the van and pitch a tent. For a while there was nothing. Small, terraced allotments, heavily cultivated, occupied every corner of open ground among the rocks and bushes. Then, at the tenth kilometer stone, a path opened off to the right into a gently sloping field sparsely planted with olive trees. Beyond it, in the distance, was a white building. The earth was dry and stony, and not very inviting, but it would do.

It was just the time of day when my hallucinations came to try me out. They were of the crassest kind possible. Usually they began with nothing more original than a cold bottle of beer. When my appetite was sufficiently inflamed I would go on to lobster, roast beef and real coffee, followed by an accidental meeting with a perfect and most loving woman in a large, clean bed. Sometimes I would conjure up the settings for these indulgences but it was hardly worth bothering. They were always roughly similar, and involved clean table linen, polished glassware, bathrooms with towels and an abundance of friendly hospitality and admiration. As the afternoons turned to evenings and I began to wonder where I would eat and sleep that night, this television set turned on in my head and subjected me to trial by advertisement, hitting me inexorably with every one of my known cravings in turn.

It was not my appetite for cold beer or perfect loving women that shamed and appalled me at those times, it was the fact that I allowed these images to oppress me when they were clearly unattainable, and to make what was there and real and within my grasp seem undesirable. Under the influence of these lobster and champagne ravings I became the perfect sucker, vulnerable to the shoddiest substitutes. For lack of cold beer I would waste money on warm Coke, and hate it. I would fall prey to any hotel sign, knowing full well that far from enjoying a clean bed and loving women I would be shut up in a dirty, fetid box with a hundred mosquitoes.

It is said that at three or four in the morning the body is physically at its lowest ebb, but it was at five in the afternoon, at the cocktail hour, that my morale slumped, and the temptations came to me in the wilderness. I fought them as best I could through all the years of the journey and always, when I won, I was handsomely rewarded. I carried a stock of memories of magical evenings out alone in the wild, completely satisfied by the simple food I had cooked, listening to the silence and toasting the stars in a glass of tea, and I used these memories as my blindfold against the gross sirens that beckoned with their neon smiles. Success was built on success, and sometimes I was able to carry through a victorious campaign for days or weeks on end, becoming hardier and happier with each succeeding day. But the war could never be truly won. Sooner or later some warm, generous person on my trail would offer, unsolicited, some or even all of the delights I had learned to ignore. Then, when it was time to leave, the struggle would begin all over again. Like a general, I was only as good as my last battle.

Yet the torment only ever lasted for an hour in every twenty-four. During the day, out in the world, no matter how hard or cold or wet the road might be, I never wished I were safe in the Ritz. More often the road was neither cold nor wet, and I felt myself to be the most privileged person on earth to be able to pass through where others saw only normality, and to think myself in paradise. While at night I swam lazily among mysterious and potent dreams.

And still . . . during the days before I met Antoine and Bruno at La Quiaca my morale had been sagging badly. I had left Santiago with a heavy heart. I wanted company, and I knew that was why I was not ready to leave them. They protected me from my five o'clock follies, and I was grateful to know they were chugging up the road behind me, pleasant and familiar friends.

So on that evening outside Abancay my cerebral TV channel was showing a different program. As clearly as if I stood before it, the white building in the distance became the stately hacienda that somewhere in South America I had always hoped to encounter. I saw the richly molded plaster work framing heavy wooden doors studded with black iron; floors of gleaming hardwood polished and hammered by generations of leather boots; ancestral portraits of Spanish swordsmen in lace and breastplate; stiff white table linen splashed with the crimson geometry of candlelight passing through cut-glass goblets of wine; and myself deep in a leather armchair, listening to my host tell tales of the Conquest, as I gazed up at the white faces of his perfect daughters flitting coyly behind the rails of the gallery beneath the coffered ceiling.

With a sigh I stopped the bike and waited. It was not many minutes before the dusty white van labored into sight. We turned into the field and chose a good spot. Antoine got out the plastic water carrier and we all drank some warmish water. I threw my red bag and jacket to the ground, and added my helmet to the pile. Bruno lifted the hood of the van and began again to wonder what he could do to the engine.

"There's a house over there," I said. They had not noticed.

"I'll see who's there and tell them what we're doing. Maybe I can get some meat," I added, thinking about the wine and the girls on the gallery. I rode along the path, about five hundred yards, past an area of thick marshy grass. The house and its courtyards were enclosed by a high wall, and as I approached, the house became hidden from view. A van stood outside the broken iron gate, and three men were talking. Two of them said "Adios," and looked at me curiously, then got into their van and drove off. The third man watched me, without expression, as I parked the bike and walked towards him. He was so placed that I still could see nothing of the house.

"*Buenos dias,*" I said. "*Buenos dias,*" he replied, and waited as I composed my Spanish.

"We are in the field down there," I said. "We are three. We hope to spend the night there."

"If you like," he said, and fell silent again. He was half Spanish and wore shabby Western clothing. His shirt was buttoned up around his neck, and I noticed a great many red dots on his skin above the collar and on his arms below the short sleeves.

"We would like to buy some meat if you please."

"There is no meat," he said, without emphasis or explanation.

"If possible, we would like to buy a chicken," I suggested.

"There is no chicken," he said.

This time I simply watched him, patiently, until he felt obliged to fill the vacuum.

"We sell all our meat to the buyer of meat. You can ask him."

"Thank you, Señor. I will try. Where is his house?"

"At thirty-three kilometers," he said.

I could not make sense of his reply as I felt sure the buyer would be in town, and pointed that way.

"No," he said. "At the thirty-third kilometer," and waved towards the mountain.

"He has a house?" I asked. It was a poor question, but I could think of nothing better. Already I was feeling slightly uneasy.

"*Si, hay una casa,*" he replied. Again silence. He was shrouded in silence. Or he was listening to sounds I could not hear.

"*Bueno. Muchas gracias.*" Slowly I turned towards the bike, hoping he might add something, but he simply stood and watched me ride away.

It meant riding nineteen kilometers. I told Bruno and Antoine what I was doing and set off up the road. It continued to climb steeply and the air grew cooler. The trees were leafier, and a pleasant brook bubbled along the roadside. Some goats, startled on their way home, skittered up an almost vertical face of rocks and bushes, and a small girl, half their size, shouted and rushed after them at the same speed, her long skirts flying. Where the road curved around a spur a few mud and wattle huts stood among banana trees on a shelf of ground overhanging the valley. An Indian woman was hoeing her corn. I asked for "the man who buys meat" but she shook her head helplessly. Beyond these huts there was no further sign of human habitation. I passed the thirty-third kilometer stone.

The vegetation thinned, and large areas of the mountainside were bare. It seemed absurd to suppose that a meat wholesaler would have his warehouse at the top of a mountain. My embarrassment and indignation welled up in a tide of fury. I had allowed myself to want the meat (and the sherry and the daughters) and it had made me stupid.

I turned around, storing up anger for the man who had sent me on this mad errand, determined to confront him, preparing phrases which would shame him into telling me the truth. I could not conceive that he had invented the meat buyer, but at the same time I imagined his laughter as he watched me roaring off and up the mountain.

As I passed Bruno and Antoine I could hardly get a word out. Astonishingly, the man was still standing near the gate. As before he watched me get off the bike and walk towards him.

"There is nobody up there, Señor," I said, tight-lipped.

"You could not find him?" he asked.

"There is nothing there," I said. "No house, no people."

"Well," he said, "*entonces*, there is some meat. Please come with me."

His face betrayed no reaction, no hint of mockery, but the voice was, I thought, faintly tinged with interest. Bewildered, I followed him through the gate.

The house was now revealed in all its glory, but it was the glory of total decay. Windows without frames stared blankly from peeling and cracked walls. Broken shutters hung drunkenly by one hinge. A once magnificent porch was littered with wrecked furniture and masonry rubbish, and the lath and plaster ceiling above it bellied down like the breastbones of a decomposing whale. We walked towards it across a muddy and unkempt yard. A wave of athletic pigs swept across our path, driving frantic hens in all directions. In a dark corner of the porch an old Indian woman bundled up in black sat spinning yarn, all her life apparently concentrated in her fingers as the floss of wool flowed from her right hand to the twirling bobbin in her left. There were a few younger men and women moving or standing but I could not tell whether they had any purpose. The sense of collapse was general and overwhelming.

The man with the spots asked me to wait a moment while he went into the house. I wish I had gone in with him, for I never saw the inside, but my attention was caught by a large blueprint pinned to the wall. It was a diagram headed *Co-operativo del 24 Junio,* and it set out the organization of the co-operative, with the chairman and his council on top and the descending chain of command and responsibility. It was sufficiently elaborate to be interesting, and simple enough to be credible. In faraway Lima I imagined this piece of paper must have impressed a number of people.

"Now here we have our *Veinte-cuatro Junio.* You see, our reforms are going well. The people are really taking the land into their own hands. They have a fine building there too, for their meetings and recreation. The original landlord described it to me. He is a friend of mine, you know – a friend of the revolution. He lives in Lima, of course, with his four perfect daughters . . ."

I wondered whether the man with spots was the chairman. Then he came out and asked me again to follow him. My cravings had subsided and I was in a much happier state. My senses now were bristling with excitement at the sights and sounds and smells that surrounded me. We walked around the main building past sheds and outhouses, and plodded uphill across some fallow grassland. Eventually we reached a cluster of huts like the ones I had seen from the road. An Indian woman came out towards us, wiping her hands on her embroidered apron. She had a nice, smiling face. I had the strange impression that we were expected, as though she had had a telephone message that we were coming, a ludicrous idea.

She wore her stiff-brimmed black hat set very square on her head, and her long black hair hung in two braids. They talked awhile in the Indian language. Then the man said to me:

"This is my wife. She will show you the meat."

She smiled at me again and led me into a smaller hut. The light outside was already fading, and inside it was very dark. A barrel stood there, on end, open at the top. She pointed to it and I saw it was full of raw meat encrusted with dried blood. She pulled out the first lump and held it up for inspection. It was a shapeless mass weighing many kilos. I could not guess which part of the animal it was, only that it was cow.

"*Es muy grande,*" I said.

She gestured that I should look for myself. I laid my gloves aside on a crate and plunged my hands into the gory mess. After a while I found a piece that I liked better than the rest. None of it smelled bad, and I could not understand how the meat stayed fresh in the heat of the day, with all the flies around, and no salt or preservative.

The problem fascinated me, but my Spanish was not good enough to resolve it.

The piece of meat I had chosen looked quite gruesome and was still too large. The man laid it on a tree stump and chopped it in half with a wood ax. His wife brought a yard arm and weighed one of the halves. It came to just under two kilos, and I paid the price, which was half the price in the butchers' shops when you could find one.

I carried the piece away in my bloodstained fingers, still convinced that it would be inedible. I felt that I was living through part two of a complex and inscrutable hoax, but by now I was a willing accomplice.

Antoine and Bruno did not, as I expected, turn pale with disgust when I held out my trophy, so I got busy on the lump with my knife and their cutting board, and found three fine big steaks inside. The bits and pieces, shorn of their crusts, I put aside for soup stock. As I worked I discovered a possible reason why my friends seemed so indifferent. When I held my head still a quivering cloud formed in front of my eyes, a curtain of shimmering dots too close for focus. I put my hand to my face and found blood on it, my own blood. The flies, for that is what they were, were small, noiseless, numerous and avaricious beyond belief. Their bodies, when you could see one, were custard yellow, but they were hardly bigger than fruit flies. They seemed to chew their way into the skin so that the blood welled out in gouts.

I have never been able to make my peace with mosquitoes, and they have troubled me in most parts of the world. Some people I know have taught themselves to be undisturbed. It used to impress me to watch Father Walsh in Fortaleza, talking calmly or watching television while several of the huge hump-backed mosquitoes they had there fed contentedly on his forehead. By comparison I was as agitated as a scarecrow in a gale. He used to say that as they were not *Anopheles* there was no danger of malaria and, furthermore, there was no point in killing them once they got started, since the irritation came from the anticoagulant they injected first. If you let them get on with it, the chances were, he said, that they would suck most of the poison out again. It seemed a most rational and saintly attitude, and represented exactly the style of pragmatic holiness they all practiced up there at São Raimundo.

One might have thought that traveling constantly and knowing that any irritations I met along the way would soon be left behind would make it easier to bear these trifling inconveniences. Not so. At least, not for me. They could be suffered, but not dismissed.

As for the anticoagulant theory, that did not work for me either. It was the Buddhists who eventually made me realize that if you are waiting for a spot to hurt, it will do its best to hurt you. When I allowed the insect to have its fill of me I could never forget that I was conducting an experiment and in consequence it always hurt. So I used my mosquito net and waved my arms, and came to a kind of dynamic equilibrium with mosquitoes.

But not with the flies of Abancay. They were for me the insect equivalent of the piranha fish, and I could almost see their saw toothed jaws tearing into me. I put up my net as fast as I could and prayed the mesh was fine enough to keep them out. I am lucky enough not to share the common horror of slimy, creepy and slippery things. Snakes, spiders, beetles and worms do not distress me, and often I find them full of interest, but these silent devourers of my flesh filled me with loathing. I swore never to stop anywhere again where there was one of the tiny monsters to be seen, and said a prayer, in passing, for the Conquistadors.

Bruno said there was a similar black fly in Paraguay, and he seemed more resigned to it, while Antoine showed no visible reaction at all that I can remember.

While twilight lasted, two men came riding past towards the house, wearing scarves and cowboy hats and broad leather chaps or *pasa montes*. At that moment I remembered that I had left my gloves behind at the hut, and I called out to them, saying I would come in the morning to collect them. At the back of my mind was the idea that they would be less likely to disappear if it was known that I was coming back for them. The next morning I discovered my mistake.

When I came to the hut I could not find my nice, smiling woman. There was a strange couple there.

"Yes," said the man, "Luis has your gloves, to give to you. Now he has gone off into the mountains to hunt for cochineal, and it is impossible to find him. But tonight or tomorrow morning, Señor, have no fear, he will bring them to you."

The long conversation that followed was merely to express my frustration. It was clearly fruitless from the start. The meat had, after all, cost me dearly, for it was a long time before I could find another pair of suitable gloves. I consoled myself with the knowledge that the experience had been priceless, but still I cursed myself and all Indians indiscriminately. Then we set off up the mountain.

The van was no better than the day before. It was never out of first gear. As soon as the sun appeared it began to overheat again, and they drove with the hood up. Since Bruno could not see where he was going, Antoine had to stand up and lean out of the open door calling directions to Bruno. In this unlikely fashion they would creep up the mountain towards me as I sat on some pleasant rock beside a river, watching and thinking. I spent a lot of time then, and later, thinking about the meat buyer. Many days later I learned that it was forbidden by decree for producers to sell meat privately. Also, every alternate week had been declared "meatless" to favor exports. I thought that explained some of it, but by no means all. And I went on listening for the sounds that the man with the spots seemed to hear. Perhaps, I thought, they also offered relief from blood-sucking flies.

The mountain got steeper, and there were dizzy drops from the road. The views in these great valleys are unequaled anywhere, and I benefited from Bruno's snail's pace to sit quietly and observe distant peaks and terraces, and then all the small detail around me. Sometimes little goat herds peered at me bashfully from behind trees, to disappear with a giggle and pop up again in seconds in a quite different place. Their strength and agility must have been extreme.

As we rose into the thinner air the van lost more and more power until at last it was exhausted and could go no farther. Yet we felt that we must be near the summit. Once there, it would be a hundred miles or more of level roads and steep descent. We had to get to the top somehow.

"I'll give you a tow," I said. "Well, why not. You've almost got enough power. The bit extra I can give you will make the difference."

It worked for a while, but then the bike began to get unpleasantly hot and I was thinking we would have to find some other way when I saw some people ahead of us on the narrow dirt road. It is a rarity, I am sure, to see a motorcycle towing a car up a hill, but they were even more odd, I thought. They were walking, but not at all the way one walks in order to get somewhere, or for the fun of walking. They were in procession and had a religious air about them. There was a man in the lead and he held an object in his hand, but I could not make out what it was, and in any case he was not carrying it with reverence. Yet there was an unmistakable aura of ecstasy about them all.

I stopped the bike, and the van stopped too. At last the leader of the procession reached us, and the others stood behind him, a random group of people enchanted by their fate. The object I had been unable to identify was the fractured steering link of a bus. The driver and his passengers had just narrowly escaped plunging thousands of feet down a mountainside. They were in a state of bliss.

When we explained what we were doing, the driver approached the van like a faith healer, and laid his hands on the distributor. With the minimum of fuss, the engine power increased by fifty per cent and we sailed away to the top of the mountain.

My greatest concern the next evening was to be out of range of the "yellow peril." Several times on the climb beyond Andahuaylas I stopped on some idyllic campsite until, after a few minutes, the first flesh-eating fly homed in and I fled farther up the mountain. Altitude was the only defense. That night we slept in a high valley, moist and green and so intensely cultivated that there was scarcely space for us. Bruno wanted to move into an empty barn, but the owner said he put his pigs there when it rained. It looked like rain, so we made do on a grass verge.

Next day I planned to make Ayacucho, a long ride, and I left the others far behind. They were much better equipped to travel in the dark and could afford to arrive later. The road plunged again into a deep valley, a phenomenal drop to the Rio Pampas, where I was once again among thorn and cactus. The climb on the other side of the river was correspondingly high, and took me after several hours to a plateau at fifteen thousand feet. I saw eagles and, for the first time, the world's biggest bird, the condor. It was soaring at some distance, and its size was not noticeable until it flapped, just once, its twelve-foot wings. The shape they made as they beat up and down left no doubt. It was an airborne monster, a thrilling sight to see.

The road ran on across this high table of rock and scrub much farther than the map indicated. Herds of llama and alpaca scattered at my arrival, a hazard because instead of running away from danger, isolated animals ran to the herd, often across my path. I could feel the cold gathering, and worried that I did not have enough fuel. The sun was almost down, hitting me in the eyes and dazzling me as always happened when I was most concerned about making good time and keeping out of potholes. Then I met a truck, the only vehicle I had seen, and miraculously the driver had spare gas.

I made the last long descent into Ayacucho in the dark. Ayacucho is an important town in Peruvian history. A great battle was fought in that valley and it has interest for tourists. There was a simple but graceful hotel with patio and fountains and tiled corridors. I was given a room to myself for seventy *soles*. The usual price was eighty *soles*.

"*Por essos que llegen en coche, ochenta. Pero essos en moto son muy hombre*," said the clerk with a grin. In other words, car drivers pay the full rate but there is a discount for heroes.

Attached to the hotel was a cafe-restaurant. It was built as an afterthought and compared with the hotel it was shoddy and fly blown. It reflected the general indifference to standards in food and drink, an indifference born of scarcity. It was pointless to work up an appetite for steak, a cold beer or an egg fried in butter. The chances were more than even that whatever you wanted you could not have.

In South America the Spanish language is called Castillano and the two most important words in Castillano say it with a brevity greater even than the Anglo-Saxon:

No hay. There isn't any.

"Beer?" I asked.

"*No hay cerveza*."

"Steak?"

"*No hay*."

"What do you have?"

"*Huevos con arroz*."

"Can I have some butter with the eggs, please.?"

"*Mantequilla no hay*."

"All right, bring me a Coca-Cola and coffee."

The waiter brought a Pepsi (which I like even less) and two jugs.

One jug contained hot water. The other jug, a small glass one, seemed to have an inch of soya sauce in the bottom.

"Where is the coffee?"

The waiter pointed scornfully at the black sauce:

"*Aqui es!*"

It was liquid coffee essence, something I hadn't seen since Hitler blockaded the British Isles. I imagined it was pumped out of the ground in times of national emergency.

I had not had a cup of real coffee since Argentina, but at least there had been powdered coffee. Usually the tin was brought to the table in the futile pretense that it was genuine Nescafé. In elegant places they had little wickerwork baskets made specially to cradle the Nescafé, as though it were a precious wine.

In Chile, Bolivia, Peru, Ecuador and even most of Colombia, real coffee *no hay*. But in Ayacucho we sank to a new low.

I fell into conversation with an American real estate operator who had decided to holiday through the American economic recession. He was quite human until I asked what he did. Then he flew into a frenzy of phrases about "golf-course communities and high-density situations facilitating magnificent view-orientation possibilities." In the Spartan circumstances of Ayacucho the unreality of real estate was extreme.

Bruno and Antoine found me there later listening to speculations on the view-orientation facilitation situation in late 1975 in the Florida area. They brought more news from the land of *No Hay*. We were in a fuel starvation situation. Ayacucho had run out of gas.

In the morning we hung about the gas stations, hoping for a miracle, and shortly before lunch we were granted one. A tanker got through. With it came the news that the usual route to Huancayo was washed out by the flooded river Mantaro. The other route was long and circuitous, and would take at least two days.

Twenty-five miles beyond Ayacucho I took a nail through my rear tire. There were two holes in the tube and I spent an hour and a half repairing them with great care, because once again I was stuck with unreliable patches and no spare tube. A truck packed with Indian passengers passed by. I heard the usual shouts of "gringo" accompanied by mocking remarks in the Indian language. As I stood up a clod of wet mud splattered against my shirt and fell into the open wallet at my waist. It did not seem funny at the time.

The Peruvian Indians, on the whole, looked very apathetic and ground down by their toil and dreary poverty. The color and vitality of their weaving always seemed in direct contradiction to their lives, as though the inspiration for it had died centuries before and the fingers were simply reproducing it by some freak genetic mutation. Sometimes the apathy gave way to resentment, directed mainly at gringos. Although it was the Spaniards who had set their heels on the necks of the Indians long ago, the *yanqui* was the enemy now. All European travelers took the brunt of it.

Bruno and Antoine had been cooking while I worked, and I ate something with them quickly. We were at a very high altitude and hoped to get a good deal lower before stopping. When I took the bike off the stand, the tire collapsed again. I tried my last resort, an aerosol puncture-repair canister carried for emergencies. It felt like an emergency.

I pumped in the latex foam, and we set off. Within fifteen minutes the tire was flat again. Life could be like that; one damn thing after another. I pumped it up and rode another fifteen minutes. So we went on for two hours; fifteen minutes of riding, six minutes of pumping, with me rushing ahead full tilt in the darkness trying to keep up a decent average speed.

The air felt appreciably warmer when we came to Pilpichaca and a small roadside café, and we stayed there enjoying the company of the owners and their children, but we were still at fourteen thousand feet and I had a chilly night in the tent.

In the morning the others went on ahead while I stuffed a nineteen-inch front-wheel tube into my eighteen-inch rear tire; the obvious solution to my problem. Then I set off to catch them.

The road ran alongside a lake, with snow caps in the distance. The views everywhere were quite extraordinary, and would have been unforgettable had there not been so many of them. The dirt roads, though, were variable and difficult, some loose and slippery, some wet, some stony and ridged, and with many sudden surprises on bends. On one of them, sure enough, I slid gently off into a muddy hole. It took me a long time to work the bike out, with everything unpacked and spread around me. Normally I might have been more stoical about it, but a truck was parked within shouting distance, and the driver saw me struggling. I called to him but he ignored me, and it was plain he wanted me to stew in my own juice. My mood became bitter as I reflected on Indian behavior and I spent a good deal of the day immersed in unworthy hatred of them.

Finally, though, the glorious landscapes around Huncavelica lifted me out of this depression. I lay for a while among rocks of bizarre and brilliant colors, sculpted by wind into the shapes of mythical creatures, and felt some sort of benign force enter me from the hillsides. It was a very long and exhausting ride to Huancayo, with mile after mile and hour after hour of sharp descents. My arms and knees ached with the effort of holding my body back in the saddle. The brakes and gears fought to hold the bike at a reasonable speed on the stony surfaces, but I was feeling strong and capable again and arrived before night happy and full of the splendors of the Andes.

It was too late to find Bruno and Antoine, who had had an address to find outside the town. I went instead to the Tourist Hotel, a rather grand place, thinking I had earned the luxury. It was a mountain resort hotel for a clientele of comfortable means seeking relief from Lima. The restaurant was roomy and correct, with the right napery and settings, and a menu in French. A middle-aged English couple entered, each with a bull mastiff on a leash. Their tweedy clothes and manner advertised their nationality before they had even spoken and I waited breathlessly for confirmation. The man glanced around the room, looked questioningly at his consort and uttered two words straight from the trenches of the first world war:

"Same hole?" he asked. It would be hard to imagine a more eloquent phrase, provided you knew the code.

Bruno, Antoine and I joined together again for the descent to Lima. It began at a final high peak, and there, at Morococha, under a shower of grimy sleet, I saw what must be the highest ecological disaster area in the world. The worst Welsh mining town could not have competed even in its heyday. Pitiful rows of slum cottages, squalid railway yards, factories belching acrid smoke, vast slag heaps oozing lurid and poisonous wastes into stagnant pools where ragged children splashed barefoot, and all among unmelted drifts of yellow snow and bitter cold. The road was broken up and treacherous, and the image of that place stayed with me as a supreme example of the way men's lives can be degraded in the midst of such rich natural beauty. To create so much filth at fourteen thousand feet is a quite diabolical achievement.

The Lucas people received me very well in Lima, and pampered me with hospitality, while Bruno went off to stay with some French embassy people. I pulled on overalls and buried myself in minor repairs, and then wandered rather aimlessly about the city.

For once my own private introductions failed me. One friend of friends said on the telephone that unfortunately she could not speak to me since she was at lunch. Others used their hospitality as a defensive weapon, in a way like saying, "We've let you sit in our splendid home, we've given you all you can eat and drink, so you have no further claim on us. Good-bye." It was not consciously intended, but there was so much jealous pride in these Lima socialites that natural feeling could find no place. Small wonder that I found them insular and snobbish, and felt a wave of sympathy for the Indians after all, who had to bear the weight of all this arrogance.

Road miles: 2970
By boat ------
By aeroplane ----

CARIBBEAN
SEA

Cartagena
TO
SAN ANDRÉS

Panama
City

PANAMA

Medellín

Bogotá

PACIFIC
OCEAN

COLOMBIA

Popayán

La Plata

Pasto

Quito

ECUADOR

Guayaquil

Talara

Paita

BRAZIL

Chiclayo

P E R U

N
W — E
S

Punta
Salinas

Lima

MILES
0   300
0   KM   300

B runo lost his passenger, Antoine, at Lima, and went on alone in the 4L. We agreed to stay together. During the four weeks we had spent in the mountains we seemed to have reached an almost perfect understanding. I no longer felt the same fear of losing contact with the people around us. With such distinctly different vehicles we spent most of the time traveling alone, and we had already demonstrated several times that neither one was prepared to fuss about the other. We were ready to take our chances, each of us in his own way, and we came together to cook, or camp together, to buy food or sometimes to halve the cost of a hotel room, and of course to talk. It was not the same as traveling alone, but I had to admit that the dour indifference of the people I had encountered so far made me glad of company. I found the people wearisome to contemplate. Traveling with Bruno was like a holiday.

And we were going to travel along the Pacific coast.

There would be fish, more fish than we had ever seen. Everybody told us. You had only to tie a safety pin to a piece of string and you would catch one. And crabs! The biggest, meatiest crabs, in abundance. Lobsters! Delicious, fresh, cheap. And oysters! The oysters, they said, were as big as dinner plates. They were extraordinary, juicy, full of flavor and each one as nourishing as a steak.

There would be hundreds of miles of empty beach, where it never, ever rained, and we were going to roll gently along the coast, sleeping out, living off the sea, saving money and having a fantastic time.

It took us too long to find our way out of Lima and onto the Pan-American Highway. We had thought it best to get as far from the capital as possible on the first day, before looking for a beach, but at dusk we had managed only a hundred miles and, what was worse, we were on a part of the road that circled away from the coast. There were dirt roads leading off to the sea, and we took one hoping we might still find a beach in time, but we seemed to be crossing an artificial wasteland or army training ground. It was crisscrossed with tracks, and signposts with names and numbers that told us nothing, and in the gathering dark we saw headlights sweeping over great distances, and heard the rumbling of engines. We went as far as we could, but found no beach. Finding two solid signposts near each other, we hitched our hammocks between the roof rack of the 4L and the signposts, fed ourselves and went to sleep. During the night, sev-

At the end of the road, there is only death. Nothing could better describe the miserable lives of the inhabitants of this Peruvian company town, dominated by what amounts to a huge burial mound, where children play, and where the

crosses trap plastic garbage blown down the street by an arid south wind. The town is San José, the industry is fish processing. On this part of the coast it never rains, sparing the company the expense of proper roofs, *(Continued)*

eral big trucks ground slowly past, thrashing their gears, and in the morning we saw we were in a great field of natural salt deposits. In fact we had come within a few hundred yards of the sea, and we scrambled over a bluff and down to the water. There was no real beach, but a lot of rocks tumbling into the ocean, and a few patches of sand. All over the rocks we saw crabs, big red and black crabs, but how were we to catch them? We had no net, or bait. We had not even bought a fishing line yet. It seemed, though, that if we were stealthy enough in coming over a rock we might catch one with a suitable weapon before it had realized its danger.

Bruno had something closely resembling a spear, and for a while we scrambled over the rocks, lashing at the crabs and missing them by a hair's breadth, but always missing. I could see Bruno was getting furious. He hated to be beaten by a crab. It was pretty obvious to both of us by this time that these were not the great, fat, juicy eating crabs we had been promised, but it had become a desperate sport. Bruno rushed off to the van and came back with a wild look and a tiny nickel-plated revolver in his hand. It was time for me to get out of the way.

Looking more like a crab himself, he crept over the rocks, and fired several times, but without success. Finally he managed to corner a big one in a cleft. We both looked and saw this insolent monster sitting there, pointing at us with its eyes and munching slowly and steadily. It was point-blank range. Bruno fired again and again, and the crab went on munching until the magazine was exhausted. Then the crab turned away contemptuously and vanished. It had not been trapped at all, merely unconcerned.

That day we traveled two hundred miles, almost to Chimbote, but passed no town big enough to sell fishing equipment. However, we did find a beach. It stretched off straight to the horizon, at low tide, with a thick blanket of sea weed defining the high-tide mark. The smell of it was invigorating beyond belief, a special quality, I always thought, of the Pacific. A little grass hut with a chimney stood alone and deserted on the beach, but there was otherwise no sign that the beach was known to man. We found driftwood and made a fire but, failing fish, we dined on eggs, rice and onions, tasty but prosaic.

In the morning we found that the van was stuck in the sand. As we worked to extricate it with shovel, ropes and brushwood, a girl

although drinking water has to be trucked in all along this coast. An old lady and a younger woman peered out suspiciously at me from their ramshackle hovel and, not surprisingly, the people of San José appeared sullen and inhospitable.   By contrast, a few miles further along the coast was another fishing community, equally poor but self-governing, where the people were cheerful, dignified and welcoming. Apparently it is not just poverty that makes a slum.

appeared unexpectedly from behind a low ridge of sandstone. She looked rather dusty, and her sleeveless black top did not quite register with her bra. She asked for a lift to Chimbote, saying that a man had dumped her there when she refused to do it.

Bruno took her in the van, and she showed us where to buy fishing lines, hooks and sinkers. Some boys sold us a handful of big gray grubs they were digging up on the beach, and we set off to find fish.

Our first efforts were not a success. At Puerto Mori we had to pay a toll just to get on the beach, and caught nothing. The following day, beyond Trujillo, we were unlucky again. There were only pebble beaches. Both of us constantly snagged our lines, and I lost mine altogether. However, this time we had thoughtfully provided against failure by buying a big fish at the market. It weighed a kilo and a half, and was like a mullet. Grilled, it was wonderful, and we gorged ourselves into a stupor. I at least was getting used to the idea that fishing was one thing, and eating fish another, but the taste spurred us on.

The following night we found a beach close to a fishing village and saw crates of the fish being brought ashore. We had no difficulty buying one, but still we could catch nothing. Absolutely determined to win some kind of free booty from the sea, I turned my greedy eyes on the small crabs that were dashing about all over the beach.

"If we got enough of them," I said, "maybe they would make a soup. I saw the same mad glint kindle in Bruno's eye.

"*Allons-y,*" he shouted. In the dark, with a hurricane lamp, we rounded up dozens of the miserable, dazed creatures. The result of all this slaughter was quite inedible. Full of shame, we swept up the litter of pathetic limbs strewn around us and buried it. The collective unconscious of the crab world was not slow to revenge itself though. The next day I stepped into the water and felt a most excruciating crunch on my foot from an enormous pincer. For an hour I suffered intense pain and thought I would probably die.

We decided then that it was time to try for some of the other delights of the Pacific.

"At Chiclayo," said Bruno, "is the Tourist Hotel, where we will eat oysters and lobsters. It will be wonderful. I have been told about it. Oysters and lobsters with cold white wine. Prepare yourself."

I had to admit the hotel looked promising. The entrance was

grand, the waiters wore starched white coats. There were table cloths and, wonder of wonders, white bread rolls.

"Waiter," I said, as one approached with a menu, "we want oysters, oysters as big as this plate."

"*No hay,*" he said.

"In that case," said Bruno grandly, "we will have lobster."

"*No hay,*" said the waiter, and offered us prawns in batter.

We looked at the menu. We knew it was no good, but could not bear to admit that the feast was canceled. The prawns were very expensive. Almost certainly they were frozen, but we ordered them.

"And a bottle of white wine," said Bruno.

"*No hay vino,*" said the waiter snootily. "It is forbidden to sell *vino* during the revolution."

That was how we first heard about the revolution. We stared at each other in amazement. It was a serious matter. The police in Lima and Callao had staged a coup. Many had been killed. The tanks were out in the streets and the fate of the country was in the balance. So far the government had managed to survive. There were rumors of chaos and bloodshed in Lima, but the only noticeable effect in Chiclayo was that you could not get wine with your prawns.

Anyway the prawns were no good. They were fried in bread dough, and the chef had forgotten to put in the prawns.

We left poorer but little wiser. At the next traffic light a dozy Peruvian driver ran into me from behind, ripping off one of my panniers, denting the oil tank and throwing me to the ground. It was that kind of day. I made a tremendous row about it and the crowd came over gradually to my side. Reluctantly the driver peeled off a 100 *sole* note, gave it to me and rushed away. I tied my broken box together and took my 100 *soles* into a wine shop where I got a bottle from a man who had seen too many revolutions. So something good came of that day, although it was not over yet, by any means.

We rode on to Paita, which surprised me by being a really graceful town of old and elegant wood-frame buildings. Unhappily the hotel was the grubbiest of all the buildings, and far too expensive, so we had a chicken dinner and decided to sleep out again. I remembered the telegraph poles lined up along the road on our way into town and we drove out to sling our hammocks between a suitable pole and opposite ends of the van.

As I was dozing off a faint creaking sound disturbed me, but before

I had time even to identify it, the pole came crashing down. My head was towards the pole, and Bruno was asleep with his head at the van end of the hammock. In the moonlight I saw the pole fall directly onto Bruno and the porcelain insulation strike his head. I was so horrified imagining the weight of the pole behind that sharp glassy knob that I did not even notice that I had fallen to the ground.

For a second or two he was deathly still as I struggled up in alarm from the tangle of bedding. Then he woke. He said he had felt nothing. Astonished but relieved, I began to consider what the police in Paita might think if they found their communications cut during a revolution, and we decided to leave the site rapidly. Pausing only to pull on our trousers and bundle all our loose things into the van, we rushed off for another five miles. Then the bike blew a fuse and stopped, without warning, for the first time on the entire journey.

Hoping we were out of range of suspicion, we stopped and slept. I rode back to the scene of our "crime" next morning to recover a piece of cord that Bruno was missing. I was puzzled by the incident, wondering why the pole had fallen, and why Bruno's head was not split open. The cord was there. The pole lay as we had left it, and I touched one end of it. It was as light as cork, having been entirely eaten away inside by termites, leaving only a thin shell.

We rode a long way north that day, and were approaching Ecuador, and still the idyllic beach had eluded us. We came then into a surreal landscape of wind-whipped sandstone shapes where petroleum wells glittered and nodded mysteriously in the wilderness, like a colony of extraterrestrial beings. When the road swung back to the ocean after Talara I looked down and saw it, a broad, gently curving bay embraced by headlands, a fine beach rising up to a cliff face, two small brightly painted fishing boats beached, two others at anchor in the bay and no other sign of people or habitation.

I rode down to it and dissolved in its beauty. The sand was soft and unspoiled up under the cliff face, and washed clean and smooth down by the ocean, with no dividing line of seaweed to attract irritating insects. Along one part of the beach some black stone thrust up through the sand. It had been lapped and hollowed by the tide into elegant geometrical forms, lovely in themselves but also so deliberate and precise that I could almost fancy nature mocking, "fit a function to this then, if you please."

Other bigger rocks stood out into the ocean and offered good platforms for fishing. Squadrons of gray pelicans cruised complacently a few yards offshore, falling now and again like feathered bombs to prove the fish were there. Frigate birds hovered above, printing their primeval black silhouettes on pure blue. The Pacific stretched calm and glorious under the afternoon sun and the cliffs around glowed rosy and warm.

Bruno followed me down and parked the Renault on a hard shelf, by the rock face, resisting the temptation for once to rush in and sink the van irrevocably into the sugary sand. I unpacked the bike and constructed a nest for myself in the sand. It was quite unnecessary, I could have done it later or not at all, but I needed to do something to mark my arrival and stake my claim.

Then we fished, I from the rocks, Bruno by swimming out to one of the anchored boats. I caught nothing but was filled with peace and pleasure. After an hour I looked up to see a police car crawl up behind the Renault, its red light still twirling on its roof. Two policemen were standing by the van, looking fairly relaxed, and Bruno was swimming in to shore. I decided to stay where I was. It was a disturbance. I could not help connecting it with the news from Lima, even the telegraph pole we had brought down, but I preferred not to speak to policemen.

I sneaked an occasional glance. Bruno seemed to be talking to them quite amicably. Two fishermen walked past me along the beach dangling several big fish at their sides, and stopped to join the discussion for a while. The fishermen walked on. The police climbed back into their car and drove off. Bruno went back to the water and swam out again to the boats.

Later Bruno showed me his fish. It was a huge thing with golden discs shining on a gun-metal skin, called a *sierra*. He had not caught it, however. The police had requisitioned two of them from the fishermen and passed one over to us.

"What did the police want?" I asked.

'Who knows." He shrugged. "Maybe they come every day for a free fish. They warned me not to go out too far. *Nada mas.*"

It was an odd, meaningless event. Nothing ever came of it, and I never forgot it either. The *sierra* was one of the most prized fish on that coast, and we must have each eaten about two pounds of it, grilled to perfection. I lay back with tea and cigarettes at exquisite peace with the world.

Even Bruno was unusually calm. He was a good traveler, tough and inquisitive and (it must be said) unusually flexible for a Frenchman. But he was in his mid-twenties with a lot of life ahead of him, and in a bit more of a hurry than I was. That night he seemed willing to let time stand still.

"Who wants to be in Paris in some shitty office," he said. "I wish I didn't have to go back."

"Why go then?" I asked.

"I don't know. It's expected. It's the system – and there's the family farm to sort out now that my father is dead. But I don't want to get fucked in that bloody machine, stuck in a box for the rest of my days," he said angrily. The French call a business a box, one of their better ideas.

"There was a man in Paraguay, out in the Chaco, a Frenchman. I really admired him. Self-made, self-taught, he lived in his own world, surrounded by books and his farm. But his mind, it was extraordinary. He thought everything out for himself, and his ideas were original, marvelous. That is a life I envy, but I could never do it alone. I suppose I'm bound to get a job for a while . . . it's not too easy these days."

Lying on that warm beach under the stars it seemed like the utmost folly even to contemplate it.

We stayed there another day and a night. Some of the time I sat and studied the crabs. They were small and lived in holes spaced about a foot apart. Around the holes was a curious pattern like the footprints of many birds which first attracted my attention. I waited to see what it was. After a while the crabs would start to emerge, popping their brightly colored periscope eyes over the top before daring to climb out. Almost invariably each crab had a small ball of sand tucked under one arm, reminding me of an American footballer about to make a run. Some crabs kicked the ball, others walked a little way and then broke it up. Either way they then went over the loose sand with their pincers, stamping it down to leave those marks I had noticed.

In front of me were three holes set to form a triangle. One crab sat confidently at the mouth of its hole watching the other two. When another crab appeared the first crab made a rush for it, but always failed to get there before the other had bunked down its hole again. After many unsuccessful attempts, the aggressor decided on a final solution. It filled up both the other holes with sand, stamping down on them until they had disappeared. I waited a long while to see if either buried crab would reappear but did not see them again. I had no idea what the game was but, for all its strangeness, the episode had an uncomfortable familiarity.

From that beach the road led almost directly into Ecuador. Right up to the frontier the country continued barren and rainless. Immediately beyond it we were enveloped by lush wet vegetation, waist high grass, marshy land, muddy roads and mile upon mile of banana plantations.

In Quito we were accommodated by two Frenchmen seeing out their military service as teachers attached to the legation. Of all their luxuries, we appreciated most the hi-fi. For an entire afternoon we both lay in their living room with the volume turned full on, playing, again and again, the same recording of Wagner's overture to *Tannhäuser,* until we were drunk and saturated with it.

The teachers themselves, for all their hospitality, were less satisfying. One of them was particularly boorish. We all joked at times about the awkwardness of South Americans, but he had no room for humor.

"*Il faut les suprimer,*" he said, again and again. "They must be put down." When I realized that he was seriously thinking of exterminating them, like vermin, I became rather uncomfortable and was glad to leave.

In Quito, at a crossroads, I encountered two Americans riding a Norton Commando. We all stopped, on a whim, and talked for a while in a cafe. The meeting led us to stay together for ten days in a hacienda that they were sharing with some others near Otavalo. It was an enchanting experience, not least because we were there long enough to know and talk to some of the Indian girls who came to help with the house and garden. Even Bruno contained his impatience well. The Americans, Bob and Annie, left a deep impression on me. They were, at that moment, contemplating marriage. Indeed they made a valiant attempt to achieve it in the next town, but were defeated by the residence qualifications. So they were happy, of course, but their happiness had an unusual quality of clarity and depth, like a clear pool that invited others to jump in and share.

After a few days they spoke to me about a ranch somewhere north of San Francisco, and some people they thought I would like to meet. I knew this was significant to them, but they were being deliberately vague and so I asked no questions. I had an address of friends where we could meet up again in California, and I put it aside until then. It always seemed strange afterwards to recall the apparently haphazard way in which we had met. It was one of those meetings which, with all the hindsight in the world, must have been a pure chance that changed my life.

The Andes resolutely refused to pall. North of the equator they became more beautiful than ever, as they spread out across Colombia. From Ipiales to Pasto to Popayan, I was prepared to swear that I would never see anything more beautiful than these great mountainsides clad in greenery and bursting with flowers and flame trees. The homes were developed, and built in the most pleasing shape of all, around patios, with red-tiled roofs running out over verandahs. Unlike Peru, Colombia was a soft, habitable country, with streams and waterfalls, and good earth apparently everywhere.

It also had the reputation of being the most dangerous country on earth. Throughout South America I had been accumulating stories of what happened to travelers in Colombia. Armed robberies at night, tourists shot in hotel rooms, fingers cut off for rings, watches ripped off wrists, every kind of daring hit-and-run theft, and a tradition of murder and violence among Colombians themselves unparalleled in modern history. From the beginning of the journey friends had suggested that I should carry some kind of weapon. Some had ideas, borrowed from political thrillers, of guns that broke down into pieces that looked like motorcycle parts, or tent poles. At least a small pistol like Bruno's, they thought, could be hidden away somewhere.

Guns never made any sense to me. When I pictured myself fighting off bandits with firearms I knew the idea was ridiculous. For one thing, if I were to be attacked at all it would almost certainly be on the road. Short of having rocket launchers slung under the handlebars it would be impossible for me to defend myself while riding. By the time I stopped the bike and got to my gun it would all be over.

But my revulsion for firearms went much deeper than that. I was convinced, from the start, that merely to carry a gun invites attack. When there is a fear of hostility my mind is torn between two kinds of response; to lick 'em or to join 'em. With a gun in my pocket I would be thinking more about licking them, and I have come to

I was unable to get close to the Andean Indians of Bolivia and Peru. They seemed eternally morose, unless stoned on *coca* or drunk on *chicha*. In Ecuador the gloom lifted somewhat, and Indians seemed more in charge of their own destinies. I stayed at a *hacienda* near Otavalo and made friends with these girls. Despite their high spirits they were very shy of the camera. Their parents still believed that the lens could steal their souls away. In a sense, they may be right.

believe firmly that what is going on in my mind is reflected in a thousand little ways by the way I behave towards others. I am not beyond believing that just having that gun in my pocket would be enough to get me shot. Anyway, there was a notion of manliness associated with weaponry that I could not understand. Guns seemed to me to speak only of fear. I would prefer my chances of walking empty-handed up to any bandit, rather than trying to shoot him first, and all the accounts I later heard seemed to bear me out.

Even so, it was impossible not to be impressed by tales of highway robbery in Colombia, and I decided at least to make life a bit more difficult for the robber. I bought three padlocks and a chain to secure my leather tank bags.

As it turned out, the only robbery I suffered in Colombia was soon after we arrived there while we were staying in Popayan. I was standing in a grocer's shop with the contents of my pocket on the counter, searching for loose change, when someone deftly pocketed my keys. It was a quite senseless theft. The keys were surely useless to the thief but I had lost the duplicates and before I could leave Popayan I had to have my three padlocks sawn off with a hacksaw.

So much for paranoia, I thought, and tried never to be bothered with it anymore.

Bruno and I had come a long way together by then. We were two thousand miles north of Lima and into our third month. He still hoped to reach Mexico with his van. It was struggling valiantly and looked like getting there against all the odds when we left Popayan for La Plata. The dirt road was winding and mountainous as they all were, but it was narrower than most and, for the first time, I had trouble with the trucks.

Normally the trucks and I co-existed. They swept along regardless of all other traffic, indifferent to accidents, noisy, filthy, painted and repainted with wonderful fairground colors and brave mottoes, spraying transistorized music and football commentaries from their cabs. They never went for me, and I never dueled with them. It was no part of my pride to fight battles with Colombian truck drivers. Where there was room, I slipped past. Where there wasn't I got out of the way.

On the road to La Plata it was distinctly harder to get out of the way, although it was really just a matter of going slower, and being ready for a truck to appear around every bend. Most of the bends were concealed and I had a lot of anticipating to do, but that was all right. That also was what my journey was about, a sort of Zen meditation on reality. I went more slowly and appreciated it all the more.

Bruno's case, however, was different. All the anticipation in the world could not get him past a truck where there was no room. I had been waiting a very long time for him at a bare-boarded cafe next to a brothel in a mountain top village when a bus driver came through and said my friend was in trouble. I found him with one wheel in a ditch and up against a concrete culvert. His half-shaft had broken its joint. We found eventually that he could still crawl along and we crept painfully back to Popayan. I was not sorry to be back. I had found Popayan to be one of the finest cities, ranking with Cuzco and Ouro Prêto as places that generated contentment. I think there must be happy occasions when the size of a community, the appreciation of the people and the shape and disposition of their dwellings all coincide at a point most favorable to the human spirit. These three cities seem to have passed through that time, and the memory lingers on.

We moved into one of the most beautiful hotels in South America, El Monasterio, and shared a room for $8.00, which we thought of as a lot of money, having lost touch with the Western world. Bruno put on a virtuoso performance for the Renault agent, and had his half-shaft replaced for pennies. We gorged ourselves on the sights, sounds, smells and tastes of Popayan, and Bruno left early next day, determined this time to drive as slowly as humanly possible, while I went looking for someone to saw through my padlocks.

I left at lunch time, in glorious weather, hoping to miss the regular afternoon storm. Then a fuse blew again and I spent too long trying to trace the fault, with the tank off and everything unpacked. I just had time to put in a temporary hot line from the coils to the battery and get packed up before the storm broke over me and made me very wet, but it the rain stopped soon enough. The sun came out, and dried me through and through.

There was so much natural beauty on that road that I swung out of control and managed a thirty-foot skid on loose dirt across a blind bend. When I thought what a truck would have done to me there, I had to chalk that one up as a life lost. But it was Bruno's day of reckoning, not mine. Incredibly, he met another truck and this time there was not even a ditch to hide in. They both braked masterfully. The impact was not enough to hurt either driver, but the Renault was converted from a rectangle into a lozenge. I was not present at this sad scene. Bruno spoke of it later with much emotion, although like a true gaucho of the highway he did not allow grief to unbalance him. Many Colombian truck drivers assembled at the scene, he said, and they were able, by force of numbers, to persuade Bruno that the accident had been his fault and that he owed six hundred *pesos* for the repair of a truck fender and the repainting of several hearts and flowers. Leading with his right wheel several inches ahead of his left, he was able to meander on along the road to La Plata, and I overtook the pathetic pair later. The geometry of the car was certainly peculiar, and his front tires were almost bald after only thirty miles.

We decided to make a camp and go on to La Plata in the morning, and I found a green field leading down to a river. We drove in, and halfway down the field sank into a bog. For half an hour or more Bruno labored to bring his crippled car back up to the gate. He could get speed up across the field but always that last short stretch when he had to turn up the hill was too much, and he slithered to a halt. Finally, in desperation, using every device we had learned on the way, we heaved the van out. The field was a horrifying sight, denuded of pasture, rutted and ripped to shreds. It seemed better to move on before the owner came and shot us. So we came to La Plata after all and took a room at the Residencias Berlin. There we made the acquaintance of Jesus and Domitila Clavijo, their ten children and Roberto the parrot.

Domitila, the mother, was a woman of great vigor and good humor. She bustled constantly, in the kitchen, the dining room, the many bedrooms scattered around the yard, issuing instructions to her small army. Her children, boys and girls ranging between eighteen and zero, seemed exceptionally bright and well mannered. We played chess with the boys, talked to them all and admired the way they supported their mother. They seemed alert and generous and sensitive to feeling to a degree far beyond what I would consider normal in a European or North American home. Something of this had already impressed me about Colombia in general, as though the very hazards and cruelties of life there were bound to generate their opposite qualities.

The father, Jesus, made a strong impression also, but of a quite different kind. He sat generally on a chair in the dining area, a middle-aged man with a spreading bulk, a lightly woven hat perched over an expressionless face and his left hand in his pocket. The hand was so firmly in the pocket that I had the feeling his sleeve was sewn to his trousers. He spoke softly and sibilantly, but he exerted great authority over his family. They clearly feared and respected him as much as they loved their mother. He did nothing in the hotel although he had some land outside La Plata which he supervised. On Saturdays he went to the billiard saloon and drank with his cronies. The Saturday I was there he returned drunk, accused one of his daughters of whoring in town, brought several of them to tears and then went to sleep it off.

One of his sons explained this to us.

There had been a time, not long before, when Jesus' family and friends had been the kings of La Plata. They ran it, in every way. They decided what would be built, what would be torn down, who could live there and who couldn't, who should pay what to whom, and who was guilty or innocent. There were no police. Government agents were sent packing with bullets at their tails. La Plata, like most small towns of the interior, was a law unto itself, and Jesus and his friends were IT.

One day, at the billiard saloon where the weekly council meetings were held, there was a disagreement. It was a trivial enough matter, something like whether the bus should stop outside Manuel's store or Jose's barber shop. But feeling was already running high between the Jesus faction and others. Jesus had his hand on the wooden frame of a billiard table when a rival drew a machete and sliced it off. Not satisfied with that, he chopped through the middle of Jesus' brother's hand as well.

When the brothers returned with their stumps sewn up, they murdered their assailant and his uncle, and narrowly missed his wife. Those were the days! They were over now, though. The government had finally found enough soldiers to bring their own brand of law to La Plata, and Jesus now exercised his authority less directly. It was later in the same conversation that I discovered that the field we had ripped up and ruined almost certainly belonged to Jesus. I decided, in the circumstances, to keep the matter to myself.

For Bruno it was a godsend that the police were back in La Plata.

His van was obviously undriveable. It had shredded two tires in thirty miles. We were already within a few days of the Caribbean coast, when the car would in any case have to be shipped to Panama at great expense. It did not add up, and after swallowing a few times, Bruno decided to let the van go.

Colombians are insane about buying things from abroad. They are convinced that everything foreign is a bargain, and there would have been no difficulty selling the van, wrecked as it was, but for the fact that it was quite illegal and the buyer would have difficulty getting license plates. A policeman solved the problem by buying it for himself.

A closing-down auction was held in the courtyard of the Residencias Berlin. Buyers came from all around. There was foam plastic, kitchenware, clothing, even an oil painting, and I added my obsolete air mattress to the display. The bargaining continued with animation through the day. Domitila and I fought well into the night over the mattress, and eventually we all fell exhausted and satisfied into our beds. Next day Bruno picked up his two leather grips and climbed onto a bus, and my life with Bruno came to an end. Both of us agreed it had been wonderful and unforgettable, and we had no problem about going our separate ways. We would meet again. No doubt.

It was March when Bruno took the bus. I rode off the following day, first to Bogotá, then to Medellin and on to the Caribbean port of Cartagena, up and down across hundreds of miles of valleys and mountains, all bewitchingly beautiful.

I bargained for space on an island trading vessel and sailed to San Andrés, known to English pirates as St. Andrews. From there, for the first and last time, I took to the air. Honduras Airlines stuffed my bike onto the flight deck of a Lockheed Electra, right behind the pilot, and flew me to Panama, looking down on the canal as we went.

Panama, I told myself, was only a hop skip and jump from the U.S.A. It was a silly mistake to deceive myself in this way, just laziness and wishful thinking. The lure and challenge of South America had always distracted me from that string of "banana republics" connecting it to North America, and I had paid no real attention to its geography.

In Panama I had to face up to the fact that there were at least six

Meet the family of Jesús and Domitila Clavijo, some of their ten children, and Roberto the parrot. That's Domitila in the background, smiling as usual. Jesús is out of the picture. As usual, he is *not* smiling. He
sits on a chair, in the courtyard of their small hotel, with his left wrist in
his pocket to hide the stump. He had his hand cut off in a power struggle over the right to govern La Plata, the small Colombian town where
Bruno and I stayed a few days. Despite the violence that constantly
erupts in Colombia, I found the people unusually warm, friendly and,
above all alert and in love with life. Could there be a connection?

distinct countries to traverse, and five thousand miles to ride, before I reached California. It made me sad to realize that what should have been an exciting prospect left me rather dispirited.

The ten thousand miles since Fortaleza had been hard but I loved the physical work of traveling and it was not that which exhausted me. More difficult to sustain, I found, was the daily grind of contact with the Latin American personality. It should not have come as a surprise. Where else in the world is the male individual so insecure, divided as he is between the Latin and Indian cultures, with the blood of both in his veins? The Latin American has no tribe to fall back on, as the African does, no reliable judiciary to defend his rights as the European does, no social ideal or sacred constitution to appeal to as the North American does, no pervasive mythology to soften life as it does in Asia, and not even an ideology to subscribe to, as does the Russian or Chinese. Without wealth, what is there left to him but his manhood, to be flaunted and defended at every occasion?

Traveling, you meet it again and again, the unspoken question: "How does this man threaten my virility"

Every day, in some little way, I had had to damp down fears, still suspicions, prove that I was not there to make a fool of anyone. All the more difficult when people do not have the information you need, cannot supply the thing you want, are reminded of their own ignorance and the chronic material shortages with which they live.

People can say *"No hay"* only so often before it changes to "Fuck off.

"In the land of *No hay,* they play Hunt the Scapegoat, and every gringo qualifies. It was a constant preoccupation to escape that label, and find a way to meet with people in a more human and personal way.

Of course, where people live in one place and get used to each other they get along fine, usually, just as they do everywhere else in the world. Nowhere could I have found warmer or more generous friends than those I stayed amongst in Rio, in Curitiba, Bariloche, Santiago, La Plata, Medellin and Cartagena. Once contact is made and the intention is clear there is no shortage of trust and warmth.

And then there are also the exceptional people who make nonsense of all generalizations. At the roadside in the southwest of Argentina I was struggling to mend a puncture on a hot dry day when a man stopped and came over with the sole purpose of encouraging me. I could see by his dress and the car he drove that his means were limited, but he put his hand in his pocket and brought out a bundle of paper pesos with several notes of a quite high denomination. "If you are short of money," he said, "please take what you need."

I needed nothing, but I was overwhelmed by such spontaneous generosity, and his single gesture helped me later to swallow a dozen rebuffs. Unfortunately there were too few like him to absorb all the punishment, and by the time I got to Panama I was feeling the cumulative effect of it.

There had been other pressures too. My relations with the *Sunday Times* seemed to have gone sour. After a promising start in Brazil, Argentina and Chile, none of my articles had been published and there were ominous signals about money. Prices were rising constantly. Inflation had made a mockery of my original budgets, and it was obvious that I would need more money, even though I was living on the slenderest of shoestrings. As I struggled in and out of ditches and became a connoisseur of cockroaches, I was bitterly aware that there were people in London who thought my journey was a frivolous waste of funds.

I had hoped for news in Panama that would at least state the position clearly. Panama was an important drop along my route. The Lucas Company had a huge depot there in the Free Zone, and it was the first forwarding address since Lima. There were tires, brake linings and tubes waiting, but no mail, no answers to questions, no news from anyone.

It was this uncertainty as much as anything, I suppose, that focused my mind on California, because I could not expect to have the future of my journey resolved until I got to the States and was once more in easy communication with England. Thinking about California, I could not resist anticipating the reception I had been promised there by Triumph. The American market was vital to Triumph's sales, and their headquarters were in Los Angeles. There had been talk of a hero's welcome, and in my depressed state I thought about it more than was healthy. So far, on my journey I had learned scrupulously to resist traveling as though to a destination. My entire philosophy depended on making the journey for its own sake, and rooting out expectations about the future. Traveling in this way, day by day, hour by hour, trying always to be aware of what was present and to hand, was what made the experience so richly rewarding. To travel with one's mind on some future event is futile and debilitating. Where concentration is needed to stay alive, it could also be disastrous. I was aware of the danger, and tried hard to recover my earlier spirit of enjoyment and optimism about the journey.

The squalor and steam heat of Panama did not help. I tried to wring some interest out of the hotel where I was staying. It was more of a boardinghouse, really, with guests, mostly single women, staying for longish periods and doing contract jobs in the city. I met Pete there, in the kitchen, cooking his lunch. One of the rules was that guests may not cook in the kitchen, but Pete was granted a special dispensation, he said, on the grounds that "if I can't cook, I'm leaving." The proprietor's wife, a knotty white lady wrapped in kimonos, took a realistic view because he lived there by the month and paid the daily rate of six dollars.

He offered me a drink, and we sat sweating and almost naked under the fan in his bedroom, drinking rum and Coke. He drank an awful lot of it. He was a construction engineer, young and good looking, but there were dark stains spreading around his eyes like a kind of rot.

I put it down to the booze, but he swore that he could leave it alone. "Never when I'm working," he said. "Only afterwards." He just happened not to be working.

In that case, I thought, it must be the screwing. Pete told me fairly quickly that he had screwed every girl in the hotel. Without exception. It was important to him to make no exceptions, although some were considerably less inviting than others.

"Staying here is like a license to screw," he told me seriously. "The girls are all very discreet, they never talk about it, but I don't mind you knowing. That's why I don't mind paying six dollars a day. It's worth it."

I was particularly interested in Pete because he had just ridden a three-cylinder Kawasaki on almost the same route from Rio to Panama as I had taken.

"Remember that bridge coming into Ecuador?" he asked.

There was only one bridge he could have meant. It was built like a railroad track, but with planks instead of rails to take the wheels of cars. The sleepers were set about eighteen inches apart, and there was nothing between them but air, and only river beneath. It might not have been so bad if the planks had not kept changing direction, so that it was impossible to build up any momentum. I had fallen halfway across and was lucky not to have gone through into the river. Bob and Annie had also fallen on it with their Norton.

"Sure I do," I said. "I fell on it."

He howled, and grabbed my hand.

"Me too, pal. Which way did you fall?"

"Into the middle."

"Jesus, I only fell against the side. Boy, that was some ride. I'm really glad to meet you, pal."

He told me more about his journey, and I was fascinated but appalled by his account. He had hated it. He hated the country and the people. A lot of the time he rode at night so that he would not have to look at things. Between rides he said he had spent most of his time "fucking and drinking in bars."

The important thing for Pete was to have done it. The whole journey had taken him two months, against my six, and he had spent $10,000 on the way. He said there wasn't anywhere where he would not rather have been in a car.

The hotel did not help me out of my depression. Nor did the slight touch of fever I felt now and then. When I was invited to stay with some people in the Canal Zone, I accepted gratefully. U. S. Navy Captain John Mallard and his wife, Anne were exceptionally kind and considerate people. They lived in quarters on a Marine base, and for two weeks they gave me total insulation from care or responsibility in that strange, artificial world of the peacetime military establishment.

Captain Mallard, a submariner, was second in command of the Canal Zone, and among the most liberal and understanding men I have met. While Panamanians were hurling insults at the U.S.A. he never allowed a prejudiced or intolerant remark to pass his lips, and he seemed deeply concerned that the American presence there should benefit Panamanians in every way possible. In the year of Watergate he was a fine and reassuring ambassador for his country.

So I tried to rebuild my morale, and to some extent succeeded, but still I could not be rid of the thought of California as the promised land where I should be able to shrug off all my cares and woes. I set off, finally, just before the rains came, with the conflicting ambitions of seeing all the remarkable things there were to see in Central America and, at the same time, to get through it all as fast as possible. It was not a very propitious program.

On my way out of Panama I ride up to Volcan at ten thousand feet for the pleasure of feeling cool. I meet a man in the street who tells me I can sleep on the porch of the motel that he manages. Free. There are two pillars under a roof where I can sling my hammock. As I'm making myself coffee, my benefactor comes across.

"What a remarkable coincidence that we should meet," he says. "If you had arrived a few minutes earlier, or later, we would have missed each other."

I agree that this is true, although he is straining my sense of the miraculous.

He has come to save me with two naive religious tracts translated into Spanish and distributed by a North American mission. One is called "*Sospendido Por Un Hilo*," the other "*Pessado y Hallado Falto*." The titles are literal translations of the English idioms "Hanging By a Thread" and "Weighed and Found Wanting."

U.S. advertising companies in South America also translate their domestic slogans into Spanish, word for word.

Coca-Cola has *Chispa de la Vida* for the Spark of Life.

McDonald's *Su Clase de Lugar* is Your Kind of Place.

Everywhere in South America I have seen these crude images imposed on the Spanish culture, like a terrible revenge. What the Spaniards did to the Indians by the force of arms is now being done to them by the mighty *yanqui* dollar.

The border crossing from Panama to Costa Rica is quick and civilized. Soon afterwards I find a small town with a small restaurant that looks irresistibly clean and appetizing. Full of meat, eggs, rice, coffee and well-being I ride on taking a rosy view of this nice country. When I run out of gas, a laughing Indian woman sells me a liter at a farmhouse door. It's all she has, and it's not enough to get me to a pump, but some telephone repair people stop and siphon a gallon out of their tank. There's something not quite right with the bike. I change plugs, which improves it, but there's still a problem. In the early afternoon a mountain range takes me by surprise, lifting me high up into a freezing fog. I wasn't expecting such dramatic features in such a small country, and have to laugh at my own foolishness. On the other side of this range it is raining. On the way into San José I stop for a coffee, feeling cold and a bit depressed. Two girls are sitting nearby, and one of them is quite beautiful. She smiles at me and instantly I am happy again. For the second time I have to laugh at myself, but this time with more pleasure.

Outside the cafe a gringo is standing by the bike. He is called Lee, and he came down with some friends on two Harley Sportsters and a truck from Boston. They have opened a restaurant next door called *La Fanega*, where you can get *hamburgesas, quesoburgesas, pescadoburgesas, machoburgesas,* draft beer and music. They have a spare bed, so why don't I stay the night?

Next day I look in my address book. Starting with friends in Argentina, I have a chain of friends of friends stretching right through Central America, and there's one here, just handy to celebrate my birthday.

Soon I am sitting at the poolside of a very swank country club with a completely different set of people, listening to an impeccably turned-out honey from Florida in tight white slacks and a "sweet American ass." Her provocatively buck-toothed cocktail sipper's mouth is dispensing gossip about the Smiths, who, it seems, are the world's ugliest and most disagreeable couple. He is a rich alcoholic, and she is a cosmetic surgery freak who has just had two inches of fat removed from her abdomen.

"She'll drop her pants anywhere just to show off the scars. Ain't she gross? Last time he drank himself almost to death she hired a Lear jet and flew him to Miami. It burns my stomach."

Costa Rica is popular with the Lear jet set, and hospitable to gringos, but I have to admit that life here seems more pleasant for just about everybody. I could stay a long time, wandering between the sea and the mountains, but the rains are close on my heels and it's time to move on.

Nicaragua has a volcano called Santiago. I have been sitting on the lip looking down into it for an hour, completely mesmerized. Next to the Iguaçu Falls, it is the most impressive natural phenomenon I have seen. First there is an enormous bowl, which funnels into an even blacker cup. At the bottom of the cup is a pipe leading to the center of the earth, and in this pipe I can see molten rock surging and splashing. It is cherry red and although it is a long way away, it seems to come very close as I stare at it, so intense is the glow and so fascinating the thought of what it is, full of mysterious implications, like a moon shot in reverse. I am told that the Somosa government uses it as a good way to make political opponents disappear without trace.

In Honduras the men seem to get a bit taller and slimmer again, and have a tendency to wear cowboy hats and walk like Gary Cooper. There's a quite wonderful Mayan ruin at Copán where I spend a day. In the grassy clearings sensuous bodies stand sculpted into stone slabs, birds sing thrilling songs and a few adventurous sightseers make pleasant company, but I can't stave off the tiredness and loneliness that is creeping up on me more and more often now.

A dirt road takes me fifty miles or so through forest to the frontier of Guatemala at a small border post. On the Honduras side I pay another dollar to some nebulous authority called Transit, for what I don't know. I paid them on the way in, as well as customs and immigration. They all pretend it's official, but you are lucky to see a receipt, and although a dollar or two is not much, it adds up when you're scraping along. On the Guatemalan side the first thing I see is a battered desk by the roadside and a little fat man who needs a shave and wears something vaguely like a uniform. He says he is the army, and I have to pay him a dollar.

"How do you say in English," he says in English, "when you have too much in the night?"

"Hangover," I say.

"Hamburger?"

"No, hangover" – and I write it out for him. I HAVE A HANG OVER.

"I have a hamburger," he reads, entertaining us both. I begin to like him a little, but I'm still pissed off about the dollar.

"Can I have a receipt?" I ask, trying to make a nuisance of myself.

He laughs happily. "Oh no, this is for me. So that tonight I can make another hamburger."

For once I don't mind losing my dollar. That's how I like my corruption – honest.

There would be marvelous things to see and do in Guatemala, and I have planned to take advantage of them, but the excitement has evaporated. It is becoming terribly difficult for me now to get interested in anything except the route north. The Pan-American Highway stretches out ahead of me, unbroken, all the way to the U.S.A., and I feel myself being swept along it, with no time, no energy, for anything more. I see the fascination of these Central American countries but can't drive my imagination to take hold. Everything in me now cries "Enough. It's time to stop. Give us a rest."

The bike is tired also, but that is only a figure of speech. I do not credit the bike with feelings. If it has a heart and soul of its own I have never found them. People I meet are often disappointed that the bike does not even have a name. They often suggest names ("The Bug" is top favorite) but none of them seem to do anything for the bike or for me. For me it remains a machine, and every attempt to turn it into something else strikes me as forced and silly.

But it is not *just* a machine, not by any means, and I respect it totally for the very special thing it is. I know that all its idiosyncrasies, the things that make it quite different from any other motorcycle, are the result of what we have gone through together. The way I sit, my touch on the throttle, the speeds I travel at and the mistakes I make are what fashioned it into something uniquely connected with me. Like those intricately sculpted slabs of stone I have been looking at in the Mayan ruins of Copán, my bike records the passage of time and events. Its surface is richly engraved by incidents of twenty months and twenty-five thousand miles. It bears major inscriptions from Benghazi, the Nile ferry, the desert, the *Zoe G*, a front wheel blow out in Brazil, a bad fall in Argentina, a ditch in Colombia, and almost every day has contributed some minor mark somewhere. It has been molded by me, and to a large extent it has become an extension of myself.

When I talk to it, which I sometimes do in moments of concern or exasperation, I am of course talking to myself. And when I say it is tired, I mean that it reflects my own fatigue. For I am tired also of looking after it, and as we approach Los Angeles, which is as much home for the Triumph as it is for me, I spend less and less time fussing over it, telling myself that it can surely manage the last four thousand miles on its own. I stop worrying about little faults, and cure symptoms rather than look for causes.

I am spending less and less time on keeping up my own systems too. My clothes are getting ragged, my boots leak badly. Since Honduras the strap on my helmet has been broken, but I won't do anything about it. My goggles are either lost or scratched or without padding. My left-hand glove has most of the leather missing on the palm, and two fingers are poking through. Only the flying jacket is actually improved, because in Buenos Aires it became so dilapidated that I had to sew a new skin over the sleeves and shoulders, equipped with glamorous-looking fur cuffs and collar.

So the bike and I are both running down. In Costa Rica I was lucky to get a new rear chain sprocket, for the old one would certainly not have lasted through, but otherwise I am no longer the fussy owner I once was. As long as it goes, I'll not ask for more.

In Guatemala, passing Lake Atitlan, I ride into heavy rain. The highway is broad and empty, but my goggles are misting up. I am so used to being in motion on the bike that it never occurs to me to stop and I'm trying to wipe the inside of the lenses with my fingers as I go along.

Suddenly I realize that I have wandered into the middle of the road, and look up to find a huge truck bearing down on me out of the rainstorm. It is far too late for me to react, and it is entirely by chance that the truck misses me, by a hair's breadth. As I realize what I did, how close I came to being literally wiped out, obliterated, I feel that fearful rush of heat and cold sweat that makes the heart nearly burst, and feel immensely grateful for the warning while wishing I knew to whom to be grateful. A God would come in useful at times like that.

I can count only two other times when I came so close to an end. I must be really tired at the back of my skull. I must be careful. I must never let that happen again.

By the time I got to Mexico City one cylinder was smoking just as it had in Alexandria, but this time I was better prepared. I had two spare pistons with me, both oversize so that I could rebore if necessary. Was it necessary with only three thousand miles to go? This time though, a friendly Triumph agent was there with all the equipment and the will to help. It seemed silly not to take advantage. Friends of Bruno put me up; Mr. Cojuc, the agent, did the rebore; I put it together again in his workshop and, if for no other reason, the close contact this gave me with Mexican workers made the experience worthwhile.

The job itself, unfortunately, was only a partial success. As well as one cylinder getting badly scored, the exhaust valve was pitted. I had no spare valve and there was only just enough metal left to grind it in again. It should have been all right, but it wasn't.

At Guanajuato I began to suspect trouble, and as I pushed north it got worse. Those June days riding up through bone-dry Mexico were probably the hottest ever. Hotter than the Sudan, hotter even than the Argentine Chaco. My face reddened in spite of all the weathering it had had, my forearms blistered and the engine ran hotter and hotter.

Somewhere after Culiacan I lost the flying jacket. It had finally become unwearable in the heat, and I had tied it on behind over the red bag, but the heat must have dulled my senses for it was not tied as it should have been. Somewhere among unnumbered kilometers of open road it blew away. I was utterly distraught when I found out, perhaps abnormally so. I searched the road for an age, finding no sign of it, and the searching intensified my grief until I had to stop looking because I could bear it no longer. It had become something of extraordinary significance to me, that jacket, closely connected as it was to the love I had left behind me, and losing it broke an important link with the past. For the first time I felt that I had gone too far ever to go back to what I had been before, and I began to understand just how much unconscious effort I had been putting into keeping my connections with the past alive. It left a bleak and empty space.

Beyond Navojoa I realized that a valve was burning out. The left cylinder was misfiring constantly, power was dropping off, fuel consumption going up. Eventually I found that by riding with the choke fully in at fifty miles an hour I could still get reasonable power. At other speeds it was pretty bad, and of course it was not going to get any better. I was afraid that the bike might soon become undrivable, and as I came closer to the U.S.A. it felt as though some malign fate was determined to keep me south of the border.

I last touched the coast at Guaymas, and swam in the ocean there knowing that I would not see the Pacific again until Los Angeles. That southern Pacific coast had come to mean a great deal to me. Ever since I first came to it in the south of Chile, at that lovely stretch around Pucatrihue, I was powerfully drawn to it, and my mind ranged over all the memories of sunsets and surf, salt and seaweed, frigate birds, pelicans and sea gulls. There were those same pelicans at Guaymas plunging into the waves around me, wearing the same self-satisfied look on their faces. In the Gold Museum at Bogotá there had been a gold necklace with a row of birds delicately fashioned from wire, and I had been delighted to recognize them as "my" pelicans, for some ancient Inca craftsman had noticed in them that same happy complacency.

Inland from Guaymas the sun was even hotter, and the land was as arid and featureless as desert. Long-distance buses roared by frequently at seventy miles an hour, sometimes closing in dangerously with their tail ends. One that had cut in on me ruthlessly stopped farther up the road. I was able to overtake it before it had picked up speed again, and I rode up alongside the driver's seat. He looked down at me with a contemptuous grin and I raised my hand to point it at his head like a pistol, and then I shot him. His whole body jerked up as though struck by a bullet and he looked very angry, but it was the only time I ever got satisfaction.

Buses and trucks all threw out quantities of unburned diesel from their exhaust systems because of a common superstition that the extra fuel would get them there faster. In the still hot air the black smoke hovered over the highway like a long coil of barbed wire and riding through it my face and clothes became black with oily droplets. I fiddled frequently at the roadside, trying to get better performance from the engine, and lost several tools through carelessness in the heat. It was obvious to me that I was letting myself get close to my limits.

Those last days in Mexico were like the beginning of the journey in reverse. Then my energy seemed to breed itself. The more I called on my resources, the more they multiplied. Now the more effort I spared myself, the more tired I became. As I left Guaymas at lunch time for Hermosillo, I knew I would probably cross the border the following day, but I became ridiculously fearful that I might not make it. It was as though all the traveling I had done had taught me nothing.

On that last day in Latin America, between Hermosillo and Nogales, I could not help noticing how much more prosperous the people were. Prices in Hermosillo had been sky-high. There was nobody I would even have called a peasant, let alone the ragged children and beggars I had been used to seeing for most of the last thirteen months. Bars and restaurants were painted and clean, nobody seemed to spit anymore, there were no old wrecks on the road, no wandering animals. Men wore boots and cowboy hats, and clean pressed shirts and even looked like Americans. I thought that by the time I crossed the border it might be hard to tell the difference between Mexico and the U.S.A.

So when I did get to Nogales the shock was stupefying. At the end of this normal, prosperous Mexican street stood an edifice in glass and concrete that seemed to my eyes so grandiose, so unnecessarily clean and modern and bloated that I felt I must be stepping out of the Middle Ages into the year 2001. Indeed I could not imagine that ordinary people would stand a chance of getting through. I prepared myself for a very rough time. U.S. border officials are not famous for their cordial treatment of ragged travelers. With my last remaining *pesos* I bought a giant paper cup of Orange Crush and studied the ramparts wondering where to attack them.

There were no outgoing formalities at all, as though Mexico had simply given up an unequal contest. I rolled warily into one of the customs bays. An agent came out with a marble chin, trousers with honed creases and hair like molded plastic. I expected him to empty the gas tank and drill out the crankshaft looking for cocaine or peyote. He dangled one hand loosely into one of my side boxes without even looking.

"O.K.," he said.

What does he mean, "O.K."?

He grinned. "That's O.K. Immigration's over there. Glad to see you."

Amazing.

The immigration man smiled at me too. I was impressed.

"What can I do for you?" he said.

"You can let me into your fair country," I said. I hadn't meant to put it that way. It just came out.

"That's good to hear," he said. "We don't hear that much these days. How long would you like to stay?"

"How long can I have?"

"I asked you first."

"Well, three months should be fine."

"O.K."

I really didn't mean to stay anything like that long.

He punched me into his computer terminal and it turned out that for once I was not a prohibited person. So that was that, and I was in the United States.

Going to the United States from Latin America is like going to a movie, the kind they like to call a major motion picture. I ride along the freeway waiting for the titles to show. All the well-known images pop up; billboards, front lawns with mailboxes on sticks, cowboy hats and blondes driving pickups. I don't know the plot, but it's bound to be a richly satisfying and professional job. The realism is extraordinary, but I can't believe it's real because everything looks so terribly relevant. All the dirty corners of life that I have got so used to south of the border have been swept clean.

Another thing: There is this incredible sense of ease. The moment I crossed the border I felt safe. Why? I didn't feel unsafe before. Not at all. I think the explanation is that here I don't even need to think about it. I can afford to stop thinking. Look at the road surface, for example. It is perfect. Not just this bit, but the next bit too, and all the way to Los Angeles. I can count on it. I don't have to worry that around the corner it will turn suddenly to dirt, or drop me into a pothole. I can almost afford to take my eyes off the road; only habit keeps them there, a useful habit I shall need again later.

And everyone speaks my language. I don't have to think about making myself understood.

"What's the best way to L.A.? Is it through Tucson?"

"That's right."

So easy!

Then there's so much fat around. Everyone is prosperous, although they might not know it, with a house and a refrigerator. There isn't anyone who couldn't afford to help me if they wanted to, and they would want to, I know it, because their minds can grasp what I am. Also I am not black or crippled or ugly, and I have this cute English accent.

In Mexico the grass was brown, but in Arizona it's green because it is watered. It must be. Surely God would not be so discriminating. The air is clean. Would you believe it? Not a wisp of exhaust do I see from any car, truck or bus. That is a miracle in itself. And here, just where I want it, is a campsite. Rio Rica; a broad grassy paddock under a clear dry sky. Clean lavatories, showers, washing machines, a shop. Cold beer.

"Five dollars."

"That's too much, I'm afraid."

"Oh. O.K. Sure. We'll only charge you two dollars."

I never doubted it. I sling my hammock between two trees. Some kids come over, easy, cool, with beer. They talk to me; I don't have to make it happen. We all go off together: To spend the evening at a girl's house in town, eating sandwiches, listening to rock, talking. One of the kids was in Vietnam. I hear the whole story in three sentences, and he isn't even talking about the war. In fact the words don't say much, but the meaning comes through like a meeting in space. I'm so tuned in to body language and inflections that I hardly need words, but having the words too is so relaxing.

It goes on like that, through Tucson and Phoenix next day. Even the bike has relaxed and runs better instead of worse. I see on my Esso map that there's a long stretch of road from Phoenix to Blythe with no town marked on it, but I am so laid back that I don't think to wonder why. Before I know it I'm in the middle of another desert, totally unexpected, hotter even than Mexico, with a cross wind blowing sand up my nose.

Well, that makes for a better movie but it doesn't prick the bubble of credibility because I'm still on a four-lane highway with plenty of gas in my tank and, sure enough, happily placed in the middle of the desert is the big, green Colorado River, and the KOA campsite with all the usual facilities, and proud mobile home owners are lining up the cold cans of Coors beer just for adventurous chaps like me.

Next day I battle my way against an even heavier head wind. The valve trouble is so bad now that I'm down at times to twenty miles an hour, and in real trouble with the big container trucks when they come past. The wind sandblasts my arms and nose and makes me really quite tired, but as an ordeal it is still completely fictional because, whatever happens inside the borders of this country, you're never more than a half-hour helicopter flip from the ultimate in medical technology.

The thing could not have been scripted better. Only two hundred miles away are Hollywood and the Triumph offices. Without any simulation or trickery whatsoever I shall be able to arrive in the world's most elaborate city as though I had just come out of the Atbara Desert.

I have given some thought to what I would like to happen next. I see marching bands, majorettes, a great arena of people rising spontaneously, irresistibly to their feet, tears streaming down their cheeks; Governor Brown, arm outstretched, apologizing for the President's absence; my own succinct keynote speech reminding the US. of her responsibilities to her poorer neighbors followed by rapturous applause and an intimate dinner with the Secretary of State.

This is beyond the resources of the Triumph Company to arrange on the spur of the moment. I turn up at their rather plush offices on the edge of Los Angeles like a bashful Battle of Britain pilot, missing presumed dead.

"Holy cow," they say. "It's Ted Simon." And they all shake my hand and bring me a beer.

I looked around Triumph's prosperous offices with an optimistic eye, anticipating some sort of unspecified "good time." Sure I wanted a beer, and a shower and a chance to change my clothes and even to rest for a bit, but what I really wanted was company, nice enthusiastic, appreciative company. As a Hero I naturally assumed that people would be tumbling over themselves to accompany me. All the keen athletic executives in the front office were extremely cordial. All the pretty girls at their stylish mahogany veneer desks smiled very nicely at me, but as the minutes passed my bright eyes glazed over. I wasn't making contact. In spite of all the niceness, I knew they couldn't really grasp who or what I was, and maybe, even, they were too preoccupied with other matters to care.

I must have been a strange sight. The desert sun had burned me very dark and printed a goggle pattern on my face. My shirt was threadbare, and my jeans were shredded across the knees and awkwardly patched. My hair was unfashionably short and disheveled and I was a bit crazy at the thought of having actually arrived. I imagined myself to look quite romantic. After all, it was the real thing, but their nice, orderly eyes gradually convinced me that I was a bit of a mess, and the best thing I could do was go and clean up.

The credibility gap widened into a yawning chasm and never closed. They were unfailingly nice to me, and materially generous. They took the bike into their workshop and promised to give it all the care that could be lavished on it. They gave me another bike, the same model, to use in the meanwhile. They took me to a hotel about ten miles away and booked me in at their expense, and left me there until the next day.

My hotel room was at ground level and had thick glass sliding doors instead of windows, with two sets of curtains. I had a square double bed with freshly laundered sheets every day. At the foot of the bed was a big color television set. There was a writing desk, itself quite a decent piece of furniture, and in the drawer was a stack of stationery and leaflets describing all the hotel's services and telling romantic tales about its supposed history. I read them all avidly.

The bathroom had apparently been delivered by the manufacturer that morning. Everything in it was still wrapped or sealed by a paper band guaranteeing 100 per cent sterility. Not even the boys from homicide could have found a fingerprint in there.

In the bedroom everything was impeccable too. It was air conditioned, of course. Not a breath ruffled my countenance. When my arm itched and I raised my hand automatically to smash at a mosquito, there was never a mosquito. There was only me.

I switched on the television, and it responded immediately with a picture of surgeons and nurses in green conclave around an operating table. The camera closed in on a human knee, and a scalpel opened it up before my very eyes. Horrified, I switched channels to an advertisement for a film called *The Bug*. A male voice promised that unless I saw this picture I would not know what horror meant. A woman screamed at me, horrified, and showed her tonsils. "The Bug eats human flesh," said the voice, and the woman screamed again.

With flesh-eating bugs I was already familiar. I switched off. There was still only me. I had everything I had been dreaming of for months. Starched linen. Room service. Steak, lobster, mutton, cold white wine, coffee, unlimited hot water, not a cockroach to be seen.

Sitting there alone I found it all quite meaningless. I went for a walk around the extensive premises, through lobby and patio, past pool and fountain, bakery and book shop and saw that same nice smile everywhere I went, and written in the eyes just as plainly the words "Otherwise Engaged."

I looked in my address books. There were a few names and telephone numbers. The friends of friends were all far too high-powered to be called on the spur of the moment like that. There was one man, though, whom I had met in England, a businessman I had found refreshingly interesting and intelligent. He lived in Malibu and even answered the phone to me. I explained how I had arrived in Los Angeles, and he asked me penetrating questions as though I were his psychiatric patient. He promised to call me back, but never did.

The hotel was on the inland edge of Los Angeles and I thought maybe I was among particularly stuffy and provincial people, so I set out on the bike to find the real Los Angeles. I never found it. I rode forever on an astounding web of freeways, four or eight lanes wide, laid out like a never-ending concrete waffle over thousands of square miles, looking for somewhere to go, but found nothing.

These first days had a profound effect. I felt completely lost, as though I had been whisked away from the earth in my sleep one night and deposited among humanoids in a simulated earth city. Alice was never so flummoxed in Wonderland, not even on that vast chessboard. In all his travels, Gulliver was never more shocked, not even when confronted by the giant Brobdingnagian nipple.

I arrived there still smelling the smell of sweat and stale urine, of unruly growth and open decay. I was used to faces that showed the imprint of emotion, the stamp of excess. I was accustomed to things being old, worn down, chipped, scratched, scuffed and patched, but real. Where I had been, people and things were forced to show the real stuff they were made of, because the superficial could not survive the battering it got. I was used to the sound of life, roars of laughter, shouts of anger, whistles, catcalls, bargaining, argument and domestic squabble; to the sight and smell of animals; to old people sunning themselves.

Where I had been, children came running.

I looked into the cars that rode alongside me on the freeway. I saw men and women staring blandly ahead with faint smiles on their carefully carefree faces. No visible signs of life there. I looked around me for a genuine house. They were all simulated. Some looked like ice cream. Some were simulated Spanish. Some pretended to be factories, or monasteries, or farmhouse cottages. All fake. Nothing original.

I saw a tiny girl, poised astonishingly at the edge of a highway, about to wander out into the traffic. There was no adult in sight. She was toddling aimlessly out into my lane, and there was no time for me to dismount and help her, so I maneuvered the bike to bar her way, hoping to change her mind. A car screeched to a halt in front of me and a woman leapt out and snatched the infant away. She looked up at me with a venomous expression and snarled: "Oh no you don't!"

After dark, police helicopters hovered above me on the freeway flashing their epileptic blue lamps and scouring the ground with hungry beams of light.

For several days I remained a total alien, and out of this alienation grew a feeling of tremendous outrage against the senseless extravagance of it all. It was entirely a matter of perspective. To a Southern Californian, his life-style and standard no doubt seemed like the least he could get by on. To me it seemed preposterous and sick. I wandered through supermarkets and along "shopping malls" disgusted and obsessed by the naked drive to sell and consume frivolities.

When I eventually came to visit Disneyland I realized that the ultimate aim, the logical conclusion for Los Angeles was that it should all become another Disney creation, a completely simulated and totally controlled "fun environment" in which life was just one long, uninterrupted ride.

From the point of view of a Bolivian Indian chewing coca on the *altiplano* I could see that it would already be pretty difficult to distinguish between the two.

The effect wore off as my tan subsided, my insect bites healed and the goggle imprint faded. Finally I was an outcast no longer, because someone invited me to his home. He was a motorcycle mechanic making a machine to beat the world's speed record. He was a gentle fellow with a slow, warm smile, and he had come from Indiana with his girl friend, who was a gorgeous nurse. They lived in a small place in Paramount and I went to stay there after a while. I discovered that life did after all still go on in Los Angeles, in a clandestine way, lurking in the corners of the waffle.

When I judged myself to be sufficiently civilized I risked launching myself on my friends of friends who were very big in Holly wood, and so finally I got right up against the Giant Nipple itself. One friend was Herbert Ross, director of a series of immaculate comedies, and he had the idea, as we sat munching chicken sandwiches in his office at M-G-M, of having me ride up on my motorcycle to a party in Beverly Hills where he was going that evening.

His touch was as sure as ever.

I rode up through Chandler country to a house full of genuine movie superstars who not only thought my arrival a pleasant surprise but actually grasped, far better than anyone at Triumph seemed to, what my journey was all about. Other invitations followed, and after a while I stopped protesting about Los Angeles and began to enjoy it, until it became difficult to recall just why I had been making all that fuss.

There was a lot of work to be done on my bike. The forks were twisted, had been since Argentina. The cylinder head turned out to be fractured. The oil scavenge pipe had been knocked sideways in South Africa, so they had to get inside the crankcase, and while they were there they replaced the crankshaft, because the head had come off one of the flywheel retaining bolts. The transmission had never given any trouble, but there were other minor irritations that needed sorting out.

One man worked on it for a week. He seemed efficient but heartless, and I could never find a way to talk about it with him. I wanted to ask, thinking that the bike really could have been much more trouble-free than it was. In most of the poorer countries Triumphs and British bikes in general had a tremendous reputation for reliability. In the sophisticated countries like the U.S.A. it was just the reverse. The story was that Triumphs were eccentric and troublesome, and you had to buy German or Japanese if you wanted reliability.

It seemed to me that this was mostly the result of superior marketing and propaganda from Japan in the richer markets. It had led to a situation in which dealers and mechanics were involved most of the time with Japanese machines. British bikes could only be a nuisance to them, with their archaic engineering, requiring different tools and a different approach. It suited them that British bikes had a bad reputation, because it excused the consequences of their own sloppy work. I thought that if I had any obligation towards Triumph for the support they were giving me, it was to demonstrate that their bike really could run clean and trouble-free.

The attitude in Los Angeles was quite the opposite. They seemed ready to swallow the unreliability story whole. Their remedy was simply to replace everything and send me on my way.

"You'll never get more than ten thousand miles out of a set of pistons anyway," they said. I found it disheartening, but plainly things had gone too far for it to be worthwhile objecting.

The truth was that in spite of all the brisk confidence in the front office, everybody was waiting for the place to crash about their ears. And if my mechanic seemed to have lost heart, it was not surprising, for he had already got himself a new job with Yamaha.

So I took what was offered and said thank you. They pretended to believe in me, and I pretended to believe in them. I thought they were nice people, and I think they liked me, but it was too late to do any good. Nobody wanted to know any more.

I left Los Angeles eventually with a bike set up to carry much more stuff. Ken Craven had written to me offering me new boxes and Dick Pierce in LA.. fitted me out with a rack and a much bigger top box than I had had before. I had abandoned the old rack in Johannesburg, and I had slung the side boxes directly on the frame. I told Dick how the old rack had fractured on the way to Nairobi and that the side struts had been too feeble, and he said they would reinforce the system support for me and put on stronger struts. It was a very fine rig in the end, offering a lot more capacity. I kept the single saddle, with the leather cover I had made myself in Argentina, and the hole burned in the back of it by my little stove when I had been cooking rice at Ipiales with Bruno.

The sun of California is like white wine and pine sap. It may be a temperate sun, but it has an ardent nature. It lifted my heart with a heady buoyancy and spiced the air with a resinous tang. It shone down on me loyally up the coast road from Los Angeles, beating at me from the concrete freeways, beckoning me from Pacific breakers, winking from wind-stirred leaves and grasses. It followed me through San Francisco, bouncing off windowpanes and shining on long golden hair. It warmed the terra-cotta ironwork of the Golden Gate Bridge, flashed off the teeth of a toll collector, hurried me over the rain grooves and up the highway until, a hundred miles farther on, it came into its own among the forests and hills of northern California.

Where the hot cement gave way to cooler asphalt and the highway began to rise and fall and curve against the hillsides, the bike transformed itself from a running animal into a bird and leaned over to swoop and curl with the contours. Somewhere there, where the highway meets the river, I wound off to the right and flew in among the mountains, looping high up towards the sun and down again into a bowl of fertile land and golden sunshine.

The air was heavily scented. I smelled blackberry and hay and resin. Waves of vivid aroma reinforced my joy at being back on the land again, and I had to recognize the craving I had created in myself for landscape and space. For a while, absorbed in the mind boggling materialism of Los Angeles, I had forgotten those thirty thousand miles of plains, mountains, rivers, forests, deserts, skies and stars, but they would never be erased from my subconscious. As with music, they could be ignored for a while in pursuit of some short-term enthusiasm, but the hunger would build up silently inside me until something as slight as a scent of pine or a snatch of piano would warn me that I was perilously close to starvation.

I rode around a slithering curve onto a straight section. The land rose to a high ridge on my left and fell away to the right in a more gentle slope that would bring it eventually to the river winding among the rocks far below.

I crossed a cattle grid, and then the county line. The land here was sparsely wooded with oak, young fir, madrone and manzanita. I saw open grassland above me where the big timber had once stood. Near the road lay heaps of rusting machinery, the leavings of a saw mill abandoned when the land had been logged and sold. I knew about it from Bob and Annie. It was one of the signs that told me I had arrived.

A yellow mailbox was planted on a post by the roadside announcing the name of the ranch and I followed the track down the hill and alongside a big sunburned meadow. The track took me past one wooden house and a newly erected barn to another bigger house. It was early afternoon. I could see a horse on the meadow but no people. The noise of the bike seemed inappropriate and I was glad to put it to rest and let the sound fade into the silence. There were ducks on a small pond. A goat stood facing away from me, obstinately refusing to recognize the interruption.

I climbed some wooden steps to the verandah of the house and went inside. A big man with unruly fair hair sat sprawled in a chair smoking a home-rolled cigarette and staring straight at me with wide, lively eyes. I thought it odd that he hadn't got up to see who was making all the noise. He wasn't busy.

"I'm a friend of Annie's," I said. Those were the words I was told to say, my credentials.

"Hi," he said. He continued to look at me with engaging curiosity, as though I might turn into a rabbit.

"I'm looking for Carol," I added.

"Oh," he said, still gazing at me quizzically. The silence gathered again. I waited. There was no hurry. A wasp buzzed against the windowpane. It was very peaceful. I knew what he was doing and I was enjoying it, two strangers alone together in a room, appraising each other, savoring each other like animals. People talk too much at first, just making publicity. It was hardly more than a significant pause. Then he got up, and walked to the window.

"They're down by the river, I guess," he said, pointing out over the meadow. Then he smiled beatifically.

"Heard about you," he said, and grabbed me in a bear hug and kissed me solidly on the cheek. That *did* surprise me.

He told me how to get to the river, over the meadow, past a volleyball net and then left by Suicide Rock. I walked over the meadow bubbling with joy. It's that damned sun, I thought, the same sun that was shining on Cape Town in the autumn and on Rio in the spring. It gets inside me and bubbles like a leaky champagne bottle. Pretty soon I shall be engulfed in ecstasy. I can feel it coming.

At the other end of the meadow a girl was walking towards me, bare-breasted and trailing her shirt through the long grass from her fingers. She saw me and put on the shirt, holding it closed with her hand. When we met in the middle of the meadow I said I was a friend of Annie's and looking for Carol.

"Oh. Hi," she said, and released the shirt. "I didn't know. We get some pretty creepy people come sometimes. Annie's down at the swimming hole with Bob, and yeah, Carol's there too, with Josie, Christine and Frog."

I found the way easily, and met Carol walking up from the river as I came down. She was with two young girls, and my first impression was that she resented me slightly. I had never met her before, but guessed who she was. Perhaps I was feeling too pleased with myself. Perhaps I looked as though I thought I was God's gift to women. Whatever it was I felt a distance between us, but it did not matter to me at the time. I felt no special attraction to her. She had straight, dark hair tied with an elastic band, a narrow oval face and a funnily shaped up-tilted nose reddened by sun. I thought she was too thin. Even so, two things about her were striking. Her coloring was dramatic, russet as the ripest apple, and her eyes were big and gray-blue. I noticed them without paying too much attention.

Bob and Annie, it seemed, had gone up ahead to the campsite, whatever that might be, and so I walked up with Carol and the two girls, who were Christine and Josie.

"And Frog?" I asked. "Who or what is Frog?"

"You'll see," she said. "That's a treat you have in store."

I noticed her dazzling smile then, but it still didn't mean anything special.

We walked up slowly, talking. We talked about Ecuador and Venezuela, and gardens and marriages and rattlesnakes, and trees and Ohio, where she was from. She had a warm voice, pitched a bit low, and a powerful Middle West accent that said "bahks" for "box," and made me want to laugh, but Josie got in first with "Are you a limey man?" and so we all laughed at my outrageous British accent instead.

I learned that the ranch was a commune although they never called it that, and that they had 670 acres of the most beautiful land in the world, bought cheap after it had been logged. I learned that people who cut down trees indiscriminately for profit were despicable, and that Carol worked the vegetable garden where, with a little help from her friends, she produced enough to feed twenty people. Also that someone we both knew in San Francisco was a nerble.

"What," I asked, "is a nerble?"

"A nerble," she said, "is one thing and a nonie is another. Ask Frog about nerbles and nonies. Frog is in charge of naming."

"Who's in charge of Frog?"

"Honk shoes," she exclaimed mysteriously, "nobody is in charge of Frog. Frog is in charge of the world."

She said it as though she meant it, but I got no further with my questions because we had climbed out of the river gorge and crossed a small clearing and we were at the campsite. Some rattan matting had been set up as screens around a room-sized space in the shelter of a group of oaks. Inside were an old stuffed sofa and some easy chairs, a low table, orange boxes set up as shelves for food and things, and old carpets on the ground. An outdoor room.

"No, it never rains in the summer – well hardly."

Annie was there and embraced me fondly. Bob, too, and some other people. Everybody looked very pleased. Frog, as I had guessed, was a small boy. He stood on the edge of the circle and looked me over very thoroughly for a while. He was only four, but very tough and self-contained, a force to be reckoned with.

They said I should sleep there at the campsite. Josie and Christine were sleeping there too, and maybe others. Carol said we should go up to the cabin in the morning and she would make pancakes for breakfast. She said she lived in a wooden cabin up the hill on the other side of the county road, and I could find it by listening for the sound of the piano.

"A piano," I cried. "You must be joking."

She smiled. I think it was the piano that made me begin to take it all seriously. A piano is a distinctly permanent thing.

Six hundred and seventy acres is a lot of land, especially when it is all up and down, laced with streams and studded with hillocks and humps of crumbling stone. I ambled around it for some time in the morning, looking for the cabin. A certain kind of countryside has always attracted me. I like streams of clear water running at a gentle pace over smooth rocks and pebbles freckled and veined with the browns and greens and yellows of mysterious minerals. I like grassy banks tied to the roots of ancient trees, and rough-hewn hillsides scattered with live and fallen timber, boulders and mosses, leaves and lichens, where creatures I have never seen can go about their business undiscovered. I love land that rises and dips, forever revealing and concealing secret places, intricate land with shelter and food for all kinds of life, big and small.

The power of this attraction was heightened enormously by my long journey. In Africa, Brazil, Chile and Argentina, Colombia, Costa Rica, so many places, I saw countryside that drew me almost with the force of destiny. It became too painful to be forever passing it by. I felt I had to stop somewhere and make some lasting connection with this earth, to become involved with it in some way. The power of the desire was overwhelming. I walked through the ranch, smelling the earth and leaves, startling deer, being startled myself by the sudden screech of peacocks roosting in a large oak, and thought, "This could be the place. This has to be the place."

I heard the piano, and found the cabin on a gently sloping shelf of land. A stream ran along one side, lost under a thriving colony of blackberry bushes, and tall trees provided shade on the other side.

It was a modest cabin, square and set on piles, made of planking with a tar-paper roof. The piano was in the front room, which overlooked the valley through a large sheet of acrylic set into the wall. Also in the front room was a big, black, cast-iron, wood-burning Franklin stove. At the back was a bed and a kitchen range. Behind the cabin was a clear space with an outhouse, a hose rigged up for a shower, and a chopping block. The water came in a tube from upstream.

The heat was beginning to build up for the day. All the doors were open and warm air moved through carrying all the scents of the woodland. Carol was alone and we talked much as we had the day before. Nobody else came. I had to admit that suited me, and Carol did not seem at all surprised. I played a few pieces, clumsily through lack of practice, while she made breakfast. The aroma of coffee (that old cliché) wafted through the cabin, followed by the smell of frying in hot butter.

"The butter is from Germany," she said. "Germany is one of our cows.

"Frog again," I said.

"You know it," she said. "Really."

We ate our way through mounds of little soft pancakes soaked in almost pure maple syrup. The simplicity of the cabin, and the golden silence all around us was affecting me profoundly. Halfway through the pancakes, I said:

"I still don't really know what you are all doing here."

She looked up with a flash of anger in her eyes. Then she snorted.

"I guess there are some people here who'd like to know too."

She tried to tell me something about the ranch, how it had come about out of the turmoil of Student Revolt, Flower Power, Civil

Rights, the Women's Movement, the Vietnam War, all those waves of energy rushing across the face of America promising a storm of change and liberation.

"Some of us got together and found this land, after it had been ripped off by the loggers. It was amazingly inexpensive. Some of the guys who were at school together, they wanted to start a school here. One day we will. It's still my dream."

"What happened?"

"I guess when we got here we found we had too much to learn ourselves."

I listened hard trying to understand, but every answer begged another question, and I didn't really want to ask questions. There were some people here, living on some land. Why or how seemed less important than the fact that they were doing it. In any case the only way to find out would be to do it with them.

Apparently there was this one annual crunch, the mortgage payment. Every year they struggled to make money, selling produce, hauling hay for a neighbor, maybe getting in money from jobs in the city, but they were not desperate. There was money among them, already inherited or in a parent's bank account. No question, one way or another the payment would be met. The Annual Mortgage Meeting was a symbolic crunch, when they looked at each other and estimated how much energy they had in the bank, and what kind of energy it was.

The Annual was coming up soon. I gathered that this year the energy was running low. There were fewer people living on the ranch than ever in its four-year history, only half of the twenty or more who had built their own small houses on various parts of the land.

"We put all our energy into our relationships, and the results are totally amazing. Really. You'd never find a more beautiful set of people anywhere. But, I don't know, we were on this big high, but it seems to be fading, which is fine but . . . it's really hard on the kids."

"Look, you know what surprised me most when I got here?" I said, bravely. "The mess. I mean, all the stuff littered round the big house. I don't understand how you put up with that ugliness. Doesn't anyone want to clear it up."

"I know," she said sadly. "It seems to be really hard for people to find that kind of energy right now."

There was no doubting Carol's energy. She worked furiously in the garden. I spent most of that day and the next with her, at the cabin or in the garden. She told me things about herself which surprised and sometimes disturbed me. The disturbing things were about love, different kinds of love for people and things. It was alarmingly honest, but exhilarating too. Sometime during those two days, her grey-blue eyes got too big for me and swallowed me up. I forgot that I was only intending to be there for a few days, that I was already booked on a ship for Australia, and that I was only halfway around the world. The next day I rode the bike up the trail to the cabin and moved in.

I don't think I ever fell in love with Carol in the way I had fallen before. Love simply wrapped itself around me. She was made of it, and the ranch, I discovered, was full of it. It was what they had really come there for, and it was what I wanted more than anything else; to be alive and in love on land like that. A week or so later I rode into San Francisco and postponed my sailing from August to November.

I claimed that long summer, immersed in love and sunshine, as my reward for two years of physical and emotional battering. Although I had stopped for a few weeks at a time in Johannesburg, Cape Town, Rio and Santiago, although I had even fallen in love once before, a part of me had always been unattached, waiting to move on. The journey had never stopped, and all the while I was soaking up information and sensation at an alarming rate.

I came to the ranch brimful of feelings and insights that had had no release on the way. Like a cargo of perishable goods they were threatening to rot in me. So I spilled my heart out on that land and among those people who had made it their business to share feelings and dreams.

There was work to do, a chance to leave something that would survive my passing. We built an extension to the cabin that widened it by a few feet towards the blackberry bushes, and gave a sense of new space that was quite palatial. We called it the East Wing, and moved the bed into it to receive the morning sun.

The blackberry bushes concealed a busy community of birds, frogs, rodents and various species of snake. The largest inhabitant was the civet cat, a kind of spotted skunk. For a while the entire wall of the cabin was down, and we lived as though in an extension of the blackberry bush, open to the stars and the moon and the cool night world. Then the civet cat took to visiting us.

I was wakened by the startling sound of someone running across the bare wooden floor in small hobnailed boots. It did not stop. In short rushes the sound traversed the cabin from end to end. There were snuffling noises. Sounds of pleasure and excitement. Boxes toppled over. A broomstick clattered to the floor. Whoever it was, was brazen beyond belief. To tell the truth I was delighted that some small wild animal should want to live its life so close to mine but, even so, there was a distinct lack of respect. A lesson would have to be taught.

"Hon," said Carol, "just be careful. If you scare it, it'll stink the place out."

I watched from the bed. The moon was bright. Something like a big white shaving brush emerged from behind the chest and went bobbing jauntily across the room. Rat-tat-tat-tat-tat-tat went the hobnails. I could just make out the lustrous black fur of the body, polka dotted with white, but it was the flouncing white tail that enticed the eye, and threatened the nose with doom.

I prowled around the cabin, naked in the moonlight, but the civet knew I was powerless. It was utterly insolent, did exactly as it liked and left in its own good time.

The second night I was bolder. Prodding it with the long handle of a mop, I tried to guide it to the door. Failure. The civet actually seemed to enjoy the game and stayed even longer. The noise it made was phenomenal.

"They have these pads of toughened skin," Carol told me. "They signal by thumping the ground." Under the civet's hammer blows the planks of the cabin resounded like a xylophone. Adorable as it was, we were losing sleep.

The third night I struck lucky. By chance I held the mop the right way around, and brandished the mop head in a way that I imagined would be very frightening to civets. The civet rushed up to the mop head and positively fawned on it, clearly in love at first sight with what it took to be the ultimately handsome civet. I drew it cunningly across the floor and out through the open kitchen door. Then I closed the door.

With the whole side of the cabin missing, that was a very thin gesture of defiance, but the civet did not return. Hideously deceived, it joined the ranks of heartbroken lovers and crept away into the bushes to pine.

Carol and I loved very deeply. It seemed inconceivable that it could come to an end and I lived my life there as though it was forever. The ranch felt like home and the people on it became my family.

I learned to know the land, walking around it and working on it. There were many more encounters with animals, including a thrilling meeting with a rattlesnake that was carried off with great dignity on both sides. The summer held out right through to the end of October, cooling slowly as the days drew in, but staying bright and clear. More and more ranchers were making trips to the city and some were staying away longer than they had expected. It was evident that some new impulse would have to be found to bring everyone back, and as the numbers diminished the prospect of a winter on the ranch became less tenable for those who remained.

Eventually Frog's mother also decided to move to San Francisco. Shortly before she left, Frog stood on the wooden steps of the communal house and declared that he was no longer Frog. His name, henceforth, would be T.A. Frog was born with the ranch, and he seemed to have grasped with extraordinary clarity that it was the end of an era.

During the last month I began to dig a drainage ditch across a hillside to intercept spring water that was flooding the foundations of the big house. As I dug it became a stream, a microcosmic river with cascades, bridges and grassy banks which I imagined might one day blossom with spring flowers. It revealed scores of forgotten memories of streams I had camped by, paddled in or simply gazed into as a child. It led me (more than I led it) in a meandering curve around the house, so that the clearing away of old junk and abandoned machinery became part of something new and exciting.

I took the experience of the stream as a parable on life, believing that as long as I did what I did wholeheartedly it could only go well, and if there was to be pain then that also must lead to better things. There would have to be pain. The journey had to be finished. I could not take the ranch with me, but I could at least leave something, a part of myself, behind.

The sailing date was November 15. I had seen the P&0 liner *Oriana*, all 42,000 tons of her, the day before when I had come over the Bay Bridge from Berkeley. She had a fairy-tale brilliance floating there in the dark winter evening. Just looking at her made me feel thousands of miles away and sad.

They loaded the bike in the morning. Carol and I were staying at a friend's house on Maple Street, and in the afternoon T.A.'s mother brought her Volkswagen beetle over to take us all to the ship. She was enormously pregnant and very happy about it, and I was allowed to put my hand on her big tummy and listen for the baby inside. It was a heartbreaking thing to do in the circumstances. The father of this as yet unborn wonder was also there with still another rancher, and the five of us, with all my luggage, completely filled the VW's egg-shaped interior.

We drove along Clay to Gough, left and right to Van Ness, left and right again past Stockton to Pier Thirty-five. I fastened on to all the details hungrily. We went through an archway past a pot-bellied guard to the luggage reception, and I joined a queue of passengers while the others made their way to my cabin. When I arrived among them other ranchers and friends had arrived. Bob and Annie were there with the biggest rolls of paper streamers I had ever seen, and Larry, another close friend, had brought two bottles of champagne.

There was a tremendous air of excitement about us all. The ship was so grand, and made such a powerful statement about romantic travel, that nobody could be immune from it. We celebrated as though all of us were going along, and it really began to feel like that. I grabbed one of the streamers and dodged crazily around and between people until I had tied us all into a great knot, and the emotional temperature rose far beyond anything I had ever known before in a group. We kissed each other, all of us, men or women regardless. I felt a distinct rush of love for every person there and knew that it was reciprocated, and I was able to say a few things that were true. It was a most moving experience created entirely by those marvelous people out of their real warmth and affection for me, and it bound me to them forever.

Australia
and Malaysia

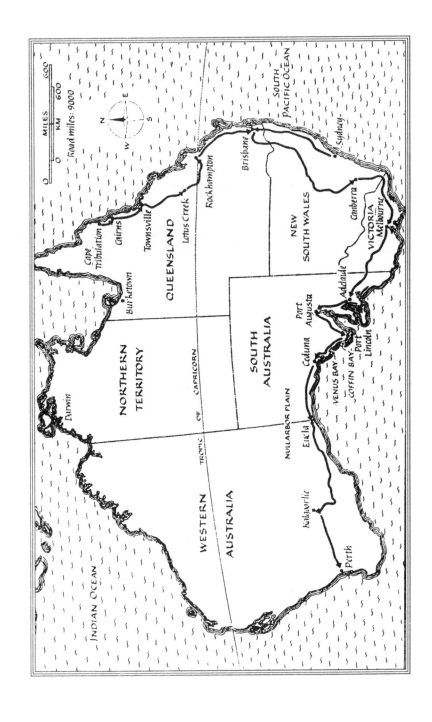

I stepped off the ship at Sydney wondering what it would be like to arrive there with no name, no past, nothing but a handful of cash and a new life to start from scratch. Until they opened up the moon, Australia was still the farthest I could get from the place I called home.

It was a continent I knew only as a caricature. Perhaps because it was so far away, the only images that seemed to travel the distance were absurdly overblown. Australians were the Ancient Gauls of the twentieth century, a good-hearted people so untouched by the niceties of civilization that with one sweep of their good intentions they could do more damage than an elephant in Bloomingdales.

Australian women, I knew, were big and brazen and went about the streets dressed and made up for the stage in the belief that the right way to catch a man was to incite him to rape. The wounds sustained during this savage form of courtship were soothed by swimming two hundred lengths before breakfast.

Australian men were big and bronzed and wore shorts and singlets from which their muscled limbs extended like four strings of sausages. At the end of one of the upper strings was attached either a tennis racket or a small bottle of beer called a "stubbie." They ambled about in hot sunshine being disgustingly frank about their natural functions and waiting to be incited to rape. If one of these King Kong figures appeared over the skyline the thing to do was run for your life.

I came ashore determined to forget all the jokes and cartoons and ridiculous stereotypes and to learn about the real Australia.

It was not easy. During the first days in Sydney, getting ready to ride up the east coast, I looked around me with the freshest eye I could manage in the dusty December heat. I saw men ambling in singlets and shorts. Their muscled limbs looked remarkably like sausages. I saw women who had apparently slipped offstage during the interval of a matinee performance of *Cabaret*. They looked as though anything less than rape might be mistaken for indifference. I noticed that many men wore tailored shorts with cute slits up the seams, like *cheongsams,* to show a little extra flash of thigh, and the obscene thought crossed my mind that maybe they were hoping to be raped as well.

I saw some men, still in their youth, with the grossest beer bellies it was possible to imagine, cultivated at great expense, and I was overcome by the noise people made and the difficulty they had in showing each other affection.

Then, one day, I set out to photograph these things I had noticed. Not one revolting beer belly came my way; not one girl was dressed in such tasteless extravagance as to be worth recording. To my annoyance I saw men and women appearing to be softly and openly appreciative of each other. The truth bore in on me that I had been seeing only extremes in the crowd; the most flamboyant, the most threatening, the most crass, just as an Australian in London would see only Poms in pin-striped suits and bowler hats.

The vast majority of Australians were not like that, and yet my first impressions had been correct too, and I wondered how a few examples of extreme behavior could so stamp and characterize a whole society. It became one of my main preoccupations.

For an Englishman, especially one who can remember how things were in England before the fifties, Australia has a disturbing familiarity. The streets straggle out of Sydney much as they do out of London, and pass through namesake suburbs. You see street furniture and municipal architecture that have since been replaced in London by something newer; like old-style post offices, libraries, and mechanic's institutes. Or so it seemed to me, for the force of nostalgia is so strong that one old lamppost can color an entire street.

Out in the New South Wales countryside, too, there are glimpses of old England. The railway system, seemingly with all its veins and arteries still intact, and local puffer trains running between model stations, is a powerful time warper. I rode up into the cozy Blue Mountains past village greens and orchards and vine-covered cottages. The strange admixture of aboriginal names only seemed to point up the quaintness of the English ones. Wentworth Falls and Katoomba; Mount Victoria, Bell and Bilpin; Kurrajong, Richmond and Windsor.

I rode past meadows and stables and ponds; butchers' shops bursting with the finest and cheapest meat in the world; languid pubs made glamorous with the fancy Victorian ironwork which we, in England, melted down for scrap in the war.

At Wiseman's Ferry a great, green river rolled by between steep cut grassy banks, and a country hotel founded in 1815 served a counter lunch for a dollar sixty which made it seem cheap at the time, piled high with lamb chops and brussels sprouts. It was hot, but not too hot. There were flies, but so far not too many. The sun put creases around the eyes and seemed to be richer in ultraviolet than any other sun I had known but it was tolerable and it was, after all, midsummer. Riding through it like this, viewing it as an outsider, it was a rural idyll, far away from the troubles of the world.

When I came back onto the coastal highway there was less to admire. All Australia seemed to be moving up the coast in trailers, and campsites were crowded. As I moved closer to people their prejudices showed through. The flies grew thicker too, and I had to eat my steak with a handkerchief waving in my hand to keep them from totally obscuring the meat. But the great green rivers kept rolling down to the sea, and the beautiful beaches stretched out for ever, and it was still the best steak in the world.

The coast road north of Sydney is called the Pacific Highway for 650 miles until it gets to Brisbane. Then it becomes the Bruce Highway. Another five hundred miles north is Rockhampton, right on the Tropic of Capricorn. I crossed the tropic (for the sixth time on my journey) four days before Christmas and headed on for Mackay. Since Brisbane the arid summer of the south had been giving way slowly to the tropical rainy season of Queensland. In the southern droughts the cattle died of thirst. In the north they drowned and floated away on the floods. Australia runs to extremes.

After Marlborough the road takes a long inland loop for 150 miles to Sarina, to avoid floods. People had told me lurid tales about this part of the road.

"You want to watch out," they said. "There's criminals on the lam from Sydney."

Only a few weeks before a married couple had been mysteriously murdered in their car on that lonely stretch. I was served the story several times, with relish. There was sometimes a ghostly quality about that land, but it was nothing to do with criminals or even ghosts. Much of the land was covered by a light forest and a high proportion of the trees were acacias called brigalow. Across broad areas of the land the brigalow was dead, and the thousands of twisted gray trunks seemed to haunt the forest. It was murder all right; they had all been slain by a poisoned ax to clear the way for pasture.

I took on gas at Marlborough and set off. It was monotonous country, and empty, but not at all sinister. After eighty miles I came to Lotus Creek. There was nothing much to distinguish Lotus Creek from the other small rivers I had crossed. It ran in a shallow bed cosseted by reeds and ferns and clumps of tall guinea grass. Several small species of gum tree, black butt, white, and stringy bark among them, grew alongside it.

The highway dipped gently to the bridge, which was simply made of huge square-cut trunks of one of the bigger species of gum tree, for some gums grow to well over three hundred feet. The trunks were surfaced with smaller wood and tarred over. The bridge had no parapet but was more than wide enough for the biggest trucks. Most of the smaller bridges were built in this way.

Beyond the bridge on the right was a roadhouse and gas pump. I filled up, on principle, and went in for a coffee. It was a small restaurant, neater and cleaner than I had expected. Behind a well-stocked counter was a door open to the kitchen. The man behind the counter was busy at something. He was a stocky fellow in a neatly pressed blue bush jacket and matching shorts. He wore woolen socks up to the knees and a cowboy hat.

"How much is coffee?" I asked. I always asked. Australia was vastly more expensive than I had expected and prices varied wildly from place to place.

"Thirty cents," said the man without looking up. There was an edge to his voice though, and a hint of Middle European accent. I guessed Polish. Thirty cents was a high price.

"Thirty cents?" I repeated, pretending mild astonishment.

Then he did look up. He had truculent blue eyes.

"Is thirty cents too much?" he demanded. "If it is, I'll make it fifty cents. I'm like that."

A touch of panic assailed me. There was something funny going on, and I could not figure it out. I made placatory noises and he let me have a cup for thirty cents after all.

"I'm up here to make money, that's all," he said. "Why else would anyone come and live up here in this wilderness. When you're still here in a couple of days you'll be grateful I don't put it up to a dollar."

"Well, it's very nice here," I said, "but . . ."

"If you're thinking of going back to Rockhampton you'd better make it soon, before Lotus comes up too," he said with a slight sneer, and then the message began to filter through.

"Too?"

There were two others in the restaurant, a man and a teen-age girl at a table. The man had got up and was walking over. He said: "When Connor's comes up, Lotus ain't far behind. Right, Andy?" "What's Connor's?" I asked, although I had guessed by now. I just wanted them to know that I hadn't known.

"You didn't know? Connor's is the next creek along to Sarina, ten miles down the road. I just came back from there. She's seven feet over the bridge and still rising. And to anticipate your next question, sometimes she's up for a day, sometimes for a week, and there's no tellin'."

I waited to see if there were any other questions I had planned to ask, but it seemed not. His curly blond hair was graying and he wore steel-rimmed spectacles. He looked old for the girl. I asked him what he was doing there, nicely.

"I'm based in Mackay," he said, "but I travel around a hell of a lot. I'm the most knowledgeable journalist in Australia about the tropics."

Between them, I thought, these two fellows could run Australia. They had the confidence for the job. However, after a bit they became quite friendly and interesting. It was just that first aggressive flash that got me. Like an Anglo-Saxon version of Latin America. The comparison pleased me. Also, the coffee when it came was very good.

I rode up to Connor's to have a look before settling in for the week. The queue was several hundred yards long, cars and trucks. It was very warm, with sun striking down between the cumulus clouds, and people were all over the place in their singlets and summer frocks, eating Fast Food and chucking the plastic containers and empty bottles into the countryside. Four truckies were playing an intense game of poker in the middle of the road. The bridge was nowhere to be seen, but the top of the "Give Way" sign was still visible. The water was black and turbulent, and still rising.

I got back to Andy's place to find four big refrigerated trucks had parked outside, their engines thrumming away to keep the coolers working. The drivers were already piling up empty beer bottles in the restaurant. There were five men, a jolly red-headed woman and a boy. I decided to get my stuff unpacked and into the tent before it started to rain, and rode the bike out to the campsite in the field.

When I walked back to the restaurant I found the drivers outside sitting at some trestle tables under a waterproof canopy. I felt like joining them and asked Andy to sell me some beer. I had a great knack for treading on Andy's toes. Either that, or his toes were a permanent mess.

"I don't sell beer," he said hotly. "I have never sold beer. I have applied for a license and you will never find sly grog sold on my premises."

"Oh well, I only thought . . ." I said, sniffing the fumes that still hung around the room, and went out to sit with the truckies. After five minutes, Andy came out with a bottle of beer he wanted to give me, the sentimental fool. But by then I'd already finished one and been given another.

Two of the truckies were doing most of the talking, and they were both comedians in their way. One of them was a brisk tubby fellow who told conventional jokes like a club comic. I could imagine him with a spotted bow tie and a microphone going "I say, I say, I say." That was Clive.

The poet among them was a man they all called Ferret. He was a slightly built man with a daft little cloth hat on his head and an expression that managed to be both sad and humorous at the same time, in the Celtic manner. He was the acknowledged leader of the truckies and was famous throughout Australia for his verse epic, "Ode to a Truckie." It was about a pal who had died overturning a truck full of empty bottles outside Gladstone, having probably emptied a good few of the bottles himself.

I liked Ferret immediately. He had a warm manner and a sympathetic way with stories. The real humor ran all the way through them, between the punch lines, and I thought them very funny and subtle and not a little astonishing. Traveling with Ferret was a handsome, athletic fellow with a wistful manner called P.J. He was going to see his mother in Sarina for Christmas. He hadn't seen her, he said, with a slight grin, since two and a half years ago when she was dying in hospital.

The fourth truckie was a chirpy little Tasmanian they called McCarthy. He had rubber legs and a concave face and played "fall guy" when one was needed. He enjoyed the role and encouraged it, and his tee-shirt showed a hand with two fingers up, meaning "Peace" or "Piss Off," depending on how you saw it.

The fifth man's name I never knew. He was husband to the redhead and they both made an appreciative audience for the others.

Even before the beer warmed them all in a deep amber glow, there was a great kinship and liking between them, a quite tangible thing. They were mates, of course, which is a powerful enough bond, but it was more than that. They were truckies, and in Australia that was tantamount to being an outlaw.

I had heard about truckies from the outside, stories of reckless violence and villainy. For respectable Australians, truckies ranked with drought, pestilence and "criminals on the lam" as one of nature's chief hazards. "No truck with a truckie" was their motto, and they locked up their daughters when the big rigs rolled in. Now from the inside I saw that they had many qualities I had missed badly on my way up the coast, and the most surprising was sensitivity. The boorishness that I had begun to accept as inevitable was absent, and in its place was a delicacy of touch that seemed little short of amazing. Yet, thinking it over, it was natural. They were all long-distance drivers, not short-haul cowboys. Anyone who spends long hours alone with himself on the road has to have more in his head than a stock of sterile prejudices.

Clive's son made regular runs to the truck for more beer.

"Are you trucking beer?" I asked Clive.

"No, I've got general groceries. He's got ice cream," he said, pointing at the fifth man.

"McCarthy's got prime Victoria rump, and Ferret's going empty."

We talked and told stories. I learned about the roads in the interior and what I heard convinced me that I must give up my idea of crossing the north in the rainy season. The only way out of Cairns would be the way I had come. I heard chilling tales of reckless driving over the roads of hell to get to the pub in time; of truckie pride and the awful falls that followed. Then the boy brought the bad news. The beer had run out.

Cars were still coming in over Lotus Creek, so without hesitation McCarthy went out to his big truck, wheeled it round and roared off across the bridge. Somewhere out there was a pub, and as long as there was a pub open in Australia they would have beer at Lotus Creek that night. The sun was fading, black clouds lowered all around. There were flashes of lightning off to the northeast. The journalist came out looking worried, and walked over with an expression that tried to look threatening but was just a bit silly.

"Have you seen my daughter?" he said. We all looked at

McCarthy's empty seat and smiled at a nice thought, although none of us believed it. The journalist sat in McCarthy's seat and gazed at the sky.

"She'll be filling up tonight," he said. "It's raining over the catchment area. We won't be out of here tomorrow." He was very authoritative, so I had no way of knowing whether he knew what he was talking about. Nor did I really care.

Andy switched on the lights in the grounds and the bulb under the canopy created a pleasing intimacy in the warm tropical evening. I heard the frogs honking down by the river. Lotus was beginning to rise now. Two tour buses came in and some cars. McCarthy was last over the bridge, with a crate of Castlemain's XXXX, the beer they all agreed was best, and with much relief they set to drinking again.

The place was filling up fast now, and looking like a refugee camp. The holiday makers were sleeping in their buses, and made a big crush with their visits to the bathrooms. The car travelers had filled Andy's annexed rooms, and others were camped in the field, but all this activity swirled around the canopied island of yellow light where the truckies sat drinking and murmuring with a low-key energy that seemed inexhaustible. Hours later I left them and slept through a heavy rainstorm.

I woke up to the sound of an old-fashioned hurdy-gurdy playing outside my tent. The melody had been coded in a secret cipher, but all the notes were there, creaking and squeaking rustily together. I looked out at what looked like a very fat magpie, waddling about and making this cheerful but extraordinary music.

I saw Ferret approaching across the field with a stubbie in his hand, his feet scarcely bending the blades of grass, his face rosy as the dawn.

"What is this amazing bird?" I asked. In a steady, sober voice, he said it was called a butcher bird, and I added it immediately to my list of top creatures.

"Come and have some breakfast," he said. "We're doing steak."

Connor's River had risen in the night to equal all previous records at thirteen feet above the bridge and McCarthy was celebrating by breaking into a fifty-pound carton of rump steak.

I wandered over to see a heap of timber blazing in the big barbecue stand and Clive cutting the rump into slices an inch thick. There was no indication that any of them had been to sleep or would ever sleep again. The refugees from the buses had come out after a cramped night in their seats and were huddled at a safe distance gazing in awe and envy at the terrible truckies. I was given half a square foot of the most delicious steak I had ever had, or would ever have, and a bottle of beer to start the day right.

The truckies were as contemptuous of the tourists as army men are of civilians, and took pride in their fearsome reputation, but as men they were too kindhearted to ignore the distress all around them. In Australia, meat-eating is a religion. P.J. and Ferret called over to them to come and get it if they wanted it. Most of them shrank back in horror as though they had been offered a cup of cyanide, but a few bold spirits risked coming in for a nip, like jackals around a campsite.

Andy came out from his house stamping his boots hard in anger as he walked.

"If I see you taking money for that meat," he shouted at Ferret, "there'll be trouble. I'm not having people doing business on my property."

He was so far out of line it was ridiculous. The truckies laughed and swore at him, and he stomped back to his overcrowded restaurant.

"He's better than the bloke up the road," said P.J. philosophically. "They were selling water at twenty cents a glass last flood."

"Who pays for this meat?" I asked.

"No worries," said Clive. "In a situation like this, they expect us to break into the load. They're happy enough if the refrigeration equipment keeps going while we're standing here.

"There should be several tons of strawberry ice cream running over the road by nightfall," he added, jerking a thumb at the fifth man. "His cooler's packed in."

It was true. The magnitude of this potential disaster fascinated me, and my mind was linked by telepathy to those slowly liquefying tons of frozen yuck for the rest of the day, hoping to be there when the first pink dribble appeared under the doors.

We had steak for lunch and for tea, and then we had steak for supper. I tried to talk to some of the bus crowd. There was a couple with a small boy who seemed nice, on their way to their home in Townsville. They asked me to come and stay on my way through. We hadn't been talking long before they wanted to tell me about the

At Lotus Creek, north of Brisbane, I ran into the monsoons and was stranded between flooded rivers with a party of Australian truck drivers. For two days and nights they drank beer and ate steaks virtually non-stop, while I did my best to keep up. Above, the amiable 'P.J' with a 'stubbie' in his hand, and the acclaimed truckie poet, Ferret. Others spent their time playing poker and watching the creek rise.

"abos." I had had only one encounter with aboriginals up to then, at a small town on the coast south of Brisbane. I had seen a couple standing barefooted in the shallow water of a lagoon fishing with a line but no rod. They were short dumpy figures, he with his trousers rolled up, she in a cotton frock. I had taken a picture of them from the jetty and he had seen me. His reaction was fierce and bitter.

"I'll fuckin' toss yer in there," he screamed, pointing at the water. I thought it a sad story and hoped these people would understand.

"You don't want to have anything to do with them," the woman said firmly. "Don't you ever trust one. Never. They'll lift anything off you. Good as the Arabs, they are."

"You know Palm Island?" said the man. I shook my head. "It's an abo reserve off the coast up here. Well, you know those flagons of cheap wine that cost a dollar fifty. Take one over there and you can flog it for forty-five dollars. They go crazy over grog."

"They're not human beings really – they're another species of animal," said the woman. "They live with animals, don't they? And it's a medical fact that every girl over three has been molested."

"If you hit them on the head," said the man, "you can only injure yourself. But they're the only people with any money in Australia."

It made me sick to listen to it. And they were really nice people. Several times coming up the coast I had heard these outpourings of filth that seemed to proceed from some deep hurt, like pus from a wound. I registered the fact that in all the hours we had spent together, not one of the truckies had ever uttered a single word of prejudice, and I was glad to get back among them as soon as I could.

The journalist's daughter came and stood by me for a while. She screeched a lot but she didn't have anything to say. The frilly bodice of her yellow cotton dress held her breasts up for my inspection, and then she disappeared again. I thought she was a disaster waiting to happen.

During the afternoon Connor's started dropping. By evening it looked promising. I was advised to be ready to cross, since it could easily start to rise again. I packed up all my stuff and slept in the back of Ferret's empty truck. P.J. spent the night in the cab with the last bottle of beer. When he had finished it I believe his eyes closed briefly. I woke to find him studying the centerfold of a magazine called *Overdrive,* gazing lustfully at a big and luscious color picture of a new Mack truck.

Soon afterwards the first car came through from Mackay and we all got ready to go. The pink ice cream was safe after all. I said goodbye and rode off to Connor's. There were still a few inches of water over the bridge, but I went across all right. Farther along the road, Ferret's big truck started hooting at me from behind. I slowed and he swung it deftly onto the verge in front of me.

"See you at the hotel in Sarina, Ted," he said. P.J. grinned, and I said O.K. I didn't feel like hurrying, and when I arrived they were already at the bar. Ferret was finishing one of his shorter stories.

"So this fellow said: 'Who did you see down there in Sydney, Dave?'

" 'Well, I was in the same room as Bishop Lennox.'

" 'Who's that then?'

" 'He's only the foremost Catholic in Australia. He's so holy he's most probably got holy water in his toilet.'

" 'What's a toilet, Dave?'

" 'How should I know. I'm not a bloody Catholic.' "

We were drinking out of dainty seven-ounce glasses at the counter instead of those stubby bottles. It didn't seem right, but the fumes were stronger in the enclosed space and Ferret and P.J. seemed to thrive in the atmosphere as though it were pure oxygen. One day, I thought, they would be leaning against a bar like this and they would just fade and dissolve into the alcoholic air. I had got to like them both very much.

I said I had to go, because I did not dare drink any more.

Ferret looked hard at me with that sad little smile on his face.

"You're a lovely person," he said. "I knew straight away. Most people don't do anything for me. They can be nice – know what I mean. I can be nice too. But it doesn't mean anything."

I knew exactly what he meant.

"You'll be right," said P.J. cheerfully.

I often thought about them afterwards but when, weeks later, by a million-to-one chance, I met Clive in a pub in Victoria I didn't know him at first.

"You know what happened to Ferret?" he said, grinning the way Australians do when there's bad news. "He turned his truck over outside Sarina that day."

"Is he all right?" I asked anxiously.

"Oh, yeah, he got away with it. Beer softened the fall."

A man I had met in Nairobi two years before had given me four elephant-hair bracelets to deliver to his sister. The hair was pulled from the elephant's tail, and was supposed to confer virility on men and fertility on women. His sister's home was in a small town near Cairns, and this romantic little mission gave my journey to "Far North Queensland" a nice human focus, but by the time I arrived the sister had long since abandoned her husband and taken her children off to England.

The husband was very kind and said that it would probably not have made any difference if I had got the bracelets there sooner. He gave me two of them to keep, but they never did much for me either.

I learned that it was still possible to go a bit farther north, with the promise of a unique rain forest to see at Cape Tribulation a hundred miles away, and I had the name of someone at a place called Noah's Creek. The first seventy miles were tar. Then came a ferry across the Daintree River, and after that, dirt. The real problem was Cooper's Creek, which crossed the dirt road. If the creek was up, "no way." If the creek was down, "no worries." We tried to get Charlie the ferry-man on the phone, but there was no reply. So I went anyway.

I found Charlie leaning against the ferry rail, waiting for customers. He was a snub-nosed, fair-haired young fellow with a wispy beard and a saucy look. He was leaning back at an easy angle but very alert and it was a moment before I noticed that one of his legs was missing.

He eyed the mud-spattered bike with amusement, following the route I had painted on one of the boxes.

"How's Cooper's?" I asked.

"No idea," he said, offhand. "Haven't had anyone through from that side. Should be O.K."

As I rode off the other side he called: "See ya later." He sold only return tickets, he knew I had to come back that way.

I rode on over red rocks and mud, laced with rivulets, slippery at times, but mostly steady going in third gear. I felt a vague thrill of apprehension thinking about Cooper's, and all the rivers I had already crossed. The worst had been in Bolivia on the *altiplano* between Potosí and La Paz. There were two rivers there, and I fell in one of them, and stopped dead in the middle of the other. It was very uncomfortable and made a terrible mess of my arrangements. I could easily conjure up a picture of my hotel room in Oruro, the floor papered from wall to wall with the pages of the Triumph workshop manual laid out to dry. Some Germans in a taxi helped to pull me out of the second river with a rope; it was all I could do to keep the bike upright against the force of the current. But what a world that was up there on the roof of the Andes!

I forded a few minor creeks and then came Cooper's. It was about twenty feet across with a bed of pebbles and boulders, and I got off the bike to have a good look. To go straight through was out of the question; there were at least three feet of water in the middle. A little farther downstream the creek widened and became more shallow. The right course to follow was a wide horseshoe shape, swinging downstream and then up again on the other side. The last bit would be the worst, with the mufflers submerged, trying to find the power to clamber up the bank.

On the other hand there could be no real disaster, because some campers from Cairns turned up in a small truck to give a hand if I made a muck of it. They crossed first and I watched their wheels to gauge the depth. Then in I went, managing all right until the last leg where I turned a bit too sharply against the current. The engine faltered and stopped, but I had both boots planted firmly on the river bed. The campers were already in the river, swimming, and we hauled the bike ashore together. I poured the water from my boots, unbolted the pipes to empty them too and then took my turn for a swim.

I found Noah's Creek just before dusk. There was a clearing by the river, with gardens and thick grasses, and a square tin-roofed house. The man I had come to see was not home, so I waited with his family. Extravagant blue butterflies flickered among the trees. At twilight insects chanted as though through amplifiers concealed in the bushes. A paraffin lamp was set, hissing, on the verandah, and suddenly into this circle of yellow light stumbled a dangerous and desperate figure. His shirt was split from collar to waist and the right sleeve was in tatters. He had four days' worth of dense black stubble on his sweaty face, and a crazy glint in his eye. In his right hand he swung a machete.

But it was only the proprietor, back from his daily chores. He had been hacking his way, painfully, along a high ridge at the limit of his property, looking for the blazes that were made to mark his boundaries in 1896. Among the picturesque obstacles to progress through this undergrowth were the Wait-a-while, with its long tendrils carrying fish-hook thorns at close intervals in sets of four, and the Stinging Bush, which has a fur of fine needles on the underside of its broad leaves that break off in the skin and hurt for a month, or so I was told.

In the morning I volunteered to go to Cape Tribulation for some provisions. It was a long walk through the forest along a track with glimpses here and there of the green ocean. The forest is a covered maze of towering tree trunks and twenty-foot ferns, knit together by massive trailing lianas and parasitic growths of all kinds. Forays into the under growth produced a fruit like a cobalt-blue egg, and another purple one with red flesh and three pits.

The Cape was a small, easy-going community with a lavishly stocked general store run by a middle aged couple and their children who had "emigrated" from Sydney. They spoke of it as of a different country, and it was true that Australia did not seem to reach up this far. I had the impression of Sydney being huddled down there some-where in the south-east corner of the continent. The family were not only happy to be where they were, they looked it. They went about helping each other and being openly warm and affectionate. Until I saw it I had not realized how cramped and undemonstrative other families had been. The father was kneading dough for the bread oven. He told me that I reminded him of a copper on the Drug Squad at Cairns.

"Drug Squad?" I asked, taken aback.

"Oh yes," he said. "They're very active. Packets of heroin are always floating ashore here. I've found some myself."

Later I helped to load a small outboard dinghy onto the truck at Noah's Creek and we went to the coast to find not heroin but mud crabs. We floated over thick brown water at the edge of a mangrove swamp and put down two wire traps. Within minutes we had a huge black crab with claws that can take off a finger. The meat of the mud crab was more delicious than any I had eaten since childhood. Obviously Australian coasts and rivers offered an abundance of good food, and I started to think it was time I bought a rod and took up fishing.

I would have been happy to stay for a few days, but the rain fell heavily all night, drumming on the tin roof louder than I had ever heard it before. By morning it was clear that if I wanted to get out across Cooper's any time soon I had better leave.

I fell once gently in a puddle of red clay on the way back but at

Cooper's I learned my lesson and got through with only my boots full. Charlie was still leaning against the side of his ferry, his one leg thrust forward just as I'd left him. This time we got talking and I asked if there were any crocodiles.

"Sure are," he said. "Used to be me livin'."

A one-legged crocodile hunter? Was he retired by one crocodile too many?

"Not a bit of it," he said. "If they made it legal again, I'd be off in the morning and no worries. 'Course, they were right to close it down. There's plenty of freshies to build up the population now they're protected, but there aren't enough salties left to keep a man in wages."

Fresh and salt, he said, referred to the water they came in.

"You might get twenty dollars for a freshie, double for a saltie. I got one saltie that was sixteen foot. It brought two hundred and forty dollars for the skin, but I'd never go after one of those again. It was too big to land in the boat. We had to drag it into shallow water and skin it there. The blood brought shoals of small shark in, and they lacerated our legs.

"There were three of us that used to shoot together. Both the others are dead. One was me wife's brother. He died of septicemia. The other one turned out to be a convicted rapist who'd killed a man. We only found out after he'd killed another man and was shot dead himself.

"Happened over in Burketown. Been there? Favorite place of mine. There was a pub and very little else. The walls and the floor were all at an angle from being hit by storms. When it flooded the clients had to row themselves to the thunder-box at the bottom of the yard.

"The host was a Yank. He was a bit 'tropo.' He had periods of sanity, then he'd become violent in a Wild West way. Used to punch his customers across the bar and come down the stairs with guns blazing. They put him away in the end. Then the pub was hit by a whirly-whirly."

I asked him how he had lost his leg.

"Cancer," he said. "But it got mashed up pretty badly first," he added laconically. "Croc shooting isn't that dangerous though. The shot is the important thing. You've got a six-inch target, quite close to. If you know your job you won't often have to swim for the corpse. You don't get rich either. You get wages and a half. But you're doing what you like best."

Three weeks later I rode into Melbourne on the Dandenong road, and turned left into St. Kilda, then again left into Robertson Street and stopped outside Number One. Dandenong is a big and busy highway, and the next road was like a neighborhood high street and Robertson Street was a quiet little backwater of terraced houses, so it was like coming into harbor.

The house was rented by Graham and Cheryl, whom I had known in London, and they shared it with Dave and Laurel and a small dog of uncertain temper. I took up residence in the meditation room.

Graham had long brown hair and cool gray eyes and seemed always to have just materialized out of a Nordic mist. He was a gardener in the grounds of a lunatic asylum. Cheryl was quick and nervous and had frequent little rows with herself in which Graham played his part patiently. She worked part-time behind the bar of a private club. Laurel was a generous, wistful girl who wished that Dave would be a bit more satisfied with life. She worked as a secretary at the Musician's Union around the corner. Dave was eager and erratic and wished he could be really good at something, but preferably the piano. At the time he was loading cases of Melbourne Bitter beer into boxcars down at the railway goods yards.

They were all within a few years of thirty, and there was much more to them than this, but it gives an idea. They were very modest in their demands on life and in several ways they failed to qualify as Australians at all. They hardly ever ate meat, for one thing, and they drank very little alcohol. They were all slim and light and did not try to conceal their anxieties under a mound of muscle turning to fat, in the usual Australian way.

The girls sometimes wore ankle-length peasant skirts and blouses without bras. Graham and Cheryl had traveled in the East, and the meditation room had a mandala and a Buddha and was scented with joss sticks. They actually used it for meditating. Their great ambition was to buy farmland and live on it. They had already saved enough to start looking for good offers and we used to sit at the kitchen table with mugs of tea and hear about the mouth-watering acres that had been snapped up too quickly by someone else. I found their situation exciting and enviable.

Every weekday morning for two weeks I went to work. I took the tram for St. Kilda to Flinders Street, where I changed onto the Coburg tram to Sydney Street. I loved Melbourne and I loved its green single-deck trams. Generally I avoided the rush hours since I was master of my own time, and I sat at ease in the tram, cruising down the center of the broad avenue that sweeps past the park and the big boys' school and the art gallery, and over the railway bridge to Flinders Street.

Flinders Street Station was built in the prewar image of a London terminus, even down to the framed spaces for advertisements and the newsboys shouting the titles of the evening papers on the corner. All about was a bustle of traffic and commerce, with crowds of office workers, shoppers and travelers from out of town weaving their way across the intersecting tram lines under the pompous facades of Victorian bank chambers and offices. It was London again in an earlier, less self-conscious time, when business still made its presence felt in the street and had not yet withdrawn behind the plate-glass doors and anonymous concrete of the modern European office block.

The prosperous and the derelict rubbed shoulders on the pavements. You could see that there were fortunes to be made and lost, and the pursuit of profit was free of shame. There was a rich mixture of city life on the streets and I lingered between trams to absorb it. For all that it was busy I never felt it was frantic; exuberant, rather, and not a little ruthless, which gave it a slight whiff of Dickensian days. The scale of the houses and streets still allowed human beings their natural place. And I was always conscious of the great, lazy expanse of Australia beyond the city, reminiscent perhaps of the empire that once lay beyond the City of London.

The Coburg tram took me down Elizabeth Street and eventually brought me out of the rectangular heart of Melbourne to pass through open park land for a while. It skirted the university and finally plunged into narrow, noisy Sydney Street, a long ribbon of small businesses that wound on and on towards the prison. Once I went out to see the prison, and stared with morbid fascination at its high walls and old-fashioned Alcatraz look. It seemed very relevant somehow to Australian life, which has more of a snakes-and-ladders feeling about it than does life in England. I often heard talk about criminals. They were mentioned as a fact of life, rather than in tones of dismay or moral outrage. They were there. If they got you, then you went down. If they were got, then they went down.

On weekday mornings though I jumped off at the second stop down

Sydney Street, or if possible at the lights before that. This is where Frank Musset has his motorcycle business. On one side of the road is the shop, where he presides over the stock with his mournful white face and brown overalls, unless he can escape into his own little workshop hidden round the back. On the other side is the repair shop where my Triumph stood stripped down on a stand. I was overhauling it, slowly, at my leisure. The barrel was being rebored. Some oversize pistons were coming from England. There were new exhaust valves to grind with the cylinder head. I was improving the supporting system for my tank panniers, rebuilding the rear wheel, repairing the oil seals in the forks and doing a host of other little things that I had thought of.

Perhaps it is not surprising that after all the moving about I should enjoy spending a fortnight in a steady, unvarying routine, but the deep satisfacton I felt could not be so easily explained. I was having a marvelous time in that shop. It was not a pretty place, maybe. It was big, and cool, and there was almost everything I needed, but what gave it the character that stamped itself on me so that I would never forget it was a transistor radio tuned in to a commercial station called THREE-X-Y.

In two weeks I became hopelessly addicted to this radio station, something that had never happened to me before. The program could hardly have been more rudimentary. It consisted of the same ten songs played over and over again, interspersed by advertisements. Three years later I have completely forgotten the ads, but the songs are clear in my memory.

A tenor screamed "Who Is That Lady All Alone?" ending on a false note. Bob Dylan sang about his wife in a Portuguese bar. David Essex did "Hold Me Tight, Don't Let Me Go." The Queen sang "Mama, I've Killed a Man...." Rod Stewart was doing something surreal on Main Street. There was a horribly mawkish song about being music and making the girls cry, and there were four or five others.

The company was congenial. I had a good mechanic working nearby who showed me a lot of dogged enthusiasm and helped me over difficulties. But it was the songs that got me. They drugged me. The radio was never switched off and I was like a cow being lulled at milking time. Once I got into that shed in the morning my day was complete, it was over before it began because I knew nothing could break that mood or change it and I had "no worries" as they are so fond of saying. Obviously the treatment was relieving me of some kind of burden. I guessed it was that I had simply spent too long on my own thinking. For two weeks I had my brain anesthetized, and I reveled in it.

At mid-day I went out into the blinding sunshine and walked to the pub for a "counter lunch." I learned to treat lunch time beer with great caution in Australia. It was drawn by the ounce in deceptively fragile glasses at a temperature that numbed the throat and delayed the action. Dave's alcoholic workmate down at the yard said the need hit him hardest in the throat, and I knew what he meant. Could see it coming.

Sometime after four in the afternoon I dipped my hands in the soap tin and got ready to leave the great greasy canyon for home. The Queen followed me into the street with a last poignant wail from the transistor ".... put my gun up to his head, pulled the trigger now he's dead. Mama, I'm leaving now.... I took my life and threw it all away."

Back on the tram, hot sun, hot upholstery, watching the girls in the street, dreaming, taking the song over in my head where the radio left off. A prim-looking woman sits opposite me. By accident, as I cross my legs, my foot touches her leg just below the knee. I'm surprised to see an enormous dusty footprint on her stocking, as though a man had climbed up under her skirt. I murmur an apology but she draws herself up in disdain and pretends not to have noticed. She can't see it and of course I'm not going to tell her now.

"Silly cow," I thought. "She'll walk around like that for the rest of the day. Typical." Everything in Australia seemed typical. Déja vu. Dreamlike. Couldn't work it out. Not at all like White South Africa, or Rhodesia. Nothing like America. I gave up and settled back into the dream.

Often at St. Kilda, on my way home, I went to the off-license at the back of a small pub and bought half a gallon of Angove's white wine, the cheapest of the nicer ones, for a knock-down price. I was a bad influence at Number One Robertson Street. I brought alcohol and meat into the house in unprecedented quantities. I could not help it. I was under a spell and the magic was most intense in the house itself.

Until very recently all Australian buildings were made, as far as possible, in the image of their British counterpart. Number One Robertson Street was the epitome of the trend, just like any suburban semi-detached villa in London, except that it had only one floor rather than two. The roof was pitched and gabled in the same way, the proportions were all familiar, the wainscoting and picture rails were molded in the same pattern and covered with the same number of layers of the same thick paint in the same colors. The same linoleum covered the same boards, and in the kitchen the doors of the built-in cupboards were even fastened by the same pieces of paint-encrusted metal.

A low brick wall divided the pavement from the little front garden where various shrubs struggled against each other, although some of the bushes were a bit florid by conservative English standards. At the back was a kitchen porch and a potting shed.

At least, that is how I saw it in 1976, and at least once a day I used to look at all this and wonder whether, somewhere on my way across the Pacific Ocean, I had unwittingly passed through a looking glass.

Naturally I had expected Australia to be influenced by English forms. What gave it the power of an enchantment, though, was the feeling of period. This was London suburbia of the thirties, not of the seventies. This same house, in New Eltham say, would since have been changed out of all recognition with wall-to-wall carpets, designer's colors, Formica kitchen units, bathroom improvements and all the appurtenances of Mr. and Mrs. 1970. In Robertson Street I had the vivid impression of having returned to New Eltham in the thirties, and since it was in just such a house in New Eltham that I did, in fact, spend the first five years of my life, the effect on me was hypnotic.

And to make any resistance impossible, there was the sun. Against all reason I remember my childhood as having conducted itself exclusively in hot sunshine. In the thirties there were no winters. Regardless of the meteorological records the sun shone on New Eltham constantly, and although it may not have been the happiest of times, in that respect it was a Golden Age. Picture then my astonishment, after decades of disillusion, at finding myself back in the imagined world of my childhood, bathed in that same eternal sun, but with the important and tantalizing difference that this time it was ME in charge.

Just like my father in the thirties, I walked out of the house every weekday morning through the swing gate, turned left down the road and went off to work. Only where he took the 8:15 to London Bridge, I took the Flinders tram from St. Kilda.

I felt a great urge to spend the rest of my life there, lost in this fantasy come true.

I sank deeper and deeper into the luxury of the illusion, which was like a balm to ancient hurts. All the pains of growing and becoming which lingered in me like the rheumatic twinges of old wounds seemed to be soothed away in hot nostalgia. To hell with all the agonies of the Western conscience, the gropings for awareness, the soul-wrenching efforts to root out unworthy prejudices. To hell with the nuclear holocaust and the coming ecological cataclysm and solidarity with the victims of totalitarian oppression.

I was in Australia, the Lucky Country, and its unofficial motto was "No Worries." A large infantile part of me grasped at this heaven-sent chance to wipe the tapes and start again. I resented bitterly every reminder that I was not here to stay, that there were plans to make.

There were enough sensitive, intelligent people in Melbourne to make the prospect of staying acceptable even to my conscious adult self. We had pleasant evenings and weekend lunches where I paid lip service to problems of conscience, but there was no obligation to take an enlightened view of anything. It was perfectly respectable in Australian society to say: Down with the Abos, Up with the Uranium, Out with the Blacks, In with the Beer, and so on. Wit was appreciated, but the maximum of vulgarity would do as well and qualified as "okker," which is Australia's revolutionary response to the tyranny of the intelligentsia. Since Australians are equal, by definition, a point may be made by quoting Virgil or by pissing on the carpet. The main difference is in the cleaning bill.

The enigma that had bothered me in Sydney was beginning to resolve itself. If Australians allowed themselves to be represented world-wide as a nation of beer-sodden boors and hysterical Amazons it must be through sheer lack of imagination. Like most people everywhere they spent most of their lives just getting by, but there was no collective dream or mythology that told them what it was they were supposed to be doing. In that respect they were far behind the aboriginals they had decimated and despised.

Yet many signs indicated that the time might not be too far away when Australians would agree on a better reason for living than to eat a pound of beef a day. When that day came, I thought, this would become one of the world's best places to be.

The faces of the old men told me there had been something once that was lost and could be found again. On a hot, quiet pavement stood a sun-dried old gent wearing loose, tobacco-brown clothes, so accustomed to the brightness that he had taken on the color of his own shadow, bent and gnarled and resilient as a tree in the desert. A small boy passed in front of him, very conscious of his grown-up little boy's trousers, while the old voice, steeped in loss and yearning, said:

"G'day, mate."

The greeting was aimed at the little boy (who appeared not to hear it) but it cracked my heart.

There is a silly sentimental dream alive in Australia, a potbellied householder's dream of security and Sunday lunch, but it is rooted in something else much older and sadder and more powerful. Sometimes the old men seemed to know what it was.

I rode the coast road from Melbourne through Geelong towards Adelaide. At one point I went inland towards Hamilton and spent a few days on a sheep station visiting the parents of the Australian I had met in Ecuador. I did a little work and bought a fishing rod, and in the Glenelg River I caught my first fish, some redfin and a salmon trout that filled me with pride.

The foreman took me to the shearing shed and showed me how to kill and slaughter a sheep, impressing me with his speed and precision. All those thousands of acres were maintained by four people, father, mother, son and foreman, but teams of men came in at crucial times to do the shearing, drenching, dipping and a gruesome operation called mulesing, which involved peeling the skin away under the tails of lambs.

In the shed, where every inch of wood had been polished by contact with hands and sheep, it was easy to imagine all that furious labor amidst a river of wool, but most of the time the broad paddocks and their great shady gum trees slumbered peacefully, and the only sounds were made by flocks of parrots scolding each other in the trees.

Going west it was getting drier. In Victoria State, fourteen inches of rain a year, in South Australia seven or less. Sheep gave way to grain. Big gums to smaller ones. Around Adelaide, high ground and a western-facing coast trapped more moisture and there was a brief greening, perfect for the grapes of Maclaren Vale and the Barrossa Valley, but beyond Adelaide the aridity gripped hard, drying out the nostrils, gritting up my chain, burning everything the color of tobacco.

All the way the coast was spectacular, empty, endlessly inviting. I dawdled along from Port Augusta to catch whiting at Lucky Bay and Tommy Ruffs at Port Neill, to go cockling in a cove at Coffin Bay and meet the pelicans at Venus Bay. The land dried farther on, the settlements thinned and by the time I got to Ceduna I could guess at the thousand miles of waterless waste that lay beyond: The Nullarbor Plain, which divided the West from the East.

People had been trying to frighten me with "The Crossing of the Nullarbor" for months.

"Watch out for the bulldust, mate!"

"The what?"

"The bulldust. It's a fine powder that fills the potholes. You can't see them until you're in them.

"And the 'roos. They come leaping across the road in droves. You don't want to hit a kangaroo, mate. They're a lot bigger than you."

I thought of the aggressive young salesman who had entertained me in Adelaide in one of those big, hermetically sealed lunch clubs that businessmen patronize there. The walls were lined with gambling machines, and men stood with their backs to the room playing two machines at once to save time. My host was crammed into a fashionable suit with yards of superfluous material at the cuffs and lapels, and despite the air conditioning he glistened with the sweat of good living. He listened to my plans, and declared ominously:

"You can perish in Australia."

Australians in cities love to shudder at the merciless hostility of their continent. I wondered whether it was a sort of apology for betraying the national ideal, an excuse for not being out there digging.

Truth to tell, the Nullarbor may have been rough once but now the road is sealed and tarred all the way from Melbourne to Perth. I was privileged to ride the last two hundred miles of dirt before the new section was opened, and they were no more than ordinarily awful. But the Nullarbor itself is a beautiful, mysterious land. A spry old gent called Gurney showed me one of its secrets. He lived halfway along the dirt stretch in a ramshackle bungalow, with a wife, a gas pump, some emus, a wombat and other more familiar animals. He said he owned eleven hundred square miles of South Australia but it did him no good because the only drinkable water on the whole property came out of a cave a mile from his house.

It was the cave I wanted to see, and he didn't usually allow visitors – "not since those three blokes with guns. They were sitting down there firing rifles at the roof. Mad drunk or something."

The Nullarbor is extremely flat, so you get into the cave by clambering down a crater. Miraculously, at the bottom of the crater among rocks and boulders Gurney had an orchard, the only place where fruit trees could survive the heat. The cave is a series of great caverns, and an important experience, for it suggests that the whole plain must be largely hollow. Indeed there's a theory – or fancy – that the Southern Ocean flows by subterranean passages to the interior of Australia. At any rate, the hollowness seemed most significant there, because you can feel the earth reverberate when you stamp on it, because emus call to each other by inflating bladders under their croups and making a noise like the underground echo of a steel drum, and because hollowness is a sign of great age. So in the night, half asleep on the ground, listening to the emus drumming and the clank of distant goat bells and not knowing what they were, I thought I was hearing the sound of a great tribal celebration drifting across the plain.

If the Nullarbor was not an ordeal, it was perhaps a last straw. Bouncing over it was too much for the spokes of the rear wheel after all they had been through in two and a half years. I had been warned. In Melbourne and again in Adelaide I had replaced broken spokes, and I checked them every time I stopped for the day.

At Eucla, where the dirt ended and the highway began they were still in order. The smooth tar enticed me to greater speed. After five hundred miles, just before Norseman, I noticed a growing vibration through the steering head. I stopped in the absolute nick of time.

Only four of the twenty spokes on one side of the wheel were left, and the rim was a terrible twisted shape. A few seconds more and it would certainly have collapsed. I shuddered to think of the mangled mess that that would have left. As it was, I spent one of the nastiest hours of the journey rebuilding the wheel in a twilight plagued by squadrons of vicious mosquitoes.

The following night I was within reach of Perth and saw the whole western sky lit up like molten lava, with white lightning and black rain tracing fantastic patterns over it. I arrived in Australia's Windy City on the first day of the winter rains, and four days later when I sailed for Singapore, it was still pouring and blowing as though it would never stop.

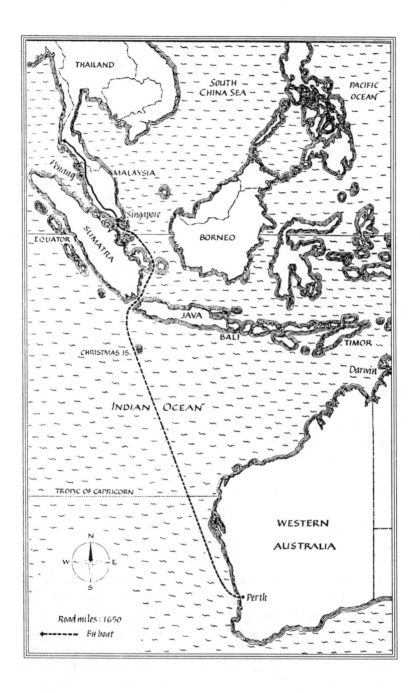

THAILAND

SOUTH
CHINA SEA

PACIFIC
OCEAN

Penang

MALAYSIA

Singapore

SUMATRA

EQUATOR

BORNEO

JAVA

BALI

TIMOR

CHRISTMAS IS.

Darwin

INDIAN OCEAN

TROPIC OF CAPRICORN

WESTERN

AUSTRALIA

N

W — E

S

Perth

Road miles: 1650

------ By boat

The most natural way to leave Australia would have been from Darwin, in a short hop across the Timor Sea and then up the islands of Indonesia to Bali. My hopes were dashed in Melbourne. Timor was at war. Darwin was still in ruins from a destructive cyclone. There was no known shipping out of Darwin at all. To go that far on the off-chance seemed out of the question.

Even from Perth the only escape was by cruise ship to Singapore. It was outrageously expensive as well as being heavily booked. It would have been cheaper to ship the bike and fly myself, but I would not let the bike travel unaccompanied. And the bookings made it impossible to delay the decision.

I raved and cursed. Indonesia had tantalized me for so long. The thought of paying so much money to sail right past it rankled in me. The whole thing was cockeyed. I could not rid myself of the feeling that something had gone seriously wrong, but in the end I had to accept it and put down my four hundred American dollars. Sailing date was April 15.

I had come most of the way through Australia with my dream of California intact, thinking of Carol and the ranch, anticipating the life I would begin when the journey was over. As I sailed for Singapore I felt that dream slipping away. Time passed. Distance increased. The pressure of everyday experiences piled up relentlessly, and I found my concentration on past and future events was interfering with the present.

I began to see my commitment to California as an obstacle to The Journey, and I realized I would have to get free of it, just as I had had to get free of my earlier commitment to Europe. The Journey was once more making its ravenous demands on me.

"You and your fucking mission," Carol had once shouted in a burst of frustration. It felt just like that; as though I had entered a priesthood.

These thoughts were always most intense when my morale was low, and the voyage to Singapore did not help. It was a disaster. The ship was called the *Kota Bali*, but it was not going to Bali and the other half of the name reminded me of sanitary napkins. I found myself with a shipload of Australian primitives goaded by a fussy, waspish Welsh captain and ministered to by an unctuous Chinese crew. The women changed their frocks four times a day, while the men poured their holiday funds into the slot machines and over the bar counter. Had it not been for the beer fumes thickening in the air and lending some support they would have all fallen down. There was better company on the lower deck where several hundred sheep were herded in pens, bound for Muslim slaughterhouses.

To dramatize my disappointment I managed to catch a virus and arrived in Singapore in feverish cold sweats. I struggled through the formalities at the docks and the shipping office feeling worse and worse, and it was perhaps no wonder that I formed a poor impression of Singapore. It struck me as a crowded metropolis entirely devoted to business and money and with no heart at all.

The streets were filled night and day with a torrent of traffic and only the most expensive hotels could put their guests out of earshot of the noise. On Bencoolen street, where I stayed, the pavements were factory space for all the carpenters, mechanics and other assorted artisans who spilled out of their lock-up shops. The rivers were clogged with filth, and the huge storm drains that ran into them down each side of the street were alive with rats.

Yet, even through my fever, I found all the startling variety and detail very exciting after the barrenness of Australian life, and knew that when the culture shock had subsided I would enjoy it. Meanwhile, in my delirium I decided that I was carrying too much stuff on the bike and decided to send a parcel home. Among the things I thought I would never use was a spare stator for the alternator, a heavy luxury in spare parts. I made up my package, wrapped and tied and sealed as the law demanded, and sent it off to England before setting off myself up the Malaysian Peninsula.

It was from Ringit in the Cameron Highlands that I wrote to Carol to tell her that the Journey was taking me over and that her Missionary would not be able to keep all his promises. It was ten miles farther along the road that the bike stopped. It took only a little time to discover that the stator coils had burned out. I roared with hysterical laughter, but thought it far from funny. It felt too much like swift retribution to be a joke.

The map told me I was only 180 miles from Penang, where I planned to stay awhile anyhow. The first thirty miles of that were a nonstop descent to the main highway from Kuala Lumpur. They could be done, if necessary, without running the engine at all. I figured that an overnight charge in the battery would get me to Penang, and as I was still lucky enough to have come to a stop just outside a village, I found a small repair shop with a battery charger. The night was not wasted. I spent it mingling with the crowd at a Chinese funeral ceremony, attracted to it by the sound of drums and gongs. I saw a coffin, massively constructed from beautiful woods, supported inside a room so that it soared into the air like the prow of a vessel. Beneath it professional mourners chanted and played strange music on even stranger instruments. Filial delegations made ritual obeisances. Some wore sackcloth hats bound with straw rope. Others had white head bands, red tabs sewn to their sleeves and carried bamboo branches trailing paper streamers.

The noise on the verandah of the house was continuous and, as I learned, was deliberately encouraged so that the deceased ancestor would know he had good company. People ate and drank, played cards and mahjong, shouted and laughed and banged happily on drums put there for the purpose. I rolled off a flourish myself, to help them along, for they planned to keep it going nonstop for four days and nights.

My plan to get to Penang worked well. The Lucas Company, which has branches everywhere in the world, arranged for the stator to be flown from England, and though my ears were burning and I still felt shaky inside, I settled down to make the best of a bad job.

What I had already seen of Malaysia appealed to me. I liked the gracious wooden houses set back from the roads in grassy clearings with decorated shutters, window frames, verandah rails and eaves. The staircases that widened towards the lower steps seemed to welcome visitors with an embrace. Always there were tall green trees to provide shelter from the sun.

In its variety of fruits it rivaled Brazil. Many I knew, many I did not. Mangostin and durian both took me by surprise. There was fruit to suit any taste.The durian was a special challenge, with its pungent odor. It is highly prized in Malaysia, although a textbook describes the taste as "French custard passed through drains."

In the streets, food stalls sold food of all kinds. They carried pineapples sculpted into wonderful spiral shapes, slices of mango, ginger, and papaya on slivers of bamboo. There were shiny mangles to crush the juice from sugar cane. Mobile Chinese kitchens with compact and versatile charcoal stoves conjured up limitless arrays of rice, noodle and soup dishes which went streaming out to purchasers up and down the street.

It was a manual civilization, everything guaranteed touched by hand, but highly sophisticated, and a powerful antidote to Western hygiene.

Penang is a polyglot place, but the main ingredients are Malay, Chinese and Indian. In the city most of the Malays I saw were pedaling trishaws and usually saw me first, shouting "Hey, Johnny, you want smack?" meaning heroin, not punishment. The Indians too were also often pedaling, but on ancient bicycles with large glass cases mounted behind the saddle containing bread and buns. Sometimes a fleet of them would pass at one time, all ringing bells or tapping pieces of metal.

But for all that there is no doubt that the life of Penang is Chinese, perhaps even more traditionally Chinese than China itself, and I was well placed to study it. From my room on the second floor of the Choong Thean Hotel, in Rope Walk, I looked down on a shop where five generations of the same family had been engaged in the management of Chinese funerals and celebrations. Every evening almost, on scooters and bicycles, they were off to some part of the town to erect their stages and screens, to play their instruments, perform their sword-swallowing and fire-breathing acts, to chant and wail in their black gowns.

Next door to the hotel was a shop where models of palatial mansions were built of paper and split bamboo. They had terraces, balconies, elaborate porches in gilt and scarlet, television in the sitting room, even a car in the garage. Resplendent with the good life, they provided everything an ancestor might need to take his correct place in the hereafter, and all of it to be consumed by flame so that it might follow his spirit across the water.

In another shop incense sticks were made, some of them three or four feet high and thick as a man's thigh, entwined with dragons. At the other end of this short street was a hall where, on certain nights, Kung Fu was taught or the "lion dance" rehearsed.

The shops themselves were impenetrable to the eye, so crammed were they with divers objects, so crowded with people and furniture and so mysteriously lit by shrines and candles. At night beds came out on the pavement in front of the shop and those who didn't fit inside slept out. At mealtimes, a space was cleared on the counter or worktable, a cloth was spread and the shop was turned into a restaurant. Generations lived, ate, worked and slept in these confined

Bruno took the picture above soon after we crossed into Colombia. The flying jacket got a new lease of life with an extra layer of Argentine leather, and I was proud of the fur cuffs and collar, but sadly I lost it in Mexico a month later. As a study in the use of wheels it makes an ironic contrast to the picture below, taken later in Penang. I was impressed, in Asia, by the time lavished on the simplest objects, and by the way entire lives were lived out in the smallest of spaces.

spaces, absorbed by the microscopic detail of their worlds. Their energy and dedication appeared to me to be phenomenal and more foreign than anything I had yet seen. There were times, when I saw them flicking rice into their mouths with that peculiarly frenzied motion of the chopsticks, that I thought I detected a kind of madness. Why choose the slowest way of eating, and then become so painstakingly proficient at doing it quickly?

At the Temple of Heavenly Mercy I watched them park their motorcycles and rush, with their candy-colored metal-flake helmets still on their heads, to the counters inside the temple where the incense sticks and bundles of paper money were sold. The temple was full of acrid smoke from the burning paper, and they raced through their ceremonies, eyes streaming, desperate to get outside again with their smoldering offerings and fling them into the big iron incinerators that stood waiting on the pavement. If there was a single thought of an ancestor in any of them it was inscrutably hidden behind expressions of irritation and impatience.

I was still not functioning well physically. The days were hot and humid. I was drinking too much cold fizzy stuff, and could not get myself really excited about doing anything. I worked at odd jobs on the bike, and one day, with the battery charged, I took it round the island thinking I would go fishing.

It had rained heavily, the sky was clearer and the air drier than usual. It was wonderful to be riding for pleasure again, on an unloaded bike. I passed over small mountains, forested and populated by monkeys and brilliant birds. The villages were quiet and unspoiled and nobody tried to sell me heroin. I watched what looked like a Chinese pantomime. Only the stage was covered. The audience, children and adults, were spread around a small area of grass, and I was able to see it from the coffeehouse across the road. An extraordinary woman appeared on the stage dressed like a Victorian huntress in bloomers and carrying a bow. She shot an arrow in the air. It went about a yard and fell to the boards, and a cloth goose came tumbling down from the ceiling. Everybody was delighted, myself included.

In late afternoon I found a quiet spot on the shore, beyond a fishing village where some men were burning the paint off their boat with bundles of flaming grass. I caught nothing, but became impatient for success. That evening in town, well after dark, I remembered that people usually went fishing off the esplanade at night and I took my rod there with my highly corrupt prawn bait.

It was still very crowded along the promenade facing the park. Brightly lit stalls selling fruit, soup, noodles and drinks made an almost uninterrupted line along the curb, and Chinese couples sat shoulder to shoulder along the sea wall sipping dayglo drinks from plastic bags. In Malaysia technology seems to boil down to three things; plastic bags, fluorescent tubes and two-stroke motorcycles. The sea bed around Penang is already lined with plastic, and for my first two catches I brought in two bags full of sea water.

Shortly before midnight the crowds thinned out, the stalls were wheeled off and only dedicated fishermen were left on either side of me. I was very inexperienced and had no real hope of catching anything, but for a moment when I felt the tug on the line I did think I had a big fish. Then I saw it was a branch of a palm. My line was a very strong one, bought in Australia for a quite different purpose, and I was able to drag the branch into the strip of beach six feet below me under the sea wall. Then I had the silly idea that I could hoist it up and disentangle my line. I had a lead sinker on the line, my last one, and I wanted to save it. I leaned over the wall, straining with all my might, and something hit me very, very hard in the right eye.

I clapped my hand over my eye and gave some token gasps, waiting for the pain to engulf me. No such thing happened. First there was a stunning shock. Then a wave of nausea as I realized what I had done. The hook had broken away, obviously, and the sinker, catapulted by a thirty-pound line under breaking strain, had scored a direct hit on my eyeball. Like a bullet in a grape, I thought. Even while shuddering with the horror of it, I was aware that the fisherman alongside me was quite unperturbed. I danced about a bit to dramatize my injury, to no effect. I dared to explore with my finger, dreading what I might feel, but the eyeball did at least seem to be a ball. Experimentally I opened my eyelid. Pitch blackness assailed me. It just seemed impossible that an eye could survive such an injury. I gave some thought to the kind of eye patch I would wear, and to whether it was possible to ride a motorcycle successfully with one eye.

I said to the fisherman: "I have been hit in the eye."

"You want me to gather your things-ah?" he replied, unmoved.

Bewildered by his priorities, I declined the offer, got my own things together with one hand (I could not, for some reason, take my hand away from my eye) and left him my bait. Then I wandered off down the esplanade, and it came to me that I should really do something about it. All the time a little voice was telling me:

"You are blind in one eye," and I felt a bit unsteady.

Two policemen stood by the Town Hall.

"I have had an accident," I said. "Is there a hospital?"

They didn't speak much English.

"Go to big police station," said one, pointing across the park into the darkness.

"No. No. Hospital," I said. By now I knew that's what I had to do.

"No car," said one, "but – ha! – here trishaw."

The trishaw stopped and I said: "To the hospital how much?"

"Three dollar. O.K.?" he said.

"Dollar fifty O.K.," I said, and off we went.

The history of Penang is all bound up with British naval history. I sat in the little wooden cab between the two front wheels while the trishaw driver pedaled behind me, and in the prow of our small craft, with my hand over my eye, I imagined myself to be Nelson as we sailed through the night. A brilliantly uniformed policeman on a flashing Motoguzzi tried to get us to make way for the Prime Minister of Kedah State who was leaving an ornate mansion in his limousine, but I pointed ahead imperiously and cried: "Hospital!" He fell back demoralized, and we swept past, raking him with a broadside.

At the hospital they put me in funny white pajamas, taped gauze pads over both my eyes and told me to hope for the best and above all not to move a muscle.

I spent a week in total darkness, being manipulated for my own good and hating it, discovering cups of cold tea on my locker hours after they had been put there and learning about the other problems blind people have with the rest of us. I spent much time contemplating the path that had led me to that bed. I could not avoid the feeling that I was there because I had lost my grip on my situation and purpose; that I was adrift here in Penang as I had been ever since I had allowed the journey to change focus in California.

The degeneration followed, it seemed, when I gave away control, believing the seductive Californian notion that only good things happen when you let it all hang out. Maybe there was another trip to be made that way, but mine was not open-ended like that. It had to be conceived and executed and completed; more like a work of art than life. The instructions had to be uncompromisingly clear and they had to be regenerated at every step, otherwise what could I expect but a drift towards decay and chaos.

The bike itself was a model for the idea I was striving towards. Only a continual desire to improve its performance, to make the systems more and more efficient and trouble-free, would keep it going to the end. There was no steady state. As soon as I lost interest, became tired of it, said that's good enough and I'm not going to bother with it for a while, things began to fall apart. I would start losing things, a wrench, a pair of goggles, a useful piece of rope. Or something would come unscrewed and fall off before I had noticed it, and I would have to do some makeshift repair. Then, to realize that my pocket universe was running down and fraying at the edges because of my own laziness made it harder to find the extra energy and enthusiasm to pull it all together again. A lazy mistake saps confidence and leads to the next mistake. I was in hospital in Penang because I had misjudged my strength in California, or so it seemed to me then.

The chain of cause and effect had not yet run its course. A few days later someone came into this ward full of sightless people and stole my wallet from my bedside locker. When I knew it had happened it was as though the last support had been kicked out from under me. The two passports, the papers, the wallet itself were precious. The bulk of the money, thank heavens, was for once in traveler's checks. But the address books.... I felt as though the whole journey had been stolen from me and I was in despair.

I came out after nine days with my sight only slightly impaired and a crazy dwarf swinging a lantern in the corner of my right eye. I was grateful to have an eye at all. I spent a lot of time at the coffeehouse opposite the Kung Fu hall, dredging my memory for the names and addresses I had lost. Those were the bitterest moments. I could have forgiven the thief everything but that.

A beautiful girl lived and worked there. She had the most delicious Chinese rosebud mouth. In the morning, when I went there for a steamed cake, she came down in a pink nightgown with the sleep still in her almond eyes. I wanted to believe she was the proprietor's sister, but she was probably his wife. In any event she had no interest in me, and I had to satisfy myself with looking at her when I could.

I was resigned to two weeks of outpatient treatment before it was safe for me to travel on, and I sadly abandoned my plans to cross over to Sumatra. There would be time for a short excursion into Thailand, and no more.

The British Embassy in Kuala Lumpur refused to send me a new passport even though there was a consul in Penang who had checked me out. They insisted that I drive the five hundred miles to Kuala Lumpur and back, a dirty and expensive ride on the main highway, but they did not even look at me when I got there. It was the kind of treatment I always heard tourists complain about. I was unused to it, and it emphasized my sense of having lost my status. All over the world tourists had their passports ripped off. In every bank there were tourists claiming refunds on stolen traveler's checks. It was never going to happen to me but now I was just another tourist after all, only fit to sign up for a package tour. I had lost my immunity, and it hurt.

When the stator arrived from England with a new rear wheel as well my spirits lifted a little. The checks were replaced without difficulty. I had another cholera shot and a smallpox scratch to get the necessary certificate. I bought some leather and sewed a new wallet to replace the old one.

The owner of the Choong Thean Hotel spoke no English but was very kind and showed real concern for me and for the safety of my things while I was in the hospital. When I returned he made sure I had the same room, and he often asked me, by gestures, to come and eat with him and his staff in the back.

He was not an old man but his face was battered and impassive. It was difficult for him to express his feelings with it. He walked around all day in pajama trousers, sometimes with a singlet, sometimes without, and scarcely ever left the hotel. There was much to keep an eye on there. Several Indian prostitutes worked in his front room looking out on the street, comfortable matronly ladies with gold teeth, most of them. They did not have to solicit, for they had regular Hindu gentlemen who called, at all times of day, usually with briefcases under their arms. A room was set aside for them at the back, and they paid a dollar twenty per customer to the house. Then there was the nightly mahjong game in the kitchen below the hotel stairs. This appeared to be hired out on a franchise to a man who also ate with us. He busied himself preparing the table with its thick pad of clean white paper sheets, and was there to tear off the top sheet after each game. It is a noisy game, played very fast and for a high stake. The clatter of the tiles and shouts of "Pong" and "Kong" went on into the early hours and I was glad my room was a long way away.

There was an old man working for the owner who spoke English, although he was literally tongue-tied. He told me that he could have been a police inspector if he had had an operation "to cut the string," but he was too frightened. When he was not dozing in his chair he asked me questions about traveling and how much things cost in France. Although he was almost destitute, he began to form the idea that his luck would change and he would be able to travel the world and visit me in France.

"But I would not be able to go as you. When you are going through the jungle and meeting dangerous animals I will not be able to run away, so it will cost me fifty thousand dollars to go around the world." Not nearly, or about fifty thousand dollars, but the precise sum, and he would of course put it all straight into "traveling checks".

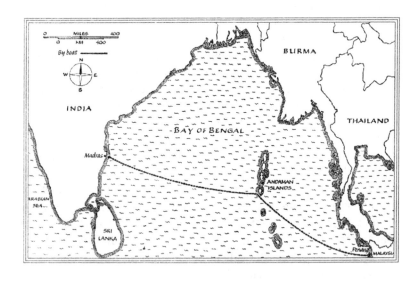

India

Before coming to India I never associated it with boats and nautical pursuits, yet the long and, for the most part, beautiful coast is busy with seagoing craft, from the most primitive to the most elaborate, often recalling our own age of sail. This picture was taken near the ferry at Karwar, just south of Goa on the road to Bombay.

India received me so well. I sat there smiling back at my own good fortune. At best I had hoped to be received by friends of friends but here I had the friend himself. Quite by chance I had come during the two weeks that he was visiting his father, and so I had been able to arrive out of the crush and confusion of the Madras docks to a peaceful welcome.

I sat on a bench in the garden close to the door of the house. There was an area of crazy paving and, rising from the middle of it, a big mature tree with fine leaves called the neem tree. My friend's father, a retired colonel, told me it was sacred and I did not doubt him. In it lived small squirrels, chocolate brown with light yellow stripes along their backs where, it was said, the fingers of Brahma had caressed them. One of them came down to the paving in front of me to see what else the hand of God might have provided.

Near the tree was a stone pedestal and on it stood a pot with a sacred plant directly facing the door. On the flagstone outside the door a design was chalked which was also sacred. It was renewed every morning by the housekeeper, and there were several patterns she could choose from. They were quite complex and were drawn in a continuous line around rows of dots with swift confidence. Inside the front door was a small reception area, and on the wall, looking out to the sacred plant, were portraits of Sai Baba, for the colonel was a devotee of Sai Baba, the holy man. Between the plant and the pictures the daily *pujas,* or services, were performed, and these few yards were the axis of the spiritual life of the colonel's household.

I sat in this shaded pool of faith under the neem looking along the path to the garden gate and at two women who were standing there and talking about the arrangements for a wedding. They wore saris of course, and it would not be worth mentioning but that it was new to me and I was trying to decide what it was about this garden, this light, these women that made the sari look so natural.

The women were the mother and the sister of the bride-to-be. The young woman wore a pink bodice under her sari, but the older woman just draped the loose folds of cotton over her breasts. The temperature was such that all clothes were mere decoration.

Nothing changed. Time passed. The squirrel nibbled, ran up the tree, came down again. The women talked, and I heard the rapid syllables of Tamil spurting out, each spurt ending on a tantalizing drawn-out vowel sound. Behind the leaves of the neem the sun broke into a thousand glittering fragments and moved slowly towards evening.

The colonel's house was humble. Once the family had lived in a big house and owned a sizable piece of Madras, but times had changed and anyway the colonel had found satisfaction in simplicity. The house was a bungalow with a flat roof. At one end was the colonel's bedroom. At the other end was an office cum spare room where I now slept. Between the two were the little hallway and the kitchen. The kitchen was mysterious and dark, with little furniture and a stone floor. The housekeeper, a tubby determined woman, sat on the floor to chop food on a board and grind the spices in a mortar. At night she slept on the floor behind the front door. She was a very religious woman and sometimes went into a trance, singing and dancing and twirling rather dangerously, and then it took the strength of several men to restrain her.

There were a few smaller buildings around the garden. My friend was housed in one. At the other end of the garden near the gate and beyond the women who were still talking was another abode attached to a garage. That was where the father of the bride to-be lived. He was a Brahmin called Rajaram, who had appeared by chance in the colonel's life some years before and had stayed to become the resident spiritual adviser.

He was coming towards me now, past the women and the neem tree, a small thin figure, perfectly erect, with a striking head and prominent features. His eyes were large and luminous, and his mouth was poised always on the brink of mirth, for the world was to him a source of constant amusement.

He wore an open shirt revealing a string of brown beads and the knotted cord of his caste. Around his waist was tied the usual cotton skirt called a *lungi*. His chest was nut brown, hairless, very spare and scarcely wrinkled at all, although he was certainly over seventy years old. There was a little wispy white hair on his head, and rather more in his ears. He was almost deaf, and I got the impression that he was quite glad to be spared from hearing so much nonsense. It certainly saved him from a lot of the fuss to do with the wedding, and he joked about the cost of it and the ceremony attached to it.

The guest list had grown to over a hundred and everyone had to be fed, with many dishes served on banana leaves.

"There are four thousand people coming," he said, spluttering with laughter. "Each one is getting a tamarind leaf with one grain of rice.

His wife scolded him for not taking it seriously, but fortunately he could not hear her. He came up to me now and greeted me gravely. Then, pointing to the motorcycle standing near his room, he held his hands out in front of him as though grasping the controls and pretended to roar off into the sky, grinning like a child.

"You are flying through the world," he said. "You must be going at two hundred miles an hour."

I laughed to see his enchantment. It was wonderful that this tiny old man could imagine himself rushing through the stratosphere, bow-legged and beads flying, astride a great machine. The bike was so familiar to me, in its capacities and limitations, that I was surprised when others saw it as a symbol of great speed and power.

The colonel came out of the house carrying a silver platter. During the day he wore English clothes. When going to town he put on his polished brown shoes and his solar topee and carried a cane. Now he was wearing a *lungi* also, and the Indian shirt. He came to me and showed me the gray powder on the plate.

"This is *vibuti*," he said. "It is holy ash. It is the custom to put this on our foreheads when we worship God." He put his finger in the ash and drew a line on my forehead, like an exclamation mark. I shuddered slightly to the touch, and then felt calmed by it. There is great power in such deliberate touching of another human being, and I had been experimenting with it, trying to recognize the force that lay in my hands.

Rajaram went through the ritual of the *puja* in front of me with the colonel standing solemnly by. The plant and the tree were part of it, and then, still chanting, the Brahmin walked to the pictures in the house and chanted in front of them too, "Hare, Hare, Krishna, Krishna," and so on, the colonel following and standing by. It was businesslike but not at all perfunctory, as so much Christian ritual seems, and as the Chinese had seemed in their temples. My friend stood by rather detached with his arms folded, looking as English here in India as he had looked Indian in England.

With no religion of my own, I had always been embarrassed when others tried to draw me into their religious exercises, saying "grace" for example at Lusaka, even making a circle of hands at the ranch, which was the least of statements. Yet here, I already felt that I was living as much in a temple as a house, and that merely by being there I was engaged in some kind of worship, and it did not offend me at all. What I objected to, what had always seemed awkward and artificial, was the separation of God from the world. "And now, a brief word to our sponsor..." – that kind of thing. If there was a god at all, then wherever he was would have to be in everything all the time, especially in me. After only twenty-four hours in India I could already feel that presence, in the tree, the plant, the animals, in Rajaram. It was the living belief of others that conjured up this feeling in me. I was excited and curious to see how it would affect me in the long run. As faith, or superstition?

"Sai Baba is quite a remarkable man," said the colonel. I could see his problem. How do you talk about such things to an English man? The word "remarkable" has a nice understated honesty about it. Might do the trick? He looked at me through his dark brown eyes, trying to gauge whether it was worth going on. The colonel was a very straightforward man, without guile. I tried to be encouraging.

"He does certain things which can only be described as miracles. For instance this holy ash now, you see, this *vibuti*. He can produce it from his hand. He will walk among his devotees and distribute the *vibuti*. In considerable quantities. I myself have seen it literally pouring out."

This is the turning point, I thought. He has committed himself now, by the evidence of his own eyes. I nodded enthusiastically.

"That is the sort of thing I have been looking for all along," I said. "In Brazil I heard about something similar..." I stopped. The colonel was listening politely but I could see that he did not want to hear about Brazil.

"Of course, many holy men can produce *vibuti*," he said. "That is nothing special. Now Sai Baba does other things much more remarkable. He can produce objects such as jewelry, and precious stones. There are recorded instances of him taking a broken watch from a devotee and returning it in perfect order after holding it in his hand. I will give you a book to read. There are many examples.

"Sai Baba has encouraged me to do my own work here. I had the idea of building a small temple devoted to him, and a hall where people may come to hear about different religions. You see, there is only one God. Christ, Buddha, Brahma, Mohammed, it is all the same.

"I asked Sai Baba, and he gave me his blessing. Every year he produces a *lingam* from his mouth. It is an important event at

On my way around India I went to many sacred places and met a number of priests, *saddhus,* pilgrims, *gurus* and other holy men, but none of them impressed me so much as Rajaram, who was there when I first landed in Madras. He seemed to me to be the embodiment of innocence, simplicity, truth and wisdom, and his influence has been important to me ever since.

Whitelands, where he has his headquarters. It is quite extraordinary. The *lingam* is very big. It is impossible to see how it can pass through his throat.

"There is always a great throng of devotees and Sai Baba passes among us, talking to some, stepping over bodies to get past. At one point he stepped on my back to pass across and you know, a quite remarkable thing, he was weightless. He had his foot on my back but there was absolutely no weight at all."

We walked through the gate and along the pavement, and then turned back behind the garden wall to where the temple was, a simple square building with a wooden floor, and at the back a shrine with two portraits of Sai Baba. In one he was garlanded and smiling, and the picture was rather faded with brown marks at the bottom edge. In the other he was standing at the top of a flight of stone steps in a vivid crimson robe. He was a small dark-skinned man with a round face appearing at the center of a mass of fuzzy black hair. The portraits were in silver frames. Beneath one was a silver bowl and beneath the other was a tray.

"Now I have brought you here to see this," said the colonel, "because it is proof. From this portrait, you see, ash falls into the tray. The *vibuti* you have on your forehead came out of this picture. Every morning there is more ash on the tray. And from the other picture honey runs into the bowl. It is quite amazing."

There was ash in the tray, but the bowl was empty.

"During the last few days, the honey has stopped. I think it is a sign that something is not right. There are certain problems. I am planning to ask Sai Baba's advice."

Just suppose, I said to myself, that I crept out here at midnight, and hid. Would I be likely to see old Rajaram slip through the window with a syringe and inject honey into that photograph? Or would the colonel appear furtively in his nightgown and shake ash into the tray? It was preposterous. I imagined myself devoting a lifetime to experiments with carbon dating and isotope tagging, infrared cameras and laser beams to prove that the colonel and the Brahmin were true or false. And never would I know any better than I knew already after only twenty-four hours that it could not be in them to deceive me in that way. Or even if I showed them false today, what is to stop them being true tomorrow?

Let the ash pour, and the honey drip. What do they prove after all? That the world is full of marvels which I don't understand? I have known that for a long time. There are subtleties here to be penetrated, but not by scientific experiments on the composition of honey and the origins of ash.

Still, I thought, I shall go and see this Sai Baba. It would be something to be present at a miracle.

My friend introduced me to the more mundane aspects of life in Madras. I tasted again the strange pleasure to be had in visiting institutions created by the British in another era, and maintained by the Indians in their original form for their own use. There was squash and ginger beer at the Madras Cricket Club, for example, and there was still a faint but original odor of mem-sahib drifting in the air of Spencer's store. All of it, though, was transformed for me by the calm of the colonel's garden and the aura of Rajaram. I was easy with the climate, hot as it was, and happy with the food. After four days I felt rested and secure, and the wounds of Penang seemed finally to have healed. I was ready to set off into India, like a ship well rigged and provisioned with a rested crew, a good wind and nothing but fair weather ahead. The blow fell that morning. A telegram arrived to tell me that my stepfather had died, suddenly and unexpectedly.

I wrestled with the problem for hours. Many times I had asked myself what I would do if my mother were to die while I was away. The answer was always: Keep going. I was obsessed by the idea that to break the journey might somehow destroy it. But it had never occurred to me that it might be Bill, who was so much younger, who would die first. The very fact that I should have got the news in Madras, where every day planes took off that could get me to England, seemed significant. What if it had happened while I was on the altiplano? In my heart I knew I could not leave my mother alone at such a time.

I asked Rajaram, writing my question down on a scrap of paper:

"YESTERDAY MY STEPFATHER DIED. WHAT SHOULD I DO FOR MY MOTHER?"

and he replied, in writing too:

"1/8 or 1/5 your profit income you may help her. It is bounden duty of human being if she helpless."

"MONEY IS NOT THE PROBLEM. I WANT TO COMFORT HER."

"There is a doctor already to look after her."

"BUT WHICH WAY SHALL I GO?"

"(We are gifted a compus in our hart) your prayer will guide you, right direction; for your all success in life.

Following my compass, it took me thirteen hours to fly back to the place that I had spent three years traveling away from. I was sucked up by the silver tube and spilled out on London Airport. Within no time I was standing next to my mother at the crematorium chapel, as the remains of her husband were consigned to the flames. I was so sickened by the soulless mechanics, the hideous in sensitivity of the whole affair, that his loss did not strike home to me until weeks afterwards. With the feeling of India still strong in me I felt I would rather be tossed out on a charnel ground for the vultures than be disposed of by remote control behind nylon curtains in a gas oven, dispatched by the rounded insincerities of a mass-destruction priest.

Best of all would be to die somewhere where my friends could dig a hole for me. I hoped that when I died I might still have friends who would do that for me.

The flight back to Madras was tedious. Police searched the 747 at Tel Aviv and again at Teheran. I missed the connection at Bombay and had to spend a night there in the monsoon. Next day the plane was delayed at take off. Engineers rooted about on the flight deck while we roasted in the cabin.

I sat next to a professor at Madras University returning from a spell in Germany. He was good company, but the remark I treasured most was about the water in Frankfurt.

"We always boiled the tap water," he said. "It is polluted and quite unsafe to drink. Fortunately in Madras we don't have this problem. Our river water is quite pure."

By coincidence, some ten days later the Bombay-Madras plane blew up, killing everyone on board.

Madras, when I got back there, felt like a different place. I was plagued by minor irritations and discomforts that I had not even noticed before, if indeed they had existed. I was bothered by the heat, the humidity and the mosquitoes. I felt weak and jet-lagged. My friend had long since left and I imagined myself less welcome than I had been before. I found people ambiguous and inefficient, waggling their heads in the absurd way they do as though the gesture alone would make everything turn out fine.

Eating with my fingers was disagreeable, and forced me to wonder why I should feel so vulnerable sitting at table with sloppy food all over my right hand. I felt a craving for meat, thinking it might restore my morale, and I bought a chicken and asked the house keeper to cook it.

It was a bad mistake. The colonel liked meat, having been raised in an English tradition, but he was now convinced that it was wrong to do so. Rajaram would never touch it, although he sweetly ignored those who did. The housekeeper was thoroughly disapproving and I could see I had made the colonel feel very guilty. What was worse, when the chicken appeared on the table in a small bowl, there seemed to be nothing left of it but the beak, neck, claws and ribs. I naturally assumed that the thrifty housekeeper was planning to stretch it over several meals, and in all innocence I asked in what way she planned to prepare the meat.

I thought Kali, the Goddess of Destruction, was going to leap at me from her eyes when the colonel translated the message.

"She says the chicken is all there," said the colonel. I was wise enough to keep quiet, but I thought I had better leave their house soon before I blundered into even deeper trouble. It was a classic example of the danger of flying between different worlds and cultures.

Obviously it was I who had changed, and not India, and I longed to feel the satisfaction and calm I had known before. Perhaps, I thought, I will find it in the temples as I ride south to Sri Lanka. There was one only fifty miles away at Kanchipuram. I said goodbye to the colonel, feeling very grateful to him and miserable at having even doubted his hospitality. I feasted my eyes on Rajaram one last time and, receiving his tranquil farewell, I rode into India.

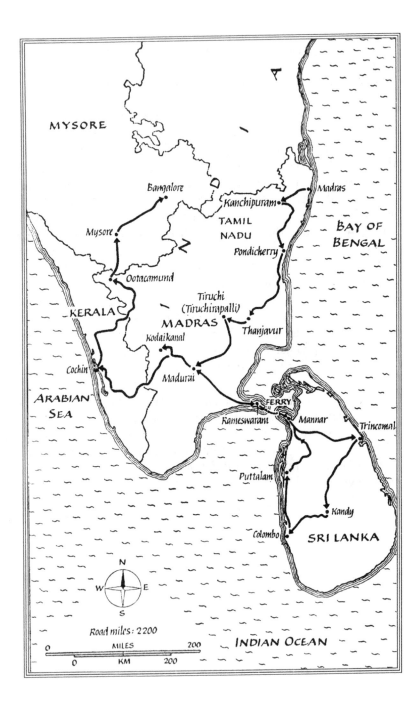

MYSORE

Bangalore

Mysore

Kanchipuram

Madras

TAMIL
NADU

BAY OF
BENGAL

Pondicherry

Ootacamund

Tiruchi
(Tiruchirapalli)

KERALA

MADRAS

Kodaikanal

Thanjavur

Cochin

Madurai

ARABIAN
SEA

FERRY

Rameswaram

Mannar

Trincomal

Puttalam

Kandy

Colombo

SRI LANKA

N

W   E

S

Road miles: 2200

0   MILES   200

0   KM   200

INDIAN OCEAN

Riding the Temple Trail is like riding into a Black Hole. Everything rushes in, squeezing, condensing, more of everything than you ever thought possible. You have only to pronounce the names to know; Ekamboreswara temple at Kanchipuram, Mahishisuramordhini cave at Mahabalipuram, Arunachala temple at Tiruvanamalai, Tiruchirapalli and Brihadeeswarer temple at Thanjavur, more syllables per word than the Western tongue can roll around, more people per tourist than the eye can see, more distance per mile, more surprises per minute, more carvings per square yard. Everything in profusion and superfluity, and somewhere in the middle of this crush they say is calm. So find it!

Not easy. A sign points down a narrow street of shops and stalls, a milling confusion of people, animals, bicycles. The bazaar. Above the seething mass, appearing to rise right out of it, as though squeezed up and petrified by the pressure of the bazaar itself, a towering wedge of masonry completely obliterated by carved figures. The temple. What causes these people to compress themselves like this? I used to think, in my airy Western way, that it was because there were so many of them. Every question about India was so easily answered by "overpopulation." Now I remember the insane knots of people around the counter of an otherwise empty shop or post office, the steady pressure of the man behind me in the queue, forcing his body against mine, drawn by a mindless magnetism. I call it insane because my sanity flourishes with space and distance. India seems like a giant condenser, everybody streaming towards the center to fuse.

I stop the bike to consider whether I can really hope to penetrate the bazaar. A ring of bodies forms instantly, and begins to thicken. The crowd is crystallizing out around me. I have to hold tight for a second, but there is no danger. I was well trained in South America, and the crowd here is just a degree or two more concentrated. I see that it is only partly curiosity that draws them, because much of the time they are not even looking at me. It's more that I might mean an opportunity, a lucky chance. The instinct is to get close to the action, that's all.

I'm not really thinking all this stuff now, though. I'm too busy making contact, making sure they know I am a human being. Thank God I wear an open helmet so that they can see my face. I take it off anyway and talk, looking out at the sea of faces with the confidence of a superstar. It is something I learned to do, like overcoming vertigo. First I was scared to death, then completely at ease. There is no middle way. Now I am quite relaxed. There are easily a hundred people gathered around me, but they are short and I can look down on them.

Where is the temple? Can I go through this way? A man in the foreground answers:

"Yes, you can go. You are coming from? Your native place is?"

A stream of questions, and as I answer I am trying to cultivate humility, because it would be so easy to think I could play games with these people. I try to remember that from their point of view, as well as being fascinating I might also seem exceptionally foolish.

I kick the engine over and the crowd opens before me. At walking pace I ride through to the outer gate of the temple. It is not a good way to arrive. There is no logical place to park a bike, and it looks very vulnerable. I am hot and absurdly overdressed in boots and jeans, and I have to carry the jacket and helmet, because there is nowhere to leave them. On top of that, a camera and a long lens.

I feel like a target, not a person. And here come the kids.

"Hello, sir, what is your name? Where you are coming from? You are going? I am collecting coins. You are having coins from your country? I am also collecting stamps. You are having? Give me one rupee."

And then the man with the sandals – and the postcards, and the beads, as I walk towards the inner gate. On the right of the gate is a sanctuary like a cave and in the doorway stands an extraordinary figure of a man with streaks of colored paint over his forehead and an expression of such solemnity that I want to laugh. He is making weird gestures with his arms, and all I can think is that he looks like a fake, like Charlton Heston acting a crazy Brahmin for Cecil B. DeMille. He is beckoning to me; any second I expect to hear:

"Hey, sport! Over here! Listen! Your soul's slipping, feller. Don't miss Siva's lingam, sport. Maybe your last chance this lifetime. See the greasy ghee pour down over the supreme prick. Hurry! The Wisdom of the Orient awaits you.

The kids are still on my trail, and I have been joined by a young man who simply walks alongside me with an ineffably sweet smile, so sweet and sad that I am sure he has been practicing it for years. He asks for nothing, but as the collectors of coins, stamps, ball pens and rupees launch yet another assault, he says: "Ah, those boys," again and again.

A scene from the temple at Thanjavur

Inside the gate the unofficial soliciting slackens off, the Wistful Smiler keeps his distance (what does he want?) and I wander about looking for inspiration. Under an enormous slab of stone supported by hundreds of carved pillars, a small family is cooking in a brass pot over a fire. A bearded man approaches also making semaphore movements with his arms. He stares hotly into the middle of my skull, and then turns away as if he's got the message. I have not got the message. My eyes are grabbing at everything, but I still don't know what I'm doing here. Either this whole gigantic affair is a fraud, or someone will have to come and tell me the truth about something.

Looking for the heart of the temple, I find a cash desk with a man sitting behind bars. There's a board up with various prices; 30 paise, 75 paise, 1 rupee 25, 2 rupees 50, but the explanation is printed in Tamil. Eventually I discover that this does not apply to me. As a non-Hindu I am a prohibited person, but a young man takes my arm and says: "Come. I will show you." As I hesitate, he says: "I am not a guide. I am a priest."

He draws me around a labyrinth of colonnaded passages, rattling away. When I listen closely I realize he is speaking English, but the syllables are colliding and leapfrogging over each other. Then we come to the Mango Tree. Partitions have been built to shield it from any casual eye, and I am led inside where a loquacious old gentleman takes over.

The Mango Tree, he says, is probably three thousand years old and has four branches. Each branch bears a different quality of fruit; bitter, sweet, sour and savory. He walks me round the tree at a fair trot.

"And now," he says grandly, arms outstretched, "you can offer something to be shared among these friends."

The friends, I see, include the priest and the Wistful Smiler.

"Ten rupees is the least you can offer."

I give two, with bad grace, and hurry off. As I emerge from the temple, the priest, who has been keeping up with me, says: "I also am collecting coins..."

But the bike is untouched, and although the kids greet me in even greater numbers I am able to keep my temper with them and even clown a bit, and all I lose is my ball pen. The Wistful Smiler smiles on me again, in the bazaar, and I have learned to do it differently next time. Anyway, the truth is waiting for me next day on the road at Chingleput.

On the main road at Chingleput is a gas and diesel station, and on the opposite side of the road, a wooden teahouse. Trucks, buses and cars stop here, and it is a busy area. One man has put himself in charge of it. How he has done so I don't know, but there is no doubt, as I watch him over a cup of milk tea, that he is in command.

He is a handsome, powerfully built man in middle age with iron gray hair close cropped on a strong head. His face is particularly striking; it has the intelligence and flair of a statesman or a soldier, lines deeply etched and showing great force and passion, even I would say genius.

Both his legs are cut off halfway along the thigh, and he sits on the stumps on a little wooden trolley, a couple of inches off the ground. He has leather pads on his hands to push himself along. It seems to me that he has all the energy and conviction it takes to run a country or command an army and he has put it into being a crippled beggar. He skates back and forth across the tarmac with immense skill, shouting his demands, roaring with laughter when he is refused, slapping his stumps with mirth and defying fate with every gesture. There is not a drop of pathos or self-pity in him anywhere. He is a blaze of vitality. When he holds out his hand to me, and I hesitate, he grunts with impatience, laughs and scoots off to the next arrival. There is no question that it was my loss, not his.

There is no one in sight who could even begin to challenge his authority, and he is the best example I have ever seen of the power of the human spirit to impose itself over fate. Is it pure coincidence, then, that I should see the next day another man who achieved as much and in a quite different way?

From a distance he is no more than a black smudge on the pavement outside the Continental Hotel in Pondicherry. When it becomes apparent that this blob has a human head on it, my inclination is to hurry by, but two small boys prevent me, and reluctantly I am drawn towards it.f

The head is about eighteen inches above the pavement, and is not nearly as handsome as the Churchill of Chingleput's, but at least it is a complete head, and it sits on shoulders. One shoulder is better developed than the other, and from it a single strong arm reaches up past the head to grasp a stick. Below the shoulders and under his shirt I can see the outline of an underdeveloped chest, which seems to be resting directly on the pavement. Whatever else is there is concealed by the shirt, but there is no room for anything much. It is utterly improbable that this person could exist at all. It seems to lack room for the most basic organs, just a head, shoulders and lungs hanging like a vine on a stick. But I must stop this callous clinical naming of parts, because he says: "Good afternoon."

I crouch down on the pavement, and we have a conversation in English. His English is limited but intelligible, and he speaks gently, with patience. He is forty years old. This alone I find incredible. With his withered arm he brings out some papers from beneath his shirt. Among them is an address book. He has friends everywhere. He corresponds with Europe and America. For some months he lived with some Germans in their rented rooms until their visas expired. There is an exchange of letters also with a wheelchair firm in Calcutta and a scheme for sponsoring the construction of a special device to wheel him around.

From this almost nonexistent being on a pavement in Pondicherry a field of consciousness reaches out around the globe. As far as I know he is not a great painter or poet or musician, although it would be wonderful if he were, but his accomplishment is much greater than that. Against all the odds, he has refused to disappear.

I'm riding awkwardly through a thicket of experience, still shaky from the flight to Europe. After three years on the move I can't mend my fences so fast. I hover between confidence and a sense of great loss, trying to understand the meaning of what has happened. It seems to me that my trials should have been over after Penang. My first days in Madras should have been the beginning of a final and marvelous chapter in India, full of discovery, significance and spiritual satisfaction. That is how I would have written it, but I have lost the strength to sustain the illusion and reality has tripped me up. I feel as foolish as if I had slipped on a banana peel.

Have I really been on a long flight from reality, trying to give meaning to something that was meaningless? Was it all just an escape that I have been trying to turn into a legend? I'm teetering on a knife edge between faith and despair. Was the purpose of that return to Europe just to show me that there was no purpose? I arrived there full of wisdom, but nothing I had seen or done or thought seemed to be relevant. I passed through pubs, offices, restaurants, supermarkets, stifled by the boredom of it, but with nothing useful to say to anyone. I felt the failure was mine, that if I had properly understood my experience in Africa, America, Asia, I should be able to apply it to people in trouble with the cost of living or career bottlenecks or sheer boredom. Some of them even asked me, thinking I should know, but my answers seemed to offer no solution. My advice always boiled down to the same thing. Don't solve the problem, just give it up.

They always assumed I was advising them to move to some tropical paradise. I saw the disillusionment growing in their eyes.

"Well, frankly, old boy, we'd love to but, with the boys just in school and the property market being what it is . . ."

I might just as well have smiled sadly and said: "Ah, those boys..."

In Pondicherry I spend a day drinking hot tea and sweating, to try to get rid of a fever. Then some days at Auroville, a city of the future that exists in the dreams of a scattered band of people, mostly Europeans and Americans, living on a great sandy site near the coast. Where else in the world could there be so much clarity amidst confusion, so much love amidst hostility, so much beauty in squalor, so much faith against all the evidence? The pioneers of Auroville are at war with their governing ashram in Pondicherry. Among themselves they hold wildly different views about how the dream of their guiding spirit, Mother Aurobindo, should be carried out.

There are some French people living as though on a luxury holiday in St. Tropez, Australians farming like aboriginals in loincloths on a diet of fermented Finger Millet, a Mexican running a market garden on the lines of a Jesuit mission in Latin America, others living more or less orthodox lives in other corners of this vast estate. Yet I feel the cohesion in all this diversity, and it is symbolized by a huge, raw, ferroconcrete skeleton, unfinished and hungry for labor, hand-built on the scale of a modern construction project, which one day, God willing, will become a shimmering sixty-foot globe enshrining the aspirations of them all. Meanwhile it is a demanding and practically useless burden without which, I feel, the whole place will fall apart.

I am more at home in the temples now, less encumbered, and at Thanjavur I find the one that sends my spirit soaring. It has a perfect form, as classical as the Piazza San Marco in Venice, and should be called the Drawing Room of India. My self-appointed guide is called Ravi. He has a fine address, very Indian, worth recording: c/o V. Balasubramanian, Accountant, Pandyan Automobiles, Tirunelveli 2. He is fourteen and very sharp. He claims that being a guide is his hobby, and plays a neat trick on me by not taking anything, and so keeping my suspicions alive all afternoon.

Later a literature student called Gopal catches me, like a fish, in a quiet backwater of Thanjavur where I'm eating a curry. By thrashing the water all around me he manages to guide me to his home where his friends come, one after another, to see what he has brought.

He is in a fever of excitement about having hooked a writer, and is determined that I must at least be Solzhenitsyn if not Shakespeare. When the expected fountain of wisdom fails to spurt from my lips, his disappointment is manifest.

"Does it not bother you that you have not made your name?" he asks in a hectoring manner; an odd question, since he does not yet know my name.

"Would you know if I had?" I reply.

"I would certainly know if you were an important journalist or writer, for I am reading always anything I can get my hands on. What about Ireland? Are the British being fair to Irish Catholics? What about the Israeli hijack? What about this inflation?"

Sitting on a bare iron bed frame in a cell-like room facing my inquisitor, I find I have not a single useful opinion in my head. I have read none of the books he mentions, know next to nothing about the authors he considers great. It is very dispiriting. He does not seem to want to talk about things, only to name names and list subjects and titles. Eventually I counterattack with a short lecture on empiricism. It is extremely feeble, but his waspishness melts under a single hot breath. Now he wants me for a godfather. I am to introduce his work to publishers in London, offer criticism and enlightenment, foster his career. With great difficulty I manage to disentangle myself without actually telling a lie.

How could I resent such opportunism, though. In this tide of humanity, where an economics degree might just get you a job on a bus, it's not good enough to open the door to opportunity. You must lasso it on the doormat.

In the night I dream that I am losing all my friends. They are running off while I am delayed, fumbling with something. I cannot catch them. There is a cat whose affection I am eager to arouse, without success. I ask whether it wouldn't be content to live with me. It looks at me and judges me. I can feel its appraisal.

"So, so," it says. "Comme ci, comme ca" – and I am left feeling quite worthless.

On to Tiruchirapalli, Dundigal, Madurai and Rameswaram. The humidity is so great that every time I reach into my pocket I pull the lining out with my hand. The soil is arid, and turns to sand. Goats nibble every struggling blade of grass. Under a clear sky I hear a shower of rain and look behind me, but it is the patter of goats hooves on asphalt. Strange. It reminds me of the time when I was camped by the roadside in Brazil and thought I heard cart wheels approaching over the gravel. I turned to see a brush fire advancing to consume me.

The fever has returned, mild but bothersome, usually in the afternoon. It has the effect of shaking my mind loose from my body, so that the meaning of things is out of focus. I hope it will go away of its own accord.

The ferry to Sri Lanka crosses from Rameswaram to Talimannar. The distance is twenty-five miles. I board it at ten in the morning and get off just after midnight. It may be the world's slowest boat. The same people keep turning up on this trail south, and they are on the ferry. The four Hari Krishna disciples are on my left, and one of them is dinging his tiny cymbals in my ear. A wild and nervous Australian "bushie" is here too. I am reading and have my helmet on the chair next to me. I'm reading because I feel sticky and sick, and I am desperately anxious to put my mind somewhere else just now, but the Australian is desperate to talk.

"Are you tired of answering the same questions?" he asks.

"Yes," I say, firmly, without looking up.

He perches on the bench opposite me, and stares fixedly to sea. I know he's uncomfortable, and so am I. At last I move my helmet and he sits beside me. He's trying not to talk, but he's like a kettle on the boil, and he can't help it.

"Would you like to hear some communism?" he says.

The sound of cymbals in one ear and communism in the other is too much. That is probably what started the backache, agitating a muscle at the bottom of my spine that goes berserk once or twice a year, at inconvenient moments. Riding the bike I hardly feel it, but when I get off the bike it hurts like hell.

At 8.30 we touch against a jetty, in the darkness, but unaccountably the boat sails off again. At ten we return, only to sail away again and return on the other side.

For this twenty-five-mile ferry ride I have to undergo all the formalities of an ocean crossing, a bill of lading, a handling charge, a port charge and a six-rupee charge to maintain the floating wharf under the wear and tear of my motorcycle. The paper work is volu-

Faces in the bazaar at Kanchipuram. Every time I paused on the bike a huge

benevolent crowd formed around me, as though I were a pop star – or a god.

minous and infuriating at each end, and I am not dealing with it well. I should consider myself fortunate to get away at midnight. The hordes of Indian passengers, I later hear, don't get ashore until 4 A.M.

For ten days I ride around the island, appreciating the calm of it. The pressure is off here, the people don't swarm in the same way. It's like a dropped-out version of India. I have come as a rainmaker. For two years they have had drought. The great reservoirs they call "tanks" are nearly dry. They need water very badly, and on my first day there the monsoon begins. I can find it in my heart to be very glad for them, but it complicates my life, because it keeps me moving when I would rather lie still. I meet many lovely people, see many beautiful things, but all against a backdrop of ache and fever. As the backache improves, the fever gets worse, and as it fluctuates I get two quite separate images of the tropics. In the morning, clear-sighted and with a clean brain, I see everything in bright and rapturous growth. The wet jungle smells fresh and exciting; the jungle birds leave notes of unbearable beauty hanging on the air; the world bursts with new forms and colors, and the people seem wisely content to accept what nature offers and not worry about shortages and bureaucracy and their political future. Later, as the heat accumulates, and the humidity thickens, as I get tired and the fever comes to dislocate my senses, I see the other side of the tropics. I see squalor and decay, smell the stench of corruption everywhere, feel the blind force of the jungle reaching out to swallow me, and the people seem morose, pathetic, sinking ever deeper into a putrefying slum.

At Puttalam, a Tamil town on the west coast, this jaundiced view of life hits bottom. As I walk along the shore of the lagoon everything I see seems fraught with degradation. A puppy hovering around a fish stall, so eaten up by worms that it is no more than a skull on match sticks; a beach stinking with refuse; some crows scrapping for morsels. One of the crows is obviously feeble, its feathers scraggy. It can't get to the food, and puts its claw pleadingly on the back of another bird, twice. I would never have thought I could break my heart over a crow. The healthy birds fly off, leaving it to stumble along on its own. Then I see, among all the filth and plastic and shredded tires, a dog, curled up and licking something. It looks at me with red mournful eyes. I see it is a bitch with distended udders, and between its front paws is the body of a dead puppy lying back on the garbage and oozing blood.

These examples of misery and death depress me profoundly. Everything seems a terrible mess. The buildings are mildewed wrecks; human effort seems futile. The people just a succession of empty headed bodies wrapped in sheets with shirt tails flapping, facile smiles signifying nothing if not envy and ingratiation. I notice only the stupidity, the inefficiency. Thinking of the early European planters who were so prone to feverish illness, I am amazed at the misery they must have endured. There are times when I would give almost anything to feel a cold wind blow.

I value these insights but they are undermining me seriously, and I must get rid of the fever. At the rest house I try again with massive doses of hot tea, and sweat enough to believe I might have broken it, but on the way to Mannar it returns to haunt me again. The rest house man at Mannar remembers me and gives me the same room I had on my arrival. I liked it here and I have come early to give myself an extra day before the ferry leaves. There is an old Portuguese fort I want to look at and a bridge where I want to try fishing. I go straight out with my rod, hoping to be left alone, but betel-chewing spectators gather around me. Then I get a bite. It feels big, and it's the first time I've felt that heavy pull on the line. A stingray. Fantastic. I don t care whether it's edible or not, I just want to look at it. My audience warns me to be careful. One of them shows me how to remove the sting, which, to my amazement, is not at the end of the tail at all, but close to the root, like a quill.

Proudly I carry my prize back to the rest house, and the cook says he will fry it for me, but "as a fish it is not famous." Returning to the lounge, I see two men come in and my heart sinks. They were on the bridge earlier and annoyed me unreasonably with their questions.

"Your native land, please? Are you a university graduate? How much does this rod cost in your country? And this jacket? And these shoes?" and on and on. Now I have to sit and take tea with them. There is no escape. One is a government clerk, and the other is the medical officer of Mannar. They have so little to say, and understand even less of the little I have to offer, that it is just a yawning ritual. "What are the principal illnesses here?" I ask the MO.

Malaria, tuberculosis, typhoid . . .

"What are the symptoms of typhoid?"

A fever building up slowly over a number of days, body aches, headache, nausea . . .

When they have finally left I tell myself it can't be typhoid because I don't feel nauseous. An hour later I am sick. The fever is in me again too. Thoroughly alarmed, I tell the rest house manager that I must go to a doctor. The rain is coming down with great force, but there is a car parked outside and the owner says it can take me to the hospital.

A young doctor receives me with great amusement.

"What do you want?" he asks, chuckling. "Do you want medicine or to be admitted?"

"I want to know what's wrong with me," I say, stiffly, irritated by his attitude. Why can't he stop grinning?

"You've got a fever," he says.

It's so ridiculous I have to smile too, although I don't want to.

"Why?" I ask.

"The climate," he says. "Take a Disprin and it will go."

"That's what I've been doing for three weeks."

He still thinks it's a huge joke, and asks several questions but doesn't listen to the answers.

"Cough," he says.

"What?"

"Cough."

I cough.

"You see," he says. "You've got a cough."

That alone almost cures me.

Back at the rest house, convinced at least that I don't have typhoid, I bring out the antibiotics for the first time to treat myself. Tetracycline might do it. I take the dose, and go fishing again.

That night a tremendous storm blows up, with sounds like cannon firing. There are pools of water on the floors, the garden is a lake and the varnish on all the furniture is as sticky as toffee. Between nine and midnight I rival the storm by sweating a lake myself. Not just the sheets but the mattress also is soaked right through, and I have to change beds. By morning I know the fever has broken.

I first thought of becoming a god as I was riding north from Madurai. The fever was gone. I felt more than just healthy, I was bursting with life and joy, floating as you do when you have put down a heavy load. Without exhaustion or discomfort to blunt my senses, without the distorting effect of fever, I saw myself to be in a paradise.

First there were the trees. Paradise would be unthinkable without trees. The neem, the peepul, the tamarind, countless others, stood at stately intervals alongside the roads and fields, like giant witnesses from another age. By their presence they transform everything, framing the landscape, giving it depth, variety and freshness, making green-glowing caverns under the sun and casting pools of dappled shade where people and animals can feel at peace.

The ox's creamy hide is made to reflect this flickering light. Under a shade tree a pair of pale oxen passed, yoked to their rumbling cart. The oxen tossed their heads, brandishing their high crescent horns painted in red and blue bands and tipped with glittering brass. The slack, velvety hide beneath their throats rippled in the sun, and the image was printed on my memory for life. Only on my memory? So intense was the image, is still, that I could not believe it was meant only for me. I felt it burning into some larger consciousness than my own.

Small groups of women walked the roads carrying vast but apparently weightless burdens of fodder, produce, pottery or household furniture. The breeze swirled the hems of their saris into the classic mold of nymphs and goddesses. Wrapped in those gauzy layers of lime green and rose red their bodies were so poised and supple, all of them, that it was sometimes a shock to see close up the deep wrinkles and gray hair of age.

From the road I saw fields of grain and paddy. Women worked in lines, advancing across the mud, stooping and rising easily, brilliantly colored against the green rice shoots. The men worked almost naked, with just a triangle of cloth between their long powerful thighs, black-skinned and gleaming. A team of six oxen harnessed together and guided by one man was churning up a paddy field, flying around at a tremendous rate. Everywhere people moved briskly and with confidence. They and the land were part of each other and had shaped each other. The harmony was so complete that it seemed to promise utter tranquillity. As I rode through it I felt it reaching for me, as if I had only to stop and let myself slide into it like a pebble into a lake.

India ⟶ *403*

I knew those Indians were most unlikely to share my vision. How could they, since they were in it? How could a fish describe water? And when I stopped the bike and stood idle by the roadside it faded for me too under the remorseless glare of so-called reality. I would have to strip naked, go hungry, live with the mosquitoes and the parasites in the paddy squelch and shed a large part of what I liked to call my personality. The very part of me that could envisage such a life would prevent me from living it. Did that make it an illusion?

Throughout the journey, as I rode through so many landscapes, passed through so many lives, forming impressions, holding them and developing them, had I just been wallowing in illusions? It seemed very extraordinary to me that, riding through southern India, observing this life around me, I could at the same time summon up vivid mental images of Africans working with sisal and sugar cane, of Americans working among corn, cattle, bananas and oil palms, of Thais and Malays working with rice, sago and pineapples. I could create living pictures of people and places as remote from these Indians as they had once been from me. If my head could only be wired to a colored print-out terminal I could have trailed a blizzard of picture postcards from the four corners of the earth.

Just to be carrying the consciousness of so much at the same time seemed to me to be miraculous, as though I were observing the earth from some far-off point, Mount Olympus, perhaps, or a planet. Riding a motorcycle at thirty miles an hour on the road to Dundigal, among people deeply involved in manual skills, so close to the earth and each other and so different from me, I could imagine myself as a mythical being, a god in disguise that might pass their way only once in a lifetime.

Memories of Madras, of ashes and honey, gods and temples, were strong in me. In India it is quite plain that there is more to life than what the senses can perceive. I was thinking about my plan to meet Sai Baba, the holy man, wondering how it could happen.

"There is no cause to bother," a devotee advised me. "He will know. Just go there. He knows everything. If he wants to see you it will happen."

Apparently he had a headquarters at a building called Whitelands, near Bangalore. At certain times of day he appeared before his followers. I would go there, but I would make no other attempt to get in touch with him. I had heard and read about his miracles, but I knew that such things could, in certain circumstances, be "arranged." It seemed very important not to go there expecting magic.

If he "knows" then let him call me out. That will be miracle enough for me.

I smiled at the idea of it happening.

Just imagine that he does know, that he knows I am riding towards him now, still several days away but coming closer all the time, until finally I ride up to this Whitelands place and Sai Baba falls to his knees beside the motorcycle and says: "My God. You have come at last."

That was how the notion of being a god came to me originally. As a joke. After all, there were so many gods in India already, in such wild and wonderful guises, why not a god on a motorcycle?

The southern hills were a great surprise, rising to nearly nine thousand feet and demolishing my notion that India south of the Himalayas was a flat hot triangle. I rode up to Kodaikanal, the more southerly hill station where log fires roar in the grates at night as they did in the White Highlands of Kenya, and then over the Cardamom Hills to Cochin to enjoy the splendor of the west coast and the green tidiness of Kerala. Then up again to Ootacamund, which the British nicknamed "Ooty."

At the foot of the last big climb to Ooty were groves of areca palms, quite improbably graceful and slender for their great height. It seemed incredible that they could support the weight of the men who clambered up them to reap the betel crop from below their feathery crowns, swinging from one to another like monkeys. There were monkeys too, silvery gray ones with long furry limbs. Halfway up the hill I stopped to contemplate them, my head light with thought, recalling all the other times I had watched them in Africa, America, Malaysia and most recently at the rest house in Mannar where I had played with one for hours.

They seemed so close to enlightenment, as though at any moment they might stumble over it and explode into consciousness. Their curiosity is extreme. They experiment with any unfamiliar object, a coin, a hat, a piece of paper, just as a human baby does, pulling it, rubbing it, sticking it in their ears, hitting it against other things. And nothing comes of it. To be so close, yet never to pierce the veil...

I looked at myself in the same light, as a monkey given my life to play with, prodding it, trying to stretch it into different shapes, dropping it and picking it up again, suspecting always that it must have some use and meaning, tantalized and frustrated by it but always unable to make sense of it.

"If I were a god that is how I would view myself," I thought. At times I felt myself coming very close to that understanding, as though I might rise above myself and see, at last, what it was all about. The feelings that had begun to form in Sudan, in the Karoo and on the *Zoe G* and at other times seemed to be coming to fruition in India. A latent power of perception was stirring in me.

I was astonished by my confidence with strangers. Often I was able to talk to them immediately as though we had always known each other. For a long time I had been training myself to want nothing from others; to accept what was offered but to avoid expectation. I was far from perfect, but even the beginnings I had made were richly rewarding. I could feel that people appreciated my presence and even drew some strength from it, and in turn that feeling strengthened me. There were the beginnings of a growth of power and I was determined to pursue it.

The journey continued, as it always had, with this close interweaving of action and reflection. I ate, slept, cursed, smiled, rode, stopped for gas, argued, bargained, wrote and took pictures. I made friends with some Germans, and some English, and some Indians. I learned about mushrooms, potatoes, cabbages, golden nematodes, Indian farmers and elephants.

The thread connecting these random events was The Journey. For me it had a separate meaning and existence; it was the warp on which the experiences of each successive day were laid. For three years I had been weaving this single tapestry. I could still recall where I had been and slept and what I had done on every single day of traveling since The Journey began. There was an intensity and a luminosity about my life during those years which sometimes shocked me. I wondered whether it might be beyond my capacity to hold so much experience in conscious awareness at one time and I was seriously afraid that I would see the fabric of the tapestry beginning to rot before I had finished it. I thought I might be guilty of some offense against nature for which I would be made to pay a terrible price. Was it improper for a mere human to attempt to comprehend the world in this way? For that was my intention. The circle I was describing around the earth might be erratic but the fact remained, it was a real circle. The ends would meet and it would enclose the earth. I would have laid my tracks around the surface of this globe and at the end it would belong to me, in a way that it could never belong to anyone else. I trembled a bit at the fates I might be tempting.

People who thought of my journey as a physical ordeal or an act of courage, like single-handed yachting, missed the point. Courage and physical endurance were no more than useful items of equipment for me, like facility with languages or immunity to hepatitis. The goal was comprehension, and the only way to comprehend the world was by making myself vulnerable to it so that it could change me. The challenge was to lay myself open to everybody and everything that came my way. The prize was to change and grow big enough to feel one with the whole world. The real danger was death by exposure.

In India I was on the last and most significant leg, and during the long hours of solitary riding my brain shuttled back and forth, delving into the past for new connections and meanings, synthesizing, analyzing, fantasizing, refining and revising my ideas and observations. The pattern on the tapestry still eluded me, although it shimmered somewhere on the edge of recognition. What must I do to see it clearly? Must I, like Icarus, strap on wax wings and fly to the sun? Whatever it was I felt ready to try because I had finally to admit it, I was in search of immortality.

The vital instrument of change is detachment and traveling alone was an immense advantage. At a time of change the two aspects of a person exist simultaneously; as with a caterpillar turning into a butterfly there is the image of what you were and the image of what you are about to be, but those who know you well see you only as you were. They are unwilling to recognize change. By their actions they try to draw you back into your familiar ways.

It would be hopeless to try to become a god among friends and relations, any more than a man can become a hero to his valet. It was chilling to realize that the sentimental qualities most valued between people, like loyalty, constancy and affection, are the ones most likely to impede change. They are so obviously designed to compensate for mortality. The old gods never had any truck with them.

Kronos, the king of the ancient Greek gods, began his career by cutting off his father's penis with a sickle and tossing it into the ocean. He went on to swallow his own children to make sure they did not unseat him. Zeus, the son that got away, put his father in chains and had him guarded in exile by monsters. There are endless tales of betrayal, bloody vengeance and fearful dismemberment. Zeus, who became Jupiter in Roman times, adopted deceitful disguises and committed rape as a cuckoo, a swan and a bull, and he reigned over Olympus more by cunning than virtue.

The Indian gods seemed little different in their own behavior but, reading the *Mahabharata*, I saw that in Indian mythology they became more closely involved with mankind than did the Greek gods. They allied themselves to various warring factions and offered advice. The best-known example was when Lord Krishna became the warrior Arjuna's charioteer, drove him to battle and encouraged him in words that have become known as the Bhagavad-Gita.

Arjuna, of course, was fighting for good against evil, but many good men had found themselves compromised and were on the wrong side. It sickened Arjuna to have to kill his own kith and kin, and he lost heart, thinking that it must be wrong to do so. What Krishna told him was that his primary duty lay in being true to what he was, a warrior, and not to be crippled by sentimental attachments to his family. There is an elemental brutality about this advice which I found as thrilling as it seemed cruel. When I read it every line struck home, and I relived episodes of the journey vividly, recalling my own fears and confusions.

Heat, cold, pain, pleasure –
These spring from sensual contact, Arjuna.
They begin and they end.
They exist for the time being,
You must learn to put up with them.
The man whom these cannot distract,
The man who is steady in pain and pleasure,
Is the man who achieves serenity.
The untrue never is,
The True never isn't.
The knowers of Truth know this.
And the Self that pervades all things is imperishable.
Nothing corrupts this imperishable self.

Lucky are soldiers who strive in a just war;
For them it is an easy entrance into heaven.

Equate pain and pleasure, profit and loss,
Victory and defeat.

And fight.
There is no blame this way.

There is no waste of half-done work in this,
No inconsistent results.
An iota of this removes a world of fear.
In this there is only single-minded consistency;
While the efforts of confused people
Are many-branching and full of contradiction.
Your duty is to work, not to reap the fruits of work....

Wanting things breeds attachment,
From attachment springs covetousness,
And covetousness breeds anger.
Anger leads to confusion
And confusion kills the power of memory.
With the destruction of memory, choice is rendered impossible
And when moral choice fails, man is doomed.

The mind is the ape of the wayward senses;
They destroy discrimination as a storm scatters boats on a
lake.

The concept of the Self seemed to connect with my own thought in
South Africa, of being made of the stuff of the universe, all-pervad-
ing and imperishable. The Truth was in the stuff itself, revealed in
the natural order of things. You have only to merge with the world
to know the Truth and find your Self.

There are shapes and forms which rise out of this natural order.
Trees, caves and animal architecture lead naturally to thatched
roofs, stone houses and mud walls. If you knew this you would not
choose to put up a roof in corrugated iron. Nor would you think of
throwing a plastic bag in a stream, not because of what you have
been told about pollution, but because the idea of a plastic bag in a
stream is offensive in itself. Without this sense of what is naturally
fitting you can be cleaning up the world with one hand and spreading poison with the other.

It surprised me to discover that this sense of rightness does not
appear naturally in people, even though they live in the heart of
nature. In my own village in France the same people who fished the

streams shoved every possible kind of refuse and sewage into them, even when offered convenient alternatives. In Nepal, where not a single engine or power line disturbs the mediaeval rusticity of the Himalayan valleys, people shit in their rivers with a dogmatic persistence ensuring that every village is infected by what the people upstream have got.

The Truth obviously does not reveal itself unaided to humans. It has to be uncovered by an effort of consciousness. Or, more likely, it exists only in human consciousness. Without man around to recognize it, there is no Truth, no God.

Yet it is not consciousness that governs the world, nor even ideology, nor religious principle nor national temperament. It is custom that rules the roost. In Colombia it was the custom to do murder and violence. In a period of ten years some 200,000 people were said to have been killed by acts of more or less private violence. Yet I found the Colombians at least as hospitable, honorable and humane as the Argentines, whose custom is merely to cheat. Arabs have the custom of showing their emotions and hiding their women. Australians show their women and hide their emotions. In Sudan it is customary to be honest. In Thailand dishonesty is virtually a custom, but so is giving gifts to strangers.

Every possible variation of nudity and prudishness is the custom somewhere as with eating habits, toilet practices, to spit or not to spit; and almost all of these customs have become entirely arbitrary and self-perpetuating. Above all it is customary to suspect and despise people in the next valley, or state, or country, particularly if their color or religion is different. And there are places where it is customary to be at war, like Kurdistan or Vietnam.

Speaking of the more vicious customs, and of men who should have known better, St. Francis Xavier said a long time ago: "Custom is to them in the place of law, and what they see done before them every day they persuade themselves may be done without sin. For customs bad in themselves seem to these men to acquire authority and prescription from the fact that they are commonly practiced."

Custom is the enemy of awareness, in individuals as much as in societies. It regularizes the fears and cravings of everyday life. I wanted to shake them off. I wanted to use this journey to see things whole and clear, for I would never pass this way again. I wanted to be rid of the conditioning of habit and custom. To be the slave of custom, at any level, is much like being a monkey, an "ape of the wayward senses." To rise above it is already something like becoming a god.

With these elevating thoughts forming in my mind I rode along narrow country roads among trees in a state bordering on ecstasy, and there did come a moment when I was actually prepared to take seriously the possibility of some semi-divine status. At that very moment, which I recognized only in retrospect, I turned a corner and came upon a traveling holy man, a *saddhu*, his forehead smeared with the colors of his profession, dragging his bundles on to the next shrine. He looked up at me as though he had expected me, and his face showed pure distaste. Then he spat vigorously in my path as I passed him by.

The comment could not have been more appropriate. It had the same electric connection with my thoughts that had so excited me about the flying fish on the *Zoe G.*

Really, I told myself, you could hardly ask for a more convincing demonstration, and I took the hint.

Even so I did go to see Sai Baba at Whitelands. There was a walled compound the size of a football field, with a rain shelter in the middle that could house a lot of people. The holy man apparently lived in an opulent villa at one end of the garden, accessible by a flight of broad stone steps. Scattered around near the villa were several keenly nonchalant young men of the kind you see working for progressive candidates at American conventions. There was a new building going up too, hand-made in the Asian tradition with women doing most of the work. When you have seen women working a coal mine in saris, nothing in the field of human labor seems improbable.

I sat on the ground among a mixed crowd of Indians and Europeans, and one of the guru's staff men asked me to take off my shoes. Eventually Sai Baba came down the steps with a small group and inspected the building operations. Later he came to look the rest of us over. He looked much as he had in the pictures, in his ankle-length robe of crimson, and his great head of frizzy black hair, but he seemed anxious and preoccupied. A thin red line of betel juice stained his lips. There were no miracles, and he did not even smile. He looked at us in the way a worried farmer might examine his crops for blight, and then he departed. I did not form the impression that he was God, and he seems to have been equally disappointed in me.

On my way up the coast from Mangalore I stopped at Karwar, a poor fishing town on the estuary of the Kalinadi river. I felt like drinking a beer, but alcohol had been banished to the edge of town, in a tumble-down eating house which I remembered afterwards mainly for a priceless fragment of conversation. The waiter brought fish and said:

"Your native place? From?"

London.

"Ah, London proper. You are going?"

I'm going to Goa.

"Ah, Goa going. Nice place. My from is Goa."

Goa is quite as beautiful as everybody says, but I found it chiefly interesting for what I learned about pigs. It is the excellent custom in India, in the villages, to go out in the morning to whichever field has been specially designated and leave your daily shit where it is most needed to fertilize the ground. In Goa also this custom is followed, but there is a special problem, because Goanese, unlike most Indians, are carnivorous and keep pigs. And pigs, as one may or may not know, eat shit. And the pigs of Goa are very hungry pigs so that many an unwary person has been knocked off his toes by a charging porker before the completion of his duties.

This kind of information, which most people are sadly conditioned to think of as disgusting, forms a basic element in the life of a traveler, just as its subject matter is a fundamental element of life itself. The extraordinary taboos that we have raised around the business of shitting has led to far more disgusting prejudices among people, and also to quite serious health problems. To be free of that sense of unreasoning distaste I found to be a major liberation, on a par with freedom in sex.

I did not realize how advanced I was until I read a story in an illustrated Indian magazine edited by Kushwant Singh. He had a little item, headed "Tailpiece," about a famous Indian operatic soprano who had just died. Her debut, many years earlier before a London audience, had failed rather miserably. She had not been able to bring any conviction to her singing. When asked afterwards what had gone wrong, she said she had not been able to get it out of her head, as she looked out over her distinguished audience in the Wigmore Hall, that all these people smeared their bottoms with pieces of dry paper.

Not only did I think it very funny, but I could sympathize entirely with her point of view. Anyone brought up, as Indians are, to use

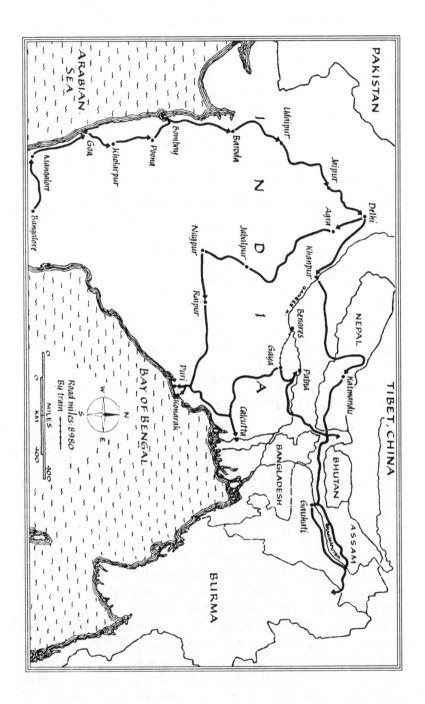

water can see that the Western method is quite barbarously inefficient, while on a long journey through poor countries it becomes uncomfortable and offensive. I was often ashamed of the mess that the civilized elite of the Western world left behind them on their trail through South America and Asia, made all the worse through being forced to spend most of their time running for the lavatory

I was lucky to have very few problems with it myself. Only once in India did I explode, and that was a clear-cut case of food poisoning in a restaurant in Bihar. I stopped in several fields on my way to Calcutta, and composed a poem while contemplating the landscape.

The food in Bihar is rather bizarre,
One should not stray far after lunch in Bihar,
Not even as far as the local bazaar,
For none can outrun the food in Bihar.

I went on through Bombay and north to Jaipur and Delhi, and from there I turned east through Khanpur, Lucknow and Faizabad to Gorakhpur, where a route runs north over the Himalayan foot hills to Pokhara in Nepal.

Luckily I did not have to waste breath or energy on things that often give visitors to India so much trouble and offense. I was used to poverty, to different standards of hygiene, to the visible effects of disease and malnutrition. I knew how to frame questions so that the other person would not know what answers I expected. I did not assume that something was possible only because it seemed easy to me. I stopped looking for objective truth and efficiency, and learned to value other things instead. And I loved the food.

I became saturated with Indian attitudes, but always there were more surprises. In Bombay I saw a newly released American film, full of violence and shootings. In Europe I would have shrugged it off, but there it made me squirm and choke with horror. What made the audience shudder most though was a happy scene in which the cowboy hero marks his cattle with a branding iron.

I saw women making a highway, by hand, circulating in vast numbers like beasts of burden with baskets of granite chips on their heads under the indifferent eye of a male supervisor. It seemed dehumanizing, but at least they had work of sorts. I saw every kind of load carried. Every kind of procession came my way. Every kind of animal drew every kind of cart, and every kind of vehicle either passed me or lay in ruins by the roadside.

In Ahmedabad, two women came towards me towing a heavily loaded trolley both dressed in uniformsaris and bodices of red and yellow, but both with their heads and faces completely wrapped in saffron muslin. They were moving with extraordinary vigor, and made an unforgettable sight. It was impossible to believe, because of their very vitality that they were suffering.

On the road from Gorakhpur to Nepal, a long, silent, empty country road, came a sight I never thought to see in this half of the century; two wiry, barefooted men in sky-blue turbans and shawls jogging along with a litter on their shoulders. I stopped, transfixed as they went past. The plush red curtains of the litter were drawn open. Inside a young man sat cross-legged, idly regarding the countryside. He was dressed in English clothes and was wearing a blazer and an old-school tie.

But I could not accept what I saw in Bombay, when I was taken past the "cages." I stared goggle-eyed at prostitutes apparently enslaved behind great iron grilles set into the doorways. I found the posturing women, the heavy iron bars, the theatrical lighting inside these prisons so grotesque that my mind would not grasp it as reality.

During those months I was exposed to such startling forms of life, in such quantity and variety, that I was drenched with images.

In Khanpur (or Cawnpore as the British spelled it in the days of the Mutiny) I stayed at the old Orient Hotel. It was in a disgraceful state of dilapidation. My room was one of a number of cardboard boxes put up inside a once grand ballroom, and I could hear the rats scampering across the dance floor. The facilities were abysmal, but one feature of the old days had been kept intact. Two beautifully maintained billiard tables gleamed under brilliant lights in a room behind the bar, and some town swells were playing a highly affected game.

One of them looked as though he belonged in a cigarette advertisement of the twenties. His black hair was plastered down flat. He wore a little patterned bow tie. His check tweed jacket was square shouldered and as immaculately pressed as though it were on a shop-window dummy. He held himself absolutely rigid above the waist, and glided back and forth like a tango dancer.

The other player wore more traditional Indian clothing; a long white shirt, baggy trousers brought in tight above the knees, a long and luxurious camel-hair waistcoat, all worn with such style and arrogance that I felt like applauding. In fascination I watched as they swaggered and sported, sipping at barely concealed illegal drinks, their faces busy with the nonstop ritual of knowing glances. They spoke Hindi, but a masterful shot was acclaimed in English with the quaint cry of "Well!" They seemed to be trapped in their own creation of some bygone sporting era, and I did not see how they would ever be able to escape.

Just before midnight I went out for a walk. The broad street was black and empty, the alleyways impenetrable. A huge advertisement leered down from the facade above my head, showing an Indian couple in swimming trunks and bikini, and announcing:

Stomach GAS & SEX Problems. Consult Dr. Whosit.

A train of wagons was coming towards me. They were drays moving silently on rubber tires, each one drawn by two water buffalo. The drays were long flat platforms without sides, and littered with sacking. There were eight of them, making a very long train, and each one had a driver, almost invisible under cotton wraps and head cloth. Only the first driver seemed to be truly awake, and his stick made a regular dull thwack against the buffalo hide.

Heaven knows how far they had come or how far they were going. Among the sacks I saw other peasants sleeping, and I guessed they were returning to their villages after delivering produce. The buffaloes looked more than usually mournful in the night, with their long necks straining out in front of them, heads lolling hopelessly, heavy black bodies plodding low to the ground, making hardly any sound on the tar.

The movement was as inexorable as it was slow, and I stood and watched until the last of the long line had vanished into the cold December night. They came into my life and left it like ghosts from the past and I was deeply moved.

On my walk back I saw a man, pathetic and shivering in threadbare cotton, praying to a demonic red figure of Kali in a tiny stone temple next to a garage. A little farther along a man with a distracted air and wearing a shirt attacked me verbally with the story of his misery.

"You have one recourse," he said, harshly. "To give me something for food. I haven't eaten all day." Something in what I had experienced that evening made it impossible for me to give anything. His last shouted appeal – "For humanity's sake" – and my desperate, dismal response – "You'll have to sort yourselves out" – stayed with me like twin echoes through the night.

It was important to me to give only when I felt like it. I tried never to let a sense of guilt or conscience drive me to it, for then I would never know whether I wanted to or not. Happily there were some occasions when I did want to give, though not very many.

I was a beggar myself, of course, in the sense that I made myself very obviously available to receive hospitality, and it was generously offered. The prize, I suppose, must have been the two nights I spent in the palace of the Maharajah of Baroda. My friend in Madras had known the maharajah (or strictly speaking, the ex-maharajah, since the title was officially extinct) and suggested I visit him in Baroda. I arrived full of curiosity, not knowing what to expect, and was directed first to the wrong palace which was full of soldiers. However, they sent me in the right direction, and I came to an apparently endless and towering railing alongside a road, and at last a gate.

It seemed odd that the gate should be open and unguarded, but I went in, down a potholed drive among trees and bushes until the palace came in sight. It was quite an overwhelming sight, not simply because it was vast and seemed to occupy my entire field of vision when I came upon it, but because of the breathtaking detail that filled every part of the facade. There were so many wings – even the wings had wings – that for a good while I could see no way to get at it. Only later did I realize that I was looking at the back of the palace and that the true and *really* impressive facade was around the other side.

As I rode and walked up and down the gravel, puzzled by the silence and the apparent absence of a doorway, two figures appeared on one of a hundred balconies overlooking the drive. They looked ragged and disreputable, and in every way inappropriate to all the magnificence around them. In fact I thought at first I had caught two housebreakers at work. They were probably having similar thoughts about me. One of them shouted down: "What do you want?" They obviously were keen to keep their distance.

"I want to see the Maharajah," I shouted back. It felt quite ridiculous. They looked like a couple of villains. I was a black and greasy biker after the long ride from Bombay. I should have been at the back of a slum tenement shouting "Tell Bert the cops are onto him." "Not here," the man replied. "His Highness not here."

I went on at the top of my voice in great detail about my connections and ambitions, knowing that he did not understand me but trying to entice him down. Eventually it worked. My authentic English accent must have done the trick.

I saw there was nothing villainous about him at all. He was the Indian version of a faithful old retainer, and he managed to explain that the estate was now managed from an office across the road, not far away. He gave me a glass of water, and a note scribbled in Gujarati. I went off to find the office, and met the Maharajah's brother and a young engineer called Ashwin Mehta. We talked pleasantly for a while, and I learned that the Maharajah, who was also an M.P., was in New Delhi, and that the palace was hardly used these days.

Ashwin said there was much to be seen in Baroda and that he would show me, and the Maharajah's brother said I should stay at the palace meanwhile if I liked. I had no difficulty accepting. In due course I went back to wash and change, and went through the front entrance into a hall big enough to contain most houses. There was no door, for it was never needed. It was never cold, and privacy began a long way away at the boundaries of the immense estate.

There were several servants, or "bearers" in white cotton livery with stylish cockades in their hats, and bare feet, although it was a skeleton crew compared with what must once have manned this monster. They padded ahead with my peculiar bits of luggage while I clumped after them in dirty boots under the disapproving stares of various ancestors. My suite had two rooms, both huge. One was the bedroom, the other the bathroom. They overlooked one of several beautiful courtyards trapped within the fabric of the building, crammed with palms and fountains.

My bed was a fourposter inside a little room of its own made of gauzy mosquito netting. A bearer slept on the floor outside my bedroom door at night. It would be pointless and unnecessary to pretend that I was enjoying the same luxury that the princes once offered to guests at the height of their power. To have tried to recreate or maintain that today would be absurd and impossible. What I saw there in that short stay, the profusion of marble, bronze and mosaic, the infinitely long corridors, the echoing halls, the huge audience room with chairs for five hundred people, and the executioner's sword hanging over them all, was enough. My imagination could supply the rest.

In Nepal I abandoned the bike for two weeks to walk in the Himalayas with Carol. In the total absence of machinery and electronics it felt like being spirited back to the Middle Ages. We saw lemons as big as footballs, lost our way at night in a rhododendron forest, and met Tibetan traders, like those above, on the pony trail from Pokhara to Jomsum.

I sat there on my second night, amidst all this magnificence, penning a letter on the Maharajah's stationery and thinking that it was just as well that I had also slept in a prison. It helped me to feel that I deserved it.

By the time I came out of Assam into West Bengal in February of 1977, my experiences in India alone were beginning to overwhelm me. My mind was a constantly changing kaleidoscope. A Royal Bengal Tiger seen stalking through the long grass at sunset. A religious procession winding down a mountainside. A wild tribal dance. Men in loincloths hunting with bows and arrows. Tibetan traders walking the trails from Mustang. A wildcat oil rig driving down into the rock on the Burmese border. The sublime music of one of India's greatest musicians playing only five feet away from me in a private celebration. A night lost in a rhododendron forest at eleven thousand feet. The astonishing open-cast coal mine at Margherita. The period opulence of the tea estates. An incredible all-night theatrical production by a touring company of Indian players in a tent. On and on they went, and I was gradually becoming exhausted by the effort to retain it all and still see what was new every day with a fresh eye.

What came every day was so startling, so interesting, always more than I could ever hope to absorb.

I came out of Assam knowing that I should go to Benares. How could I possibly not go to Benares? Yet I was actually going to Calcutta, and once in Calcutta it would be twice as far to come back up to Benares and down again. And still I wanted to go to Calcutta. I was tired. I wanted European company. But somewhere along the road fate grabbed me and sent me to Benares anyway.

I surrendered, to India and to the multitude. That was something else I had learned, to surrender. Vast crowds gathered around me when I stopped, but as long as they gave me room to breathe I did not mind. I got used to considering my life as public property.

"Excuse me, sir? Your native place is? London proper, is it? May I introduce? I. J. Krishnan, currently completing Bachelor of Science at B.H.U. And your good name, sir? You are married? I see, you are bachelor? Your age is please? Why are you not married? Where is your family? What are your qualifications? How are you able to leave your family for so long? Your journey must be costing a lot of money? Are you in government service? Then how please are you paying for all this?"

When it got to the marriage question I was often tempted to plead impotence or homosexuality, but the joke would certainly have failed. I let the waves wash over me. Pointless to waste effort in trying to beat them back. But gradually they wore me down anyway, and the waves grew stronger, the multitude thicker, as I advanced into Bihar, one of the poorest and most populous states in the Indian union.

But the magic was still working too, harder than ever. Why else should I have been led to a hotel in Patna whose owner was a glider pilot, and who insisted on taking me up with him? For breathless minutes I found my escape from India by whirling above it in the company of those big brown birds called Kites. Why else would I have been invited, by pure chance, to a party at which the heads of the mighty Congress Party of Bihar reveled and revealed themselves so soon before lurching into oblivion at the famous elections of '77? And why else should I find myself now having my future told to me at a Rajput wedding?

"You are Jupiter," he said.

Of all the gods in the pantheon, Jupiter is the one I fancy most. A lovely name, Jupiter, like cream and honey in the mouth. And a sense of great distance and closeness at the same time.

He was a rainmaker, and I have definitely made my share of rain. I rained all over the Southern Hemisphere in unprecedented quantities. Then he was famous for his thunder, which is appropriate too for a god on a motorcycle, and (if it's fair to mix him up a bit with Zeus) then I like the idea of appearing in all those disguises. I have been changing my shape quite often as well.

All in all I would quite like to be Jupiter, if it is not too late....

"You are Jupiter," he said, and for a flash I was, "but for seven years you have been having conflict with Mars." Of course. It was just a misunderstanding. He was talking about the planet.

"This troubling influence will go on for two more years." His grip on my hand remained firm and convincing, and I did not resist. I wanted it to be important.

"During these two years, you will have two accidents. They will not be major accidents, but they will not be minor either."

Really, I thought, that's stretching my credulity a bit. I hardly need a fortuneteller to predict accidents, with ten thousand miles still to ride. But he did say two. Not major? Not minor?

"After this period, when you are no longer influenced by Mars, all will be well. You will have great success and happiness."

I absorbed the message. Two years of strife and accident, and then prosperity and happiness ever after.

"You owe everything to your mother," he said. Did I tell Raj I was the only son of a divorced mother? I must have told someone.

"You have a weak hold on the affections of women. She is the only one who will give you whole-hearted support."

I gazed hard then at this grave, composed man in the brown business suit sitting next to me in the front seat of his car outside a wedding tent, trying to penetrate his meaning. It sounded wrong, absolutely wrong, like the reverse side of a familiar coin. Yet there was something very right hidden in it somewhere. I was impressed by him, I felt he was really trying, and after all it was nothing to him. None of them would ever see me again. He was just a businessman about to leave for his office in Patna.

There were more pleasant remarks about my strength and determination. We exchanged solemn compliments and he drove off.

Ten miles beyond Gaya is Boddhgaya, the place where Buddha preached his first sermon under a tree. A tree stands on the spot now, although not, I think, the same tree. Above and around the tree a great temple and *stupa* have been built. Somewhere nearby every Buddhist nation is also represented by a temple and a refuge for pilgrims. The refuges are austere and cheap to live in. They offer shelter and tranquillity, and in the dry hot spring of Bihar that is all one needs.

The first of these refuges on the road from Gaya is the Burmese Vihar, and it had been recommended to me. Two monks made me welcome and I took the bike in through the big wrought-iron gate. The original building on my right faced a square garden of rather straggly shrubs and vegetables, and along each side, between the garden and the high walls that enclosed the Vihar, ran two rows of small brick cubicles. It was very popular, and the place was full of people from every continent, but a remarkable atmosphere of good natured calm pervaded all of it.

I had one of the cubicles to myself, which gave me a wide plank to sleep on and room to put down my things and cook for myself. It was all I needed. In the area around the house was a table under a big shade tree, and I sat there and wrote an article for the approaching elections in India. A Thai monk was offering courses in yoga and meditation, and I took those too. There was time for everything, and time to spare. Those were the last perfectly peaceful days I spent on the journey and among the most promising of all.

I arrived in Calcutta slightly weakened by food poisoning, and went to ground in Sudder Street, at the Salvation Army hostel, where so many poor travellers stay. My health was easily restored but I had to acknowledge that my energy was not replenishing itself anymore. The feeling, like the climate, was reminiscent of Panama, two years earlier and thirty thousand miles back, but I had to recognize that this time the lethargy was more deeply established.

There was no easy remedy, so I tried self-indulgence. In a corner of Sudder Street facing the hostel stood, and no doubt will stand forever, a two-star bastion of the Raj, the Fairlawn Hotel. By my standards it was far too expensive. Even if I had thought it worth the price to stay there and confirm that the empire was past its prime, I did not actually have the money.

However, I could afford to sit in the garden and drink a lemon soda. I breached the big wooden gates and sat at an iron table under a spray of blossom, alone in the grounds and soothingly remote from the city's business. It took the bearer a long time to find me among all the trees and trellises, although I had seen eyes peering in my direction from the reception desk for some while. Was I perhaps unsuitably dressed for the Fairlawn, I wondered. After all, I had shaved, and the pattern of my shirt was still recognizable through the grime. And I might be down on my luck but, dammit, I was still an Englishman.

"Bring me a lemon juice and a bottle of soda," I said, almost adding, "And make it snappy!"

The bearer returned with my order (what else could he do?) and opened the bottle on the table. I waited for the cheerful sparkle, the gay effervescence that would zestfully challenge Calcutta's soggy noon. Nothing happened. One bubble struggled wearily up through the liquid and lodged itself in the meniscus, lacking the will to burst.

India —————➤ *423*

It was an unimportant matter, and I would have left it, except that it gave me an opportunity for conversation and I was curious. I had already noticed an elaborately coifed head of hair bobbing about briskly in the reception area. I knew the hotel belonged to an old Indian Army man, and I thought this must be the mem-sahib herself. I thought she might be amused by my story and I sauntered over with the bottle dangling from my fingertips.

She was dressed and made up in a manner that left no doubt about how she saw her usefulness in this world. Here, I told myself, is a woman who likes to maintain standards, and I resolved to help her. I mentioned the paucity of bubbles in my soda water, and she flew into a rage.

I was amazed. My remark had been as light and debonair as I could manage it, as if to say, "What's in a bubble? After all, we're British."

Her rage was all the more violent for being fearfully controlled.

"There has never been any sickness here from water," she cried. Never once in living memory, not since the Mutiny, not since John Company first set foot on this subcontinent, not once ever had anybody challenged the water at the Fairlawn.

"And you are not even staying with us!"

Useless to explain that the purity of the water was not in question; that I was merely reporting a minor matter of bubble trouble. She shook and went livid and puce by turns. I began to suspect other roots to her distress. Perhaps she had detected a working-class inflection in one of my vowels. She gathered herself up finally, in her full fury, to administer the blow that would send me reeling off the premises.

"All our water, I'll have you know, comes directly from the Saturday Club."

I was rendered speechless, since I had never heard of it. It was the *coup de grâce*, but she could not leave well alone.

"And if that is not good enough," she went on, "you can speak to my husband."

"Ah," I said, "that's a good idea. Where is the colonel?"

"Upstairs," she said grimly. I got one foot on the first step, but her staff surrounded me.

"No, sir. Please. No. This way, sir, please come" – and with a fresh bottle of soda they enticed me back to my table.

I tried on another day to drink a beer in the garden, knowing that others had succeeded, but the bearer informed me frigidly that it was a dry day at the bar. I dared not approach the desk again. A dog with eyes like cartwheels I can face, but an irate mem-sahib, never. I could not get a grasp of Calcutta. It seemed to elude me. Only afterwards did I wonder whether perhaps I had been misled by its reputation into expecting something else. I visited that kindest of institutions, the Home for the Destitute and Dying set up by Mother Theresa, but far from finding it shocking I thought it was a good deal more pleasant and better ordered than an average Indian railway platform. I dragged myself out across the awful Howrah Bridge into various poor areas, but saw nothing that was conspicuously worse than what I was already accustomed to.

I was not overcome by grisly sights or intolerable smells. Nobody fell dead at my feet. When I came to read *Freedom at Midnight* and other dramatic Western accounts of Indian life, with their constant emphasis on reek and stench and teeming masses, death, disease and subhuman squalor, I was outraged by the careless assumption that only the Western nose and eye can judge what is fit for humans.

Several times on my way through India I had asked to be taken to the worst slum, expecting the worst. Each time, as I entered among the colony of makeshift shacks, I could see only individual families doing what they could with what they had, and I became absorbed in the detail of their lives. It was a shock to recall that thirty years before I had visited families in London in a North Kensington slum area whose circumstances had certainly been much worse, for they had to cope in addition with cold winters and living in underground basements.

But at that time, in Calcutta, my spirits being a bit deflated, I assumed my own judgment was at fault in not appreciating the epic quality of Calcutta's miseries, and I decided to get out.

The route I had planned took me back one more time to the Bay of Bengal at Puri and at Konarak. Powerful winds were blowing in from the bay, and a thin veil of sand particles hovered over the long beaches to give the light an unearthly feeling. Through this eerie brightness I gazed at abandoned summer villas half buried in dunes, turreted and crenellated, pastel-colored Indian Gothic remains, seemingly untouched for decades and in terminal decay, except that being in India it would not have surprised me to see the family resume occupancy at any time.

I fought brief battles with enormous waves, gazed at mildly erotic carvings and slept a lot, gathering strength for the last curl in my spiral course through India. I was deeply conscious of the fact that from here on I would be heading directly towards Europe, but first I had to cross to Nagpur, at the geographical center of India. Those fifteen hundred miles from Puri to Delhi worried me. Already, on my way from Calcutta, I had felt the heat in the air, greater than I had imagined possible for April. In the heart of India, on the Deccan Plain, it would be hotter still, much hotter.

Shortly after I set out the chain broke, a unique event in my experience. It was nothing like the disaster I had always anticipated. No damage was done. Anyway, it had broken on the joining link, which was easily replaced, but it drew my attention again to the state of the rear sprocket. All the teeth were badly blunted, worn down, as it were, almost to the gums, and some were broken off altogether. Now I had something to worry about. Sprocketlessness, like scurvy, sounds funny, but in advanced stages it can prove fatal. As I repaired the chain I recalled the two accidents I had been promised and added them to my anxieties. Soon after, the heat became unbearable. It struck me as though from a blast furnace, and for the first time I found that the faster I rode the hotter I got.

I took refuge in a roadside teahouse, and ate portions of curried peas and spinach and dhal from chipped enamel plates, scooping it up with puri and chapati. It was after four in the afternoon before the heat wavered and dipped. I had never traveled by night before. It had seemed pointless and dangerous, but now I realized that there was no other way, and I started with very real misgivings.

The unfamiliarity was frightening at first. I had never liked to put faith in road surfaces, and here it was unavoidable. One could not hope to pick up every pothole in such poor light. There were many big trucks moving at night, and they were as unpredictable at night as by day. In addition the roads were all under reconstruction. For hundreds of miles they were regularly interrupted by culvert constructions to channel floodwater, and temporary diversions dived off into the sand and stone of the surrounding countryside. It seemed to me that all this, combined with an almost bald front tire and a worn chain on a toothless sprocket, must conspire to produce an accident somewhere.

Perhaps the clairvoyant saved me. I was damned if I was going to fulfill his prophecy so quickly. As the hours passed I grew more adept at recognizing hazards, and began to feel more confident. I was surprised to find I had covered more than three hundred miles in the first leg, and the night journey developed into a relaxed and interesting experience.

Life in the towns and villages continued far into the night, and I came out of the dark flat scrub land into brilliant city streets or bustling village corners.

On the first day I found a room in the Inspection Bungalow at Pithora. The other room was occupied by a CARE official. He said he was a doctor helping the government of Maharashtra to set up a nutrition program. And he was himself a sleekly obese advertisement for nutrition.

"You are from?" he said.

"You mean now," I asked, "or originally?"

"No, no," he said, irritably. "You are *from?*"

After that he seemed to lose interest. I went to the back to cook breakfast and found that a crow had broken and eaten one of my eggs. I slept through the afternoon, and left at dusk, making a de tour through Bagbhara to get gas. At Ghorari I stopped at a chai shop for tea and curry.

"So, how do you like my India?" inquired my neighbor, a retired tax inspector with a wizened face and a patronizing manner. I tried to give some kind of answer to his question, but it was neither expected nor wanted.

"You will not be able to understand," he said with smug certainty, "it will take you too long.

"In the course of my duties," he went on, "I also have been traveling. I have been to Australia. There are minor differences of custom naturally but otherwise I would say we are the same. Yes, Indians and Australians are the same."

It was an astonishing suggestion.

"You must have been in Australia a long time to have known them so well," I said, but of course he did not hear me.

At the *pan* stall next door I tried to buy cigarettes, but there was nobody to serve me. I lingered a bit and then asked my new-found mentor whether I might leave the money and take a packet. He threw up his hands.

"Oh, no, good gentleman," he said. "This is India."

I rode on to Raipur and found cigarettes at a shop outside a hotel. While there I thought I might as well use the lavatory. The cubicle was already occupied by a man aiming a jet of urine into the bowl. He had left the door open and looked up as I approached.

"I am making water," he told me solemnly. "You wish to do so?"

The whole of India suddenly struck me as wildly funny, and I went on laughing most of the way to Nagpur.

The following evening at Jabalpur I met another Indian who had been to Australia. I had no idea so many Indians had gone there. He was a prosperous-looking fellow riding a scooter the way a merchant banker might sometimes bicycle to the City. We had a beer together in an Indian honky-tonk behind a wine store. He was very nostalgic about Australia, and had just bought a farm – "Just as a hobby to remind me."

"I am going to train monkeys to shoo off the neighbor's cattle," he told me. My surprise must have shown on my face. "Well, why not? If dogs, why not monkeys?"

Eventually I came to Agra by way of Khajurao. The Taj Mahal was entirely worth visiting, exceeding expectations, and even more worth listening to. The sighs of a million spirits drifted down inside from the echoing dome.

I watched young Indian couples come in, noisily alive, wanting to make their mark on this sacred cow of architecture. If they could have carved their names into the marble, they would have had the building in shreds very quickly. Instead they flung their voices at the ceiling, young men drunk with power, young women drunk with hope, wanting that moment of immortality when the Taj would speak with *their* voices. But no sooner was the voice launched than everything that was sharp, personal and assertive in it was lost and it became a mournful ghost to mingle forever with the gray legions above.

I walked around the grounds, talked to some stonemasons and watched their deft work on the big red slabs of stone they were decorating. In the arcade outside, after three and a half years of thinking about it, I bought a pair of sandals that I could actually wear, and walked in them to see the fort.

But the fort was closed to the public and surrounded by army.

"A hundred and twenty ministers from foreign countries are visiting," an officer told me. I walked on letting my annoyance dissolve in the melting pot of the bazaar, among ox carts, horse carts, cabs, hand barrows, cycles and rickshaws. Knowing that I would not be a part of this confusion for much longer, I sat on a box in an open store with a bottle of lemonade and watched the street. The bottle had a pinched neck and a glass marble as a valve, a brilliant device, almost forgotten since my childhood. Indian life flowed past me, a feast of color and detail, wonderful in the sheer breadth of the spectrum of human circumstance that is paraded there.

I walked on up the hill in the throng of vehicles and pedestrians. A portion of noise slightly louder than the rest made me turn, and I saw a horse cab coming up the rise.

The horse was a powerful white beast, full of nervous energy, thrashing in the shafts and tossing its head. The driver too was young and flushed with energy and excitement, urging the animal up the hill, a young Muslim in robe and turban, sleeves swept back, rising up and reaching forward with his whip, eyes glowing with pride. The cab was heavily loaded with passengers and sacks of grain, all Muslims in turban and robe.

The components of the tragedy came together before my eyes. The cab was going too fast, the horse was too wild. I saw three tiny girls, scarcely knee high, although they were graded, one, two, three, a few inches apart, perhaps sisters separated by a year, all identically dressed as miniature mothers in ankle-length red dresses, voluminously pleated from the waist with machine embroidered bodices, cheap dresses for they were clearly poor girls and barefooted, but happily clutching each other and chattering madly together as they darted across the road among the legs of the crowd, a few feet from where I had stood and turned. The crowd parted, swiftly, to reveal the horse they had not heard and they fell in a single bundle, as though their dresses were stitched together, one, two, three, and I watched the wheel of the heavy cab rise slowly over their bodies.

The moment froze. The big wooden-spoked, iron-tired wheel bore down. Then time flowed on and the wheel slipped back to the ground. Men started forward to rescue the girls. The driver stumbled to the ground and horror overwhelmed him. He clasped his hands and fell to his knees and raised his arms and face to the sky shouting for mercy. His passengers slipped quietly from the cab, pressed a few coins on the driver and discreetly disappeared, no expression visible on their faces.

Two of the girls, miraculously, were able to stand. The third, the smallest of them, lay in a shopkeeper's arms. Bright blood appeared at her lips. He passed the child to a boy of fifteen or so, and gave him some instruction. The boy just stood and grinned awkwardly as though embarrassed. The man shouted and pushed the boy, and the boy turned reluctantly and walked up the street carrying his unwanted bundle.

He had not very far to go. I saw him turn through a doorway marked "Dipty X-Ray Clinic." A man came out again a few moments later carrying the girl and got astride the pillion of a scooter, which another man drove away.

The incident had an effect on me far beyond the merely shocking. There was also something very familiar about the wheel crushing those small bodies, as though it were an ever-recurring theme of life, an accident that was *made* to happen, that had *already* happened countless times over many thousands of years. I even felt as though I had seen it myself often before.

For a few minutes I thought of finding out where they had gone and following them; of learning everything there was to know about those three girls and their family. Then I sighed at the impossibility of it, and walked on.

Although the Triumph behaved faultlessly all the way to Delhi, I knew that there was no question of riding much farther without a new sprocket. I had long ago written to England about it, and expected to find a new one waiting for me at the Lucas depot. It was a great disappointment to find nothing there.

For all their charm and helpfulness, the Lucas people could not conjure a sprocket out of thin air, and as I sat it out, waiting for packages that did not arrive, sitting by telephones that did not ring, I fought a losing battle with my own exhaustion. I had counted heavily on being able to get out of New Delhi and on my way in a few days, before the heat came down, before I lost the momentum I had built up.

The days stretched into weeks, and I became bogged down in delays and absurd misunderstandings. Many good things happened to me while I was there, but eventually they were all lost under the crushing weight of frustration. In the muggy heat of a Delhi summer I began to feel India closing in on me, and I fought furiously to escape from its cloying embrace. Indian friends indulged my antics as if they were the tantrums of a spoilt child.

When the sprocket finally arrived at New Delhi airport, I had been waiting four weeks. Nervously I sweated my way through the hours of rigmarole at customs, where I was already well known. After their own fashion they were kind to me. The sprocket passed into my

Years of traveling amidst poverty protected me from the shock that overwhelms most Western visitors to India. The average Indian family is as strict, morally, as any other, but the extremes of life and death intrude more frequently, and prudery is kept in its place. Though Hindi pop films scarcely even permit kissing, the temple walls of Khajarao, *below,* celebrate the joys of procreation with frank exuberance. In Benares, by contrast, death touched me in the form of a corpse floating past on the Ganges, with a pecking crow perched on its forehead. Later I was able to recall the image of this body, resting in the the river as though in a deep armchair, and find in it a source of comfort. It diminished my fear of death – perhaps the only way to find peace in this world.

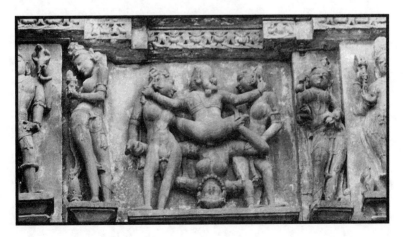

hands the same day, and I paid neither tax nor bribe nor fee. When I got it, I had only one ambition: To make a bolt for the border, and home.

My fear of being trapped in India was not entirely fanciful. There was news of great upheavals in Pakistan, and with the overthrow of Bhutto's government, martial law was declared. There were curfews and riots, and I feared that the border might be closed at any time. All overland routes to Europe go across Pakistan.

But I had other deeper fears, although I could not describe them. I was in an advanced state of rootlessness and it was becoming plain to me that these were not just words, but a real condition that threatened to break me down unless I found some stability and peace soon. Meanwhile, just being on the move towards Europe alleviated it.

The Prophecy Fulfilled

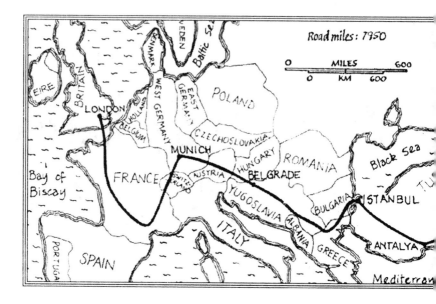

On the map: Road miles: 7950 · MILES · KM · Baltic Sea · SWEDEN · DENMARK · EAST GERMANY · POLAND · EIRE · BRITAIN · LONDON · HOLLAND · BELGIUM · WEST GERMANY · CZECHOSLOVAKIA · MUNICH · HUNGARY · ROMANIA · Black Sea · FRANCE · SWITZERLAND · AUSTRIA · BELGRADE · YUGOSLAVIA · ISTANBUL · Bay of Biscay · ALBANIA · BULGARIA · PORTUGAL · SPAIN · ITALY · GREECE · ANTALYA · Mediterranean

On May the fifth, with 26,300 miles on the clock since L.A., I left New Delhi. I shot up the trunk road to Amritsar like an arrow from a bow, and had three narrow escapes with buses before I was able to cool down sufficiently to ride with my usual caution. In retrospect those seemed like the most dangerous miles of the journey.

The urge to move westward was irresistible. I had to keep going. I had seen and done more than enough.

The Pakistan border was open and I rode in an armed convoy of cars to Lahore. The entire population of this great and crowded city had vanished and the streets were deserted, and charged with unease. There were soldiers on every street corner to enforce the stringent curfew at gun point, but the only other life I saw was a herd of dairy buffalo making their own way with leisurely condescension down the middle of the broad and empty avenue.

There was no reason to stay, for I would only have been sequestered in an expensive hotel, and I set off alone for Rawalpindi. In less than two hours I arrived at the Jhelum River. Outside Lahore the atmosphere was much lighter, and already I was experiencing a relief from India. I had stopped briefly to drink some tea, and was struck immediately by the humor of the people around me. They made jokes that I could laugh at. How long was it since I had heard a joke?

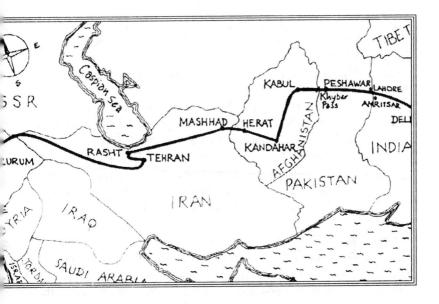

The Jhelum Bridge is a toll bridge. As I stopped at the booth a voice called to me.

"Sir. Sir. Please. Come and rest. Have a cup of tea."

I saw a man at the roadside looking at me with a cheerful smile. He wore the pale gray pajama suit of northern Pakistan, long tunic with tails over trousers that ballooned out and came in sharply at the ankles. His face was weathered and creased with lines of mischief at the eyes and mouth.

His family had paid for the franchise on the toll bridge. They lived in quarters on the riverbank, all males, brothers and cousins, and were Pathans from the Kohat region not far from the Khyber Pass.

Hamid was the eldest of them, and therefore honored although he was otherwise the least qualified. He told me that he liked to offer comfort to foreign travellers, and he set about comforting me with a will. He gave me tea, heated water for my bath, laid out my bed and bedding, gave me supper and treated me to a hundred courtesies which, in the context of my journey, were great luxuries. All the while he entertained me with fragments of wit and wisdom garnered from all corners of human life. He quoted Freud and Einstein and Shaw, and spoke himself with such impish eloquence that I could close my eyes and imagine I was with an Irishman. He even said "Sorr."

"Now tell me, Sorr, about the inert gases. I mean what is the use of them? Do they lead us anywhere at all? And where would you say God is in all this?"

I said I thought God may well have been a nineteenth-century chemist.

"Yes, Sorr, well maybe now he is a psychologist. That would be my choice if I were capable. It was a great misfortune for me, Sorr, that in my childhood I was hit many times on the head. It has damaged my brain. I am unable to remember the first five years of my life."

He produced a copy of *The Psychologist* for May 1952, a faded tomato-red pamphlet, and wrote his name, "HAMID, ABDUL, Kohati," on the cover above the words "The Way to Get to the Root of Your Worries."

"Please keep this, Sorr, as a remembrance. I get it every month. I also study homeopathy and natural medicine. Would you not say, Sorr, that modern medicines are very dangerous?"

He showed me plants and herbs along the riverbank, including the castor-oil seed, which I had not noticed before, and offered to massage my arms and legs before going to bed.

The beds, charpoys and quilts, were set out on the hillside. I had put my mosquito net up, but the enemy was already within. Before I could get to sleep my waist was a mass of fiery blisters. Hamid was equal to the situation. Instead of wasting time on apologies and mortification, he fetched kerosene to soothe the bites and deter the creatures. He insisted on changing beds because he said he was impervious to bedbugs, and I fetched out my own sleeping bag. He sailed through this contretemps with an aplomb that is the hallmark of ultimate hospitality in my opinion. No fuss, no embarrassment, a minor problem solved and forgotten. He lay under the mosquito net, a fine green nylon mesh made in the U.S.A. Before I went to sleep I heard him ask: "Where did you get this mosquito net, Sorr?"

I told him it came from San Francisco, and waited for the next, inevitable question.

"It is very marvelous," he whispered, almost to himself. "I have never seen the moon in so many colors."

The dreaded question, the one I had become so resigned to for so long, never came. He did not ask me what it cost. Happily, I closed my eyes. Good-bye, India.

Every day I climbed higher towards the mountains, leaving the multitudes of India behind me. I had the impression of rising above a great bowl teeming with life, a vast and vaporous swamp of fecundity. Up here in the colder air the crowd thinned and resolved itself into individuals, aloof from each other, cherishing their apartness.

I had no idea how far I had adjusted myself to the press of people in India and the absence of privacy. Suddenly I felt space opening all around me and I was afraid of exploding into a vacuum, like a diver in decompression. The feeling became even more intense as I rode on through the Khyber Pass into Afghanistan. In Kabul I felt I had to stop for a few days until I had regained control of myself. I was in a sort of dizzy rapture and afraid it could lead to an accident.

I hung around the curio shops dickering with samovar salesmen, amazed at their toughness in bargaining. After a night of serious discomfort, I treated myself to a canister of insecticide, but my greatest indulgence was to buy a loaf of real bread, half a pound of cold imported butter, a large lump of cheese and a bottle of Italian wine made in Afghanistan. With these I retired to my hotel room, and among the bedbugs now lying dead on their backs all around the floor, I consumed all my purchases in an orgiastic feast.

Only six thousand miles to home.

The road ran on through a thousand miles of barren and severe waste, Kandahar, Herat, and into Iran. My thoughts turned in on themselves more and more. I was so close to the end now. What had I to show for four years of my life? What was it all about?

As my mind scratched restlessly back over the journey my dismay grew to panic. I really didn't seem to know anything anymore.

I remembered a snatch of conversation from the hotel at Kassala, when I came out of the Atbara Desert on the way to Gondar. How strong I was feeling then.

There was a tea boy with dreadful suppurating sores on his ankles. They would not heal. He had shown them to a chemistry teacher who happened to be sharing my dormitory.

"Have you got anything to help this boy?" he asked me.

Together we washed and dressed the sores, and I pulled a seven day dose of ampicillin from my battery of wonder drugs, glad to put them to some use.

"You must take them all, or not at all," I said sternly, putting twenty-eight shiny red and black capsules in the boy's hand. They looked fearsomely potent in that grubby palm. He gulped and promised. I told his employer to make sure, and he brought us free tea for our trouble.

"What are you doing this long journey for?" the teacher asked me.

"To find out," I answered, weary of my usual long-winded explanations.

"But what is it you wish to find out?" he persisted.

"Why I am doing it."

It was a frivolous reply, but I was so free and easy about it then, with most of it still ahead of me.

Now, running for home across this bleak land, I had to face the same question.

Did I find out, after all, why I was doing it?

It seemed to me that there were times during those four years when I did know, and those were the times when the Journey needed no justification.

When I was floating free.

Then I needed no better reason for the journey than to be exactly where I was, knowing what I knew. Those were the times when I felt stuffed full of natural wisdom, scratching at heaven's very door.

The days of Jupiter.

What had become of him since? Where was all that wonderful assurance and enlightenment now? As I moved mechanically through the landscape, undeviating, incurious, hugging my last reserves of energy, I felt bereft and ignorant, cast down to the depths, no more than "a pair of ragged claws scuttling across the floors of silent seas."

Scuttling towards home. I called it home. I told myself: "Just another five thousand miles to home. In only three weeks you can be there."

I was drawn as if by a magnet past glittering mosques, perfumed bazaars, mountain eyries and troglodytic retreats, all the ages and splendors of civilization, hardly willing even to turn my head. In my mind's eye the same picture flashed again and again. A Mediterranean avenue, and myself on the Triumph riding up it, with the sun flicking between the trunks of the plane trees, towards my home. I played it over and over like a clip from an old black and white film. My "homecoming."

It was an illusion, and I knew it. There was a house there still, of course, that was mine, but it would never mean to me again what it once did. How many times I had renounced it already! Only a year before I was sure I would return to California and Carol. Now I was besotted by a nostalgic memory more than four years old. All the fine freedom I had known since had evaporated. All the brilliant and unrepeatable experience of four years was lifeless as ashes. I was burned out, and I could think only of getting to my little stone castle and slamming the door.

Rage could still kindle a fire of sorts, as I accused myself of stupidity, betrayal, waste, weakness, every failing under the sun.

How could I have let it go? How could I have let it shrivel away like this? The whole thing was preposterous and frightening. I must have something to say after four years and sixty thousand miles, after all I had seen and done in forty countries.

"Excuse me, Mr. Simon, but can you tell me please what message you will be carrying back to your country when you return?"

I did not have a message. I seemed to have lost it on the way.

"But surely, Mr. Simon, you have learned something. What about death, for example."

Yes. True. I did learn something after all.

It was at the end of my two weeks at Boddhgaya that I packed a small bag, hired a rickshaw to Gaya and took a train to Benares. I stayed there only one full day and towards the end of that day I shared a small boat with a New Zealander and floated on the Ganges, as everyone does, to the ghats where the bodies are burned.

As we approached the ghats, going upstream, an unburned corpse drifted slowly past us. I did not, at first, recognize it for what it was. It lay back in the water as though in a very deep, soft armchair, with only the knees, toes, arms and head above water. A crow was perched on its forehead, pecking.

Nobody in normal times could be indifferent to the sight of a dead human body. I certainly was not, and to see it being ripped into by a bird was even more shocking. Yet the shock lasted hardly a second. I had been preparing for this sight a long time, and Benares itself gave my conditioning a last, powerful shove.

What was there to be shocked by? Nothing could suggest greater peace or purity than the Ganges. To watch that broad body of shining water, so massive and unruffled in the evening light, is like watching life itself slide past. No Indian could wish a better fate on the poor clay of his body than that it should float away on this river. Was I going to be shocked then by considerations of hygiene? Hardly, knowing what is pumped regularly, if invisibly, into the world's rivers.

Was it the bird then? But why should a bird be harder to contemplate than a worm? So it must have been that I simply didn't like being reminded of death.

In time that body floating down the river was transformed for me into an image of great beauty and simplicity. It allowed me to think more calmly about the prospect of death. Unless I could do that, I thought, how could I possibly hope to appreciate without fear the pleasures of being alive.

"Thank you, Mr. Simon, but what about God? It is reported that at one time you considered yourself to be God. Do you not think that to be rather blasphemous?"

No. I do think it is possible to be God for brief moments. I am certainly not God now.

"But surely, in your country, most people believe there is only one God?"

I think God is the composite creation of large numbers of people being good for a moment – the way football fans keep a steady glow going in a stadium because there is always someone lighting a match. If people stopped being good altogether God would vanish.

"This is all rather airy-fairy, isn't it? Don't you have anything more specific to tell people?"

I could tell them to refuse to be afraid, and to try always to do what is right. It comes with practice, but unfortunately it goes away again with preaching, as in my own case. However, we are gifted with a compass in our hearts which will guide us to all success in life.

"Mr. Simon, after your many experiences people will certainly want something more concrete and pertinent to the world we live in. What can you suggest?"

They can always leave a tip for the starving millions on their way out.

The eastern border of Turkey was the halfway mark. Only three and a half thousand miles to go. So far it had been easy. The worst I'd had to face were an oil leak in Afghanistan and some filthy weather by the Caspian Sea. I had steered my way safely between all the wrecked tankers and trucks littering the side of the highway and, so far, had successfully outwitted the fate prophesied for me.

The entrance to Turkey was a yellow stucco gateway, built presumably for horse-drawn traffic. In this wasteland between Turkey and Iran it stood as a romantic relic of the Ottoman Empire, comprehensively stuck in an age of bound ledgers entered by hand with scratchy nibs. Waiting to go past was a mile-long queue of forty-ton TIR trucks parked two abreast in the hot sun. The drivers, mostly Hungarians, Bulgarians, Yugoslavs, Englishmen and Scandinavians were out sunning themselves in singlets and shorts, and playing interminable games of cards. They expected to be there for two days or more, but private traffic passed through quite quickly and easily.

When I asked travelers about the Asian route they had always made a song and dance about this part of the world. Australian bikies riding their ex-factory BMW's home from Berlin told me chilling tales about the high passes in eastern Turkey.

"And if they don't freeze your balls off, then the locals will probably knock 'em off for you," they said, referring to the belligerent and oppressed Kurds, who have a reputation for stone throwing.

Now the crowds at the frontier and the familiar, old-fashioned architecture made Europe seem comfortably close. Nobody threw stones. A restaurant in a garden at the next small town served a delicious and civilized meal. The sun was shining. I decided the rest of the story was exaggerated too.

For once the traveler's tale was right and I was wrong. As the road rose up into the mountains the cloud took the sun away and sent a fine drizzle down through the cold air. I had expected to cross one or two high passes and then come down again but the road stayed up on this broken and uninhabited plateau and turned to dirt, and rock slides and mud, with snow-capped peaks all around until I began to realize that this was becoming an ordeal. Astonished that I should run into such extreme conditions so close to home, I rode on 150 miles through the freezing drizzle without seeing so much as a house, and wondering whether I would ever know the welcoming warmth of a tea shop again.

The cold struck deep into me, and my body stiffened. I tried every trick, singing, flexing my muscles, thinking warm, not realizing how far gone I actually was. When I did reach the gas pump before Horasan it was just in time.

Hypothermia happens easily on a motorcycle. The body temperature sinks before you know it.

In the wood-frame cafe there was a coke stove burning, and I sat

The Prophecy Fulfilled ——————➤ *441*

by it drinking glasses of hot tea one after another, shaking and laughing at my own spectacle, but it was still half an hour before my teeth stopped chattering. I had never been so cold before, and this was in spite of wearing a waxed and lined Belstaff suit over a padded leather jacket.

I put on more underclothes for the last fifty miles to Erzerum and then it was all downhill. The mountain range was the last major hazard of the journey, the dog with the cartwheel eyes, and it caught me unawares.

If I was able to enjoy myself in Turkey the credit is due, mainly, to two fellows and a girl who were going the same way on two bikes. We met in a restaurant in Sivas. Perhaps they could see how close I was to the end of my tether. They seemed to treat me gently and bore me along with them, so instead of taking the shortest possible route I saw the extraordinary conical rocks of Cappadocia (like a petrified rally of the Ku Klux Klan) and lingered for a few days on the warm Mediterranean coast between Mersin and Antalya.

The ride up through the middle of Turkey to Istanbul took three days. Once we camped out, and the second night we stayed at a small hotel. In the teahouses I spoke German with Turkish men, admiring their opulent mustaches, wondering at their baggy striped shirts with detachable collars and their heavy old-style suits and flat hats that reminded me of the Depression years. Turkey surprised me in many ways, by its size and by a culture which inspires a special quality of nostalgia for the period one is just too young to remember. Turkey was one country I knew I would have to come back to and see properly. Then I was in Istanbul, and only two thousand miles from home.

My friends and I parted company and at this point I gave up all pretense of being on a journey. I stayed in Istanbul just long enough to give the Triumph one last, thorough overhaul, and then I rode as fast as I could for home, in the grip of a kind of madness. It was lucky for me, perhaps, that the engine had begun to vibrate badly, and it was too painful to ride over sixty miles an hour.

The roads were heavy with holiday traffic and big trucks, a dangerous mixture. Most of the cars were German and I met them in an unending stream flowing south through Yugoslavia to Greece, until I felt I must be in the new German Empire. There were some obscene and terrible accidents on the Yugoslav Autoput, which must be a serious contender as the world's worst road. I felt fortunate to get through unscathed.

For three nights I camped by the roadside, and the fourth night I was in Munich, staying with a friend. A day's riding took me to another friend's house in Switzerland. There, only a day's ride from my house, it felt safe to believe that I was really going to make it.

One morning in June 1977, I rode over the Jura Mountains into France. The Triumph had stopped protesting and was running freely. All my equipment was in working order. I sat in the saddle with the same ease that others find in an armchair, and could main tain that position comfortably for twelve hours or more. I was very light, at 126 pounds I was some thirty pounds below the weight I set out at four years earlier, but my body functioned better than ever except in one respect: My right eye was less efficient after the accident in Penang. To read a telephone directory in twilight I needed glasses. I still smoked cigarettes, and still wished I didn't.

I was carrying rice from Iran, raisins and dried mulberries from Afghanistan, tea from Assam, curry spices from Calcutta, stock cubes from Greece, halva from Turkey and some soya sauce from Penang.

In a polythene screw-top bottle bought from a shop in Kathmandu was the rest of the sesame-seed oil I had bought in Boddhgaya. The rice and raisins were in plastic boxes from Guatemala. My teapot was bought at Victoria Falls, and my enamel plates were made in China and inherited from Bruno at La Plata. A small box of henna leaves from Sudan, a vial of rose water from Peshawar and some silver ornaments from Ootacamund were all tucked into a Burmese lacquered bowl. This in turn sat inside a Russian samovar from Kabul.

My leather tank bags and saddle cover were made in Argentina. The tent and sleeping bag were original from London, but the bag had been refilled with down in San Francisco. I had a blanket from Peru and a hammock from Brazil. I was still wearing Lulu's silver necklace and an elephant-hair bracelet from Kenya. The Australian fishing rod was where the sword from Cairo had once sat, and an umbrella from Thailand replaced the one I had lost in Argentina.

By far the most valuable of all my things was a Kashmiri carpet, a lovely thing smothered in birds and animals to a Shiraz design, but it would have been hard to say which of my possessions was the most precious.

I came down through Lyons and stayed off the motorway, crossing the Rhône at St. Esprit and heading off for Nîmes. I was still playing that clip of film in my head; the avenue, the plane trees, the sun flicking between the trunks and leaves. Within hours, even within a modest number of minutes, the film would merge with reality. I would be riding up that avenue, and by that single act I would be sealing off forever the four most eventful years of my life.

Any minute now . . . The End.

It should have been intolerable. I should have turned and fled the other way. It was after all a kind of death. The only Ted Simon I knew was the one who moved on. The Hello-Goodbye Man. From person to person, country to country, continent to continent. Half man, half bike; if not Jupiter, then Pegasus, perhaps, or at least a centaur. At least that.

But soon, no more. I would take my things off the bike and put them away in cupboards. I would wear ordinary clothes. And this bike, which had been 60,600 miles around the world, I would ride to the shops. And most of my days, from then on, I would spend trying to remember. Yes, it would be a bit like death, but I welcomed it. I rode on through the sunshine until I came to the avenue, and the sun flickered through the plane trees exactly as I had remembered.

The end of the journey was even more confusing than the beginning. In fact it was just as arbitrary and meaningless as any of the other milestones along the way. Did it end in France, or in England? In my own way I had even ended it in Istanbul, when I crossed the Bosporus into Europe.

My friends welcomed me back. I could feel their excitement, and I enjoyed it. As long as I was in their company I could feel some satisfaction through them. Alone, though, I was in great trouble, tossed on a storm of conflicting emotions. I felt exactly as though I were at the mercy of great waves, without the strength to hold on to anything firm. The one task which might have centered me on something steady and reliable was the book I had to write, but I found it impossible. The memories I had relied on refused to come to life, and I knew that to try to force them into the open might cripple them. These things of the imagination are so delicate, they can be strained and fractured just as easily as the muscles and bones of one's body. And they can grow old and lifeless too. I was afraid.

During this bad, mad time, the wedding prophecy came to my mind quite often. I had never before been specially superstitious, but the experiences of the journey had changed the way I viewed things.

In particular, the incidents with the flying fish and the saddhu had affected me profoundly. I saw that things could happen in other ways than according to the physical laws I had been taught, and I found the world a much richer and more satisfying place because of that.

All the same, astrology and fortune-telling did not fill me with confidence. They seemed far too deliberate and much too vulnerable to ordinary wishful thinking to have a firm place in my new mythology. If I thought about the prophecy it was mainly because I had lost control over my own future so completely that there was a vacuum which had to be filled with something.

The prophecy had promised me two years of trouble and internal conflict, and I was certainly getting a full dose of that. It had promised me two accidents "not major, not minor," and I had not had either of those. It had promised me great happiness and prosperity from 1979, and that was what I was looking forward to. I allowed myself to believe that, however bad things felt now, happiness and prosperity were on their way.

At the end of August I put all my bags and boxes back on the bike, re-assembled my gear and rode off to London to appear at the Motorcycle Show. Once again, The End. Finally, I rode the bike up the Motorway to Meriden and was received by the factory work force assembled inside the gates. Although it had been arranged for television and newspapers, this last arrival, which was really the end of The End, was the one that moved me most.

While I had been riding their bike around the world, most of these men had been fighting a bitter battle to keep their factory going, and had wound up as proprietors of their own business. Triumph was now a workers' co-operative, the first in the motorcycle industry, and I was very proud to be representing them. I had always hoped that they would understand that, and draw some value from the publicity I was giving their motorcycle. When they gave me three old-fashioned but rousing cheers, I thought they meant it, and the questions they asked afterwards seemed to confirm my feeling. It was a difficult time. The bike would be theirs now. There was talk of putting it in a museum. I knew it was the sensible thing to do, but I was immensely relieved to feel that it meant something to them too.

They gave me an almost new Triumph 750 in its place. Craven gave me new boxes and a windscreen to fit on it. It felt very strange, and I struggled to get used to it. Most difficult of all was the switch of gear lever and brake pedal to opposite sides of the bike. Four years of living with the old Triumph had made my reflexes instinctive, and it was hard to relearn them. I put a thousand miles on the bike before taking it back to France, and by then I felt more comfortable with it, but I was riding with great care. It had always seemed to me that, having ridden so many miles without a serious accident, the period after my return would be the most dangerous of all.

In the South of France near Avignon, I came to a crossing. There were no traffic lights, and I was on the minor road. I stopped the bike completely and looked up and down the major road. I saw no traffic, and set out to cross it. I could hardly have been doing five miles an hour when I saw myself within yards of a big van coming straight for me very fast. It should have hit me side-on and I would undoubtedly have been killed if it had, but I braked and the driver didn't, and so his van was just past my front wheel when I hit it. The bike was torn away from underneath me, and the front end was smashed beyond repair. I fell on the tarmac with all the bones in my body shaken in their sockets, but otherwise unharmed.

The worst was having to face that I could look directly at a speeding van and not see it. My confidence was more shattered even than the bike. After all that I had done, with all the care I was taking, I could not explain how I could ride blindly into such a disaster. If ever an accident qualified as "not major and not minor" that was it.

I felt positively glad that I would have no bike to ride for a while. It was time to give it a rest. From my friend Peter Mayle, I borrowed a little open Citroen with a plastic body and a soft canvas top, and drove around in that during the winter.

It was a very hard winter. Emotionally I was as disturbed as ever. The house still did not feel like home, the book would not come, nothing was right. I took shelter with friends and hoped for an early spring. Then Carol came to see me.

One day we went to visit my house. The weather was very bright, winds were tearing the clouds across the blue sky. While we were there I decided to bring the Indian rug back with me to protect it. We drove back up a steep road on a stony hillside to rejoin the main road. I stopped the car at the crossing, to look for traffic. We were stationary when a giant hand plucked the car off the ground, raised it four feet up in the air, rolled it over and threw it down the hillside.

The violence was so great, so terrifying and unexpected, that I knew only afterwards what had happened. At the time I had the impression of whirling in hell and being hit. It seemed to go on for a long time, and I was sure I would die. Carol had the same recollection. I was thrown from the car on my head. Carol fell into the back of the car. Fortunately the car did a complete roll in the air, for if it had fallen upside down she would have been crushed. It fell with its front wheels hooked over a big boulder some ten feet below the road. The boulder held it, otherwise it might have bounced and rolled a long way down the mountainside. Carol escaped with a bruised arm. I was drenched in blood from a scalp wound.

The only possible explanation was that a gust of wind had filled the car from behind, through the open back, and whisked it away like a parachute. The strength of a wind that would be capable of lifting a car four feet in the air was beyond my ability to compute. It had an element of the supernatural about it, of course.

There was one other strange coincidence. The Indian rug was never found. Many people searched for it, but it had disappeared.

A week later Carol flew back to the ranch, and I went to work. Things improved, gradually, and my confidence returned. The memories flooded back and the book got written. It is now the winter of 1978. The prospects for prosperity in 1979 seem quite good. I have a letter from Carol saying that she is thinking of getting married. Franziska, the policewoman in Fortaleza, has qualified as a lawyer and is working in Brasilia. Bruno is a buyer for the French tobacco monopoly, and travels to tobacco auctions all over the world. Tan, the old man at the Choong Thean Hotel, has sought refuge with the Little Sisters of the Poor. The family on the farm near Lusaka has been violently over-run, after all, by Mr N'Komo's freedom fighters, and driven out. Equally sad is the news that the Black Mountain Inn in Rhodesia is now a ruin of broken brick walls and naked rafters. There is no news of the Van den Berghs.

The Triumph 500-cc model T100-P, known as XRW 964M, is in the Alfred Herbert Museum in Coventry, and remains unwashed since Istanbul. Some day soon I plan to visit it.

Meanwhile I dream a lot. Often I dream of riding over the hard red floor of a great forest, beneath a high canopy of translucent green, spreading on and on. An enchanted forest, perhaps, where men may still sometimes play at being gods.

The End   ⟶   447

The Jupiter Trilogy

This is the first of three books in which
Ted Simon, as "Jupiter", explores his
relationship to planet earth
over a period of a quarter of a century

The others are

Riding High, $16.95
and
Dreaming of Jupiter, $24.95

All three books are available through
bookstores or directly from the author.
For more information, go to
Jupitalia.com

Now to complete the experience consider getting
Jupiter's Travels in Camera

On that first epoch-making journey Ted also took photographs, as
and when he could, purely for his own sake. This large and
beautifully designed book, with more than 300 images and
new text by the author himself shows us what he saw so long ago.
This book is only available from the author, at
Jupitalia.com/teds-books/jupiters-travels-in-camera/

Other books by Ted Simon:

The River Stops Here, Random House and
UC Press, Berkeley.

The Gypsy in Me, Random House, now only
available as an eBook. Visit Jupitalia.com